ACCA
STUDY TEXT

Paper 2.6

Audit and Internal Review

IN THIS JUNE 2002 EDITION

- Targeted to the syllabus and study guide

- Quizzes and questions to check your understanding

- Clear layout and style designed to save you time

- Plenty of exam-style questions with NEW detailed guidance from BPP

- Chapter Roundups and summaries to help revision

- Mind Maps to integrate the key points

- SAS 610 *Communication of audit matters to those charged with governance*

FOR EXAMS IN DECEMBER 2002 AND 2003

BPP Publishing
June 2002

First edition 2001
Second edition June 2002

ISBN 0 7517 0237 4 (Previous edition 0 7517 0739 2)

British Library Cataloguing-in-Publication Data
A catalogue record for this book
is available from the British Library

Published by

BPP Publishing Ltd
Aldine House, Aldine Place
London W12 8AW

www.bpp.com

Printed in Great Britain by WM Print Ltd

We are grateful to the Association of Chartered Certified Accountants for permission to reproduce past examination questions and questions from the pilot paper. The answers have been prepared by BPP Publishing Limited.

Contents

BPP PUBLISHING

Contents

THE BPP STUDY TEXT

Aims of this Study Text

To provide you with the knowledge and understanding, skills and application techniques that you need if you are to be successful in your exams

This Study Text has been written around the **Audit and Internal Review** syllabus.

- It is **comprehensive**. It covers the syllabus content. No more, no less.

- It is written at the **right level**. Each chapter is written with the ACCA's **study guide** in mind.

- It is targeted to the **exam**. We have taken account of the **pilot paper**, questions put to the examiners at the recent ACCA conference and the assessment methodology.

To allow you to study in the way that best suits your learning style and the time you have available, by following your personal Study Plan (see page (ix))

You may be studying at home on your own until the date of the exam, or you may be attending a full-time course. You may like to (and have time to) read every word, or you may prefer to (or only have time to) skim-read and devote the remainder of your time to question practice. Wherever you fall in the spectrum, you will find the BPP Study Text meets your needs in designing and following your personal Study Plan.

To tie in with the other components of the BPP Effective Study Package to ensure you have the best possible chance of passing the exam (see page (vi))

Recommended period of use	Elements of the BPP Effective Study Package

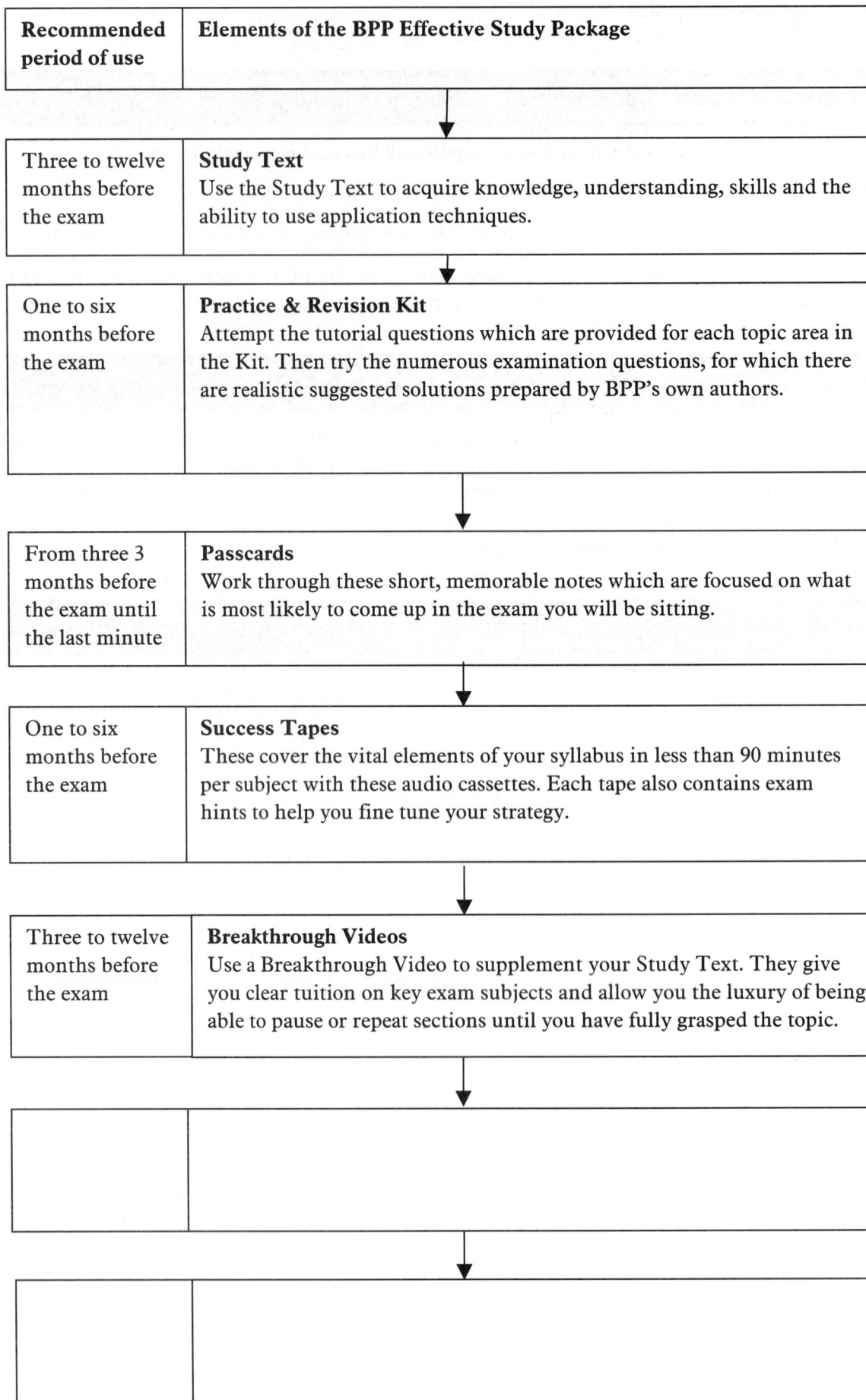

Three to twelve months before the exam	**Study Text** Use the Study Text to acquire knowledge, understanding, skills and the ability to use application techniques.

One to six months before the exam	**Practice & Revision Kit** Attempt the tutorial questions which are provided for each topic area in the Kit. Then try the numerous examination questions, for which there are realistic suggested solutions prepared by BPP's own authors.

From three 3 months before the exam until the last minute	**Passcards** Work through these short, memorable notes which are focused on what is most likely to come up in the exam you will be sitting.

One to six months before the exam	**Success Tapes** These cover the vital elements of your syllabus in less than 90 minutes per subject with these audio cassettes. Each tape also contains exam hints to help you fine tune your strategy.

Three to twelve months before the exam	**Breakthrough Videos** Use a Breakthrough Video to supplement your Study Text. They give you clear tuition on key exam subjects and allow you the luxury of being able to pause or repeat sections until you have fully grasped the topic.

HELP YOURSELF STUDY FOR YOUR ACCA EXAMS

Exams for professional bodies such as ACCA are very different from those you have taken at college or university. You will be under **greater time pressure before** the exam – as you may be combining your study with work as well as in the exam room. There are many different ways of learning and so the BPP Study Text offers you a number of different tools to help you through. Here are some hints and tips: they are not plucked out of the air, but **based on research and experience**. (You don't need to know that long-term memory is in the same part of the brain as emotions and feelings – but it's a fact anyway.)

The right approach

1   The right attitude

Believe in yourself	Yes, there is a lot to learn. Yes, it is a challenge. But thousands have succeeded before and you can too.
Remember why you're doing it	Studying might seem a grind at times, but you are doing it for a reason: to advance your career.

2   The right focus

Read through the Syllabus and Study guide	These tell you what you are expected to know and are supplemented by Exam Focus Points in the text.
Study the Exam Paper section	The pilot paper is likely to be a reasonable guide of what you should expect in the exam.

3   The right method

The big picture	You need to grasp the detail – but keeping in mind how everything fits into the big picture will help you understand better. • The **Introduction** of each chapter puts the material in context. • The **Syllabus content, Study guide** and **Exam focus points** show you what you need to **grasp**. • **Mind Maps** show the links and key issues in key topics.
In your own words	To absorb the information (and to practise your written communication skills), it helps **put it into your own words.** • **Take notes.** • Answer the **questions** in each chapter. As well as helping you absorb the information you will practise your written communication skills, which become increasingly important as you progress through your ACCA exams. • Draw **mind maps**. We have some examples. • Try 'teaching' to a colleague or friend.

Give yourself cues to jog your memory	The BPP Study Text uses **bold** to **highlight key points** and **icons** to identify key features, such as **Exam focus points** and **Key terms.** • Try **colour coding** with a highlighter pen. • Write **key points** on cards.

4 The right review

Review, review, review	It is a **fact** that regularly reviewing a topic in summary form can **fix it in your memory**. Because **review** is so important, the BPP Study Text helps you to do so in many ways. • **Chapter roundups** summarise the key points in each chapter. Use them to recap each study session. • The **Quick quiz** is another review technique to ensure that you have grasped the essentials. • Use the **Key term** index as a quiz. • Go through the **Examples** in each chapter a second or third time.
Review, review, review	It is a **fact** that regularly reviewing a topic in summary form can **fix it in your memory**. Because **review** is so important, the BPP Study Text helps you to do so in many ways. • **Chapter roundups** summarise the key points in each chapter. Use them to recap each study session. • The **Quick quiz** is another review technique to ensure that you have grasped the essentials. • Go through the **Examples** in each chapter a second or third time.

Developing your personal Study Plan

One thing that the BPP Learning to learn accountancy book emphasises (see page (iv)) is the need to prepare (and use) a study plan. Planning and sticking to the plan are key elements of learning success.

There are four steps you should work through.

Step 1. How do you learn?

First you need to be aware of your style of learning. The BPP Learning to learn accountancy book commits a chapter to this **self-discovery**. What types of intelligence do you display when learning? You might be advised to brush up on certain study skills before launching into this Study Text.

BPP's **Learning to Learn Accountancy** book helps you to identify what intelligences you show more strongly and then details how you can tailor your study process through your preferences. It also includes handy hints on how to develop intelligences you exhibit less strongly, but which might be needed as you study accountancy.

Are you a **theorist** or are you more **practical**? If you would rather get to grips with a theory before trying to apply it in practice, you should follow the study sequence on page X. If the reverse is true (you like to know why you are learning theory before you do so), you might be advised to flick through Study Text chapters and look at questions, case studies and examples (Steps 7, 8 and 9 in the **suggested study sequence**) before reading through the detailed theory.

Step 2. **How much time do you have?**

Work out the time you have available per week, given the following.

- The standard you have set yourself
- The time you need to set aside later for work on the Practice & Revision Kit and Passcards
- The other exam(s) you are sitting
- Very importantly, practical matters such as work, travel, exercise, sleep and social life

Note your time available in box A.

A [Hours]

Step 3. **Allocate your time**

- Take the time you have available per week for this Study Text shown in box A, multiply it by the number of weeks available and insert the result in box B.

B [ ]

- Divide the figure in Box B by the number of chapters in this text and insert the result in box C.

C [ ]

Remember that this is only a rough guide. Some of the chapters in this book are longer and more complicated than others, and you will find some subjects easier to understand than others.

Step 4. **Implement**

Set about studying each chapter in the time shown in box C, following the key study steps in the order suggested by your particular learning style.

This is your personal **Study Plan**. You should try and combine it with the study sequence outlined below. You may want to modify the sequence a little (as has been suggested above) to adapt it to your **personal style**.

BPP PUBLISHING

Suggested study sequence

Tackle the chapters in the order you find them in the Study Text. Taking into account your individual learning style, you could follow this sequence.

Key study steps	Activity
Step 1 **Topic list**	Each numbered topic is a numbered section in the chapter.
Step 2 **Introduction**	This gives you the **big picture** in terms of the **context** of the chapter. The content is referenced to the **Study Guide**, and **Exam Guidance** shows how the topic is likely to be examined. In other words, it sets your **objectives for study.**
Step 3 **Knowledge brought forward boxes**	In these we highlight information and techniques that it is assumed you have 'brought forward' with you from your earlier studies. If there are topics which have changed recently due to legislation for example, these topics are explained in more detail.
Step 4 **Explanations**	Proceed methodically through the chapter, reading each section thoroughly and making sure you understand.
Step 5 **Key terms and Exam focus points**	• **Key terms** can often earn you *easy marks* if you state them clearly and correctly in an appropriate exam answer (and they are indexed at the back of the text). • **Exam focus points** give you a good idea of how we think the examiner intends to examine certain topics.
Step 6 **Note taking**	Take brief notes if you wish, avoiding the temptation to copy out too much.
Step 7 **Examples**	Follow each through to its solution very carefully.
Step 8 **Case examples**	Study each one, and try to add flesh to them from your own experience – they are designed to show how the topics you are studying come alive (and often come unstuck) in the real world.
Step 9 **Questions**	Make a very good attempt at each one.
Step 10 **Answers**	Check yours against ours, and make sure you understand any discrepancies.
Step 11 **Chapter roundup**	Work through it very carefully, to make sure you have grasped the major points it is highlighting.
Step 12 **Quick quiz**	When you are happy that you have covered the chapter, use the **Quick quiz** to check how much you have remembered of the topics covered.
Step 13 **Question(s) in the Question bank**	Either at this point, or later when you are thinking about revising, make a full attempt at the **Question(s)** suggested at the very end of the chapter. You can find these at the end of the Study Text, along with the **Answers** so you can see how you did. We highlight those that are introductory, and those which are of the standard you would expect to find in an exam.

BPP PUBLISHING

Short of time: *Skim study technique?*

You may find you simply do not have the time available to follow all the key study steps for each chapter, however you adapt them for your particular learning style. If this is the case, follow the **skim study** technique below (the icons in the Study Text will help you to do this)

- Study the chapters in the order you find them in the Study Text.

- For each chapter, follow the key study steps 1-3, and then skim-read through step 4. Jump to step 11, and then go back to step 5. Follow through steps 7 and 8, and prepare outline answers to questions (steps 9/10). Try the Quick quiz (step 12), following up any items you can't answer, then do a plan for the Question (step 13), comparing it against our answers. You should probably still follow step 6 (note-taking), although you may decide simply to rely on the BPP Passcards for this.

Moving on...

However you study, when you are ready to embark on the practice and revision phase of the BPP Effective Study Package, you should still refer back to this Study Text, both as a source of **reference** (you should find the list of key terms and the index particularly helpful for this) and as a **refresher** (the Chapter roundups and Quick quizzes help you here).

And remember to keep careful hold of this Study Text – you will find it invaluable in your work.

More advice on Study Skills can be found in the BPP **Learning to Learn Accountancy** book

BPP PUBLISHING

SYLLABUS

Aim

To develop knowledge and understanding of the audit process and its application in the context of the external regulatory framework and for business control and development.

Objectives

On completion of this paper, candidates should be able to:

- understand the nature, purpose and scope of auditing and internal review, including the role of external audit and its regulatory framework, and the role of internal audit in providing assurance on risk management and on the control framework of an organisation

- identify risks, describe the procedures undertaken in the planning process, plan work to meet the objectives of the audit or review assignment and draft the content of plans

- describe and evaluate accounting and internal control systems and identify and communicate control risks, potential consequences and recommendations

- explain and evaluate sources of evidence, describe the nature, timing and extent of tests on transactions and account balances (including sampling and analytical procedures) and design programs for audit and review assignments

- evaluate findings, investigate inconsistencies, modify the work program as necessary, review subsequent events, and justify and prepare appropriate reports for users within and external to the organisation, including recommendations to enhance business performance

- discuss and apply the requirements of relevant Statements of Auditing Standards

- demonstrate the skills expected in Part 2.

Position of the paper in the overall syllabus

Paper 2.6 builds on the knowledge and understanding by Paper 1.1 Preparing Financial Statements and to a lesser extent Paper 1.2 Financial Information for Management.

Candidates will be expected to be familiar with Paper 2.5 Financial Reporting, including the requirements of the accounting standards examined within it. They will also be expected to be familiar with Paper 2.1 Information Systems.

Paper 2.6 provides the knowledge and understanding of the audit process which is then developed in Paper 3.1 Audit and Assurance Services.

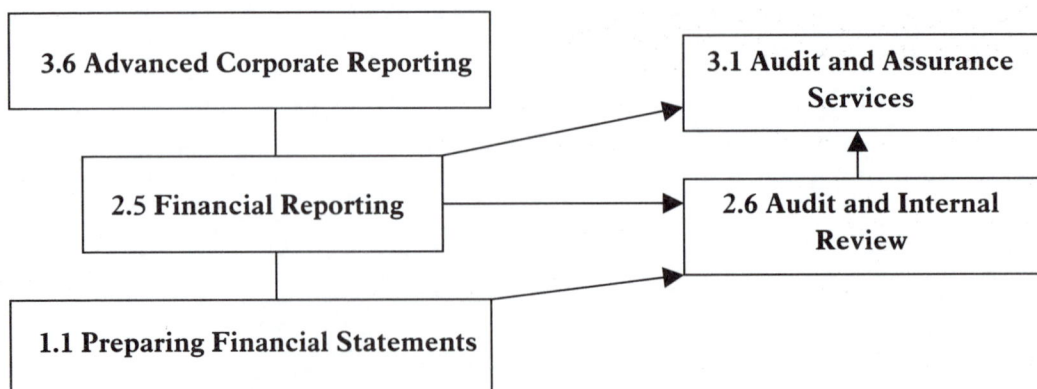

SYLLABUS

1 Audit framework

(a) The development and changing nature of audit, the social role of audit.

(b) Statutory audits, accountability, stewardship and agency.

(c) Professional ethics and codes of conduct, their application to external audit and internal audit, responsibility for fraud and error.

2 Internal audit and internal review

(a) The role of internal audit and internal review and their relationship with:

(i) Corporate governance
(ii) Risk management
(iii) Organisational control
(iv) Corporate objectives

(b) Scope and functions of internal audit, the nature and extent of internal audit assignments.

(c) Outsourced internal audit functions.

(d) The nature and extent of internal review assignments including operational, systems, value for money and financial reviews.

3 Regulation

(a) Statements of Auditing Standards:

(i) Their development and role
(ii) Their relationship with International Standards of Auditing.

(b) Auditors:

(i) Regulation and supervision
(ii) Their relationship with Government
(iii) The role of the Auditing Practices Board and other UK standard-setting bodies.

4 Planning and risk

(a) Objectives of audit and review assignments, the relevance of stakeholder dialogue.
(b) Communicating the objectives of audit and review assignments.
(c) Analytical procedures.
(d) Risk assessment.
(e) Materiality, tolerable error, and sample sizes.
(f) Design and documentation of the plan and work program.
(g) Co-ordination of the work of others.
(h) Information Technology in planning and risk assessment.

5 Internal control

(a) Objectives of internal control systems.

(b) Inherent weaknesses in internal control systems.

(c) The use of internal control systems by auditors.

(d) Transaction cycles (revenue, purchases, payroll, inventory, capital expenditure).

(e) The use of internal control systems by auditors including ICQs, ICEQs and tests of control.

(f) Communication with management.

6 Other audit and internal review of evidence

(a) Financial statement assertions: assets, liabilities, income and expenditure, including accounting estimates.

(b) Assertions reported on and opinions provided in review assignments.

(c) Analytical procedures as substantive evidence.

(d) Balance and transaction testing.

(e) Computer-assisted audit techniques, their uses and limitations.

(f) Management representations.

(g) Audit sampling and other selective testing procedures.

(h) Subsequent events review.

(i) Going concern reviews.

(j) The overall review of evidence obtained.

(k) Modifications to the plan and work program in the light of findings.

7 Reporting

(a) Format and content of unmodified and modified external audit reports on financial statements.

(b) Format and content of review reports and other reports on assignment objectives.

(c) Recommendations for the enhancement of business performance

Excluded topics

Audit of groups is not examinable at this level. Candidates should be aware of the content, wording and meaning of audit reports and they may be asked to prepare the explanatory paragraphs for inclusion in a modified audit report. However, candidates are not expected to draft full audit reports.

KEY AREAS OF THE SYLLABUS

The key topic areas are as follows:

- Professional ethics as they apply to accountants working in public practice and internal audit departments

- Risk assessment

- Internal controls

- The practical application of audit techniques

BPP PUBLISHING

Paper 2.6

Audit and Internal Review
(United Kingdom)

Study Guide

1 THE NATURE, PURPOSE AND SCOPE OF AUDIT AND REVIEW

Syllabus reference 1a, 1b, 2a, 4a

Explain the:

- Nature, development and social role of audit and review

- Concepts of accountability, stewardship and agency

- Reporting as a means of communication to different stakeholders and the importance of stakeholder dialogue

- High level of assurance provided by audit assignments and risk-based approaches; the moderate level of assurance provided by review assignments and procedural approaches; assignments in which no assurance is provided

- Recent extension in the scope of audit and review

NB: Students are expected to be aware of the nature and purpose of non-financial audit and review services as described in Session 4. Questions will focus on financial and systems audits and reviews in the context of companies and small not-for-profit organisations.

2 STATUTORY AUDITS

Syllabus reference 1b, 3, 7a, 4a

Describe the:

- UK regulatory framework in which statutory audits take place

- Development and status of the Auditing Practices Board Statements of Auditing Standards and their relationship with International Standards on Auditing

- Reasons for, and mechanisms for, the regulation of auditors by Government and other regulatory agencies including other UK standard-setters

- Types of opinion provided in statutory audit assignments

- Limitations of statutory audits

3 INTERNAL AUDIT AND INTERNAL REVIEW I

Syllabus reference 2a, 2c

Explain the:

- Development and role of internal audit in achieving corporate objectives and as part of good corporate governance practice

- Function of internal audit in the context of corporate risk management and organisational control

- Relative merits outsourcing internal audit and internal review services to external auditors and others, and the associated problems

- Difference between the role of external audit and internal audit

4 INTERNAL AUDIT AND INTERNAL REVIEW II

Syllabus reference 2, 2b, 3d, 4a, 6b

Describe the:

- Scope of internal audit work and the limitations of the internal audit function

- Nature and purpose of internal review assignments including:
  - value for money
  - best value
  - IT
  - financial

- Nature and purpose of operational internal audit and review assignments including:
  - procurement
  - marketing
  - treasury
  - HR

- Types of report provided in internal audit and internal review assignments

5 PROFESSIONAL ETHICS AND PROFESSIONAL CODES OF CONDUCT I

Syllabus reference 1c

- Describe the sources of, and enforcement mechanisms associated with, professional ethics and professional codes of conduct

- Define the fundamental concepts of professional ethics

- Describe the components of risk and the use of information technology in risk analysis

– service organisations

BPP PUBLISHING

- Explain and illustrate how structural and operational weaknesses in sales and purchases systems should be reported to management

- Explain and illustrate how structural and operational weaknesses in stock systems should be reported to management

- Explain and illustrate how structural and operational weaknesses in bank and cash systems should be reported to management

**18 OTHER AUDIT AND
REVIEW EVIDENCE III -
STOCK**

**21 OTHER AUDIT AND
REVIEW EVIDENCE VI
– TANGIBLE FIXED
ASSETS AND LONG-
TERM LIABILITIES**

24 AUDIT FINALISATION

BPP
PUBLISHING

28 **NOT-FOR-PROFIT**
   ORGANISATIONS

THE EXAM PAPER

The examination is a three hour paper constructed in two sections. The bulk of the questions will be discursive but some questions involving computational elements will be set from time to time.

Section A is compulsory. The questions will cover the key elements of the syllabus relevant to both internal and external audit assignments. Section B requires candidates to answer two out of three questions. The questions will cover all areas of the syllabus.

		Number of Marks
Section A:	3 compulsory	60
	scenario-based questions	
	(no single question will exceed 25 marks)	
Section B:	Choice of 2 from 3	40
	questions (20 marks each)	100

ADDITIONAL INFORMATION

This paper encompasses:

1   Internal review, which may be provided either by internal auditors or may be outsourced to external auditors.

2   External audit and external review services, which are provided by external auditors only.

References to audit and auditors mean both internal and external audit and auditors, except where otherwise indicated. Detailed knowledge of external audit is currently more important than external review in this syllabus. However, students are expected to keep up-to-date with the development of alternatives to the statutory audit

Candidates need to be aware that questions involving knowledge of new examinable regulations will not be set until at least six months after the last day of the month in which the regulation was issued.

The Study Guide provides more detailed guidance on the syllabus. Examinable documents are listed in the 'Exam Notes' section of the Students' Newsletter.

Analysis of past papers

December 2001

Section A

1   Role of internal/external auditors, outsourcing
2   Risk, audit work
3   Purchase controls, report to management

Section B

4   Debtors' audit, circularisation
5   Analysis of audit and review report
6   Auditing standards, audit regulations

Pilot Paper

Section A

1   Professional ethics
2   Audit risk and going concern
3   Role of internal audit

Section B

4   Fixed assets, depreciation
5   Internal controls, sales and debtors
6   Stock, management letter

OXFORD BROOKES BSc (Hons) IN APPLIED ACCOUNTING

The standard required of candidates completing Part 2 is that required in the final year of a UK degree. Students completing Parts 1 and 2 will have satisfied the examination requirement for an honours degree in Applied Accounting, awarded by Oxford Brookes University.

To achieve the degree, you must also submit two pieces of work based on a **Research and Analysis Project**

- A 5,000 word **Report** on your chosen topic, which demonstrates that you have acquired the necessary research, analytical and IT skills.

- A 1,500 word **Key Skills Statement,** indicating how you have developed your interpersonal and communication skills.

BPP was selected by the ACCA to produce the official text *Success in your Research and Analysis Project* to support students in this task. The book pays particular attention to key skills not covered in the professional examinations.

> AN ORDER FORM FOR THE NEW SYLLABUS MATERIAL, INCLUDING THE OXFORD BROOKES PROJECT TEXT, CAN BE FOUND AT THE END OF THIS STUDY TEXT.

OXFORD INSTITUTE OF INTERNATIONAL FINANCE MBA

Plans for a new joint MBA have been announced by the ACCA and Oxford Brookes University, who have set up the Oxford Institute of International Finance as a partnership. BPP has been appointed the provider of materials and electronic support. This new qualification has been available worldwide from January 2002.

The MBA is available to those who have completed the professional stage of the ACCA qualification (subject to when this was achieved), as the ACCA's Professional exams contribute credits towards the MBA award.

The qualification features an introductory module (*Markets, Management and Strategy*). This is followed by modules on *Global Business Strategy, Managing Self Development* and *Organisation Change and Transformation*. The MBA is completed by a **research dissertation.**

For further information, please see the Oxford Institute's website: www.oxfordinstitute.org

BPP PUBLISHING

Part A
Framework

Chapter 1

THE NATURE AND PURPOSE OF ASSURANCE

Topic list	Syllabus reference
1 The purpose of assurance	1
2 The nature of assurance services	1
3 Assurance and reports	1
4 The chronology of an audit	1

Introduction

Firstly we need to consider **why there is a need for assurance in relation to financial and non-financial information**. You learnt about the nature of a company in Paper 2.2 (old Paper 2). The main reason an assurance is required is the fact that the ownership and management of a company are not necessarily the same thing. We will introduce concepts of **agency, accountability** and **stewardship**.

Secondly, it is important to understand **what assurance services exist**. The key assurance services which your syllabus concentrates on are the audit (statutory and non-statutory), reviews, and internal reviews. Although it is strictly defined, many people do not understand what an audit is and what it is designed to achieve. This results in an **expectations gap**, which is discussed more in Chapter 19.

The effect of audits and reviews is that people interested in the accounts of an entity are given a level of **assurance** as to the quality of the contents of the accounts. The audit report focuses on the truth and fairness of the accounts. It gives reasonable assurance, rather than an absolute assurance. The degrees of assurance given by audits and reviews are discussed in section 3.

While audits will vary according to the nature of the clients' businesses, most will follow standard stages overall. The chronology of a typical statutory audit is set out in section 4.

The rest of the text builds on themes identified in this chapter. This is shown in the table below.

Part A	The regulations and codes of practice surrounding auditors
Part B	Planning audit and other assurance work
Parts C+D	Carrying out audit work
Part E	Reporting

Study Guide

Section 1

Explain the:

- Nature, development and social role of audit and review
- Concepts of accountability, stewardship and agency
- Reporting as a means of communication to different stakeholders and the importance of stakeholder dialogue

BPP PUBLISHING

- High level of assurance provided by audit assignments and risk-based approaches; the moderate level of assurance provided by review assignments and procedural approaches; assignments in which no assurance is provided
- Recent extension in the scope of audit and review assignments

Section 2

- Types of opinion provided in statutory audit assignments
- The limitations of statutory audits

Exam guide

This chapter explains the basis of auditing and explains the distinction between audit and review. The mechanics of these issues are explained throughout the text. Questions in the exam could draw on matters in this chapter, **in conjunction** with the knowledge you will obtain later in the text.

1   THE PURPOSE OF ASSURANCE

1.1   The key reason for having an audit or review can be seen by working through the following scenario.

Purpose of assurance scenario

Laine decides to set up a business selling flowers. She gets up early in the morning, visits the market, and then sets up a stall by the side of the road. For the first year, all goes well. She sells all the flowers she is able to buy and she derives some income from the business.

However, Laine feels that she could sell more flowers if she was able to transport more to the place where she sells them, and also knows that there are several other roads nearby that she could sell flowers, if she could be in two places at once. She could achieve these two things by buying a van, and by employing other people to sell flowers on the other roads.

Laine needs more money to achieve this expansion of her business. She decides to ask her rich friend Glyn to invest in the business.

Glyn can see the potential of Laine's business and wants to invest, but he doesn't want to be involved in the management of the business. He also does not want to have ultimate liability for the debts of the business if the business fails. He therefore suggest that they set up a limited company. He will own the majority of the shares and be entitled to dividends. Laine will be managing director and be paid a salary for her work.

At the end of the first year of trading as a limited company, Glyn receives a copy of the financial statements. Profits are lower than expected, so his dividend will not be a large as he had hoped. He knows that Laine is paid a salary so does not care as much as him that profits are low.

Glyn is concerned by the level of profits and feels that he wants further assurance on the accounts. He doesn't know whether they give a true reflection on the last year's trading, particularly as the profits do not seen as high as those Laine had predicted when he agreed to invest.

1.2   The solution is that the **assurance** Glyn is seeking can be given by an independent **audit or review** of the financial statements. An auditor can provide the two things that Glyn requires:

- A **knowledgeable review** of the company's business and of the accounts
- An **impartial view,** since Laine's view might be partial.

1.3   Other people will also view the company's accounts with interest, for example:

- Creditors of the company
- The Inland Revenue

1.4 The various people interested in the accounts of a company are sometimes referred to as **stakeholders**. Although they will all judge the accounts by different criteria, **they will all gain assurance** from learning that the accounts they are reading have been subject to an independent report.

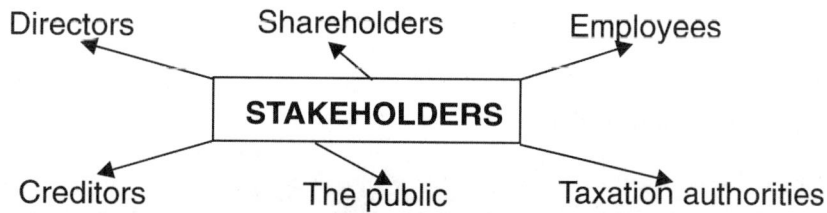

```
   Directors        Shareholders        Employees
        ↖                ↖                   ↗
          ┌──────────────────────────────┐
          │        STAKEHOLDERS          │
          └──────────────────────────────┘
        ↙                ↓                   ↘
   Creditors         The public       Taxation authorities
```

1.5 The example of Glyn and Laine is a simple one. In practice companies may have thousands of shareholders and may not know the management personally. It is therefore important that directors are **accountable** to shareholders. Directors act as **stewards** of the shareholders' investments. They are **agents** of the shareholders.

KEY TERMS

Accountability is the quality or state of being accountable, that is, being required or expected to justify actions and decisions. It suggests an obligation or willingness to accept responsibility for one's actions.

Stewardship is the practice of being a steward, that is, someone employed to manage another person's property.

Agents were introduced in paper 2.2 *Corporate and Business Law*. Agents are people employed or used to provide a particular service. In the case of a company, the people being used to provide the service managing the business also have the second role of being people in their own right trying to maximise their personal wealth.

An **assurance engagement** is one where a professional accountant evaluates or measures a subject matter that is the responsibility of another party against suitable criteria, and expresses an opinion which provides the intended user with a level of assurance about that subject matter.

1.6 Continuing the example above, we see the following relationship.

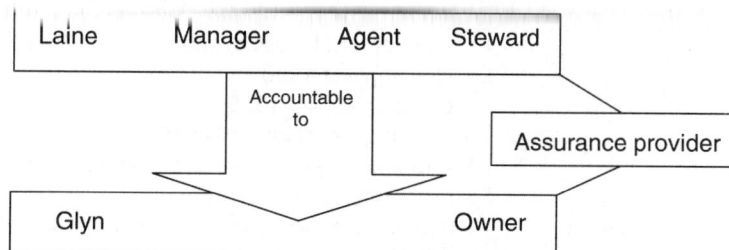

```
┌─────────────────────────────────────────┐
│ Laine    Manager    Agent    Steward     │
│               ┌──────────┐           │
│               │Accountable│          └────────┐
│               │    to    │      ┌──────────────────────┐
│               │          │      │  Assurance provider  │
│               │          │      └──────────────────────┘
│         ┌─────┴──────────┴─────┐   ↗
│         │ Glyn            Owner │
└─────────────────────────────────┘
```

1.7 The **auditor can give assurance** to the owners that their agents have accounted properly for their actions, so that owners can assess how well management have discharged their stewardship.

1.8 In order to give this assurance, it is important that the assurance providers are **independent** from both the owners and the managers so that the opinion they give is **objective**. This is discussed more in Chapter 4.

2 THE NATURE OF ASSURANCE SERVICES

2.1 A definition of an assurance service was given above. It is an engagement **to express an opinion giving assurance** to a set of people **on information which is the responsibility of others**.

2.2 That definition sums up two of the major features of the audit and internal review syllabus, audits and reviews.

Statutory and non-statutory audits

> **KEY TERM**
>
> An **audit** is an exercise whose objective is **to enable auditors to express an opinion** whether the financial statements
>
> - Give a **true and fair view** (or equivalent) of
>   - The entity's affairs at the period end, and of
>   - Its profit and loss (or income and expenditure) for the period then ended
>
> - And have been **properly prepared** in accordance with the applicable reporting framework (for example relevant legislation and applicable accounting standards) or, where the specific requirements prescribe the term, whether the financial statements 'present fairly'.

2.3 In an audit, the auditor gives an opinion to the members (shareholders in a company) of an organisation on the financial statements which are the responsibility of the directors. It is important to remember that the auditors only have a **duty** to report to the shareholders.

2.4 Audits are required under statute in the case of a large number of undertakings, including the following.

Undertaking	Principal Act
Limited companies	Companies Act 1985
Building societies	Building Societies Act 1965
Trade unions and employer associations	Trade Union and Labour Relations Act 1974
Housing Associations	Various acts depending on the legal constitution of the housing association, including: Industrial and Provident Societies Act 1965 Friendly and Industrial and Provident Societies Act 1968 Housing Act 1980 Companies Act 1985 Housing Association Act 1985.
Certain charities	Various acts depending on the status of the charity, including special Acts of Parliament.
Unincorporated investment businesses	Regulations made under the Financial Services Act 1986

2.5 **Non-statutory audits** are performed by independent auditors because the owners, proprietors, members, trustees, professional and governing bodies or other interested parties want them, rather than because the law requires them. In consequence, auditing may extend to every type of undertaking which produces accounts, including:

- Clubs
- Charities (some of these will require statutory audits as well)
- Sole traders

- Partnerships

2.6 The audit of **not for profit organisations** will be considered in more detail in Chapter 21.

2.7 Auditors may also give an **opinion** on **statements other than annual accounts**, including:

- Summaries of sales in support of a statement of royalties
- Statements of expenditure in support of applications for regional development grants
- The circulation figures of a newspaper or magazine

2.8 In all such audits the auditors must take into account any **regulations** contained in the internal rules or constitution of the undertaking. Examples of the regulations which the auditors would need to refer to in such assignments would include:

- The rules of clubs, societies and charities
- Partnership agreements

Advantages of the non-statutory audit

2.9 In addition to the advantages common to all forms of audit, including the verification of accounts, recommendations on accounting and control systems and the possible detection of errors and fraud, the audit of the accounts of a **partnership** may be seen to have the following advantages.

(a) It can provide a means of **settling accounts** between the partners.

(b) Where audited accounts are available this may make the **accounts more acceptable** to the **Inland Revenue** when it comes to agreeing an individual partner's liability to tax. The partners may well wish to take advantage of the auditors' services in the additional role of tax advisers.

(c) The **sale of** the business or the **negotiation of loan** or overdraft facilities may be facilitated if the firm is able to produce audited accounts.

(d) An audit on behalf of a 'sleeping partner' is useful since generally such a person will have little other means of checking the accounts of the business, or confirming the share of profits due to him or her.

Question 1

Some of the advantages above will also apply in the audit of the accounts of a sole trader, club or charity. Which ones? And can you think of others?

Reviews

2.10 Some of the benefits discussed above might also be obtained through a review, which is an **exercise similar to audit**.

KEY TERM

The objective of a **review engagement** is to enable an auditor to state whether, on the basis of procedures which do not provide all the evidence that would be required in an audit, anything has come to the auditor's attention that causes the auditor to believe that the financial statements are not prepared, in all material respects, in accordance with an identified financial reporting framework.

2.11 The major result for recipients of a review engagement is that the **level of assurance** they gain from a review engagement is not as high as from an audit. This is discussed in Section 3.

2.12 However, the procedures carried out in a review engagement are similar to an audit. There is a higher reliance on the use of analytical procedures (discussed in Chapter 12) but otherwise, the approach is similar. Therefore, the procedures discussed later in this text are relevant to both reviews and audit.

2.13 In the UK, guidance on how to audit is produced by the Auditing Practices Board. This is discussed further in Chapter 2. There is currently no UK guidance from the APB on undertaking a review. Auditors need to use their professional judgement to ascertain the level of work required to give the appropriate level of assurance on a review assignment.

Internal audit

KEY TERM

Internal audit is an appraisal or monitoring activity established by management and directors, for the review of the accounting and internal control systems as a service to the entity. It functions by, amongst other things, examining, evaluating and reporting to management and the directors on the adequacy and effectiveness of components of the accounting and internal control systems.

2.14 Up to now in this Chapter we have discussed assurance services where an independent outsider provides an opinion on financial information. However, the syllabus is also concerned with the assurance that can be provided to management (an by implication, to other parties) by **internal auditors**.

2.15 The management of an organisation will wish to establish systems to ensure that business activities are carried out efficiently. They will institute clerical, administrative and financial controls.

2.16 Larger organisations may appoint full-time staff whose **function is to monitor and report on the running of the company's operations**. Internal audit staff members are one type of control. Although some of the work carried out by internal auditors is similar to that performed by external auditors, there are **important distinctions** between the nature of the two functions.

DIFFERENCES BETWEEN EXTERNAL AND INTERNAL AUDITS		
	External	*Internal*
Independence	Independent of organisation	Appointed by management
Responsibilities	Fixed by statute	Decided by management
Report to	Members	Management
Scope of work	Express an opinion on truth and fairness of accounts	Consider whatever financial and operational areas management determines

2.17 Internal audit will be discussed in more detail in Chapter 3.

3 ASSURANCE AND REPORTS

Dec 01

3.1 External auditors give an opinion on the **truth and fairness** of financial statements. This is not an opinion of absolute correctness. 'True' and 'fair' are terms used in legislation, but they are not defined in law. The following definitions are generally accepted definitions.

> **KEY TERMS**
>
> **True.** Information is factual and conforms with reality, not false. In addition the information conforms with required standards and law. The accounts have been correctly extracted from the books and records.
>
> **Fair.** Information is free from discrimination and bias and in compliance with expected standards and rules. The accounts should reflect the commercial substance of the company's underlying transactions.

3.2 An auditor obtains evidence 'on a test basis', he does not check everything. He is therefore giving 'reasonable' not 'absolute' assurance.

> **KEY TERM**
>
> An audit gives the reader **reasonable assurance** on the truth and fairness of the financial statements. The audit report does not guarantee that the financial statements are correct, but that they are true and fair within a reasonable margin of error.

3.3 One of the reasons that an auditor does not give absolute assurance is the **inherent limitations** of audit.

Limitations of audit

3.4 The assurance auditors give is governed by the fact that auditors use **judgement** in deciding what audit procedures to use and what conclusions to draw, and also by the limitations of every audit.

(a) The fact that auditing is **not** a purely **objective** exercise. Auditors have to make judgements in a number of areas including risk assessment, what constitutes a significant error, what tests to perform and ultimately what opinion to give.

(b) The fact that **auditors do not check every item** in the accounting records. We shall see that for many tests auditors only check a sample of items.

(c) The **limitations** of **accounting** and **internal control systems.** We shall discuss these further in Chapter 9, but for example the systems may not be able to deal with unusual transactions, and may not be flexible enough to cope well with changing circumstances.

(d) The possibility that **client management or staff** might **not tell the truth,** or **collude in fraud.** One important control may be a division of responsibilities so that one member of staff checks another's work, but the control will be ineffective if the two collude.

(e) The fact that audit **evidence indicates** what is **probable** rather than what is **certain.** Some figures in the accounts are estimates, some require a significant degree of judgement and some are affected by uncertainty.

(f) The fact that auditors are **reporting** generally **some months after** the balance sheet date. The client's position may be changing, and the position shown in the accounts at the last year-end may be significantly different from the up-to-date position. If on the other hand auditors do report soon after the balance sheet date, evidence about certain figures in the balance sheet may be insufficient.

(g) The **limitations** of the audit report. Although work has been done to make the report more informative, the standard format is unlikely to reflect all aspects of the audit.

Hence auditors can only express an opinion; they cannot certify whether accounts are completely correct.

3.5 Misstatements which are significant to readers may exist in financial statements and auditors will plan their work on this basis, that is, with **professional scepticism.** Auditing guidance makes it clear that, even where auditors assess the risk of litigation or adverse publicity as very low, they must still perform sufficient procedures according to auditing standards, that is, there can never be a reason for carrying out an audit of a lower quality than that demanded by the auditing standards

3.6 Another reason is the concept of **materiality,** which will be discussed in Chapter 6. The auditors' task is to decide whether accounts show a true and fair view. The auditors are **not responsible for establishing whether the accounts are correct in every particular** for the following reasons.

- It can take a great deal of time and trouble to check the correctness of even a very small transaction and the resulting benefit may not justify the effort.

- Financial accounting inevitably involves a degree of estimation which means that financial statements can never be completely precise.

KEY TERM

Materiality is an expression of the relative significance or importance of a particular matter in the context of financial statements as a whole.

A matter is material if its omission or misstatement would reasonably influence the decisions of an addressee of the auditors' report.

Materiality may also be considered in the context of any individual primary statement within the financial statements or of individual items included in them.

Materiality is not capable of general mathematical definition as it has both qualitative and quantitative aspects.

3.7 Although the definition refers to the decision of the addressees of the audit report (the company's members), their decisions may well be influenced by other entities who use the accounts. For example, if the accounts are to be used to secure a bank loan, what is significant to the bank will influence the way members act.

3.8 Therefore the views of other users of the accounts must be taken into account if they influence the members of the company.

Question 2

Define the term 'not material' and state in which context it might be used.

Answer

Generally speaking, transactions or other events will be seen as material in the context of an enterprise's financial statements, if their omission or misstatement would reasonably influence the decisions of an addressee of the auditors' report. The report lends some credibility to those statements which will have been prepared by the management of the enterprise.

In order to form an opinion on truth and fairness, the auditors will need to exercise their professional judgement and experience in relation to the question of materiality. It will be important for the auditors to assess materiality not merely in monetary terms but also in the overall context of the company's financial statements, statutory requirements and recognised best accounting and auditing practice.

Levels of assurance

3.9 'Assurance' here means **the auditors' satisfaction as to the reliability of the assertion made by one party for use by another party (ie by the management for use by the readers of the accounts)**.

3.10 To provide such assurance, the auditors must assess the evidence collected as a result of procedures conducted and then express a conclusion. The degree of satisfaction achieved and, therefore, **the level of assurance which may be provided**, is **determined by** the **procedures performed** and their results.

3.11 An **audit** can be distinguished from other assurance engagements in the following ways.

(a) **Audit engagement:** the auditor provides a high, but not absolute, level of assurance that the information audited is free of material misstatement. This is expressed positively in the audit report as **reasonable assurance**.

(b) **Review engagement:** the auditor provides a moderate level of assurance that the information subject to review is free of material misstatement. This is expressed in the form of **negative assurance**.

KEY TERM

Negative assurance is when an auditor gives an assurance that nothing has come to his attention which indicates that the financial statements have not been prepared according to the framework. In other words, he gives his assurance in the absence of any evidence to the contrary.

(c) **Agreed-upon procedures:** the auditor simply provides a report of the actual findings, so **no assurance** is expressed. Users of the report must instead judge for themselves the auditor's procedures and findings, and draw their own conclusions from the auditor's work.

(d) **Compilation engagement:** users of the compiled information gain some benefit from the accountant's (as opposed to auditor's) involvement, but **no assurance** is expressed in the report.

4 THE CHRONOLOGY OF AN AUDIT

4.1 The chart below outlines the **normal** main stages of a statutory audit.

A DIAGRAMMATIC REPRESENTATION OF THE SYSTEMS AUDIT

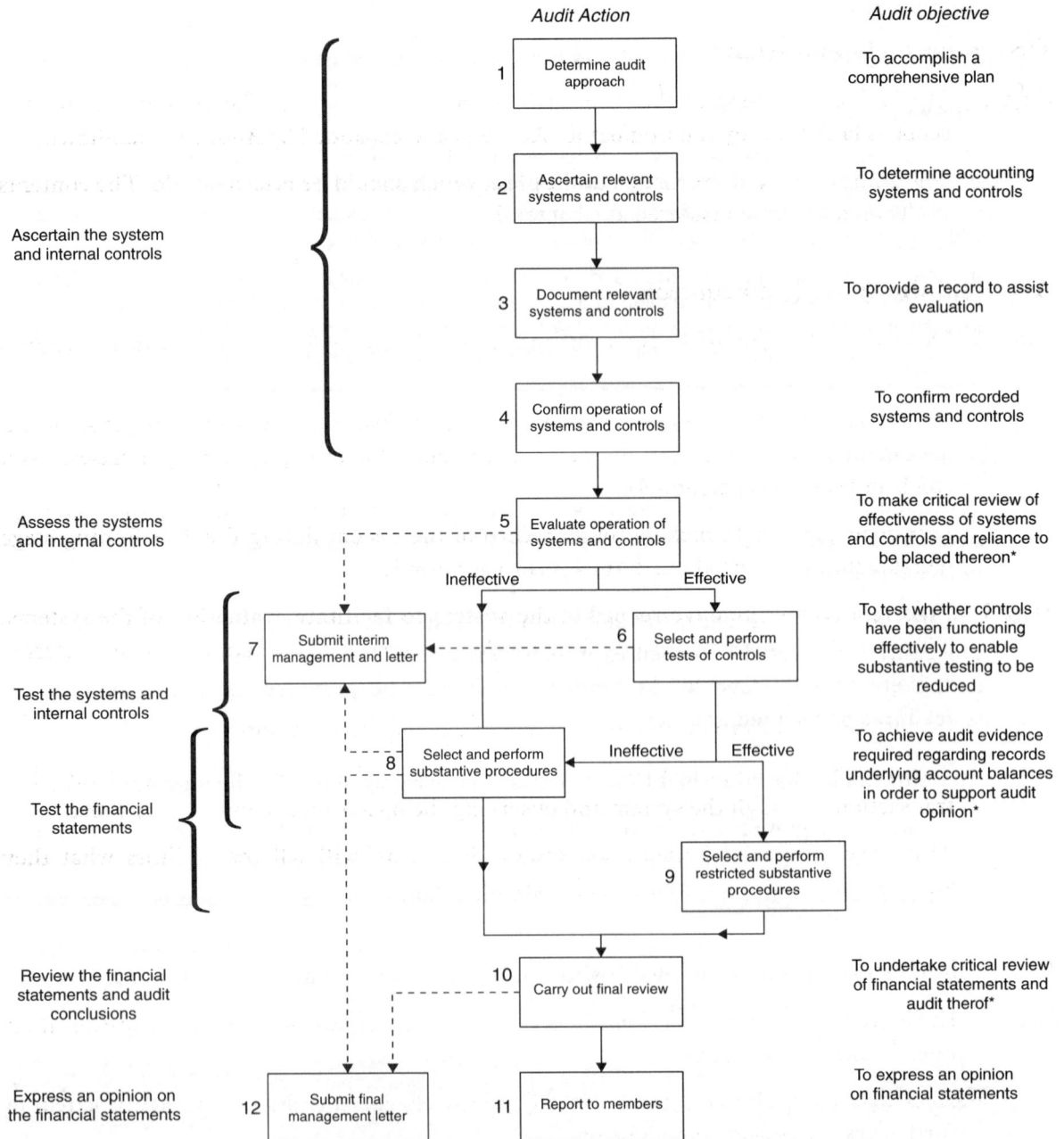

	Audit Action	Audit objective
Ascertain the system and internal controls	1 Determine audit approach	To accomplish a comprehensive plan
	2 Ascertain relevant systems and controls	To determine accounting systems and controls
	3 Document relevant systems and controls	To provide a record to assist evaluation
	4 Confirm operation of systems and controls	To confirm recorded systems and controls
Assess the systems and internal controls	5 Evaluate operation of systems and controls	To make critical review of effectiveness of systems and controls and reliance to be placed thereon*
Test the systems and internal controls	7 Submit interim management and letter — Ineffective / Effective — 6 Select and perform tests of controls	To test whether controls have been functioning effectively to enable substantive testing to be reduced
Test the financial statements	8 Select and perform substantive procedures — Ineffective / Effective	To achieve audit evidence required regarding records underlying account balances in order to support audit opinion*
	9 Select and perform restricted substantive procedures	
Review the financial statements and audit conclusions	10 Carry out final review	To undertake critical review of financial statements and audit therof*
Express an opinion on the financial statements	12 Submit final management letter 11 Report to members	To express an opinion on financial statements

⟶ Stages in audit procedures

------➤ Contact with management

* A secondary objective of this audit action is to recommend to management improvements in systems controls and in accounting procedures and practices

4.2 Certain common elements form a major part of the auditors' work on any client.

(a) **Making such tests** and enquiries as they consider necessary to form an opinion as to the reliability of the accounting records as a basis for the preparation of accounts

(b) **Checking the accounts** against the underlying records

(c) **Reviewing the accounts** for compliance with the Companies Act and accounting standards

4.3 We will now look at the various stages identified in the diagram.

Determine audit approach

Stage 1   Determine the **scope** of the audit and the auditors' approach. For statutory audits the scope is laid down by the Companies Act 1985 and expanded by Auditing Standards.

The auditors should prepare an **audit plan,** which should be placed on file. The contents of the plan will be considered at Chapter 6.

Ascertain the system and controls

Stage 2   Determine the **flow of documents** and **extent of controls** in existence in the client's system.

This is a fact finding exercise which is achieved by discussing the accounting system and document flow with all the relevant departments (for example, sales, purchases, cash, stock and accounts personnel).

It is good practice to make a rough record of the system during this fact finding stage which will be converted to a formal record at Stage 3.

Stage 3   Prepare a **comprehensive record** of the **system to facilitate evaluation** of the systems. The records may be in various formats (for example, charts, narrative notes, internal control questionnaires and flowcharts).

Stage 4   Confirm that the **system recorded** is the same as that **in operation.**

This is achieved by performing walk-through tests. These involve tracing a handful of transactions through the system and observing the operation of controls over them.

This check is useful because sometimes client staff will tell the auditors what they **should be doing** rather than **what is actually done.**

Assess the system and internal controls

Stage 5   **Evaluate the systems** to gauge their reliability and formulate a basis for testing their effectiveness in practice.

Auditors will be able to recommend any improvements and also determine the extent of further tests at Stages 6 and 8 below.

Test the system and internal controls

Stage 6   *(This should only be carried out if the controls are evaluated as effective at Stage 5. If not, Steps 6 and 7 should be omitted.)*

If controls are effective, tests should are designed to establish compliance with the system should be selected and performed.

Tests of controls, which cover a larger number of items than walkthrough tests and cover a more representative sample of transactions through the period, should be carried out.

If **controls are strong,** the records should be reliable and the amount of detailed testing can be reduced. If **controls are ineffective** in practice, more extensive substantive procedures will be required.

Stage 7 After evaluating the systems and testing controls, auditors normally send an interim **report to management** identifying weaknesses and recommending improvements.

Test the financial statements

Stages 8 and 9 These tests are concerned with **substantiating the figures** given **in the final financial statements.**

Substantive tests also serve to assess the effect of errors, should errors exist.

Before designing a substantive procedure it is essential to consider whether any errors produced could be significant. If the answer is no, there is no point in performing a test.

Review the financial statements

Stage 10 The financial statements should be reviewed to determine the overall reliability of the account by making a **critical analysis of content and presentation.**

Express an opinion

Stage 11 The auditors evaluate the evidence that they have obtained and they **express their opinion** to members in the form of an **audit report.**

Stage 12 The **final report to management** is an important **non-statutory end product** of the audit. The purpose of it is to make further **suggestions for improvements** in the systems and to **place on record specific points** in connection with the audit and the accounts.

Risk based audits

4.4 In recent years there has been a shift towards risk-based auditing. This refers to the development of auditing techniques which are responsive to **risk factors** in an audit. Auditors apply judgement to determine what level of risk pertains to different areas of a client's system and devise appropriate audit tests. This approach should ensure that the greatest audit effort is directed at the riskiest areas, so that the chance of detecting errors is improved and excessive time is not spent on 'safe' areas.

4.5 The increased use of risk-based auditing reflects two factors.

(a) The growing **complexity** of the business environment increases the danger of fraud or misstatement. Factors such as the developing use of computerised systems and the growing internationalisation of business are relevant here.

(b) Pressures are increasingly exerted by audit clients for the auditors to keep **fee levels down** while providing an improved level of service.

Risk-based auditing is responsive to both factors. The stages of the audit shown in the diagram will still be followed in a risk-based audit.

Exam focus point

Your answers on the specific practical situations you are given in the exam should reflect the major risks relevant to the client. We shall consider audit risk further in Chapter 6.

Chapter roundup

- An assurance engagement is essentially an **impartial**, **knowledgeable** scrutiny and review.

- This syllabus is particularly concerned with **audit** (both statutory and non statutory), **review** and the assurance provided to management by **internal audit**.

- The auditors' report on company accounts is in terms of **truth** and **fairness**. This is generally taken to mean accounts are:

  ° Factual
  ° Free from bias
  ° Reflect the commercial substance of the business's transactions

- The APB also points out that audits at best give **reasonable assurance** that the accounts are free from material misstatement.

- As well as audits of accounts, there are various other types of audits and reviews, statutory and non-statutory. The level of assurance given in such an exercise may be lower than for a statutory audit.

- **Internal auditors** are employed as part of an organisation's system of controls. Their responsibilities are determined by management and may be wide-ranging.

- The **key** stages of the audit process are:

  ° Determine audit approach
  ° Ascertain the accounting system and internal controls
  ° Assess the accounting system and internal controls
  ° Test the accounting system and internal controls
  ° Test the financial statements (substantive testing)
  ° Review the financial statements
  ° Express an opinion

Quick quiz

1   Complete the APB's **definition** of an audit:

An audit is an exercise whose objective is to enable auditors to ....
whether the financial statements give .... (or equivalent) of the entity's
affairs at .... and of .... for
the period then ended and have been .... in accordance with
.... (for example relevant legislation and applicable accounting
standards) or, where other specific requirements prescribed their terms, whether the financial statements
'present fairly'.

2   Link the correct definition to each term.

(i)   Accountable   (iv)   True
(ii)   Steward   (v)   Fair
(iii) Agent   (vi)   Materiality

(a)   An expression of the relative significance or importance of a particular matter in the context of the financial statements as a whole.

BPP PUBLISHING

(b)   A person employed to provide a particular service.

(c)   Factual and conforming with reality. In conformity with relevant standards and law and correctly extracted from accounting records.

(d)   A person employed to manage other people's property.

(e)   Free from discrimination and bias and in compliance with expected standards and rules. Reflecting the commercial substance of underlying transactions.

(f)   Being required or expected to justify actions and decisions.

3   For which of the following is an audit a statutory obligation? (There is more than one correct answer.)

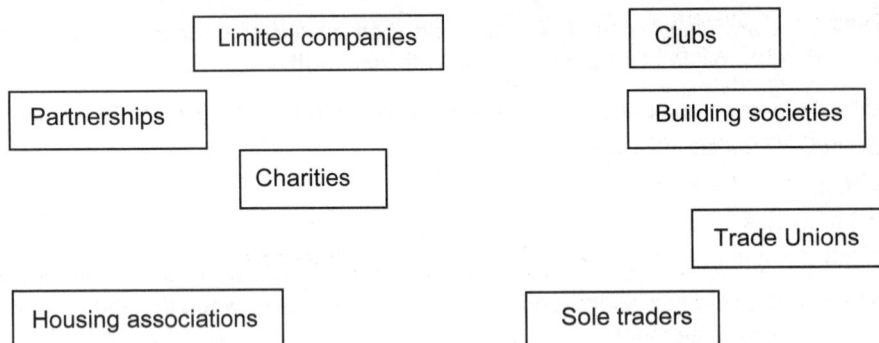

Limited companies	Clubs
Partnerships	Building societies
Charities	
	Trade Unions
Housing associations	Sole traders

4   Put the following stages of an audit in the correct order.

- Assess the system and internal controls
- Test the financial statements
- Determine audit approach
- Express an opinion
- Ascertain the system and controls
- Review the financial statements
- Test the system and internal controls

5   Tests of control cover a large number of transactions while walkthrough tests will be limited to one or two.

True   ☐

False   ☐

6   A partnership might benefit from having an audit even though it is not required to do so by law. Tick the correct advantages below.

(a)   Means of settling accounts between partners   ☐

(b)   Ensures that partners' remuneration will be made public   ☐

(c)   May make the accounts more acceptable to the Inland Revenue   ☐

(d)   The individual partners will not have to prepare tax returns   ☐

(e)   May facilitate the negotiation of a loan   ☐

(f)   May benefit a 'sleeping partner' who otherwise has little knowledge of partnership affairs   ☐

Answers to quick quiz

1   Express an opinion, a true and fair view, the period end, the profit or loss (or income and expenditure), properly prepared, the applicable reporting framework.

2   (i)   (f)   (Iv) (c)
     (ii) (d)   (v)   (e)
     (iii) (b)   (vi) (a)

3   Limited companies, building societies, trade unions, housing associations, **some** charities.

4   •   Determine audit approach
     •   Ascertain the system and controls
     •   Assess the system and internal controls
     •   Test the system and internal controls
     •   Test the financial statements
     •   Review the financial statements
     •   Express an opinion

5   True

6   (a), (c), (e) and (f). (b) would not necessarily be a result of an audit and would not be an advantage anyway. (d) is simply untrue.

Now try the question below from the Exam Question Bank

Number	Level	Marks	Time
1	Introductory	n/a	15 mins

Chapter 2

STATUTORY AUDIT AND REGULATION

Topic list	Syllabus reference
1 The statutory audit requirement	1
2 Audit regulation	3
3 Rights and duties of auditors	3
4 Auditing standards	3
5 The statutory audit and corporate governance	1

Introduction

This chapter describes the **statutory requirement** for certain companies to have an audit, and the discussion which exists over exemption from that requirement.

It also examines the main bodies and the major factors which govern auditing. You should particularly note how the **audit monitoring regime** works and what inspectors are looking for.

The legal **rights and duties** of auditors are outlined in section 3.

The chapter then goes on to discuss the role of the Auditing Practices Board and the scope of the guidance it issues. You should understand the authority of **SAS's, Practice Notes** and **Bulletins**. The detailed requirements of the SAS's you are required to know (most of them) are discussed throughout the rest of this Study Text.

Study guide

Section 2

Describe the:

- UK regulatory framework in which statutory audits take place

- Development and status of the Auditing Practices Board Statements of Auditing Standards and their relationship with International Standards on Auditing

- Reasons for, and mechanisms for, the regulation of auditors by Government and other regulatory agencies including other UK standard-setters

- Types of opinion provided in statutory audit assignments

Exam guide

The regulatory framework for auditors discussed in this chapter and the ethical framework discussed in Chapter 4 are very important. They could be examined together as part of a scenario question on planning or accepting appointment.

The examiner has stated that an understanding of the overall regulatory regime is essential to an understanding of external audit and could be examined in the compulsory section of the exam in the future.

1 THE STATUTORY AUDIT REQUIREMENT

1.1 The majority of companies are required to have an audit under the Companies Act 1985. Members of companies which are dormant have the right to dispense with an audit.

1.2 There are some exceptions to this requirement, notably the exception for small, limited companies.

Small company audit exemption

1.3 The following exemption is given to small companies:

(a) A company is **totally exempt** if it qualifies as a small company under s 246 of the Companies Act 1985, its **turnover is not more than £1m** and its **balance sheet total is not more than £1.4m**. The turnover limit is expected to go up to £4.8 million at some time in the future.

(b) These **exemptions do not apply to public companies, banks, insurers, insurance brokers, those authorised under the Financial Services Act, trade unions, employers' associations, parent companies or subsidiaries**.

(c) Members of **groups** can claim exemption from audit.

(d) A company is not exempt if **members holding 10%** or more of its shares **demand an audit** at least a month before the end of the financial year.

(e) Where a company takes advantage of an exemption its directors must make a **statement on the balance sheet**. Among other things, this statement must acknowledge the directors' responsibility for ensuring that proper accounting records are kept, and for preparing accounts that give a true and fair view and comply with the Companies Act.

1.4 This exemption was extended to companies with a turnover of £1m in 2000. Prior to that, the turnover limit had been £350,000. It is anticipated that the exemption limit could rise as high as £4.8m, which is the maximum level permissible under EC law.

1.5 There has long been a **debate over the benefits of an audit to small companies**. Many small companies are owned by the same people that manage them, and the benefit of an independent review of the stewardship of those managers has significantly less value than in a company where ownership and management are divorced.

1.6 As part of raising the threshold for audit exemption to £1m, the government have been developing an alternative form of assurance for smaller companies, which would be voluntary. It is called the **Independent Professional Review (IPR)**. Preliminary indications are that the IPR has not been welcomed wholeheartedly.

1.7 The traditional arguments for and against changing the requirement to have an audit in small companies are set out below.

(a) *Shareholders*	
Against change	Shareholders not involved in management need the reassurance given by audited accounts. Furthermore, the existence of the audit deters the directors from treating the company's assets as their own to the detriment of minority shareholders.

		Audited financial statements are invaluable in arriving at a fair valuation of the shares in an unquoted company either for taxation or other purposes.
	For change	Where all the shareholders are also executive directors or closely related to them, the benefit gained from an audit may not be worth its cost.

(b)	*Banks and other institutional creditors*	
	Against change	Banks rely on accounts for the purposes of making loans and reviewing the value of security.
	For change	There is doubt whether banks rely on the audited accounts of companies to a greater extent than those of unincorporated associations of a similar size which have not been audited.
		A review of the way in which the bank accounts of the company have been conducted and of forecasts and management accounts are at least as important to the banks as the appraisal of the audited accounts.
		There is no reason why a bank should not make an audit a precondition of granting a loan.

(c)	*Trade creditors*	
	Against change	Creditors and potential creditors should have the opportunity to assess the strength of their customers by examining audited financial statements either themselves or through a credit company.
	For change	In practice, only limited reliance is placed on the accounts available from the Registrar of Companies as they are usually filed so late as to be of little significance in granting short term credit.

(d)	*Tax authorities*	
	Against change	The Inland Revenue and Customs & Excise rely on accounts for computing corporation tax and checking VAT returns.
	For change	There is little evidence to suggest that the tax authorities rely on audited accounts to a significantly greater extent than those, which, whilst being unaudited have been prepared by an independent accountant.

(e)	*Employees*	
	Against change	Employees are entitled to be able to assess audited accounts when entering wage negotiations and considering the future viability of their employer.
	For change	There is little evidence to suggest that, in the case of small companies, such assessments are made.

(f)	*Management*	
	Against change	The audit provides management with a useful independent check on the accuracy of the accounting systems and the auditor is frequently able to recommend improvements in those systems.
	For change	If the law were changed, the management of a company could, if they so desired, still elect to have an independent audit. It is

likely, however, that a systems review accompanied by a management consultancy report would represent a greater benefit for a similar cost.

The statutory audit opinion

1.8 The Companies Act requires the auditors to state **explicitly** (s 235) whether in their opinion the annual accounts have been properly prepared in accordance with the Act and in particular whether a **true and fair view** is given:

EXPLICIT OPINIONS
In the balance sheet, of the **state of the company's affairs** at the end of the financial year
In the profit and loss account, of the **company's profit or loss** for the financial year

1.9 In addition certain requirements are reported on **by exception**. The auditor only has to report if they have not been met. The following are matters with which the auditors **imply** satisfaction in an unqualified report under s 237 of the Companies Act 1985.

IMPLIED OPINIONS
Proper accounting records have been kept and proper returns adequate for the audit received from branches not visited.
The **accounts** are in **agreement** with the **accounting records** and returns.
All information and **explanations** have been **received** as the auditors think necessary and they have had access at all times to the company's books, accounts and vouchers.
Details of directors' emoluments and other benefits have been correctly **disclosed** in the financial statements.
Particulars of loans and other **transactions** in favour of **directors** and others have been correctly **disclosed** in the financial statements.
The **information** given in the **directors' report** is **consistent** with the **accounts**.

Directors' emoluments

1.10 The auditors should include in their report the required disclosure particulars of directors' emoluments and transactions with directors, if these requirements have not been complied with in the accounts (s 237).

1.11 This means that the auditors will carry out various procedures to ensure that they are aware of all such emoluments and transactions by reference to directors' service contracts, board minutes, cash book payments and so on. Benefits received in kind may be particularly hard to identify. See Chapter 17 for further details.

The standard report

1.12 A standardised report is required by Statement of Auditing Standards 600 *Auditors' report on financial statements*. This report will be looked at in detail in Chapter 19. A list of the Statement of Auditing Standards relevant to this syllabus is given in section 4.

2   AUDIT REGULATION

2.1   In the UK, the audit profession is self-regulating. This right has been devolved by the Government in statute, primarily the Companies Acts 1985 and 1989, which implement the EC's 8th Directive.

2.2   In the UK there are a large number of different accountancy, or accountancy-related, institutes and associations, such as the Association of Chartered Certified Accountants (ACCA) or the Chartered Institute of Management Accountants (CIMA).

2.3   All these bodies vary from each other, depending on the nature of their aims and the specialisms their members wish to attain. They are all, however, characterised by various attributes, stringent entrance requirements (examinations and practical experience), strict codes of ethics and technical updating of members.

2.4   The membership of all these bodies is scattered through practice, industry, government and public bodies.

Eligibility as auditor

2.5   Membership of a Recognised Supervisory Body (discussed below) is the main prerequisite for eligibility as an auditor. An audit firm may be either a body corporate, a partnership or a sole practitioner.

2.6   The Companies Act 1985 also requires an auditor to hold an '**appropriate qualification**'. A person holds an 'appropriate qualification' if he or she has gained one of the following.

- Acknowledgement that he or she has met **existing criteria** for appointment as an auditor under CA 1985

- A **recognised qualification** obtained in the UK

- An **approved overseas qualification**

Ineligibility as auditor

2.7   The Companies Act sets out the following reasons that a person would be **ineligible** for appointment as company auditor.

Being an **officer** or **employee** of the company
Being a **partner** or **employee** of such a person
Being a **partnership** in which such a person is a partner
Ineligible by any of the above three reasons for appointment as auditor of any parent or subsidiary undertaking or a subsidiary undertaking of any parent undertaking of the company
There exists between him or her or any associate (of his or hers) and the company (or any company) a **connection** of any description as may be specified in regulations laid down by the Secretary of State

2.8   The legislation does **not** disqualify the following from being an auditor of a limited company:

- A shareholder of the company
- A debtor or creditor of the company

- A close relative of an officer or employee of the company

2.9 However, the regulations of the accountancy bodies applying to their own members are stricter than statute in this respect.

2.10 Under the Companies Act 1985, a person may also be ineligible on the grounds of 'lack of independence'. The definition of lack of independence is to be determined by statutory instrument following consultation with the professional bodies.

2.11 Under s 389 CA 1985, if during their term of office a company auditor becomes ineligible for appointment to the office, he must vacate office and give notice in writing to the company.

Recognised Supervisory Bodies

2.12 The EC 8th Directive on company law requires that persons carrying out statutory audits must be approved by the authorities of EU member states. The authority to give this approval in the UK is delegated to Recognised Supervisory Bodies (RSBs). An auditor must be a member of an RSB and be eligible under its own rules. The ACCA is a RSB.

2.13 The RSBs are required to have rules to ensure that persons eligible for appointment as a company auditor are either (4(1), Sch 11, CA 1989):

- Individuals holding an appropriate qualification
- Firms controlled by qualified persons

2.14 A number of other requirements concern the procedures which RSBs must follow to **maintain** the **competence** of **members**.

2.15 Professional qualifications, which will be prerequisites for membership of an RSB, will be offered by Recognised Qualifying Bodies ('RQBs') approved by the Secretary of State.

Question 1

Outline the role of the Recognised Supervisory Bodies (RSBs).

Answer

See Paragraphs 2.11 - 2.14.

Supervisory and monitoring roles

2.16 RSBs must also implement procedures for inspecting their registered auditors on a regular basis. A Monitoring Unit was set up for this purpose by the ACCA.

2.17 The frequency of inspection will depend on the number of partners, number of offices and number of listed company audits (these factors are also reflected in the size of annual registration fees payable). The length of the inspections depends on the size of the firm and may be combined with Financial Services Act based inspections where necessary.

2.18 The following features should be apparent in each practice visited by the monitoring unit.

- A **properly structured audit approach**, suitable for the range of clients served and work undertaken by the practice

- Carefully instituted **quality control procedures,** revised and updated constantly, to which the practice as a whole is committed. This will include:
  - ° Staff recruitment
  - ° Staff training
  - ° Continuing professional development
  - ° Frequent quality control review

- **Commitment to ethical guidelines,** with an emphasis on independence issues

- An emphasis on **technical excellence**

- Adherence to the '**fit and proper**' criteria by checking personnel records and references

- Use of internal and, if necessary, external **peer reviews** or consultations

- **Appropriate fee** charging per audit assignment

Legal requirements on appointment to a company audit

2.19   The Companies Act 1985 requires that the auditors should be appointed by and therefore be **answerable** to the **shareholders**.

RIGHTS OF APPOINTMENT	
Members	Appoint auditors at each **general meeting** where accounts are laid by **positive resolution** (re-appointment of existing auditor not automatic)
	Auditors hold office until conclusion of next general meeting at which accounts are laid
Directors	Can appoint auditor:
	(a) Before company's **first general meeting** at which accounts are laid; auditors hold office until conclusion of that meeting
	(b) To fill **casual vacancy**
Secretary of State	Can appoint auditors if **no auditors** are **appointed** or reappointed at general meeting at which accounts are laid

Special notice of appointment

2.20   In certain cases relating to appointment of an auditor **special notice** (28 days) is required for the appropriate resolutions at a general meeting (ss 388(3) and 391 A(1)(b) CA 1985).

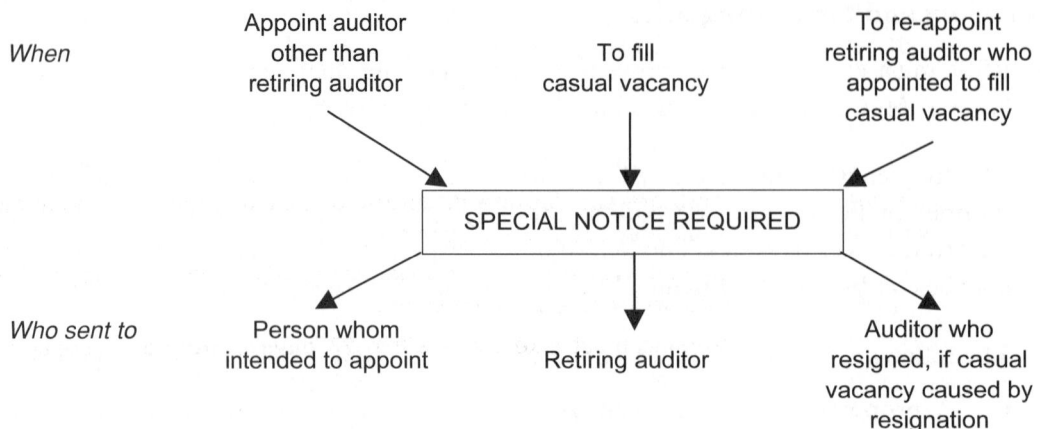

Elective regime for private companies

2.21 The Companies Act 1989 introduced a regime whereby a private company may elect not to comply with some of the statutory requirements of the Companies Act. Such an election is called an elective resolution.

2.22 A private company may by elective resolution elect not to be required to appoint auditors annually (s 386 CA 1985). In such a case, the auditors in office will be deemed to be re-appointed annually.

2.23 A private company may also elect not to lay accounts before the members in general meeting. If the company makes such an election without making an election not to reappoint auditors annually, it must hold a general meeting annually to re-elect the auditors (s 385A CA 1985).

Remuneration

2.24 The remuneration of the auditors, which will include any sums paid by the company in respect of the auditors' expenses, will be fixed (s 390A CA 1985) either by **whoever made** the **appointment** or in **such manner** as the **company in general meeting** may determine.

2.25 However the auditors' remuneration is fixed, it must be disclosed in the annual accounts of the company (s 390A(3) CA 1985).

Legal requirements at the end of an audit relationship

2.26 You will have learnt the legal requirements for resignation and removal of auditors in your studies for paper *2.2 Corporate and Business Law* (old paper 2).

2.27 However, it is relevant to revise them briefly here. It is important that auditors know the procedures because as part of their client acceptance, they have a duty to ensure the old auditors were properly removed from office.

RESIGNATION OF AUDITORS	
1 Resignation procedures	Auditors deposit **written notice** together with **statement of circumstances** relevant to members/creditors or statement that no circumstances exist
2 Notice of resignation	Sent by company to Registrar of Companies within 14 days
3 Statement of circumstances	Sent by: (a) Auditors to Registrar of Companies within **28 days** (b) Company to everyone entitled to receive a copy of accounts within **14 days** (unless company applies to court because statement of circumstances defamatory)
4 Convening of general meeting	**Auditors** can **require directors** to call extraordinary general meeting to discuss circumstances of resignation Directors must send out notice for meeting within **21 days** of having received requisition by auditors Meeting must take place within **28 days** of **notice** of meeting being sent out
5 Statement prior to general meeting	**Auditors** may require company to circulate (different) **statement of circumstances** to everyone entitled to notice of meeting

6	Other rights of auditors	Can **receive all notices** that relate to: (a) A general meeting at which their term of office would have expired (b) A general meeting where casual vacancy caused by their resignation to be filled Can **speak** at these meetings on **any matter** which **concerns them as auditors**
		REMOVAL OF AUDITORS
1	Notice of removal	**Either special notice** (28 days) with copy sent to auditor **Or** if elective resolution in place, **written resolution** to terminate auditors' appointment Directors must convene meeting to take place within 28 days of notice
2	Representations	**Auditors** can make **representations** on why they ought to stay in office, and may require company to state in notice representations have been made and send copy to members
3	If resolution passed	(a) Company must **notify registrar** within **14 days** (b) Auditors must **deposit statement of circumstances** at company's registered office **within 14 days** of ceasing to hold office. Statement must be sent to registrar within **28 days** of deposit
4	Auditor rights	Can **receive notice** of and **speak** at: (a) General meeting at which their term of office would have expired (b) General meeting where casual vacancy caused by their removal to be filled

3 RIGHTS AND DUTIES OF AUDITORS

3.1 The audit is primarily a statutory concept, and eligibility to conduct an audit is set down in statute. Similarly, the rights and duties of auditors are set out in statute, to ensure that the auditors have sufficient power to carry out an effective audit.

Duties

3.2 The principal statutory duties of auditors in respect of the audit of a limited company are set out in ss 235 and 237 CA 1985. The auditors are required to report on every balance sheet and profit and loss account laid before the company in general meeting.

3.3 As we have seen in section 1, only compliance with legislation and **truth** and **fairness** of accounts need to be explicitly referred to in the audit report; the other matters can be reported **by exception only**.

Rights

3.4 The Companies Act provides statutory rights for auditors to enable them to carry out their duties.

3.5 The principal rights, excepting those dealing with resignation or removal, are set out in the table below, and the following are notes on more detailed points.

s 389A(1)	*Access to records*	A right of access at all times to the books, accounts and vouchers of the company
s 389A(1)	*Information and explanations*	A right to require from the company's officers such information and explanations as they think necessary for the performance of their duties as auditors
s 390(1)(a) and (b)	*Attendance at/notices of general meetings*	A right to attend any general meetings of the company and to receive all notices of and communications relating to such meetings which any member of the company is entitled to receive
s 390(1)(c)	*Right to speak at general meetings*	A right to be heard at general meetings which they attend on any part of the business that concerns them as auditors
s 381B(2)-(4)	*Rights in relation to written resolutions*	A right to receive a copy of any written resolution proposed
s 253	*Right to require laying of accounts*	A right to give notice in writing requiring that a general meeting be held for the purpose of laying the accounts and reports before the company (if elective resolution dispensing with laying of accounts in force)

Rights to information

3.6 If auditors have not received all the information and explanations they consider necessary, they should state this fact in their audit report.

3.7 The Act makes it an offence for a company's officer knowingly or recklessly to make a statement in any form to an auditor which:

- Purports to convey any information or explanation required by the auditor
- Is materially misleading, false or deceptive

The penalty is a maximum of two years' imprisonment, a fine or both (s 389A(2)).

4 AUDITING STANDARDS

Rules governing audits

4.1 We discussed in Chapter 1 the various stakeholders in a company, and the number of people who might read a company's accounts. Consider also that a number of these readers will not just be reading a single company's accounts, but will also be reading the accounts of a large number of companies, and making comparisons between them.

4.2 Readers **want assurance** when making comparisons **that the reliability of the accounts does not vary from company to company.** This assurance will be obtained not just from knowing each set of accounts has been audited, but knowing that each set of accounts has been audited to **common standards.**

4.3 Hence there is a need for audits to be **regulated** so that auditors follow the same standards. As we see in this chapter, auditors have to follow rules issued by a variety of bodies. As we saw above, some obligations are imposed by **Parliament,** for company auditors by the Companies Act 1985. Some obligations are imposed by the professional bodies to which auditors are required to belong (such as the **ACCA**).

4.4   The detailed requirements that auditors are obliged to follow are set by the **Auditing Practices Board** (APB).

The APB and Statements of Auditing Standards (SASs)

4.5   Auditing standards are set by the Auditing Practices Board (APB). The APB:

- Can issue auditing standards in its own right without having to obtain the approval of all the professional accounting bodies

- Has strong representation from outside the accounting profession

- Has a commitment to openness, with agenda papers being circulated to interested parties, and an annual report being published

4.6   The APB issued a document in May 1993 entitled *The scope and authority of APB pronouncements*. The APB makes three categories of pronouncement.

- Statements of Auditing Standards (SASs)
- Practice Notes
- Bulletins

4.7   The scope of **SASs** is as follows.

'SASs contain basic principles and essential procedures ('Auditing Standards') which are indicated by bold type and with which auditors are required to comply, except where otherwise stated in the SAS concerned, in the conduct of any audit of financial statements.

4.8   The APB also publishes SASs which apply to:

- Audits and related services provided by auditors other than audits of financial statements

- Specific types of audits, for example audits of specialised industries

4.9   Apart from statements in bold type, SASs also contain other material which is not prescriptive but which is designed to help auditors interpret and apply auditing standards. The APB document also states that auditing standards need not be applied to immaterial items (items which are not significant to the accounts. We shall discuss what is material and what is immaterial in later chapters.)

4.10   The authority of SASs is given in the document.

'Auditors who do not comply with Auditing Standards when performing company or other audits in Great Britain make themselves liable to regulatory action by the RSB with whom they are registered and which may include the withdrawal of registration and hence of eligibility to perform company audits.'

4.11   **Practice Notes** are issued 'to assist auditors in applying Auditing Standards of general application to particular circumstances and industries'.

4.12   **Bulletins** are issued 'to provide auditors with timely guidance on new or emerging issues'.

4.13   Practice Notes and Bulletins are persuasive rather than prescriptive, but they indicate good practice and have a similar status to the explanatory material in SASs. Both Practice Notes and Bulletins may be included in later SASs.

4.14 The APB standards are listed below along with old APC standards and guidelines which may also be examinable as they have yet to be replaced.

Statements of Auditing Standards (SASs): APB		*Issue date*
Series 001/099	*Introductory matters*	
010	Scope and authority of APB pronouncements	May 93
Series 100/199	*Responsibility*	
100	Objective and general principles governing an audit of financial statements	Mar 95
110	Fraud and error	Jan 95
120	Consideration of law and regulations	Jan 95
130	The going concern basis in financial statements	Nov 94
140	Engagement letters	Mar 95
150	Subsequent events	Mar 95
160	Other information in documents containing audited financial statements	Mar 95
Series 200/299	*Planning, controlling and recording*	
200	Planning	Mar 95
210	Knowledge of the business	Mar 95
220	Materiality and the audit	Mar 95
230	Working papers	Mar 95
240	Quality control for audit work	Sep 00
Series 300/399	*Accounting systems and internal control*	
300	Accounting and internal control systems and audit risk assessments	Mar 95
Series 400/499	*Evidence*	
400	Audit evidence	Mar 95
410	Analytical procedures	Mar 95
420	Audit of accounting estimates	Mar 95
430	Audit sampling	Mar 95
440	Management representations	Mar 95
450	Opening balances and comparatives	Mar 95
460	Related parties	Nov 95
470	Overall review of financial statements	Mar 95
480	Service organisations	Jan 99
Series 500/599	*Using the work of others*	
500	Considering the work of internal audit	Mar 95
510	The relationship between principal auditors and other auditors	Mar 95
520	Using the work of an expert	Mar 95
Series 600/699	*Reporting*	
600	Auditors' report on financial statements	May 93
601	Imposed limitation of audit scope	Mar 99
610	Communication of audit matters with those charged with governance	Jun 01
620	The auditors right and duty to report to regulators in the financial sector	Mar 94

Notes

Questions will be based on the principles and good practice set out in the Statements of Auditing Standards and Guidelines.

Auditing Guidelines: APC

308   Guidance for internal auditors
405   Attendance at stocktaking

Practice Notes

13   The audit of small businesses
16   Bank reports for audit purposes

Other documents

Bulletin 2001/02 Revisions to the wording of auditors' reports on financial statements and the interim review report.

Briefing paper Providing assurance on the effectiveness of internal control

Accounting standards

The accounting knowledge required for Paper 2.6 is the same as that for Paper 1.1.

Exam focus point

SASs are quoted throughout this Text and you must understand how they are applied in practice. Not all of the above SASs are examinable. The list of examinable documents is available on the ACCA's website in the student section. Of the documents listed above, those which **are not examinable** are:

- SAS 240 Quality control for audit work
- SAS 460 Related parties
- SAS 510 The relationship between principal auditors and other auditors
- SAS 620 The auditors' right and duty to report to regulators in the financial sector

SAS 100 Objectives and general principles governing an audit

4.15   The APB give general guidance about an audit of financial statements in this SAS.

SAS 100.1

In undertaking an audit of financial statements auditors should:

(a)   carry out procedures designed to obtain sufficient appropriate audit evidence, in accordance with Auditing Standards contained in SASs, to determine with reasonable confidence whether the financial statements are free of material misstatement;

(b)   evaluate the overall presentation of the financial statements, in order to ascertain whether they have been prepared in accordance with relevant legislation and accounting standards; and

(c)   issue a report containing a clear expression of their opinion on the financial statements.

4.16   The SAS's explanatory material highlights the credibility given to financial statements by the auditors' opinion; it provides '**reasonable assurance** from an **independent** source that they present a true and fair view'. That is to say the audit report reassures readers of the accounts that the accounts have been examined by a **knowledgeable, impartial** professional. SAS 100 goes on to stress further the importance of auditors acting **independently** and **ethically**.

> **SAS 100.2**
>
> In the conduct of any audit of financial statements auditors should comply with the ethical guidance issued by their relevant professional bodies.

4.17 Ethical guidance is discussed in Chapter 4.

4.18 There are provisos, of course. The auditors' opinion is **not**:

- A **guarantee** of the future viability of the entity
- An **assurance** of **management's effectiveness and efficiency**

4.19 Most importantly, the standard makes clear that the auditors do not bear any responsibility for the preparation and presentation of the financial statements.

> The responsibility for the preparation and presentation of the financial statements is that of the directors of the entity. Auditors are responsible for forming and expressing an opinion on the financial statements. The audit of the financial statements does not relieve the directors of any of their responsibilities.

Application of SASs to small businesses

4.20 The Auditing Practices Board published in July 1997 Practice Note 13 *The Audit of Small Businesses*. Although the detailed contents of this Practice Note are not examinable, it does make some important general points which you should remember.

4.21 The Practice Note states that the audit of small businesses is influenced by a number of factors. These include:

(a) The **characteristics of small businesses**. The most important characteristics are **concentration of ownership** and **management** in a few/single individual(s), the business having few sources of income and uncomplicated activities and limited internal controls and the potential for management override.

(b) The **professional relationship** between the business and its auditors. Auditors will often provide a range of **other services** as well as auditing, particularly accounting services. The Practice Note stresses the importance of the auditors maintaining objectivity despite providing other services, and not taking over the role of management.

(c) Audits of small businesses may also be affected by the fact that **small teams of auditors** may be **involved** and the rules governing the content of small businesses' financial statements.

4.22 The Practice Note then goes on to give a detailed commentary on how specific SASs impact upon the audit of small businesses.

SAS 110 Fraud and error

4.23 Amongst the signs of fraud that may be particularly relevant to small businesses are the owner-manager making no distinction between business and personal transactions and the owner-manager's lifestyle being materially inconsistent with remuneration levels.

SAS 130 Going concern

4.24 The Practice Note points out that a small business's continuation as a going concern may depend on a single factor, for example funds not being withdrawn.

SAS 230 Working papers

4.25 If accountancy work is being used as audit evidence, the work performed, the evidence obtained and the conclusions drawn are recorded as for normal audit work.

SAS 400 Audit evidence

4.26 The Practice Note emphasises that accountancy work can provide audit evidence for certain objectives, but is unlikely to provide sufficient evidence of completeness and valuation.

International Audit and Assurance Standards Board (IAASB)

4.27 Similar in nature to the International Accounting Standards Committee (IASC), the IAASB issues International Standards on Auditing (ISAs).

4.28 Recently the International Organisation of Securities Commissions (IOSCO) gave measured approval to ISAs, so that multi-national accounts which are audited in compliance with ISAs are now acceptable to securities regulatory authorities around the world. The EC has stated that all listed companies in the EC should report their group results in accordance with ISAs from 2005.

4.29 These developments are important as it they provide an incentive for countries to bring their standards into line with international ones. The APB pays great attention to ISAs in its review of existing UK auditing pronouncements, to ensure that these reflect all the basic precepts of the international standards.

4.30 The following list of ISAs is not directly examinable in the UK paper, but is included here for interest and comparison with the APB's current standards.

No	Title
100	Assurance engagements
110	Glossary of terms
120	Framework of ISAs
200	Objective and general principles governing an audit of financial statements
210	Terms of audit engagement
220	Quality control for audit work
230	Documentation
240	Fraud and error
250	Consideration of laws and regulations in an audit of financial statements
260	Communication of audit matters with those charged with governance
300	Planning
310	Knowledge of the business
320	Audit materiality
400	Risk assessments and internal control
401	Auditing in a computer information systems environment
402	Audit considerations relating to entities using service organisations
500	Audit evidence
501	Audit evidence – additional considerations for specific items

510	Initial engagements – opening balances
520	Analytical procedures
530	Audit sampling and other selective testing procedures
540	Audit of accounting estimates
560	Subsequent events
580	Management representations
610	Considering the work of internal auditing
620	Using the work of an expert
700	The auditor's report on financial statements
710	Comparatives
720	Other information in documents containing audited financial statements
910	Engagements to review financial statements

5   THE STATUTORY AUDIT AND CORPORATE GOVERNANCE

5.1   We have already noted in this Chapter that the object of the statutory audit is to **provide assurance to the shareholders** on the truth and fairness of the **financial statements**. It is vital that you understand the statutory audit in these terms and see that it is this which **distinguishes** it from other assurance services.

5.2   One of the major issues in companies at the current time is the issue of **corporate governance**. This will be discussed further in Chapter 3, but it is simply the issue of company **management**, and the **position of trust** which is held by directors. It is an increasing concern of the investing world that companies have **good corporate governance**.

5.3   The government have commissioned reports on corporate governance in the wake of some major management frauds in the 1990s. These reports, particularly the **Cadbury Report**, have identified the statutory audit as a significant tool in ensuring good corporate governance. The Cadbury Report describes audit as '**one of the cornerstones of corporate governance**'.

5.4   However, critics would say that the **statutory audit is insufficient** in its report to members on the truth and fairness of the financial statements, and that the **audit should provide more assurance** on matters which reflect the governance of the company.

5.5   Such matters might include reporting on the **internal controls** of a company for instance. As we shall see in Part C, the auditors consider the internal controls of a company for the purposes of their audit, but they do not directly report on their effectiveness as part of their statutory audit.

5.6   Another area in which people believe that the auditors' responsibilities could be extended is the area of **fraud**. Auditors do not have a duty to prevent or detect fraud – although many people think that they do.

5.7   As you read through the rest of this book and consider the other forms of assurance that exist and can be provided in addition to the statutory audit, you should **consider the limitations of the statutory audit as a check on the quality of corporate governance in the UK**. This is a topical issue, and one which could come up as a discussion element in your exam.

Chapter roundup

- The Companies Act requires the majority of companies to have an audit. Some small companies and dormant companies are exempt from the requirement.

- Auditors must hold an **appropriate qualification** and to be a member of a **recognised supervisory body.**

- A person is **ineligible** to act as auditor if he is an **employee** or officer or has various other close connections with the company.

- Recognised supervisory bodies must follow a number of procedures to ensure their members are **fit** and **proper** and **competent** and that audit work is conducted **properly.**

- Legislation affecting auditors is introduced by the government on its own initiative or in response to European Commission **directives.**

- Details concerning the appointment and removal of auditors, and their rights and duties, can be found in the Companies Acts.

- The Auditing Practices Board issues:

    ° SASs
    ° Practice Notes
    ° Bulletins

- SASs contain **basic principles** and **procedures** with which auditors must comply as well as other material designed to help auditors.

- **Accounting standards** are set by the **Accounting Standards Board** and have a direct impact on the accounts on which auditors are reporting.

- The Auditing Practices Board takes account of standards set by the **International Auditing Practices Committee** when setting auditing standards.

Quick quiz

1   People can be ineligible to be company auditors under

- The Companies Act 1985
- The requirements of their RSB

Using the reasons given, fill in the table below.

Reasons

(a)   Officer or employee of the company
(b)   Creditor of the company
(c)   Not a member of an RSB
(d)   A partner of someone in (a)
(e)   A close relative of an officer of the company
(f)   Does not hold a recognised qualification

Ineligible under law	Ineligible under RSB rules

2   Match the APB document to its status.

Statements of Auditing Standards
        - bold script

PERSUASIVE

Statement of Auditing Standards
        - other materials

PERSUASIVE

Practice notes

	EXPLANATORY

Bulletins

	PRESCRIPTIVE

3   (a)   A person does not have to satisfy membership criteria to become a member of a Recognised Supervisory Body

   True   ☐

   False   ☐

   (b)   Auditing is regulated by the government in the UK.

   True   ☐

   False   ☐

   (c)   The Auditing Practices Board issues auditing standards which auditors are require to follow.

   True   ☐

   False   ☐

4   Which of the following features should the JMU not expect to find when visiting audit firms?

   (a)   Properly structured audit approach
   (b)   Quality control procedures
   (c)   Peer reviews
   (d)   Charging of unsubstantiated fees

Answers to quick quiz

1   **Ineligible under law**

   (a)   Officer/employee
   (c)   Not a member of an RSB
   (d)   A partner of someone in (a)
   (f)   No appropriate qualification

   Ineligible under RSB rules

   (a)   Officer/employee
   (b)   Creditor
   (d)   A partner of someone in (a)
   (e)   Close relative of officer

2   Statement of Accounting Standards
         - bold script   PRESCRIPTIVE

   Statement of Auditing Standards
         - other materials   EXPLANATORY

   Practice notes   PERSUASIVE

   Bulletins   PERSUASIVE

3   (a)   False. All RSBs have stringent membership requirements.
   (b)   False. It is regulated by RSBs.
   (c)   True. Auditors face discipline by their RSB if they do not.

4   (d)

Now try the question below from the Exam Question Bank

Number	Level	Marks	Time
2	Introductory	n/a	30 mins

Chapter 3

INTERNAL AUDIT

Topic list		Syllabus reference
1	Internal audit	2
2	Outsourcing the internal audit function	2
3	Internal audit assignments	2
4	Operational internal audit assignments	2
5	Fraud	1

Introduction

Internal auditing is **different from external auditing**, although the **techniques used** for many of the assignments internal audit will are carry out are very **similar** to those which will be outlined in detail in Parts B, C and D of this Study Text.

Internal audit is **established by management** to **assist in corporate governance** by assessing internal controls and helping in risk management. It can be a department of employees, or, as discussed in Section 2, can be **outsourced** to expert service providers.

The **ethical requirements** of internal auditors are different from those of external auditors due to the nature of the function. This will be discussed in Chapter 4.

Various **assurance assignments** which may be undertaken by internal auditors are outlined in Sections 3 and 4, and their role with regard to **fraud** is discussed briefly in Section 5. While the techniques used may be similar to external auditors, the **focus and reasons** behind the audit may **differ**.

There are no statutory requirements in relation to internal audit reports. Reporting will be discussed in detail in Part E of this Study Text.

Study guide

Section 3

Explain the:

- Development and role of internal audit in achieving corporate objectives and as part of good corporate governance practice

- Function of internal audit in the context of corporate risk management and organisational control

- Relative merits of outsourcing internal audit and internal review services to external auditors and others, and the associated problems

- Difference between the role of external audit and internal audit

Section 4

Describe the:

- Scope of internal audit work and the limitations of the internal audit function

- Nature and purpose of internal audit and internal review assignments including:

  - Value for money
  - Best value
  - IT
  - Financial

  audit and review assignments

- Nature and purpose of operational internal audit and review assignments including:

  - Procurement
  - Marketing
  - Treasury
  - HR

  audit and review assignments

Section 5

- Describe the responsibilities of internal auditors for fraud and error

Exam guide

Internal review is an important part of the syllabus, and there was a complete question on internal audit in the pilot paper (in the exam question bank) and the ethics question had a section on internal auditors. The role of internal audit was explored in the December 2001 paper, particularly with regard to fraud.

---

1   INTERNAL AUDIT

Dec 01

1.1   The following definition of internal audit was given in Chapter 1, for comparison with other forms of assurance service and providers.

> **KEY TERM**
>
> **Internal audit** is an appraisal or monitoring activity established by management and directors, for the review of the accounting and internal control systems as a service to the entity. It functions by, amongst other things, examining, evaluating and reporting to management and the directors on the adequacy and effectiveness of components of the accounting and internal control systems.

1.2   Internal audit is generally a feature of large companies. It is a function, provided either by employees of the entity of sourced from an external organisation to assist management in **achieving corporate objectives.**

Internal audit and corporate governance

1.3   In recent years, a great deal of emphasis has been placed on the importance of **good corporate governance.** The importance of good corporate governance is based in the fact that companies, particularly larger ones, are owned by one set of people and managed by another set.

1.4   In recent years, some high profile frauds and questionable business practice have led to attention being cast on business management. In the 1990s, a series of committees were set up to consider the matter.

BPP PUBLISHING

1.5   The key committees were:

- Cadbury Committee 1992 (corporate governance)
- Greenbury Committee 1995 (directors' remuneration)
- Hampel Committee 1995 (corporate governance)
- Turnbull Committee 1999 (corporate governance)

1.6   The findings of these committees give us an insight into

- What corporate governance is
- Internal audit's role in corporate governance

> **KEY TERM**
>
> '**Corporate governance** is the system by which companies are directed and controlled'.
> *Cadbury Committee report*
>
> 'Good governance ensures that constituencies (stakeholders) with a relevant interest in the company's business are fully taken into account.'
> *Hampel Committee report*

Combined Code

1.7   In 1998, the Stock Exchange issued a 'combined code' of corporate governance requirements arising from the various committees and reports. This is mandatory for listed companies, but can also be seen as best practice for all UK companies.

Provisions of the Combined Code	
Directors' responsibilities	
The board	Should **meet regularly,** and have a **formal schedule of matters** reserved to it for its decision.
	There should be clear division of responsibilities between chairman and chief executive.
	Non-executive directors should comprise at least a third of the board. Directors should submit themselves for re-election every three years.
	Directors should submit themselves for re-election at regular intervals (at least every three years).
The AGM	Companies should propose **separate resolutions** at the AGM on each substantially different issue. The chairman should ensure that members of the audit, remuneration and nomination committees are available at the AGM to **answer questions**. Notice of AGMs should be sent out at least 20 days before the meeting.
Remuneration	There should be remuneration committees composed of non-executive directors to set directors' pay, which should provide pay which attracts, retains and motivates quality directors but avoids paying more than is necessary for the purpose.
	The company's annual report should contain a statement of remuneration policy and details of the renumeration of each director.

Directors' responsibilities (cont'd)	
Accountability and audit	The directors should **explain** their **responsibility for preparing accounts**. They should **report that the business is a going concern**, with supporting assumptions and qualifications as necessary.
Internal control	The directors should review the **effectiveness of internal control** systems, at least annually, and also **review the need for an internal audit function**.
Audit committee	The board **should establish an audit committee**.
Auditors' responsibilities	
Statement of responsibilities	The auditors **should include** in their report a statement of their reporting responsibilities.

1.8 The Turnbull report sets out some key guidelines for the Board.

TURNBULL GUIDELINES
Have a **defined process** for the **review** of effectiveness of **internal control**.
Review **regular** reports on **internal control**.
Consider **key risks** and how they have been **managed**.
Check the **adequacy** of **action taken** to remedy weaknesses and incidents.
Consider the **adequacy** of **monitoring**.
Conduct an **annual assessment** of risks and the effectiveness of internal control.
Make a **statement** on this process in the **annual report**.

1.9 The traditional definition of internal audit given at the start of the section shows how internal audit can help the directors achieve these objectives; the traditional purpose of internal audit was to review controls.

Internal audit and risk management

1.10 The third of the Turnbull guidelines refers to risk. All companies face risks arising from their operational activities. Risks arise in different areas.

- Risk the company will go bankrupt
- Risks arising from regulations and law
- Risks arising from publicity

1.11 Turnbull requires that risk be managed. This gives rise to another role for the internal audit function, relating to **risk management**.

1.12 Risk awareness and management should be the role of everyone in the organisation. The extended role of internal audit with regard to risk is the **monitoring of integrated risk management** within a company, and the reporting of results to the Board to enable them to report to shareholders.

1.13 It is generally the responsibility of individual departments in a business to assess the risks arising to that department and to design operating systems to reduce those risks. Persons working in the department are best placed to know the specific risks that will arise.

1.14 Internal audit may assist in the development of systems. However, their key role will be in **monitoring the overall process** and in **providing assurance** that the **systems** which the departments have designed **meet objectives** and **operate effectively**.

1.15 It is important that the internal audit department retain their **objectivity** towards these aspects of their role, which is another reason why internal audit would generally not be involved in the assessment of risks and the design of the system.

Distinction between internal and external audit

1.16 The best way to see the difference between internal and external audit is to revise a key term.

> **KEY TERM**
>
> An **external audit** is an exercise whose objective is to enable auditors to express an opinion whether the financial statements give a rue and fair view (or equivalent) of the entity's affairs are the period end and of its profit and loss for the period then ended and have been properly prepared in accordance with the applicable reporting framework.

1.17 Contrast the definition of external audit with the definition of internal audit given at the beginning of this chapter. The **external audit** is **focused on** a very small item, the **financial statements**, whereas the **internal audit is focused on the operations of the entire business**.

1.18 The following table **highlights the differences** between internal and external audit.

	Internal audit	External audit
Reason	Internal audit is an activity designed to **add value** and improve an **organisation's operations**.	An exercise to enable auditors to **express an opinion on the financial statements**.
Reporting to	Internal audit report to the **board of directors**, or other people charged with governance, such as the audit committee.	The external auditors report to the **shareholders**, or members, of a company on the stewardship of the directors.
Relating to	As demonstrated in the reason for their existence, internal audit's work relates to the **operations of the organisation**.	External audit's work relates to the **financial statements**. They are concerned with the financial records that underlie these.
Relationship with the company	Internal auditors are very often **employees of the organisation**, although sometimes the internal audit function is outsourced.	External auditors are **independent of the company and its management**. They are appointed by the shareholders.

1.19 The table shows that although some of the procedures that internal audit undertake are very similar to those undertaken by the external auditors, **the whole basis and reasoning of their work is fundamentally different**.

2   OUTSOURCING THE INTERNAL AUDIT FUNCTION   Dec 01

2.1   While, as we have just discussed, the scope of the internal auditor's work is different to that of the external auditor, there are many features that can link them.

2.2   The key linking factor is that the **techniques** which are used to carry out audits are the same for internal and external auditors.

2.3   It can be expensive to maintain an internal audit function consisting of employees. The Turnbull guidelines state that the directors should consider the need for them annually. However, the directors may conclude that the cost is prohibitive.

2.4   It is possible that the monitoring and review required by a certain company could be done in a small amount of time and full-time employees cannot be justified.

2.5   It is possible that a number of internal audit staff are required, but the cost of recruitment is prohibitive, or the directors are aware that the need for internal audit is only short-term.

2.6   In such circumstances, it is possible to **outsource the internal audit function**, that is, purchase the service from outside.

2.7   Therefore, many of the **larger accountancy firms offer internal audit services**. It is possible that the same firm might offer one client both internal and external audit services. In such circumstances the firm would have to be aware of the independence issues this would raise for the external audit team.

Question 1

Paragraph 2.7 refers to the independence issues which would arise through the audit firm offering both internal and external audit services to the same client.

(a)   What do you think are the independence issues?
(b)   Why should the issues affect the external audit team rather than the internal audit team?

Answer

(a)   External auditors are employed to give an assurance to the members of a company about the stewardship of the directors and the management of that entity. They are **independent verifiers**. If the firm provides internal audit services to the entity, two issues arise:

   (i)   Internal auditors report to the director so there is a **link between the firm and the directors** which is a block to independence.

   (ii)   The firm provides 'other services' to an external audit client, and they must consider the effects of that on their audit, particularly with regard to the ACCA's guidance on fee levels.

   The specific guidance about auditor independence will be considered in more detail in Chapter 4.

(b)   The issues arise for the external audit team as independence is a key ethical issue for external auditors. **As internal auditors provide a service to the directors, independence is not an ethical requirement for them, or even necessarily a possibility!**

   Ethical issues for internal auditors are also discussed in Chapter 4.

Advantages of outsourcing

2.8   The advantage of outsourcing internal audits is that outsourcing can overcome all the problems mentioned above.

   • Staff need to be recruited, as the **service provider has good quality staff.**

- The service provider has specialist skill and can assess what management require them to do. As they are external to the operation, this will not cause operational problems.

- Outsourcing can provide an **immediate** internal audit department.

- The service contract can be for the **appropriate time scale** (a two week project, a month, etc)

- Because the **time scale is flexible**, a **team of staff** can be provided if required.

- The service provider could also provide less than at team, but, for example, could provide one member of staff on a full-time basis for a short period, as a **secondment.**

2.9 Outsourced internal audit services are provided by many audit firms, particularly the big five. This can range from a team of staff for a short term project, or a single staff member on a long term project.

2.10 However, the fact that internal audit services are typically provided by external auditors can raise problems as well:

- The company might wish to **use the same firm** for internal and external audit services, but this may lead to **complications for the external auditors.**

- The **cost** of sourcing the internal audit function might be high enough to make the directors choose not to have an internal audit function at all.

2.11 A key advantage of outsourcing internal audit is that **outsourcing can be used on a short term basis,** to:

- Provide immediate services
- Lay the basis of a permanent function, by setting policies and functions
- Prepare the directors for the implications of having an internal audit function
- Assist the directors in recruiting the permanent function.

3 INTERNAL AUDIT ASSIGNMENTS

3.1 In the next two sections we will consider a number of the detailed assignments which an internal auditor could get involved in.

Exam focus point

You should read through these two sections now to learn **what an internal auditor does** and to reinforce the **difference between an internal audit and the statutory (external) audit** introduced in Chapter 2. However, don't worry too much about the mechanics of **how** they test the following things – you are going to be introduced to the techniques of auditing in the next few parts of this Text.

Value for money

3.2 EXAMPLE

A good example of value for money is a bottle of Fairy Liquid. If we believe the advertising, Fairy is good 'value for money' because it washes half as many plates again as any other washing up liquid. Bottle for bottle it may be more expensive, but plate for plate it is cheaper. Not only this but Fairy gets plates 'squeaky' clean. To summarise, Fairy gives us VFM because it exhibits the following characteristics.

- Economy (more clean plates per pound)
- Efficiency (more clean plates per squirt)
- Effectiveness (plates as clean as they should be)

These are the three Es of VFM.

The three Es

3.3 A 1990 CCAB Audit brief on VFM audit defined the three Es as follows.

(a) **Economy**: attaining the appropriate quantity and quality of physical, human and financial resources (**inputs**) at lowest cost. An activity would not be economic, if, for example, there was over-staffing or failure to purchase materials of requisite quality at the lowest available price.

(b) **Efficiency**: this is the relationship between goods or services produced (**outputs**) and the resources used to produce them. An efficient operation produces the maximum output for any given set of resource inputs; or it has minimum inputs for any given quantity and quality of product or service provided.

(c) **Effectiveness**: this is concerned with how well an activity is achieving its policy objectives or other intended effects.

3.4 The internal auditors will **evaluate these three factors** for any given business system or operation in the company. Value for money can often only be judged by **comparison**. In searching for value for money, present methods of operation and uses of resources must be **compared with alternatives**.

3.5 Economy, efficiency and effectiveness can be studied and measured with reference to the following.

Inputs	Outputs
Inputs means money or resources - the labour, materials, time and so on consumed, and their cost. For example, a VFM audit into state secondary education would look at the efficiency and economy of the use of resources for education (the use of schoolteachers, school buildings, equipment, cash) and whether the resources are being used for their purpose: what is the pupil/teacher ratio and are trained teachers being fully used to teach the subjects they have been trained for?	Outputs mean the results of an activity, measurable as the services actually produced, and the quality of the services. In the case of a VFM audit of secondary education, outputs would be measured as the number of pupils taught and the number of subjects taught per pupil; how many examination papers are taken and what is the pass rate.
Impacts	**Economy**
Impacts are the effect that the outputs of an activity or programme have in terms of achieving policy objectives. Policy objectives might be to provide a minimum level of education to all children up to the age of 16, and to make education relevant for the children's future jobs and careers. This might be measured by the ratio of jobs vacant to unemployed school leavers.	Economy is concerned with the cost of inputs, and it is achieved by obtaining those inputs at the lowest acceptable cost. Economy does not mean straightforward cost-cutting, because resources must be acquired which are of a suitable **quality** to provide the service to the desired standard. Cost-cutting should not sacrifice quality to the extent that service standards fall to an unacceptable level. Economising by buying poor quality materials, labour or equipment is a 'false economy'.

Efficiency	Effectiveness
Efficiency means the following. (a) Maximising output for a given input, for example maximising the number of transactions handled per employee or per £1 spent (b) Achieving the minimum input for a given output	Effectiveness means ensuring that the outputs of a service or programme have the desired impacts; in other words, finding out whether they succeed in achieving objectives, and if so, to what extent.
	In a profit-making organisation, objectives can be expressed financially in terms of target profit or return.
	In NFP (not-for-profit) organisations, effectiveness cannot be measured this way, because the organisation has non-financial objectives. The effectiveness of performance in NFP organisations could be measured in terms of whether targeted non-financial objectives have been achieved.

Selecting areas for investigation

3.6 Value for money checklists can be used. The following list identifies areas of an organisation, process or activity where there might be scope for significant value for money improvements. Each of these should be reviewed within individual organisations, with a view to assessing its economy, efficiency and effectiveness.

- Service delivery (the actual provision of a public service)
- Management process
- Environment

3.7 An alternative approach is to look at areas of spending. A value for money assessment of economy, efficiency, and effectiveness would look at whether:

- Too much money is being spent on certain items or activities, to achieve the targets or objectives of the overall operation.

- Money is being spent to no purpose, because the spending is not helping to achieve objectives.

- Changes could be made to improve performance.

3.8 An illustrative list is shown below of the sort of spending areas that might be looked at, and the aspects of spending where value for money might be improved.

- Employee expenses
- Premises expenses
- Supplies and services
- Establishment expenses
- Capital expenditure

Problems with VFM auditing	
Measuring outputs	For example, the outputs of a fire brigade can be measured by the number of call-outs, but it is not satisfactory to compare a call-out to individuals stuck in a lift with a call-out to a small house fire or a major industrial fire or a road accident etc.
Defining objectives	In not for profit organisations the quality of the service provided will be a significant feature of their service. For example, a local authority has, amongst its various different objectives, the objective of providing a rubbish collection service. The effectiveness of this service can only be judged by establishing what standard or quality of service is required.

Problems with VFM auditing	
Sacrifice of quality	Economy and efficiency can be achieved by sacrificing quality. Neither outputs nor impacts are necessarily measured in terms of quality. For example, the cost of teaching can be reduced by increasing the pupil:teacher ratio in schools, but it is difficult to judge the consequences of such a change on teaching standards and quality.
Measuring effectiveness	For example, the effectiveness of the health service could be said to have improved if hospitals have greater success in treating various illnesses and other conditions, or if the life expectancy of the population has increased, but a consequence of these changes will be overcrowded hospitals and longer medical waiting lists.
Overemphasis in cost control	There can be an **emphasis** with VFM audits on **costs and cost control** rather than on achieving more benefits and value, so that management might be pressurised into 'short term' decisions, such as abandoning capital expenditure plans which would create future benefits in order to keep current spending levels within limits.
Measuring efficiency	In profit-making organisations, the efficiency of the organisation as a whole can be measured in terms of return on capital employed. Individual profit centres or operating units within the organisation can also have efficiency measured by relating the quantity of output produced, which has a **market value** and therefore a quantifiable financial value, to the inputs (and their cost) required to make the output. In NFP organisations, output does not usually have a market value, and it is therefore more difficult to measure efficiency. This difficulty is compounded by the fact that, since NFP organisations often have many different activities or operations, it is difficult to compare the efficiency of one operation with the efficiency of another. For example, with the police force, it might be difficult to compare the efficiency of a serious crimes squad with the efficiency of the traffic police.

Best value

3.9 'Best value' is a new performance framework introduced into local authorities by the government. They are required to publish annual best value performance plans and review all of their functions over a five year period.

3.10 As part of 'Best value' authorities are required to strive for continuous improvement by implementing the '4 Cs':

- **Challenge.** How and why is a service provided?

- **Compare.** Make comparisons with other local authorities and the private sector.

- **Consult.** Talk to local taxpayers and services users and the wider business community in setting performance targets.

- **Compete.** Embrace fair competition as a means of securing efficient and effective services.

3.11 The **external auditors** will report on the annual best value performance plan.

Internal auditors and best value

3.12 One of internal audit's **standard roles** in a company is to **provide assurance that internal control systems are adequate to promote the effective use of resources and that risks are being managed properly.**

3.13 In relation to best value, **this role can be extended** to ensure that the authority has arrangements in place to achieve best value, that the risks and impacts of best value are incorporated into normal audit testing and that the authority keeps abreast of best value developments.

3.14 As best value depends on assessing current services and setting strategies for development, **internal audit can take part in the 'position audit'**, as they should have a good understanding of how services are currently organised and relate to each other.

3.15 As assurance providers, they key part internal audit will play is in **giving management assurance that their objectives and strategies in relation to best value are being met.**

Information technology

3.16 An information technology audit is a **test of control in a specific area of the business**, the computer systems.

3.17 Increasingly in modern business, computers are vital to the functioning of the business, and therefore the controls over them are some of the most important in the business.

3.18 It is **likely to be necessary to have an IT specialist in the internal audit team** to undertake an audit of the controls, as some of them will be programmed into the computer system.

3.19 The diagram below shows the various areas of IT in the business which might be subject to a test of controls by the auditors.

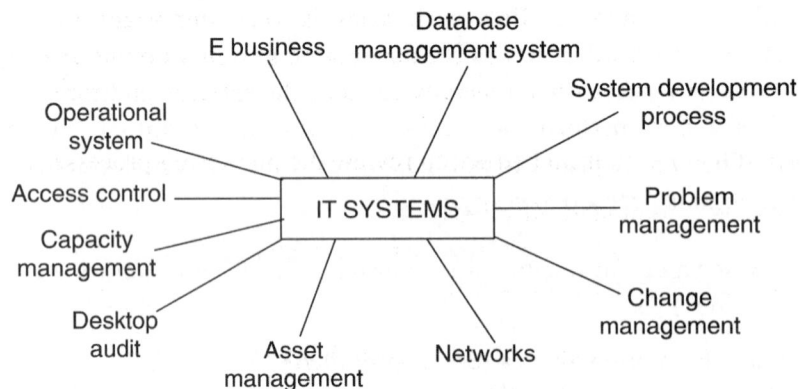

Financial

3.20 The financial audit is internal audit's **traditional role**, which involved reviewing all the available evidence (usually the company's records) to substantiate information in management and financial reporting.

3.21 This role in many ways echoed the role of the external auditor, and was not a role in which the internal auditors could add any particular value to the business. **Increasingly, it is a minor part of the function of internal audit.**

4 OPERATIONAL INTERNAL AUDIT ASSIGNMENTS

> **KEY TERM**
>
> Operational audits are audits of the operational processes of the organisation. They are also known as management or efficiency audits. Their prime objective is the monitoring of management's performance, ensuring company policy is adhered to.

Procurement

4.1 Procurement is the process of **purchasing** for the business. A procurement audit will therefore concentrate on the **systems of the purchasing department**(s).

4.2 The internal auditor will be checking that the system achieves key objectives and that it operates according to company guidelines.

4.3 The control objectives and systems will be similar to those to be discussed in Chapter 10, where we look at the purchases and expenses system. However, internal audit will also be concerned with considerations beyond the scope of the external auditor.

Marketing

4.4 Marketing is the **process of assessing and enhancing demand for the company's products**. Marketing and its link with sales is very important for the business, and therefore, the internal auditor but as the **associated systems do not directly impact on the financial statements**, they do not usually concern the external auditor.

4.5 It is important for the internal auditor to review the marketing processes to ensure:

- The process is **managed efficiently**
- **Information is freely available** to manager demand
- **Risks** are being **managed** correctly.

4.6 An audit may be especially critical for a marketing department which may be complex with several different teams, for example:

- Research
- Advertising
- Promotions
- After sales

4.7 It is vital to ensure that information is passed properly within the department, and activities are streamlined.

Treasury

4.8 Treasury is a function within the finance department of a business. It **manages the funds of a business**. It is vital to a business that funds are managed so that cash is available when required.

4.9 There are risks associated with treasury, in terms of interest rate risk and foreign currency risk, and the auditor must ensure that the **risk is managed in accordance with company procedures**.

4.10 As with marketing audits, it is vital to ensure that **information is available** to the treasury department, so that they can **ensure funds are available when required**.

Human resources

4.11 The human resources department on one hand **procures a human resource** (employee) for the operation of the business and on the other **supports those employees in developing the organisation**.

4.12 It is important to ensure that the processes ensure that people are available to work as the business requires them and that the overall development of the business is planned and controlled.

4.13 Again, **ensuring company policies are maintained and information is freely available are key factors for internal audit to assess**.

Approaching operational internal audit assignments

4.14 There are two aspects of an operational assignment:

- Ensure policies are adequate
- Ensure policies work effectively

Adequacy

4.15 The internal auditor will have to review the policies of a particular department by:

- Reading them
- Discussion with members of the department

4.16 Then the auditor will have to assess whether the policies are adequate, and possibly advise the board of improvements which could be made.

Effectiveness

4.17 The auditor will then have to examine the effectiveness of the controls by:

- Observing them in operation
- Testing them

4.18 This will be done on similar lines to the testing of controls to be discussed in Section C, where the control objectives for these areas will be set out.

> **Exam focus point**
>
> All these cycles are looked at in more detail in Chapter 11.

5 FRAUD   Dec 01

5.1 Fraud is a **key business risk**. It is the responsibility of the directors to prevent and detect fraud.

5.2 As the **internal auditor has a role in risk management** he is involved in the process of managing the risk of fraud.

5.3 The internal auditor can help to **prevent** fraud by their work **assessing the adequacy and effectiveness of control systems** and **detect** fraud by **being mindful** when carrying out their work and **reporting any suspicions**.

5.4 The very **existence of an internal audit** department may act as a **deterrent** to fraud.

Question 2

The growing recognition by management of the benefits of good internal control, and the complexities of an adequate system of internal control have led to the development of internal auditing as a form of control over all other internal controls. The emergence of the internal auditors as experts in internal control is the result of an evolutionary process similar in many ways to the evolution of independent auditing.

Required

(a) Explain why the internal and independent auditors' review of internal control procedures differ in purpose.

(b) Explain the reasons why internal auditors should or should not report their findings on internal control to the following selection of company officials:

(i)   The board of directors
(ii) The chief accountant

(c) Explain whether the independent auditors can place any reliance upon the internal auditors' work when the latter's main role is to be of service and assistance to management.

Answer

(a) The internal auditors review and test the system of internal control and report to management in order to improve the information received by managers and to help in their task of running the company. The internal auditors will recommend changes to the system to make sure that the management receives objective information which is efficiently produced. The internal auditors will also have a duty to search for and discover fraud.

The external auditors review the system of internal control in order to determine the extent of the substantive work required on the year end accounts. The external auditors report to the shareholders rather than the managers or directors.

External auditors usually however issue a letter of weakness to the managers, laying out any areas of weakness and recommendations for improvement in the system of internal control. The external auditors report on the truth and fairness of the financial statements, not directly on the system of internal control. The auditors do not have a specific duty to detect fraud, although they should plan their audit procedures so as to detect any material misstatement in the accounts on which they give an opinion.

(b) (i)   *Board of directors*

A high level of independence is achieved by the internal auditors if they report directly to the Board. There may be problems with this approach.

(1)   The members of the Board may not understand all the implications of the internal audit reports when accounting or technical information is required.

(2)   The Board may not have enough time to spend considering the reports in sufficient depth. Important recommendations might therefore remain unimplemented.

A way around these problems might be to delegate the review of internal audit reports to an audit committee, which would act as a kind of sub-committee to the main board. The audit committee might be made up largely of non-executive directors who have more time and more independence from the day-to-day running of the company.

(ii) *Chief accountant*

It would be inappropriate for internal audit to report to the chief accountant, who is largely in charge of running the system of internal control. It may be feasible for him or her to receive the report as well as the Board. Otherwise, the internal audit function cannot be effectively independent as the chief accountant could suppress unfavourable reports or could just not act on the recommendations of such reports.

(c) The internal audit function is itself part of the system of internal control: it is an internal control over internal controls. As such, the external auditors should be able to test it and, if it is found to be reliable, they can rely on it.

To check the reliability of the work of the internal auditors, I would consider the following matters.

(i)   *The degree of independence of the internal auditors*

I would assess the organisational status and reporting responsibilities of the internal auditors and consider any restrictions placed upon them. Although internal auditors are employees of the enterprise and cannot therefore be independent of it, they should be able to plan and carry out their work as they wish and have access to senior management. They should be

BPP
PUBLISHING

free of any responsibility which may create a conflict of interest, and of a situation where those staff on whom they are reporting are responsible for their or their staff's appointment, promotion or pay.

(ii) *The scope and objectives of the internal audit function*

I would examine the internal auditors' formal terms of reference and ascertain the scope and objectives of internal audit assignments.

(iii) *Quality of work*

I would consider whether the work of internal audit is properly planned, controlled, recorded and reviewed. Examples of good practice include the existence of an adequate audit manual, plans and procedures for supervision of individual assignments, and satisfactory arrangements for ensuring adequate quality control, reporting and follow-up.

(iv) *Technical competence*

Internal audit should be performed by persons having adequate training and competence as auditors. Indications of technical competence may be membership of an appropriate professional body or attendance at regular training courses.

(v) *Reports*

I would consider the quality of reports issued by internal audit and find out whether management considers and acts upon such reports.

If I find that where the internal auditors' work is reliable, I will be able to place reliance on that work when appropriate. This may mean that I will need to carry out less audit work.

However, it should be emphasised that I cannot rely totally on the internal auditors' work in relation to any particular audit objective. Internal audit work provides only one form of evidence, and the internal auditors are not independent of company management. I may be able to reduce the number of items which I test, but I will not be able to leave a particular type of test (for example, a debtors' circularisation) entirely to internal audit. I remain responsible for the opinion which I form on the accounts.

Chapter roundup

- Internal audit is a function set up to assist management monitor and appraise internal controls and manage business risk

- As such, it plays a part in ensuring good corporate governance.

- The key differences between internal and external auditors are based on who they report to and therefore, their relationship with the company.

- Internal audit can be outsourced.

- Internal audit can be involved in many different assignments as directed by management. Examples include:
  - Best value for money
  - Best value
  - IT
  - Financial

- They traditionally undertake operational audits, examples of which include:
  - Procurement
  - Marketing
  - Treasury
  - HR

- When carrying out operational audits, internal auditors will
  - Assess adequacy of company policies
  - Assess their effectiveness in practice

- As part of their function, internal auditors have a role in preventing and detecting fraud.

Quick quiz

1   What is internal audit?

2   Complete the Turnbull Guidelines

TURNBULL GUIDELINES
Have a .... for the ....of effectiveness of ....
Review .... reports on ....
Consider .... and how they have been ....
Check the .... of .... to remedy weaknesses and incidents.
Consider the .... of ....
Conduct an .... of risks and the effectiveness of internal control.
Make a .... on this process in the ....

3   Name three key differences between internal and external audit.

    1   ....

    2   ....

    3   ....

4   It is possible to buy in an internal audit service from an external organisation.

    True   ☐

    False   ☐

5   Link the value for money 'E' with its definition.

    (a)   Economy
    (b)   Efficiency
    (c)   Effectiveness

    (i)   The relationships between the goods and services produced (outputs) and the resources used to produce them.

    (ii)   The concern with how well an activity is achieving its policy objectives or other intended effects.

    (iii)   Attaining the appropriate quantity and quality of physical, human and financial resources (inputs) at lowest cost.

6   Name five areas of the computer system which might benefit from an IT audit.

    1   ....

    2   ....

    3   ....

    4   ....

    5   ....

7   Define the following areas of a business, which an internal auditor might conduct a review of:

    (a)   Procurement   (c)   Treasury
    (b)   Marketing   (d)   Human resources

8   Internal auditors are not required to consider fraud.

    True   ☐

    False   ☐

Answers to quick quiz

1   **Internal audit** is an appraisal or monitoring activity established by management and directors, for the review of the accounting and internal control systems as a service to the entity.

2   defined process, review, internal control
    regular, internal control
    key risks, managed
    adequacy actions taken
    adequacy, monitoring
    annual assessment
    statement, annual report

3   1   External report to members, internal to directors
    2   External report on financial statements, internal on systems, controls and risks
    3   External are independent of the company, internal often employed by it

4   True

5   (a) (iii), (b) (i), (c) (ii)

6   See para 4.11

7   (a)   The purchasing department

    (b)   The process which assesses and enhances demand for a product.

    (c)   Function (often within finance department) which manages funds.

    (d)   Department which procures a human resource and manages development of the organisation.

8   False

Now try the question below from the Exam Question Bank

Number	Level	Marks	Time
3	Exam	20	36 mins

Chapter 4

PROFESSIONAL CODES OF ETHICS AND BEHAVIOUR

Topic list	Syllabus reference
1 Due care, skill and competence	1
2 *Rules of Professional Conduct*	1
3 Statement 1: *Integrity, objectivity and independence*	1
4 Threats to integrity, objectivity and independence	1
5 Statement 2: *The professional duty of confidence*	1
6 Areas of controversy	1
7 Internal audit ethics	1

Introduction

In Chapter 2 we looked at some of the regulation surrounding the auditor. Here we look at the (sometimes more stringent) **requirements of the RSBs, specifically the ethical guidance from ACCA**, the association you are studying to join. **Internal auditors** are subject to the requirements of any professional body to which they belong. The only professional body specifically for internal auditors is the Institute of Internal Auditors. We will look briefly at their guidance.

The ethical matters covered in this chapter are **very important**. Ethical matters could arise in almost every type of exam question. You must be able to apply the ACCA's guidance on ethical matters to any given situation, but remember that **common sense** is usually a good guide.

We firstly examine what a client has the legal **right to demand** from their auditors under the terms of their **contract** with them. The most important qualities are that the auditors carry out their work with due **professional care**.

Auditors are also subject to ethical requirements imposed by their professional bodies. The principle of **independence**- that auditors must not only be independent but must be seen to be independent- is very important.

In a number of cases whether a particular situation is a threat to independence is not clear-cut; is auditor independence compromised by providing services other than audit to an audit client, for example.

One area where client requirements may conflict with the requirement for auditors to act ethically is whether the auditor should keep the affairs of clients secret, or disclose them to others without obtaining the client's consent. We shall see that professional guidance tries to strike a balance between stressing the importance of keeping the affairs of clients **confidential**, and stating that in certain instances auditors should consider (or have to) disclose client details to third parties.

Lastly we shall consider the position of the **internal auditor** with regard to professional ethics.

BPP
PUBLISHING

Study guide

Section 5

- Describe the sources of, and enforcement mechanisms associated with, professional ethics and professional codes of conduct

- Define the fundamental concepts of professional ethics

- Define the detailed requirement of, and illustrate and analyse the application of, professional ethics in the context of independence, objectivity and integrity

- Distinguish between the elements of professional ethics applicable to internal auditors and those applicable to external auditors

Section 6

- Define the detailed requirements of, and illustrate and analyse the application of, professional ethics in the context of confidentiality and conflict of interest.

Exam guide

Questions about independence often involve discussion of topical, controversial issues, for example provision of services other than audit to audit clients. You should keep an eye open for articles in *Student Accountant* and financial press in these areas. Exam questions will generally require you to consider both sides of a controversial topic. The ethics question on the pilot paper examined independence and the practical issue of other services.

1   DUE CARE, SKILL AND COMPETENCE

ACCA's *Rules of Professional Conduct*

'Members should carry out their professional work with due skill, care, diligence and expedition and with proper regard for the technical and professional standards expected of them as members.'

1.1   All accountants (not just auditors) in public practice are obliged by law to provide services of appropriate quality. Unless an accountant and client have agreed otherwise, there is an implied duty of care that an accountant owes to a client under s 13 Supply of Goods and Services Act 1982.

1.2   The professional guidance statement *Professional Liability* published in 1994 makes the following further points.

(a)   The degree of skill and care will depend on the work: a higher degree will be required for work:

- Of a **specialised nature**
- Where negligence is likely to **cause substantial loss**

These particularly apply where the accountant represented himself as being experienced.

(b)   The duty will not be absolute; opinions or advice will not give rise to claims just because they are proved wrong in the light of later events.

The auditors' duty of care

1.3   Thus auditors must employ **reasonable care** in all they do, in particular:

(a) Auditors must use **generally accepted auditing techniques** when seeking to satisfy themselves that the matters upon which they reports accurately reflect the true financial state of his client's business.

(b) If auditors come across any matter which puts them **upon enquiry** then they have a duty to investigate such a matter until they are able to resolve it to their own reasonable satisfaction. Auditors should not accept any explanation unless they have first carried out such investigations as will enable them properly to assess whether the explanation offered a reasonable one.

2 RULES OF PROFESSIONAL CONDUCT   Pilot paper

2.1 There are a number of ethical issues which are of great importance in the client-auditor relationship. This onus is always on the auditor not only to be ethical but also to be **seen** to be ethical. To this end, the Association publishes *Rules of Professional Conduct*.

2.2 **All** members **and** students of the ACCA must adhere to these rules. Guidance is in the form of:

- Fundamental principles
- Specific guidance
- Explanatory notes

The Fundamental Principles	
Integrity	Members should behave with integrity in all professional, business and personal financial relationships. Integrity implies **not merely honesty but air dealing and truthfulness.**
Objectivity	Members should strive for **objectivity** in all professional and business judgements, (objectivity is the **state of mind** which has **regard to all considerations relevant** to the task in hand **but no other**, it presupposes **intellectual honesty**).
Competence	Members should not accept or perform work which they are not **competent** to undertake **unless** they obtain such **advice and assistance** as will enable them competently to carry out the work.
Due skill and care	Members should carry out their professional work with **due skill, care**, **diligence** and **expedition** and with **proper regard** for the **technical** and **professional standards** expected of them as members.
Courtesy	Members should behave with courtesy and consideration towards all with whom they come into contact during the course of performing their work.

3 STATEMENT 1: INTEGRITY, OBJECTIVITY AND INDEPENDENCE

ACCA Statement

'A member's objectivity must be beyond question if he (or she) is to report as an auditor. That objectivity can only be assured if the member is, and is seen to be, independent.'

'The threat to independence may be reduced by the nature and extent of the precautions taken by the practice to guard against loss of objectivity.'

BPP PUBLISHING

3.1   The statement points out that, although the rules refer specifically to company audits under the Companies Acts, 'the spirit of the guidance applies equally to other audit situations'.

> ### Exam focus point
>
> You should note that legal independence is a set of relationships which are prohibited (see Chapter 2). Professional independence is however an attitude of mind; the detailed guidelines listed below are just guidelines and audit firms may feel justified in taking stricter measures than the guidelines suggest.

Why do independence and objectivity matter so much?

3.2   Independence and objectivity matter because of:

   (a)   The **expectations** of those directly affected, particularly the members of the company. The audit should be able to provide **objective** assurance that the directors can never provide on the accounts.

   (b)   The **public interest**. Companies are public entities, governed by rules requiring the disclosure of information.

3.3   Threats to independence and objectivity could arise for the following reasons.

The auditors' own **personal interest**. The auditors may fear, for example, the loss of fees.
When carrying out the audit, the auditors **review work** that their **own firm** has **done previously**, for example, preparing accounts or making a valuation.
If the auditors get involved in **disputes** concerning the client. They may end up **acting for or against** the **client**, which undermines the appearance of objectivity.
If the auditors are involved with the client for a long time, they may become **unduly sympathetic** towards directors and management, and thus too inclined to trust their unsupported word.
The auditors may be **intimidated** by a **dominant** or **aggressive atmosphere** at the clients.

3.4   What can the auditor do to preserve objectivity? The simple answer is to **withdraw from any engagement** where there is the **slightest threat** to objectivity. However there are disadvantages in this strict approach.

- Clients may lose an auditor who knows their business
- Denies clients the freedom to be advised by the accountant of their choice.

3.5   A better approach would be as follows

- **Consider** whether the **auditors' own objectivity** and the **general safeguards** operated in the professional environment are **sufficient** to offset the threat

- Consider whether **safeguards over and above** the general safeguards are required, for example specified partners or staff not working on an assignment.

- However the ultimate option must always be **withdrawing** from an **engagement** or refusing to act.

4 THREATS TO INTEGRITY, OBJECTIVITY AND INDEPENDENCE

4.1 Section A of Statement 1 deals with **independence and the audit**. Most of the section is taken up by discussions and **recommendations** about **areas of risk**.

Undue dependence on an audit client

ACCA Statement

'Objectivity may be threatened or appear to be threatened by undue dependence on any audit client or group of connected clients.'

4.2 The statement recommends that, in general, the recurring work paid by one client or group of connected clients should not exceed **15%** of the gross practice income. In the case of **listed** and other **public interest** companies, the figure should be **10%** of the gross practice income.

4.3 New practices may not be able to satisfy such criteria and extra care will be necessary in such circumstances to safeguard independence.

4.4 A review of the risk to independence should be instituted for all large fees, certainly 10% (public interest 5%) and greater of gross practice income.

4.5 The statement also suggests that **non-recurring fees might affect independence** if they are large enough.

Overdue fees

ACCA Statement

'The existence of significant overdue fees from an audit client or group of associated clients can be a threat or appear to be a threat to objectivity akin to that of a loan.'

4.6 Financial self-interest is obviously involved here. Firms must therefore ensure that overdue fees, along with fees from current work, could not be construed as a loan.

Actual or threatened litigation

ACCA Statement

'A firm's objectivity may be threatened or appear to be threatened when it is involved in, or even threatened with litigation in relation to a client.'

4.7 Litigation of certain sorts will represent a 'breakdown of the relationship of trust' between auditor and client. This would impair the independence of the auditor or cause the directors of the client to become unwilling to disclose information to the auditor. A dispute which is only in relation to audit fees may not cause such problems.

4.8 The point at which the firm should cease to act as auditors will vary from case to case. Auditors should be wary whenever it appears that litigation might occur.

Associated firms/influences outside the practice

ACCA Statement

'A firm's objectivity may be threatened or appear to be threatened as a result of pressures arising from associated practices or organisations, or from other external sources, such as bankers, solicitors, government or those introducing business.'

4.9 The problems of independence in relation to large and prestigious clients may arise in connection with the activities of an associated practice or organisation of the client. Factors to be considered by the firm include the closeness of the association and the strength of the associate's interest in the firm's retaining the client.

Family and other personal relationships

ACCA Statement

'A member's objectivity may be threatened or appear to be threatened as a consequence of a family or other close personal or business relationship.'

4.10 Problems arise if an officer or senior employee of an audit client is **closely connected** with the partner or senior staff member responsible for the conduct of the audit.

KEY TERM

The following people will normally be regarded as **closely connected** with a person.

(a) His (or her) spouse or cohabitee other than a spouse from whom the person is separated, or, in the case of a shareholding, a spouse or cohabitee of whose financial affairs the person has been denied knowledge

(b) His (or her) minor children, including stepchildren

(c) A company in which he or she has a 20 per cent interest or more

The following persons will normally be regarded as being closely connected with a practice.

- A partner or, in the case of a corporate practice, a director or shareholder
- A person closely connected with the above
- An employee of the practice

Note. The categories in these paragraphs are not exhaustive of the relationships which might threaten independence.

4.11 It also includes any relative to whom regular financial assistance is given or who is indebted to the staff member or partner.

4.12   Proximity needs to be taken into account, including whether the partner or staff member is involved in the audit and the position of the person in the client's office (the more junior, the less risk).

4.13   Problems can also arise if partners or staff have been involved on the audit for too long, as illustrated by the Robert Maxwell affair.

Case example

The Joint Disciplinary Scheme report on the case suggested that the senior partner, who had been involved with Maxwell for many years, placed excessive trust in Maxwell and influenced the attitude of other Coopers and Lybrand personnel.

4.14   S 27 CA 1989 prevents an officer or employee of a company (or their partner) from becoming an auditor of that company. The statement extends this prohibition for its members to two years after ceasing to be an officer or employee of the company.

Beneficial interests in shares and other investments and trusts

ACCA Statements

'A member's objectivity may be threatened or appear to be threatened where he (or she) holds a beneficial interest in the shares or other forms of investment in a company upon which the practice reports.'

'The objectivity of a practice may be threatened or appear to be threatened where a partner or a person closely connected with the partner has a beneficial interest in a trust having a shareholding in an audit client company.'

'A member's objectivity may be threatened or appear to be threatened by trustee shareholdings and other trustee investments.'

'Where a partner or staff member holds shares in any capacity in a company which is an audit client of the practice they should not be voted at any general meeting of the company in relation to the appointment, removal or remuneration of auditors.'

4.15   Staff and partners should not have shareholdings in client businesses. (This includes beneficial shareholdings held by a spouse or minor child.)

   (a)   If shares are acquired involuntarily (by marriage or inheritance) then they should be disposed of at the earliest opportunity.

   (b)   Where an Act of Parliament or the articles of the client company require the auditor to be a shareholder, then the auditor should hold only the minimum number of shares and the holding should be disclosed in the accounts of the client company.

4.16   Beneficial holdings in unit trusts and so on are not precluded, nor are modest personal savings in a client building society or other similar institution.

4.17   Where a trust, in which a partner or a person closely connected with a partner is a beneficiary, holds or acquires shares in a company audited by the practice where:

   (a)   The partner is and wishes to remain a trustee; the shareholding should be regarded as equivalent to a beneficial shareholding, and the practice should cease to report.

(b) The partner is not a trustee; he should cease personally to report as soon as he becomes aware of the shareholding.

4.18 Where an employee has an interest in a trust having a shareholding in an audit client, that employee should not be employed on the audit of that client.

4.19 The practice should not have a public company as an audit client if a partner (or the spouse of a partner) is a trustee of a trust holding shares in that company and the holding is in excess of **10% of**:

- The **issued share capital** of the company, or
- The **total assets comprised** in the trust

4.20 A trust holding of 10% or more (as described above) of **any** company will indicate problems with independence.

Loans

ACCA Statement

'Objectivity may be threatened or appear to be threatened by a loan to or from an audit client.'

4.21 No loans or guarantees should be undertaken unless they are with client financial institutions in the normal course of business (but the loan cannot be applied for partnership capital and the partner concerned must not be the engagement partner).

Goods and services/hospitality

ACCA Statement

'Objectivity may be threatened or appear to be threatened by acceptance of goods, services or hospitality from an audit client.'

Acceptance on normal commercial terms, or with only a modest benefit, is acceptable.

Provision of other services to audit clients   **Pilot Paper**

ACCA Statement

'There are occasions where objectivity may be threatened or appear to be threatened by the provision to an audit client of services other than the audit.'

4.22 This issue is discussed in section 6 of this chapter.

Safeguards against loss of integrity and objectivity

4.23 There are a number of factors in the professional environment which should help maintain members' independence. **Training** is important, as is the support given by the ACCA in the form of the Code of Ethics and advice in specific instances.

4.24 Independence is also very carefully considered by the **Joint Monitoring Unit**, and sanctions may be imposed against firms or individuals who breach guidance.

4.25 The situation within firms is also important. Firms should regard their **reputation** for independence as crucial, and there should be strong internal pressures towards independence.

4.26 Specific measures should also be introduced by firms. Ethical issues should be considered as part of **training** and **quality control procedures**. Firms should carefully consider whether **clients** should be **accepted** (this is discussed further in Chapter 5), and before each audit starts, whether there are any **threats to independence**. **Review** and **consultation** procedures are also important.

> ## ACCA Statement
>
> 'Every audit firm should establish adequate review machinery, including an annual review, in order to satisfy itself that each engagement may properly be accepted or be continued having regard to the guidance given in this statement, and to identify situations where independence may be at risk and where the appropriate safeguards should be applied.'

4.27 SAS 240 *Quality Control for Audit work* was re-issued in September 2000. It takes a broader approach to quality control than its predecessor, recognising the need for quality control in all aspects of the firm.

4.28 One of the principal reasons for this is to maintain independence and ethics. The introduction to the SAS states.

> '... quality control policy and processes are defined as those "designed to provide reasonable assurance as to the appropriateness of the auditors' report and adherence to auditing Standards, **ethical** and other regulatory requirements".'

4.29 In other words, quality control processes are a safeguard to independence and other professional ethics such as those mentioned above.

4.30 As a result of review procedures, specific safeguards may be applied on certain clients, for example involvement of an extra partner at the reporting stage.

Question 1

Southern Engineering Ltd has undergone a period of substantial growth following its establishment five years ago by two engineers. Because of a lack of accounting expertise within the company it has traditionally looked to its auditors, Smith and Jones, for accounting services in the preparation of annual financial statements as well as for the statutory audit function. Smith and Jones have also provided advice in connection with the company's accounting and internal control systems.

Smith and Jones is a two partner firm of certified accountants whose clients are mainly sole traders, partnerships and small limited companies. Although Southern Engineering Ltd was originally a typical small company client, its growth over the last five years has meant that it now accounts for approximately 20% of Smith and Jones' gross fee income and the company has indicated that it may wish to issue shares on the Alternative Investment Market in the near future.

Required

(a) Discuss the extent to which it is acceptable and desirable that Smith and Jones have in the past provided the three services of statutory audit, advice in connection with systems, and accountancy services in the preparation of annual financial statements to Southern Engineering Ltd.

(b) Discuss the acceptability and desirability of Smith and Jones continuing to act in the future as auditors to Southern Engineering Ltd while continuing to provide the other services.

Answer

(a) Auditors, especially of small companies, often provide other, non-audit services. The risk arises that, in such cases, the auditor's objectivity may be impaired. This is particularly possible where the auditor is involved in advising the client on systems, as it becomes difficult for the auditor to remain sufficiently detached to comment critically on any weaknesses or shortcomings which appear when systems are implemented. A clear distinction must be drawn between the auditor's advisory capacity - in systems or accountancy work - and the executive responsibility, which is still that of the company's management. Undue involvement with non-audit services must be avoided, lest it detracts from the auditor's essential independence and objectivity.

(b) The ethical guidance of the accounting bodies recommends that fee income from a single client should not exceed 15% of a practice's total gross fees. As Southern Engineering's fees now represent 20% of fee income (and would, presumably, increase when the company makes an issue on the AIM) it seems Smith and Jones have to consider ways of reducing their dependence on this one client. This might well be done by continuing as auditors but ceasing to provide accounting services and systems advice. (In any case, the ethical guidelines suggest that the auditors of a public company should not assist with accountancy save in exceptional circumstances.)

Smith and Jones should keep the situation under review, even after they have moved to a pure audit role, to ensure that they are not again becoming unduly dependent on Southern Engineering as it expands.

4.31 Many proposals have been put forward to help safeguard the independence of auditors and these are discussed in the following paragraphs.

Rotation of auditor appointments

4.32 It has been argued that the long-term nature of the company audit engagement tends to create a loss of auditor independence, due to an increasing familiarity with the company's management and staff, which works against the shareholders' and the public's interest.

4.33 For this reason, it has been argued that there should be a rotation of the audit appointment every few years, preventing any unnecessary loss of independence which the present situation is thought to cause.

4.34 However, rotation of auditors may not be very popular in practice, owing to:

(a) The disadvantages of **upsetting** the **client company** with continual changes of audit staff

(b) The **high costs** of **recurring first audits**

(c) The ability of auditors to retain a fresh approach to the audit by **rotating members** of the **audit staff** internally so that no member is permanently assigned to it, including the reporting partner

(d) The loss of **trust** and **experience** built up over time and the risk to audit effectiveness it would entail

Audit committees

4.35 One American innovation which had an impact in this country is the audit committee.

4.36 One of the main reasons for audit committees arises from the difficulty auditors have in combating instances where the executive directors of a company are determined to mislead them. As a result it is felt that an audit committee, preferably drawn from '**non-executive**'

directors of a client company, would provide an **invaluable independent liaison** between the board and the auditors, thus strengthening the auditors' position and improving communication.

4.37 Other advantages that are claimed to arise from the existence of an audit committee include:

(a) It will lead to **increased confidence** in the credibility and objectivity of financial reports.

(b) By specialising in the problems of financial reporting and thus, to some extent, fulfilling the directors' responsibilities in this area, it will **allow** the **executive directors to devote their attention to management.**

(c) In cases where the **interests** of the company, the executive directors and the employees **conflict**, the audit committee might provide an **impartial body** for the auditors to consult.

4.38 **Opponents** of audit committees **argue** that:

(a) There may be **difficulty selecting sufficient non-executive directors** with the necessary competence in auditing matters for the committee to be really effective.

(b) The establishment of such a **formalised reporting procedure** may dissuade the auditors from raising matters of judgement and limit them to reporting only on matters of fact.

4.39 In the UK, the *Cadbury Report* recommended that **audit committees should be compulsory under Stock Exchange rules** in the UK and that the committee should consist entirely of non-executive directors, the majority of whom are independent of the company (this has been adopted by the Stock Exchange). The audit committee should have explicit authority and the resources to investigate any matters within their terms of reference.

5   STATEMENT 2: THE PROFESSIONAL DUTY OF CONFIDENCE

Statement 23

5.1 Statement 23, which deals with confidentiality in general terms, makes it clear that information acquired in the course of professional work should not be disclosed except where

- **Consent has been obtained** from the client, employer or other proper source, or
- There is a **public duty** to disclose, or
- There is a **legal** or **professional right or duty** to disclose.

5.2 A member acquiring information in the course of professional work should neither use nor appear to use that information for his **personal advantage** or for the **advantage of a third party.**

5.3 In general, where there is a right (as opposed to a duty) to disclose information, a member should only make disclosure in pursuit of a public duty or professional obligation. Statement 2, discussed below, expands on the duty of confidence in relation to the defaults and unlawful acts of clients and others.

BPP PUBLISHING

Statement 2

5.4 A member must make clear to a client that he may only act for him if the client agrees to disclose in full to the member all information relevant to the engagement.

5.5 Where a member agrees to serve a client in a professional capacity both the member and the client should be aware that it is an **implied term** of that agreement that the **member will not disclose** the client's affairs to any other person save with the client's consent or within the terms of certain recognised exceptions.

RECOGNISED EXCEPTIONS
Obligatory disclosure
If a member knows or suspects his client to have committed **treason, drug-trafficking** or **terrorist** offences, he is obliged to disclose all the information at his disposal to a competent authority.
Under SAS 120 *Consideration of law and regulations* auditors should consider whether **non-compliance with laws and regulations** affects the accounts. Auditors may have to include in their audit report a statement that non-compliance has led to significant uncertainties, or non-compliance means that the auditors disagree with the way certain items have been treated in the accounts.
Voluntary disclosure
Disclosure is reasonably necessary to **protect** the **member's interests**, for example to enable him to sue for fees or defend an action for, say, negligence.
Disclosure is **compelled** by **process of law**, for example where in an action a member is required to give evidence or discovery of documents.
There is a **public duty** to disclose, say where an offence has been committed which is contrary to the public interest.
Disclosure is to **non-governmental bodies** which have statutory powers to compel disclosure.

5.6 If an ACCA member is requested to assist the police, the Inland Revenue or other authority by providing information about a client's affairs in connection with enquiries being made, he should first enquire under what **statutory authority** the information is demanded.

5.7 Unless he is satisfied that such statutory authority exists he should decline to give any information until he has obtained his client's authority. If the client's authority is not forthcoming and the demand for information is pressed the member should not accede unless so advised by his solicitor.

5.8 If a member knows or suspects that a client has committed a wrongful act he must give careful thought to his own position. He must ensure that he has not prejudiced himself by, for example, relying on information given by the client which subsequently proves to be incorrect.

5.9 However, it would be a **criminal offence** for a **member to act positively**, without lawful authority or reasonable excuse, in such a manner as **to impede with intent the arrest** or prosecution **of a client whom he knows or believes to have committed an 'arrestable offence'**.

6 AREAS OF CONTROVERSY

6.1 Auditing as a profession and as a concept has developed rapidly over the last 20 to 30 years. The demands on auditors have changed, as have the expectations of shareholders, creditors and managers about the audit role.

6.2 Areas of controversy will be mentioned throughout this Study Text, but here we will concentrate on some of the matters which are directly related to the auditors' independence, confidentiality and other qualities.

Multiple services   Pilot paper

6.3 One of the more controversial independence arguments raging at the moment is the **provision of other services** to audit clients.

- The perception that a company gave its auditors some lucrative consultancy work **in exchange** for a clean audit report.

- The auditors may end up making **management decisions** for the company which would harm their independence

- The auditor undertaking **self-review**, that is auditing his own work.

6.4 However the provision of other services may have **advantages** to the audit firm

- Auditors would have more confidence in work prepared by their firm.
- Carrying out accounting and tax work enhances audit staff's expertise.
- Non-audit services may smooth out seasonal audit work.

6.5 The problem exists for both large and small auditing firms, but in different ways. Small firms provide accountancy and taxation advice to their client, as well as general advice.

6.6 Audit firms **cannot** perform accountancy work for public companies, but the auditors in these case provide consultancy services, corporate finance and taxation advice instead. Audit firms should also not provide specialist valuations for the accounts of any company that they audit.

6.7 The problem with small or sole practitioners auditing very small companies is probably insurmountable. The DTI has now removed the requirement for some small companies to have an audit, and so for such companies this problem has been solved. Otherwise, the auditors must ensure that the **audit** work (as opposed to any accountancy or tax work) is **planned** and **executed**, and perhaps most importantly, properly **recorded**.

6.8 Larger audit firms have countered the problem by the use of **separate departments** for each service within the firm (consultancy, audit, taxation and so on).

6.9 The response of the profession to the criticisms about the provision of other services to audit clients has been limited.

BPP PUBLISHING

6.10 Some smaller firms which undertake both accountancy and audit work on clients have responded to the potential independence problem by **requiring different staff** to **prepare** and **audit** the accounts.

6.11 **Another important safeguard** is the **engagement letter**, which should separately identify the non-audit services provided, make clear the extent of directors' responsibilities (responsibility for accounting records, ensuring accounts give a true and fair view, taxation matters are disclosed and so on). The engagement letter is discussed further in Chapter 5.

6.12 Recent developments may have decreased some of the problems in this area. Some companies do now have a policy of using different audit firms for audit and non-audit work. Other companies make separate decisions as to who should provide audit and non-audit services. In some circumstances they may consider that one firm will provide the best audit service but another firm may be better at providing other services.

> **Exam focus point**
>
> Questions on independence often focus on provision of other services, as this has continued to be a controversial area. This was the case on the pilot paper.

Opinion shopping

6.13 If a company is unhappy with the audit opinion which it receives (or may receive) from its current auditors, then it might approach other audit firms for a second opinion. The problem will be if the current auditors are pressurised into accepting the (more favourable) second opinion.

6.14 To avoid such a situation there should be constant communication between both sets of auditors. The second firm of auditors has a **professional duty to seek permission** for an approach to the current auditors from the client (this is discussed in Chapter 5). Without such communication, the second opinion may be formed negligently.

Conflicts of interest

6.15 In some ways conflict of interest problems are similar to the difficulties firms have in maintaining independence. Conflicts of interest can arise in a variety of circumstances and each problem has to be dealt with on its own merits. There are no rules to deal with most of the situations, outside the Association's rules about independence and integrity, and the solution will usually be based on common sense as much as ethical behaviour.

6.16 We have already dealt with conflict of interest in terms of auditor independence, particularly in situations where there is a financial or personal interest in a client company.

6.17 Conflicts of interest can arise when a firm has two (or more) audit clients, both of whom have reason to be unhappy that their auditors are also auditors to the other company. This situation frequently arises when the companies are in **direct competition** with each other, and particularly when the **auditors have access to** particularly **sensitive information**. These situations are difficult for the auditors: it may involve the loss of a substantial client, even though the staff and engagement partners on each of the audits are different.

6.18 Most of these companies have this attitude because of the highly competitive nature of their industry. Others may be sensitive because of the work they do for governments in defence or other controversial areas.

Avoidance of conflicts of interest

6.19 In general, where conflicts of interest arise, there should be **full** and **frank explanation** to those involved by the audit firm, coupled with any action necessary to disengage from one or both positions.

6.20 Conflicts should, so far as possible, be avoided by **not accepting** any appointment or assignment in which conflict seems likely to occur.

6.21 This avoidance of clients causing a conflict of interest is more important for smaller audit firms. The larger firms can overcome a conflict by building a 'Chinese wall' within the firm. This would mean that the respective audits are undertaken by different audit 'groups', the engagement partners are different and all the other audit staff are allowed to work on one of the clients only.

Case example

An example of very competitive companies which appeared to agree with this type of arrangement was that of **British Airways** and **British Caledonian** (before they merged). Both companies were audited by the same large accountancy firm and yet the airline business is one of the most competitive in the world and confidential information is held at a premium.

6.22 It is possible, of course, that some clients might not agree to such an arrangement. The increasing number of mergers which have taken place within the accountancy profession recently have caused conflict of interest problems.

Case example

British Telecom was not happy when its auditors merged with the firm which audited Cable and Wireless. The new firm was forced to drop one of the audits.

6.23 Two recent cases have also cast doubt on the ability of accountants to rely on Chinese walls.

Case example

Prince Jefri of Brunei had been a client of KPMG and he argued that the firm's forensic department had a full knowledge of his personal finances. The client relationship with the prince ended, and subsequently the firm was hired by the Brunei Investment Agency (BIA) to investigate the Sultanate's financial affairs. Prince Jefri argued successfully that this meant that in effect KPMG would be investigating his affairs, and that information obtained from the firm's earlier relationship with the prince might be given to the BIA.

The House of Lords, in reaching this decision, commented that the position of accountants was similar to that of solicitors and 'it is the solicitor's (and hence accountant's) duty to ensure that the former client is not put at risk that confidential information that the solicitor has obtained from the relationship may be used against him in any circumstances.'

The Lords commented that large firms would have to introduce established organisational arrangements including physical separation of personnel, to protect former clients, The judgement did however suggest that the courts might be more likely to believe that effective Chinese walls were in place if different departments were involved with the different clients; a major problem in the Prince Jefri case was that the same department was involved with the prince and the BIA.

6.24 A further conflict of interest arose over the planned merger between the Top 20 firms Pannell Kerr Forster and Robson Rhodes.

BPP PUBLISHING

Case example

Three Robson partners and senior staff members were due to act as expert witnesses on Behalf of a group of Lloyds names who had brought an action against Pannell Kerr Forster, but had resigned as witnesses when the merger was announced.

The Names attempted to take out an injunction preventing the merger from going ahead. The injunction was not granted; however the judge imposed restrictions on the Robsons individuals for the duration of the action by the Names against Pannells. These included working in different premises and not associating professionally with anyone who in the firm who might be involved in the action. As things turned out, the injunction proved to be unnecessary, as the merger talks between the two firms were subsequently abandoned.

6.25 The Institute of Chartered Accountants in England and Wales has issued guidance for its members on the implications arising from the recent cases. The guidance says that whenever accountants are acting for two clients who are in a **directly adversarial** situation, both should be informed and asked to **give consent** for the accountant to continue to act for both. Other situations, for example clients in competition, might be covered by a paragraph in the **engagement letter.**

6.26 If consent has not been given in an adversarial situation, a Chinese wall may be effective providing the departments concerned are **physically separated** and there are **strict procedures** and **monitoring** in place. The Chinese wall needs to be part of the organisational culture of the organisation.

6.27 The guidance suggests firms can avoid the need for a Chinese wall in these circumstances by a paragraph in the engagement letter saying that information will be kept confidential except as required by law, regulatory or ethical guidance, and the client permits the firm to take such steps as the firm thinks fit to preserve confidentiality.

6.28 Another situation which can arise is where two audit clients fall into dispute with each other. The auditors might be asked to arbitrate, but this would leave the auditors open to accusations of conflict of interest.

6.29 It would be better to advise the companies to obtain arbitration from an independent accountant. The auditors should not investigate one client on behalf of another, nor pass on any knowledge of either client in such a situation. This is not always easy, particularly when the auditors can see the whole picture, but the companies cannot. The auditors must be extremely tactful and firm.

Question 2

An auditor must ensure that his independence is not being compromised by providing other services to audit clients, and by other actions.

The additional services an auditor may provide include:

(a) Taxation, preparing the company's corporation tax computation and negotiating with the Inland Revenue; dealing with the tax affairs of the company's directors

(b) Preparing periodic management accounts of the company, quarterly and annual accounts

(c) Advising the directors on legal and accounting matters in relation to the company, for example, preparing submissions to the bank to obtain additional finance, advising on changes in share ownership and capital structure of the company and valuation of the company's shares

(d) Attending meetings of the board of directors

Required

In relation to a private company, of which you are auditor, consider:

BPP
PUBLISHING

(i) The benefits which may arise to the auditor and client in providing *each* of the above services

(ii) The extent to which providing *each* of these services may compromise your independence, and the action you would take to minimise the risk to your independence of providing these services

Answer

In all cases, the auditor will of course enjoy income additional to the audit fee. The client will probably benefit from a saving in using the same professional for all these types of work, because information gained on one assignment can be used on others, and the client will not be paying for the learning time of a new advisor. The client's staff and management should also save time, as they should not need to explain the business repeatedly to different people. (It has to be admitted, however, that changes in audit and other staff do often result in the client's needing to explain the same point in successive years.) The following individual comments may be made.

(a) *Taxation.* It is customary for the company's taxation liability to be at least checked, and often computed, as part of routine audit work. It is unlikely that independence would be impaired by this, or by routine correspondence with the Inland Revenue. Similarly, it is normal for an auditor to deal with directors' tax affairs. A problem would, however, arise here if there were any dispute between the company and its directors, as the auditor would suffer a conflict of interests and would probably be best advised to relinquish either the audit or the tax advisory role.

(b) *Accounts preparation.* This clearly gives the auditor a very good opportunity to keep in touch with the company's performance during the year and to take note of any possible audit problems as soon as they arise. There is, however, a risk that the auditor will not be as detached in carrying out the audit of accounts he or she has prepared as would be the case if the client had produced the accounts.

(c) *Advice to directors.* Clearly, the auditor will be able to draw on knowledge of the company in giving advice. There is a significant risk, however, that independence will be compromised, particularly if the advice turns out to have been mistaken. If the auditor has prepared a profit forecast for submission to the bank which subsequently proves over-optimistic, he or she may find it difficult to require the client to reflect the actual result in the year end accounts.

(d) *Board meetings.* There is a risk here that the auditor may completely forfeit independence by becoming too closely involved in the running of the company. The Companies Act regards as a director anyone who carries out the functions of a director, and an auditor would be exposed to this presumption if he or she attended meetings regularly. It would therefore be advisable for the auditor to attend only the board meetings at which the annual accounts are approved by the board.

Exam focus point

Ethics is a key topic area. It is likely to be examined regularly.

7   INTERNAL AUDIT ETHICS

7.1   There are two important items to consider with regard to internal auditors and ethics.

- If the internal auditor is a member of ACCA, he is subject to the ACCA's ethical guidance, just as if he was an external auditor.

- Codes of ethics for internal auditors.

ACCA's ethical guidance

7.2   An essential feature of the ACCA's ethical guidance is that it applies to members and students of ACCA, regardless of their employment and the nature of the job they do.

7.3   Clearly, as can be seen from the analysis in the rest of this Chapter, much of the detail of the guidance relates to external auditors. However, all members of ACCA are bound by the general ethical principles and are **expected to adhere to the spirit of the guidance.**

7.4   Therefore an internal auditor who is a member of ACCA must abide by ACCA's ethical guidelines. In particular, the issue of **objectivity** is as important for internal auditors as for external auditors. In order to ensure a professional standard, internal auditors should have care for the task in hand and no other.

Exam focus point

Remember in exam question that an internal auditor who is a member of ACCA is bound by the guidelines of ACCA. You might also want to refer to ethical guidelines that are more directly applicable to internal audit.

Specific ethical guidance for internal auditors

7.5   The Institute of Internal Auditors (IIA) is another professional body of which it is possible to become a member. There are a number of joining requirements, as there are for people seeking to join ACCA.

7.6   The IIA is a body which **relates specifically to internal audit**. It issues an ethical code to its members which is useful to refer to when considering specific ethical guidance for internal auditors.

7.7   However, it is important to your to understand that an internal auditor is only bound by the following code of ethics if he is a member or student of the IIA. They are useful for other internal auditors as a **reference point only**.

Ethical guidance of the Institute of Internal Auditors

1	Members shall exercise honesty, objectivity and diligence in the performance of their duties and responsibilities.
2	Members shall exhibit loyalty in all matters pertaining to the affairs of their organisation or to whomever they may be rendering a service. However, members shall not knowingly be a party to any illegal or improper activity.
3	Members shall not knowingly engage in acts or activities which are discreditable to the profession of internal auditing or to their organisation.
4	Members shall refrain from entering any activity which may be in conflict with the interests of their organisation or which would prejudice their ability to carry out objectively their duties and responsibilities.
5	Members shall not accept anything of value from an employee, client, customer, supplier or business associate of their organisation which would impair or be presumed to impair their professional judgement.
6	Members shall undertake only those services which they can reasonably expect to complete with professional competence.
7	Members shall adopt suitable means to comply with the standards for the professional practice of internal auditing.
8	Members shall be prudent in the use of information acquired in the course of their duties. They shall not use confidential information for any personal gain nor in any manner which would be contrary to law or detrimental to the welfare of their organisation.
9	Members, when reporting on the results of their work, shall reveal all material facts known to them which, if not revealed, could either distort reports of operations under review or conceal unlawful practices.

10	Members shall continually strive for improvement in the proficiency, effectiveness and quality of their service.
11	Members, in the practice of their profession, shall be ever mindful of their obligation to maintain the high standards of competence, morality and dignity promulgated by the Institute. Members shall abide by the Articles and uphold the objectives of the Institute.

Exam focus point

You are studying for a qualification from ACCA, not IIA. You do not have to learn this code of ethics. It is reproduced here to help you to think about the ethics of auditing from the point of view of the internal auditor.

Chapter roundup

- The auditors' **duty of care** has been defined by case law over time.

- **Independence** and objectivity are the most important characteristics of auditors. Guidance is given in the *Rules of Professional Conduct.*

- Current discussion is focused on the **other services** auditors sell to audit clients, **opinion shopping,** conflicts of interest and the recommendations of the *Cadbury Report.*

- Potential **threats** to objectivity include:

  - Undue dependence on an audit client
  - Family and other personal relationships
  - Beneficial interests in shares
  - Acceptance of hospitality
  - Provision of other services

- Auditors have a professional duty of **confidentiality**. However they may be compelled by law or consider it desirable in the **public interest** to disclose details of client's affairs to third parties.

- Internal auditors who are members of a professional body (say ACCA) are bound by that body's professional guidance. However, the key issue of **independence is less critical** for internal auditors who are employed by the people they report to. **Objectivity** in each situation is a key issue for internal auditors.

Quick quiz

1   Match each ethical principle.

(a)   Integrity
(b)   Objectivity
(c)   Competence
(d)   Due skill and care
(e)   Courtesy

(i)   Strive for .... in all professional and business judgements. .... is the state of mind which has regard to all considerations relevant to the task in hand but no other, it presupposes intellectual honesty.

(ii)   Carry out their professional work with ...., ..., diligence and expedition and with proper regard for the technical and professional standards expected of them as members.

(iii)   Behave with .... in all professional, business and personal financial relationships, (........................... implies not merely honesty but fair dealing and truthfulness).

(iv)   Behave with .... and consideration towards all with whom they come into contact during the course of performing their work.

(v) Not accept or perform work which they are not .... to undertake unless they obtain such advice and assistance as will enable them to competently carry out the work.

2 Statement 1: *Integrity, objectivity and independence* applies only to statutory audits.

True ☐

False ☐

3 Fill in the blanks.

In general, the recurring work paid by the client or group of connected clients should not exceed ....% of the gross practice income.

In the case of .... or other .... companies, the figure should be ....% of gross practice income.

4 Of the following list of people who would not normally be considered a closely connected person for audit independence purposes.

(a) Spouse
(b) Personal doctor
(c) Company in which person holds 59% of shares
(d) Company in which person holds 22% of shares
(e) Company in which person holds 8% of shares
(f) Minor stepchild
(g) Estranged spouse
(h) Sister
(i) Adopted minor child

5 Using the factors given, complete the table.

(a) Forms an independent liaison between board and auditors
(b) Leads to increased confidence in creditability and objectivity of reporting
(c) Formalised reporting procedure may dissuade auditors from raising matters of judgement
(d) Impartial body for auditors to consult in the event of conflicts of interest
(e) Difficulty in selecting sufficient non-executive directors with the necessary competence

Advantages of an audit committee	Disadvantages of an audit committee

6 (a) Which of the following are legitimate reasons for breach of client confidentiality?

(i) Auditor **suspects** client has committed treason
(ii) Disclosure **needed** to protect auditor's own interests
(iii) Information is **required** for the audit of another client
(iv) Auditor **knows** client has committed terrorist offence
(v) There is a **public duty** to disclose
(vi) Auditor **considers** there to be non-compliance with law and regulations
(vii) Auditor **suspects** client has committed fraud

(b) Of the above reasons, which are voluntary disclosures and which are obligatory disclosures.

Answers to quick quiz

1   (a)   (iii)
       (b)   (i)
       (c)   (v)
       (d)   (ii)
       (e)   (iv)

2   False. 'The spirit of the guidance applies equally to other audit situations.'

3   15, listed, pubic interest, 10

4   (b)

       (e)   The percentage guide is 20%

       (g)

       (h)   Sister is not mentioned in the generally accepted definition but auditor judgement would have to be exercised; depending on the closeness of the relationships etc.

5

Advantages	Disadvantages
(a), (b), (d)	(c), (e)

6   (i)   O
       (ii)   V
       (iv)   O
       (v)   V
       (vi)   O

(*NB.* In the case of (vii), the auditor should not take action outside the company until he is certain. When he is certain, he should seek legal advice.)

Now try the question below from the Exam Question Bank

Number	Level	Marks	Time
4	Exam	20	36 mins

Chapter 5

AUDIT ACCEPTANCE

Topic list	Syllabus reference
1 Tendering and obtaining work	1
2 Appointment ethics	1
3 Client screening	1
4 Fraud and error	1
5 Law and regulations	1
6 The engagement letter	1

Introduction

In Chapter 2, we looked at some of the legal requirements in relation to statutory audits. In this Chapter, following on from the overview of professional ethics in Chapter 4, we look at some of the **practical and ethical matters an external auditor has to consider when accepting professional work**.

ACCA have issued guidance on **advertising** and **obtaining professional** work. Setting fees for new clients can be controversial. **Lowballing** is a particular area where problems can arise.

The **procedures** to be carried out both **before** and **after** the **acceptance** of a new client are straightforward and easy to learn. These are outlined in section 2.

In the current climate, the **acceptance of a new client can entail** the undertaking of a **significant amount of risk**. Audit firms, particularly larger firms, now tend towards fairly stringent **client acceptance procedures**. This client screening helps to establish good 'high level' controls in a (potential) client.

Accepting an audit engagement includes an element of risk. In sections 3 and 4 we look at two **specific areas of auditing guidance** which look at the **risky areas** of fraud and error, and compliance with law and regulations. The issues raised in these SASs are matters which should be **considered at an initial stage** as well as during the course of audits.

The **engagement letter** is an audit document of fundamental importance as it lays out the **scope** of the auditor's work and it **highlights the respective responsibilities of directors and auditors**.

Study guide

Section 6

- Describe the requirements of professional ethics and other requirements in relation to the acceptance of audit and review assignments.

- Describe the importance of engagement letters and describe their contents.

Exam guide

Risk and ethics are both important topics on this syllabus. Client acceptance is likely to be examined in the context of professional ethics, as it was on the pilot paper.

1 TENDERING AND OBTAINING WORK

Statement 3: Advertising, Publicity and Obtaining Professional Work

1.1 Guidance is given as follows.

(a) Members should not obtain or seek work in an **unprofessional manner**.

(b) Members can advertise but should have regard to **relevant advertising codes** and standards.

(c) Members should **not make disparaging references** to or comparisons with the services of others.

(d) Members should **not quote fees** without great care to not mislead as to the precise range of services and time commitment that fees are intended to cover, but they can offer free consultations to discuss level of fees.

(e) **No fees, commission** or reward should be given to third parties in return for the introduction of clients.

Fee negotiation and lowballing

1.2 The audit fee is a sensitive subject for most companies. It represents a cost for something the company often does not really want and the fees may be perceived as too high just for this reason.

1.3 The directors of other companies may have a more positive attitude towards the benefit of an audit, but even they will often feel duty bound to obtain 'an audit' for as low a price as possible. The auditors, on the other hand, must ensure that they can provide a proper audit service for the fee negotiated.

1.4 There are various rules concerning the resignation or replacement of the auditors, but here we are merely concerned with how fee negotiations take place when obtaining the services of **new** auditors, whatever the reason for the change. There will, of course, be situations where newly formed companies will require auditors for the first time, but most appointments of auditors are through a change of auditors.

Tendering

1.5 Many large companies invite **tenders** for their audit work. The directors then have the opportunity to compare directly a range of offers. This is the type of situation usually faced by the larger auditing firms, although tenders can be invited for companies of any size.

1.6 Generally, a tender will take the form of detailed written proposals and a presentation. Although the proposed level of **fees** charged will be a very important factor (and perhaps the deciding one), other aspects will be considered by the directors of the company concerned, including:

- The **level** of **expertise** each firm has in the industry
- **Similar companies** audited by each firm (good for expertise, worrying for confidentiality)
- **National** and **international presence** and so on

Audit firms which tender for such audits will usually give at least an indication of the level of fees in the next few years, including likely overall rate rises.

1.7 In all situations, the auditors should quote a fee based on the estimated hours worked by each member of staff required on the audit, multiplied by the hourly rate commensurate with their grade, plus any expenses to be incurred during the audit (travel, subsistence and so on). Many audit firms will add a premium to the normal hourly charge out rate for specialist audits, such as banking or financial services.

Lowballing

1.8 Problems can arise when auditing firms appear to be charging less than this, or at least less than the 'market rate' for the audit. The practice of undercutting, usually at tender for the audit of large companies, has been called **lowballing**. In other cases, the audit fee has been reduced even though the auditors have remained the same. The problem here is that, if the audit is being performed for less than it is actually worth, then the **auditors' independence is called into question**.

1.9 This is always going to be a topical debate, but in terms of negotiating the audit fee the following factors need to be taken into account.

(a) The audit is perceived to have a **fluctuating 'market price'** as any other commodity or service. In a recession, prices would be expected to fall as companies aim to cut costs everywhere, and as auditors chase less work (supply falls). Audit firms are also reducing staffing levels and their own overhead costs should be lower.

(b) Companies can reduce external audit costs through various **legitimate measures**:

- Extending the size and function of internal audit
- Reducing the number of different audit firms used world-wide
- Selling off subsidiary companies leaving a simplified group structure to audit
- The tender process itself simply makes auditors more competitive
- Exchange rate fluctuations in audit fees

(c) Auditing firms have **increased productivity**, partly through the use of more sophisticated information technology techniques in auditing.

1.10 These factors will all be taken into account when the audit fee is negotiated. As far as undercutting or lowballing is concerned, the relevant professional bodies may issue new ethical rules to prevent it.

1.11 In any case, an auditing firm lays itself open to accusations of loss of independence if it reduces its fees to below a certain level, particularly if it is difficult to see how such fees will cover direct labour costs. This is also true of firms which use the audit as a 'loss leader' to obtain profitable consultancy work from audit clients.

1.12 There is also a risk of a conflict of interest when non-audit services are offered to a client by the auditors. The possibility arises that the price of an 'acceptable' audit opinion is lucrative taxation or consulting work.

1.13 Where clients face difficulties paying an audit fee all at once, the auditors might offer to receive the fee over several months, or even the whole year, probably by direct debit.

2 APPOINTMENT ETHICS

2.1 This section covers the procedures that the **auditors must** undertake to **ensure that their appointment is valid** and that they are clear to act. These matters are also covered in Statement 5: *Changes in Professional Appointment* in the ACCA's *Rules of Professional Conduct*.

Before accepting nomination

2.2 Before a new audit client is accepted, the auditors must ensure that there are no **independence** or **other ethical problems** likely to cause conflict with the ethical code. Furthermore, new auditors should ensure that they have been appointed in a proper and legal manner.

2.3 The nominee auditors must carry out the following procedures:

ACCEPTANCE PROCEDURES	
Ensure **professionally qualified** to act	Consider whether disqualified on legal or ethical grounds
Ensure **existing resources adequate**	Consider available time, staff and technical expertise
Obtain references	Make independent enquiries if directors not personally known. See Section 4 of this chapter
Communicate with present auditors	Enquire whether there are reasons/circumstances behind the change which the new auditors ought to know, also courtesy See flowchart over page for process

Example letters

2.4 This is an example of a initial communication.

> To: Retiring & Co
>   Certified Accountants
>
> Dear Sirs
>
> Re: New Client Co Ltd
>
> We have been asked to allow our name to go forward for nomination as auditors of the above company, and we should therefore be grateful if you would please let us know whether there are any professional reasons why we should not accept nomination...... .
>
> Acquiring & Co
>
> Certified Accountants

2.5 Having negotiated these steps the auditors will be in a position to accept the nomination, or not, as the case may be. These procedures can be demonstrated most easily in a decision chart, as shown on the next page.

Appointment decision chart

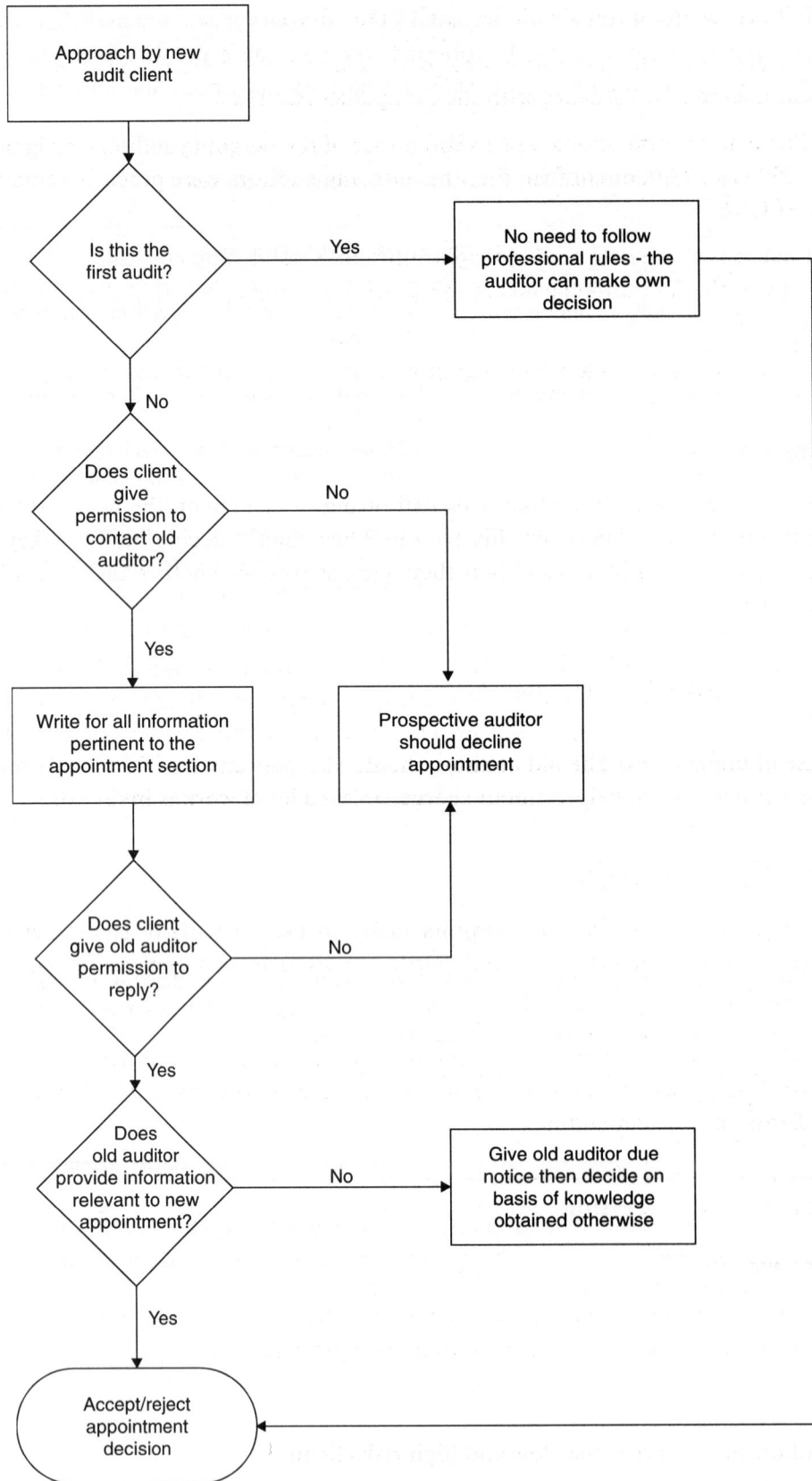

```
                    ┌─────────────────┐
                    │  Approach by new │
                    │   audit client   │
                    └────────┬─────────┘
                             │
                             ▼
                        ╱────────╲                          ┌──────────────────────┐
                       ╱  Is this  ╲         Yes            │  No need to follow    │
                      ╱  the first   ╲──────────────────────│ professional rules - the│
                       ╲   audit?    ╱                       │ auditor can make own  │
                        ╲──────────╱                         │      decision         │
                             │                               └───────────┬──────────┘
                            No                                           │
                             │                                           │
                             ▼                                           │
                        ╱────────╲                                       │
                       ╱  Does     ╲        No                           │
                      ╱  client give ╲──────────────┐                    │
                     ╱  permission to ╲             │                    │
                      ╲ contact old   ╱             │                    │
                       ╲  auditor?   ╱              │                    │
                        ╲──────────╱                │                    │
                             │                      │                    │
                            Yes                     │                    │
                             │                      ▼                    │
                             ▼              ┌──────────────────┐         │
                    ┌─────────────────┐     │  Prospective     │         │
                    │ Write for all   │     │  auditor should  │         │
                    │ information     │     │     decline      │         │
                    │ pertinent to the│     │   appointment    │         │
                    │ appointment     │     └──────────────────┘         │
                    │ section         │              ▲                   │
                    └────────┬────────┘              │                   │
                             │                       │                   │
                             ▼                       │                   │
                        ╱────────╲                   │                   │
                       ╱  Does     ╲      No          │                   │
                      ╱ client give ╲─────────────────┘                   │
                     ╱ old auditor   ╲                                     │
                      ╲ permission to ╱                                    │
                       ╲  reply?     ╱                                     │
                        ╲──────────╱                                       │
                             │                                             │
                            Yes                                            │
                             │                                             │
                             ▼                                             │
                        ╱────────╲                    ┌──────────────────┐ │
                       ╱  Does     ╲      No          │ Give old auditor │ │
                      ╱ old auditor ╲─────────────────│ due notice then  │ │
                     ╱ provide info  ╲                │ decide on basis  │ │
                      ╲ relevant to  ╱                │ of knowledge     │ │
                       ╲ new appt?   ╱                │ obtained otherwise│ │
                        ╲──────────╱                  └──────────────────┘ │
                             │                                             │
                            Yes                                            │
                             │                                             │
                             ▼                                             │
                    ┌─────────────────┐                                    │
                    │  Accept/reject  │◄───────────────────────────────────┘
                    │  appointment    │
                    │    decision     │
                    └─────────────────┘
```

Procedures after accepting nomination

2.6 The following procedures should be carried out after accepting nomination.

(a) **Ensure** that the **outgoing auditors' removal** or **resignation** has been **properly conducted** in accordance with the Companies Act 1985.

The new auditors should see a valid notice of the outgoing auditors' resignation (under s 392 CA 1985), or confirm that the outgoing auditors were properly removed (under s 391 CA 1985).

(b) **Ensure** that the **new auditors' appointment is valid**. The new auditors should obtain a copy of the resolution passed at the general meeting appointing them as the company's auditors.

(c) Set up and **submit a letter of engagement** to the directors of the company (see section 5).

Other matters

2.7 Where the previous auditors have fees still owing by the client, the new auditors need not decline appointment solely for this reason. They should decide how far they may go in aiding the former auditors to obtain their fees, as well as whether they should accept the appointment.

2.8 Once a new appointment has taken place, the **new auditors should obtain all books and papers which belong to the client from the old auditors**. The former accountants should ensure that all such documents are transferred, **unless** they have a lien over the books because of unpaid fees. The old auditors should also pass any useful information to the new auditors if it will be of help, without charge, unless a lot of work is involved.

3 CLIENT SCREENING

3.1 As well as contacting previous auditors many firms, particularly larger firms, carry out **stringent checks** on potential client companies and their management. There are a number of reasons for this, as we will see shortly.

3.2 The procedures laid out here are tailored to the extreme case of a large audit firm and a large (probably public) company audit, but the **procedures may be adapted for smaller audit firms** and smaller audits.

Basic factors for consideration

Management integrity

3.3 The integrity of those managing a company will be of great importance, particularly if the company is controlled by one or a few dominant personalities.

Risk

3.4 The following table contrasts low and high risk clients.

BPP
PUBLISHING

LOW RISK	HIGH RISK
Good long-term prospects	Poor recent or forecast performance
Well-financed	Likely lack of finance
Strong internal controls	Significant control weaknesses
Conservative, prudent accounting policies	Evidence of questionable integrity, doubtful accounting policies
Competent, honest management	Lack of finance director
Few unusual transactions	Significant related party or unexplained transactions

3.5 Where the risk level of a company's audit is determined as anything other than low, then the specific risks should be identified and documented. It might be necessary to assign specialists in response to these risks, particularly industry specialists, as independent reviewers. Some audit firms have procedures for closely monitoring audits which have been accepted, but which are considered high risk.

Engagement economics

3.6 Generally, the expected fees from a new client should reflect the **level of risk** expected. They should also offer the same sort of return expected of clients of this nature and reflect the overall financial strategy of the audit firm. Occasionally, the audit firm will want the work to gain entry into the client's particular industry, or to establish better contacts within that industry. These factors will all contribute to a total expected economic return.

Relationship

3.7 The audit firm will generally want the relationship with a client to be **long term**. This is not only to enjoy receiving fees year after year; it is also to allow the audit work to be enhanced by better knowledge of the client and thereby offer a better service.

3.8 Conflict of interest problems are significant here; the firm should establish that no existing clients will cause difficulties as competitors of the new client. Other services to other clients may have an impact here, not just audit.

Ability to perform the work

3.9 The audit firm must have the **resources** to perform the work properly, as well as any **specialist knowledge or skills**. The impact on existing engagements must be estimated, in terms of staff time and the timing of the audit.

SOURCES OF INFORMATION ABOUT NEW CLIENTS	
Enquiries of other sources	Bankers, solicitors
Review of **documents**	Most recent annual accounts, listing particulars, credit rating
Previous accountants/auditors	Previous auditors should disclose fully all relevant information
Review of **rules and standards**	Consider specific laws/standards that relate to industry

Approval

3.10 Once all the relevant procedures and information gathering has taken place, the company can be put forward for approval. The engagement partner will have completed a client acceptance form and this, along with any other relevant documentations, will be submitted to the managing partner, or whichever partner is in overall charge of accepting clients.

Exam focus point

In the exam you may be given a 'real-life' client situation and asked what factors you would consider in deciding whether to accept appointment. The ethical considerations covered in Chapter 4 and in this chapter are likely be relevant.

---

4 FRAUD AND ERROR   Dec 01

4.1 Look back at the table of risk factors on page 80 and remind yourself of some of the high risk factors which are listed there.

4.2 Many of the high risk factors listed are issues which could potentially result in a high risk of fraud and error arising.

Significant control weaknesses

Questionable integrity

Doubtful accounting policies   **FRAUD?**

Lack of finance director

Unexplained transactions

4.3 Fraud is an emotive issue. If news of a major fraud on a company hits the headlines, the question that is often asked is 'how did this happen?' Invariably when questions like that are asked, people raise **questions about the audit** that has taken place on that company's financial statements.

4.4 A major problem for the auditor can be that the public does not understand the auditors' role with regard to fraud. This forms part of an **'expectations gap'** which exists between what auditors actually do and what people think that they do.

4.5 We are going to briefly consider here what the auditors' role in relation to fraud and error, and consider when the **risk** of fraud and error arising is **too great** for the auditor **to accept** the engagement.

SAS 110 *Fraud and error*

SAS 110.2

Auditors should plan and perform their audit procedures and evaluate and report the results thereof, recognising that fraud or error may materially affect the financial statements.

4.6 The first half of the sentence from SAS 110 given above summarises the content of an external audit. Auditors must plan and perform their work, they must evaluate it, and then report to members. The second half summarises their professional requirements in relation to fraud and error: they must **recognise** that **it may exist** and **materially affect** the financial statements.

4.7 The most important thing to understand with regard to fraud is that **the auditor has no duty** (specifically no statutory duty) **to prevent or detect fraud**.

4.8 With regard to the statutory audit, the auditor must be aware that two potential causes of the financial statements being misstated are fraud or error existing.

> **KEY TERMS**
>
> **Fraud** comprises both the use of deception to obtain an unjust or illegal financial advantage, and intentional misrepresentation by management, employees or third parties.
>
> **Error** is an unintentional mistake.

4.9 EXAMPLES

The SAS gives the following list of examples of what fraud may involve:

- Falsification or alteration of accounting records or other documents
- Misappropriation of assets or theft
- Suppression or omission of the effects of transactions from records or documents
- Recording of transactions without substance
- Intentional misapplication of accounting policies, or
- Wilful misrepresentations of transactions or of the entity's state of affairs

4.10 What this list of 'fraudulent behaviour' might help you to see is that the detection of fraud committed by management is going to be extremely difficult because it is designed not to be found. Particularly where the fraud is fraud by omission, the auditor is unlikely to detect fraud as part of an audit.

4.11 The standard does not expect the auditors to detect fraud as a matter of course. Rather, it requires auditors to be **aware**, when planning and performing their audit, that fraud may exist, and more particularly, it highlights a number of **factors which the auditor should be alert to**, which could point to fraud being perpetrated.

Planning

> **SAS 110.2/3**
>
> When planning the audit the auditors should assess the risk that fraud or error may cause the financial statements to contain material misstatements. (SAS 110.2)
>
> Based on their risk assessment, the auditors should design audit procedures so as to have a reasonable expectation of detecting misstatements arising from fraud or error which are material to the financial statements. (SAS 110.3)

4.12　The factors which may indicate fraud or error are given in an appendix to the SAS, which is reproduced here:

Fraud and error	
Previous experience or incidents which **call into question** the **integrity** or **competence** of **management**	Management dominated by one person (or a small group) and no effective oversight board or committee
	Complex corporate structure where complexity does not seem to be warranted
	High turnover rate of key accounting and financial personnel
	Personnel (key or otherwise) not taking holidays
	Significant and prolonged under-staffing of the accounting department
	Frequent changes of legal advisers or auditors
Particular financial reporting pressures within an entity	Industry volatility
Weaknesses in the **design** and **operation** of the **accounting and internal controls system**	A weak control environment within the entity
	Systems that, in their design, are inadequate to give reasonable assurance of preventing or detecting error or fraud
	Inadequate segregation of responsibilities in relation to functions involving the handling, recording or controlling of the entity's assets
	Indications that internal financial information is unreliable
	Evidence that internal controls have been overridden by management
	Ineffective monitoring of the operation of system which allows control overrides, breakdown or weakness to continue without proper corrective action
	Continuing failure to correct major weakness in internal control where such corrections are practicable and cost effective
Unusual transactions	Unusual transactions, especially near the year end, that have a significant effect on earnings
	Complex transactions or accounting treatments
	Unusual transactions with related parties
	Payments for services (for example to lawyers, consultants or agents) that appear excessive in relation to the services provided

Fraud and error	
Problems in **obtaining sufficient appropriate audit evidence**	Inadequate records, for example incomplete files, excessive adjustments to accounting records, transactions not recorded in accordance with normal procedures and out-of-balance control accounts
Some factors unique to an **information systems environment** which relate to the conditions and events described above	Inability to extract information from computer files due to lack of, or non-current, documentation of record contents or programs
	Large numbers of program changes that are not documented, approved and tested
	Inadequate overall balancing of computer transactions and data bases to the financial accounts

4.13 Auditors are therefore 'put on enquiry' when such factors exist – in other words, they have a **professional duty to satisfy themselves** that **any concerns raised** have been **answered** to their satisfaction.

When fraud or error are indicated

4.14 The SAS then goes on to outline what the auditors should do if their suspicions are raised.

SAS 110.4-6

When planning the audit the auditors should assess the risk that fraud or error may cause the financial statements to contain When auditors become aware of information which indicates that fraud or error may exist, they should obtain an understanding of the nature of the event and the circumstances in which it has occurred, and sufficient other information to evaluate the possible effect on the financial statements. If the auditors believe that the indicated fraud or error could have a material effect on the financial statements, they should perform appropriate modified or additional procedures. (SAS 110.4)

When the auditors become aware of, or suspect that there may be, instances of error or fraudulent conduct, they should document their findings and, subject to any requirement to report them direct to a third party, discuss them with the appropriate level of management. (SAS 110.5)

The auditors should consider the implications of suspected or actual error or fraudulent conduct in relation to other aspects of the audit, particularly the reliability of management representations. (SAS 110.6)

Reporting

4.15 Lastly the SAS goes on to consider what the auditors should do, or rather, to whom they should report, in the event of them uncovering a fraud. Remember that, as you learnt in Chapter 4, the auditors have a professional duty of confidentiality.

SAS 110.9

The auditors should as soon as practicable communicate their findings to the appropriate level of management, the board of directors or the audit committee if

(a) they suspect or discover fraud, even if the potential effect on the financial statements is immaterial, or

(b) material error is found to exist.

4.16 Such a discovery might also have an impact on the audit report, which we shall consider in Chapter 19.

4.17 If auditors do detect a management fraud, they may consider it to be so serious that it is necessary to report it to the relevant authority in the public interest. Such a decision would not be taken lightly, and should only be taken once **legal advice** had been sought. The auditors have a duty of confidentiality, but in **exceptional circumstances**, where the matter is one of **public interest,** they may have to make such a disclosure.

SAS 110.10-12

Where the auditors become aware of a suspected or actual instance of fraud they should

(a) consider whether the matter may be one that ought to be reported to a proper authority in the public interest: and where this is the case

(b) except in the circumstances covered in SAS 100.12, discuss the matter with the board of directors, including any audit committee   (SAS 110.10)

Where, having considered any views expressed on behalf of the entity and in the light of any legal advice obtained, the auditors conclude that the matter ought to be reported to an appropriate authority in the public interest, they should notify the directors in writing of their view and, if the entity does not voluntarily do so itself or is unable to provide evidence that the matter has been reported, they should report it themselves.   (SAS 110.11)

When a suspected or actual instance of fraud casts doubt on the integrity of the directors auditors should make a report direct to a proper authority in the public interest without delay and without informing the directors in advance.   (SAS 110.12)

Fraud and audit acceptance

4.18 Several issues have been raised here from the point of view of the audit firm:

- Auditors should plan and perform procedures whilst being **aware** that fraud may exist

- Fraud, however, may be extremely **difficult to discover**

- Auditors must **satisfy themselves** if put on enquiry

- If the auditors detect or suspect fraud, they must consider whether it is in the public interest to **report** it, having sought **legal advice.**

- Fraud is an emotive issue, which may bring bad **publicity** to the firm, deserved or not

4.19 Cast your mind back to the high risk factors which were identified on page 80. **It might be that an audit firm would choose not accept a client** which was identified as **high risk** at the outset, because the chances of conducting a cost effective audit which fulfils professional requirements might be too low, even if the indicators were false, and there was no fraud being perpetrated at the company.

5   LAW AND REGULATIONS

5.1   Another issue raised by the risk factors on page 80 is the issue of the auditors' consideration of law and regulation. This issue has two aspects:

- Areas of non-compliance where the matter may **materially affect the financial statements**

- Areas where the **auditors could unwittingly become liable** for failing to report matters arising, for example, money laundering

5.2   The auditing standard approaches this issue in a similar way to the standard on fraud and error.

SAS 120 *Consideration of law and regulations*

5.3   The standard sets out the respective duties of directors and auditors in relation to compliance with law and regulations. The directors have a duty to ensure that the company complies with any relevant legislation and regulation.

5.4   The auditors do not have a duty to prevent non-compliance. However, similarly to their duty in relation to fraud and error, they have a **duty to plan, perform and evaluate** their audit work in order to have a **reasonable expectation** of **detecting material misstatements** which may arise through non-compliance.

Planning

SAS 120.1-4

Auditors should plan and perform their audit procedures, and evaluate and report on the results thereof, recognising that non-compliance by the entity with law or regulations may materially affect the financial statements.   (SAS 120.1)

The auditors should obtain sufficient appropriate audit evidence about compliance with those laws and regulations which relate directly to the preparation of, or the inclusion or disclosure of specific items in, the financial statements.   (SAS 120.2)

The auditors should perform procedures to help identify possible or actual instances of non-compliance with those laws and regulations which provide a legal framework within which the entity conducts its business and which are central to the entity's ability to conduct its business and hence to its financial statements by

(a)   obtaining a general understanding of the legal and regulatory framework applicable to the entity and the industry and of the procedures followed to ensure compliance with that framework

(b)   inspecting correspondence with relevant licensing or regulatory authorities

(c)   enquiring of the directors as to whether they are on notice of any such possible instances of non-compliance with law or regulations, and

(d)   obtaining written confirmation from the directors that they have disclosed to the auditors all those events of which they are aware which involve possible non-compliance, together with the actual or contingent consequences which may arise therefrom.   (SAS 120.3)

When carrying out their procedures for the purpose of forming an opinion on the financial statements, the auditors should in addition be alert for instances or possible or actual non-compliance with law or regulations which might affect the financial statements.   (SAS 120.4)

When non-compliance is indicated

5.5 If the auditors' suspicions are raised, the SAS goes on to say that they should **gain an understanding** of what has happened so that they can evaluate the effect on the financial statements. They should also **document their findings** and **discuss them with management**, unless they are required to report them directly to a third party.

5.6 They should also consider the implications of this non-compliance on representations made to them by management during the course of the audit.

Reporting

5.7 The reporting requirements of SAS 120 are very similar to SAS 110:

Auditors suspect or detect non-compliance with law and regulations	1. Discuss with management or the audit committee, or ensure that they are aware of the issue.	(SAS 120.8)
	2. If the non-compliance appears to be material or intentional, they should discuss it with management without delay.	(SAS 120.9)
There is a statutory duty to report.	Make the report to the relevant authority without delay.	(SAS 120.12)
There is no statutory duty to report.	1. Consider whether it is in the public interest to report and discuss it with the directors.	(SAS 120.13)
	2. Take legal advice, and report it to the relevant authority if it is in the public interest	(SAS 120.14)
	3. If the suspicion causes them to no longer have confidence in the integrity of the directors, report it to the relevant authority without delay or discussion with the entity.	(SAS 120.15)

Compliance with law/regulations and audit acceptance

5.8 Similarly to the issue of fraud, this is an area which can bring **complexity** to the audit and a severe risk of **bad publicity**. If high **risk factors** such as the entity operating in a highly regulated environment, or a complex corporate structure exist, an **audit firm may decline appointment** feeling that a cost effective audit will be difficult to achieve.

5.9 Another risk arising to the audit firm is the risk of personal liability arising if the entity is a mask for illegal activities such as money laundering. SAS 120 mentions money laundering in paragraph 19.

5.10 Auditors are **required by law** to **disclose suspicions** of the laundering of money deriving from drug trafficking or relating to terrorist offences. It is also a criminal offence to disclose such reporting. Auditors have a **statutory duty not to let their client know if they have made such a report.**

5.11 While risk factors such as **complex corporate structures** and doubts over the **integrity of management** may not (and often are not) based in the fact that the company is operating for illegal purposes, an **audit firm may decline appointment** to entities with such factors, as the risk to the audit firm of the reverse being true is too great to take on.

BPP
PUBLISHING

6 THE ENGAGEMENT LETTER

6.1 An engagement letter should:

- Define clearly the **extent** of the **auditors' responsibilities** and so minimise the possibility of any misunderstanding between the client and the auditors

- Provide **written confirmation** of the **auditors' acceptance** of the appointment, the scope of the audit, the form of their report and the scope of any non-audit services

6.2 If an engagement letter is not sent to clients, both new and existing, there is scope for argument about the precise extent of the respective obligations of the client and its directors and the auditors. The contents of an engagement letter should be discussed and agreed with management before it is sent.

6.3 Guidance is available in the form of the SAS 140 *Engagement letters*, which applies to **audit** engagements. The statements made by the standard are as follows.

SAS 140.1

The auditors and the client should agree on the terms of the engagement, which should be recorded in writing.

SAS 140.2

Auditors should agree the terms of their engagement with new clients in writing. Thereafter auditors should regularly review the terms of engagement and if appropriate agree any updating in writing.

SAS 140.3

Auditors who, before the completion of the audit, are requested to change the engagement to one which provides a different level of assurance, should consider the appropriateness of so doing. If auditors consider that it is appropriate to change the terms of engagement, they should obtain written agreement to the revised terms.

SAS 140.4

Auditors should ensure that the engagement letter documents and confirms their acceptance of the appointment, and includes a summary of the responsibilities of the directors and of the auditors, the scope of the engagement and the form of any reports.

Timing

6.4 The auditors should send an engagement letter to all new clients soon after their appointment as auditors and, in any event, **before the commencement of the first audit** assignment.

Content of letter

6.5 This is shown in the example given in an Appendix to the SAS, which is reproduced below. The main emphasis is on the 'principal relevant responsibilities of the directors and the auditors and the scope of the audit.'

Form of reports

6.6 The letter should identify any reports which the auditors will submit **in addition to** the statutory audit report, such as reports to the directors/managers on material internal control weaknesses. Confidentiality aspects of such reports should be mentioned.

Other matters

6.7   The other matters which the SAS highlights for possible inclusion in the engagement letter are as follows.

Fees and billing arrangements

Procedures where the client has a complaint about the service

Where appropriate, arrangements concerning the involvement of:

- Other auditors and experts in some aspect of the audit
- Internal auditors and other staff of the entity

Arrangements, if any, to be made with the predecessor auditors, in the case of an initial audit

Any restriction of the auditors' liabilities to the client (when such possibility exists; not possible with limited companies)

Where appropriate, the country by whose laws the engagement to be governed

A reference to any further agreements between the auditors and the client

A proposed timetable for the engagement

6.8   The following example of an engagement letter for a UK limited company client. Remember that it is not necessarily comprehensive or appropriate to every audit as each client is different; it must be tailored to meet the specific requirements of the engagement.

AN EXAMPLE OF AN ENGAGEMENT LETTER

To the directors of..

The purpose of this letter is to set out the basis on which we (are to) act as auditors of the company (and its subsidiaries) and the respective areas of responsibility of the directors and of ourselves.

Responsibility of directors and auditors

1   As directors of the above company, you are responsible for ensuring that the company maintains proper accounting records and for preparing financial statements which give a true and fair view and have been prepared in accordance with the Companies Act 1985. You are also responsible for making available to us, as and when required, all the company's accounting records and all other relevant records and related information, including minutes of all management and shareholders' meetings.

2   We have a statutory responsibility to report to the members whether in our opinion the financial statements give a true and fair view of the state of the company's affairs and of the profit or loss for the year and whether they have been properly prepared in accordance with the Companies Act 1985 (or other relevant legislation). In arriving at our opinion, we are required to consider the following matters, and to report on any in respect of which we are not satisfied:

(a)   whether proper accounting records have been kept by the company and proper returns adequate for our audit have been received from branches not visited by us;

(b)   whether the company's balance sheet and profit and loss account are in agreement with the accounting records and returns;

(c)   whether we have obtained all the information and explanations which we think necessary for the purposes of our audit; and

(d)   whether the information in the directors' report is consistent with the financial statements.

In addition, there are certain other matters which, according to the circumstances, may need to be dealt with in our report. For example, where the financial statements do not give full details of directors' remuneration or of their transactions with the company, the Companies Act requires us to disclose such matters in our report.

3 We have a professional responsibility to report if the financial statements do not comply in any material respect with applicable accounting standards, unless in our opinion the non-compliance is justified in the circumstances. In determining whether the departure is justified we consider:

(a) whether the departure is required in order for the financial statements to give a true and fair view; and

(b) whether adequate disclosure has been made concerning the departure

Our professional responsibilities also include:

(a) including in our report a description of the directors' responsibilities for the financial statements where the financial statements or accompanying information do not include such a description; and

(b) considering whether other information in documents containing audited financial statements is consistent with those financial statements.

4 Our audit will be conducted in accordance with the Auditing Standards issued by the Auditing Practices Board, and will include such tests of transactions and of the existence, ownership and valuation of assets and liabilities as we consider necessary. We shall obtain an understanding of the accounting and internal control systems in order to assess their adequacy as a basis for the preparation of the financial statements and to establish whether proper accounting records have been maintained by the company. We shall expect to obtain such appropriate evidence as we consider sufficient to enable us to draw reasonable conclusions therefrom

5 The nature and extent of our procedures will vary according to our assessment of the company's accounting system and, where we wish to place reliance on it, the internal control system, and may cover any aspect of the business's operations. Our audit is not designed to identify all significant weaknesses in the company's systems but, if such weaknesses come to our notice during the course of our audit which we think should be brought to your attention, we shall report them to you. Any such report may not be provided to third parties without our prior written consent. Such consent will be granted only on the basis that such reports are not prepared with the interests of anyone other than the company in mind and that we accept no duty or responsibility to any other party as concerns the reports.

6 As part of our normal audit procedures, we may request you to provide written confirmation of oral representations which we have received from you during the course of the audit on matters having a material effect on the financial statements. In connection with representations and the supply of information to us generally, we draw your attention to section 389A of the Companies Act 1985 under which it is an offence for an officer of the company to mislead the auditors.

7 In order to assist us with the examination of your financial statements, we shall request sight of all documents or statements, including the chairman's statement, operating and financial review and the directors' report, which are due to be issued with the financial statements. We are also entitled to attend all general meetings of the company and to receive notice of all such meetings.

8 The responsibility for safeguarding the assets of the company and for the prevention and detection of fraud, error and non-compliance with law or regulations rests with yourselves. However, we shall endeavour to plan our audit so that we have a reasonable expectation of detecting material misstatements in the financial statements or accounting records (including those resulting from fraud, error or non-compliance with law or regulations), but our examination should not be relied upon to disclose all such material misstatements or frauds, errors or instances of non-compliance as may exist.

9 (Where appropriate). We shall not be treated as having notice, for the purposes of our audit responsibilities, of information provided to members of our firm other than those engaged on the audit (for example information provided in connection with accounting, taxation and other services).

10　Once we have issued our report we have no further direct responsibility in relation to the financial statements for that financial year. However, we expect that you will inform us of any material event occurring between the date of our report and that of the Annual General Meeting which may affect the financial statements.

Other services

11　You have requested that we provide other services in respect of ... . The terms under which we provide these other services are dealt with in a separate letter. We will also agree in a separate letter of engagement the provision of any services relating to investment business advice as defined by the Financial Services Act 1986.

Fees

12　Our fees are computed on the basis of the time spent on your affairs by the partners and our staff and on the levels of skill and responsibility involved. Unless otherwise agreed, our fees will be billed at appropriate intervals during the course of the year and will be due on presentation.

Applicable law

13　This (engagement letter) shall be governed by, and construed in accordance with, (English) law. The Courts of (England) shall have exclusive jurisdiction in relation to any claim, dispute or difference concerning the (engagement letter) and any matter arising from it. Each party irrevocably waives any right it may have to object to an action being brought in those Courts, to claim that the action has been brought in an inconvenient forum, or to claim that those Courts do not have jurisdiction.

14　Once it has been agreed, this letter will remain effective, from one audit appointment to another, until it is replaced. We shall be grateful if you could confirm in writing your agreement to these terms by signing and returning the enclosed copy of this letter, or let us know if they are not in accordance with your understanding of our terms of engagement.

Yours faithfully

Certified Accountants

Recipient of letter

6.9　The letter should be addressed to the board of directors or audit committee of the organisation to be audited. The terms of the letter should be evidenced as accepted by the organisation by the signature of an appropriate senior person.

Changes in terms or nature of an engagement

6.10　Once it has been agreed by the client, an engagement letter will, if it so provides, remain effective from one audit appointment to another until it is replaced.

6.11　However, the engagement letter should be reviewed annually to ensure that it continues to reflect the client's circumstances. The SAS suggests that the following factors may make the agreement of a new letter appropriate.

- Any indication that the client **misunderstands** the objective and scope of the audit
- A **recent change of management,** board of directors or audit committee
- A **significant change in ownership,** such as a new holding company
- A **significant change in the nature or size** of the client's business
- Any **relevant change in legal or professional requirements**

6.12 It may be appropriate to remind the client of the original letter when the auditors decide a new engagement letter is unnecessary for any period.

6.13 In the case of a change in the terms of engagement prior to completion, this may result from:

- A **change in circumstances** affecting the need for the service

- A **misunderstanding** as to the nature of an audit or of the related service originally requested

- A **restriction** on the **scope** of the **engagement**, whether imposed by management or caused by circumstances

6.14 The auditors should consider such a request for change, and the reason for it, very seriously, particularly in terms of any restriction in the scope of the engagement. Auditors may have to withdraw from the engagement.

Question 1

You are a partner in Messrs Borg Connors & Co, Certified Accountants. You are approached by Mr Nastase, the managing director of Navratilova Enterprises Ltd, who asks your firm to become auditors of his company. In return for giving you this appointment Mr Nastase says that he will expect your firm to waive fifty per cent of your normal fee for the first year's audit. The existing auditors, Messrs Wade Austin & Co have not resigned but Mr Nastase informs you that they will not be re-appointed in the future.

Required

(a) What action should Messrs Borg Connors & Co take in response to the request from Mr Nastase to reduce their first year's fee by fifty per cent?

(b) Explain the procedure a company must go through to remove its auditors and appoint another firm of auditors in their place.

(c) Are Messrs Wade Austin & Co within their rights in not resigning when they know Mr Nastase wishes to replace them? Give reasons for your answer.

Answer

(a) The request by Mr Nastase that half of the first year's audit fee should be waived is quite improper. If this proposal were to be accepted it could be held that Borg Connors & Co had sought to procure work through the quoting of lower fees. This would be unethical and would result in disciplinary proceedings being taken against the firm.

It should be pointed out to Mr Nastase that the audit fee will be determined, in accordance with normal practice, by reference to the work involved in completion of a satisfactory audit taking into consideration the nature of the audit tasks involved and the level of staff required to carry out those tasks in an efficient manner. Mr Nastase should further be informed that if he is not prepared to accept an audit fee arrived at in this way and insists on there being a reduction then regrettably the nomination to act as auditor will have to be declined.

(b) Under the provisions of ss 391 to 393 Companies Act 1985 there are certain statutory procedures which must be followed by a company if it wishes to remove its existing auditors and appoint another firm of auditors in their place. The main rules relevant to this situation are summarised below.

(i) The general rule is that every company shall at each annual general meeting (AGM) appoint an auditor to hold office from the conclusion of that meeting until the conclusion of the next AGM.

(ii) Removal of the auditors requires the passing of an ordinary resolution of which special notice (28 days) has been given, the auditors being entitled to receive a copy of this resolution. If the resolution is passed then the company must notify the Registrar within 14 days of the date of the meeting.

(iii) Where an attempt has been made to remove the auditors during their term of office, or where notice of a resolution to appoint other persons in their place has been received by the company, the auditors may make representations as to why they think they ought to stay in office.

Provided they are not received too late and are of reasonable length they may require the company to:

(1)   State in any notice of the resolution given to the members that representations have been made, and

(2)   Send a copy of the representations to the members

(iv)   If the representations are not sent out, either because they were received too late or because of the company's default, the auditors may require that they are read at the meeting. This will not prejudice their normal right to speak at the meeting.

(v)   The auditors' representations need neither be sent out nor read at the meeting if, on the application of the company or any other person who claims to be aggrieved, the court is satisfied that the auditors' right is being abused to obtain needless publicity for defamatory matter.

(vi)   The removed auditors have two further rights which are:

(1)   They are entitled to receive all notices relating to the general meeting at which their term of office would have expired and of any general meeting at which it is proposed to fill the casual vacancy caused by their removal.

(2)   They are entitled to attend such meetings and to speak at them on any part of the business which concerns them as former auditors.

Finally it should be emphasised that the power to remove an auditor rests with the members and not with the directors.

(c)   Wade Austin & Co have every right not to resign even though they may be aware that Mr Nastase, the managing director of the company, wishes to replace them. The auditors of a company are appointed by, and report to, the members of a company and the directors are not empowered, as directors, to remove the auditors.

If the reason for the proposed change arises out of a dispute between management and the auditors then the auditors have a right to put forward their views as seen above and to insist that any decision should be made by the members, but only once they have been made aware of all pertinent facts concerning the directors' wishes to have them removed from office as auditors.

Chapter roundup

- Auditors have guidance from ACCA on advertising and obtaining professional work. They most controversial area is often fee-setting, with such problems as **lowballing.**

- The **present** and **proposed auditors** must **communicate** about the client prior to the audit being accepted.

- The client must be asked to give permission for this communication to occur. If the client **refuses** to give **permission,** the proposed auditors must **decline nomination.**

- The proposed auditors must also ensure they:

  - Are **professionally qualified** to act
  - Have **sufficient resources**
  - Seek **references**

- Most firms have **client acceptance procedures** reviewing the **management integrity** and **risk** of the prospective client, as well as the **likely profitability** of the engagement.

- **Investigations** may be carried out for high-risk clients

- Two issues which may be highlighted by risk factors are **fraud and error** and **the auditors' consideration of law and regulation**.

- These issues can bring such **complexity** to the audit that the audit firm may choose to decline the audit if it appears particularly high risk

BPP PUBLISHING

- Auditing guidance in these areas requires auditors to **plan and perform** their audits so as to have a **reasonable chance of detecting problems which cause material misstatements**. It also sets out the **reporting requirements** in the event of fraud or non-compliance being uncovered.

- An engagement letter should be sent to all new clients. The letter should:

  ° **Specify** the **respective responsibilities** of directors and the auditors
  ° Lay down the **scope** of the **auditors' work**

- Auditor **duties** include the duties to report explicitly on the **truth** and **fairness** of the accounts audited and their **compliance** with legislation. Auditors have a duty to **report** on other matters, such as whether proper accounting records have been kept, by **exception.**

- Auditor rights include the rights of **access** to **records** and to receive **information** and **explanations**, also rights relating to **attendance** and **speaking** at **general meetings**.

- Auditors should be aware of the legal procedures to remove auditors, or when auditors resign.

Quick quiz

1 Complete the following definition of **lowballing.**

The practice of ...., usually at ...., for the audit of large companies.

2 Complete the questions that should be in the diagram.

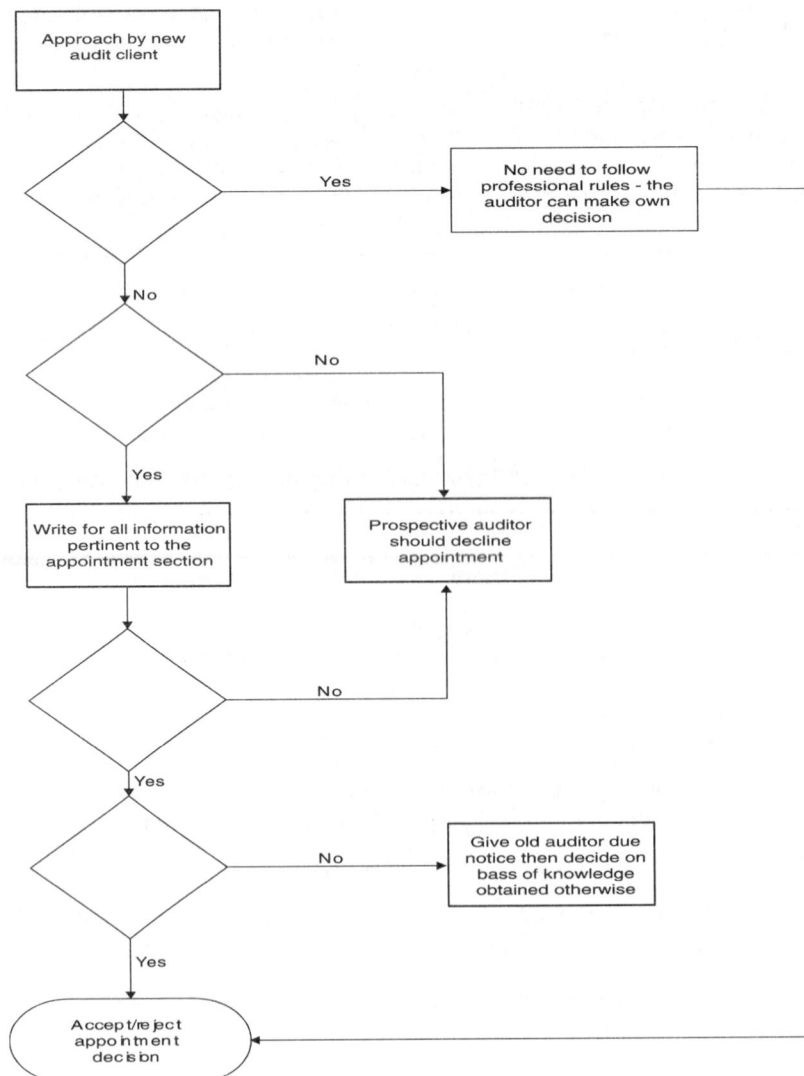

3 Auditors have a duty to detect fraud

True ☐

False ☐

4 Auditors should always report non-compliance with law and regulations to the statutory authority.

True ☐

False ☐

5 An engagement letter is only ever sent to a client before the first audit.

True ☐

False ☐

6 Ring the items that are unlikely to be found in an engagement letter.

(a) Responsibilities of directors and auditors
(b) Detailed audit procedures
(c) Other services
(d) Agreed fee
(e) Reference to applicable law

Answers to quick quiz

1 undercutting, tender

2 • Is this the first audit?
• Does the client give permission to contact the old auditor?
• Does client give old auditor permission to reply?
• Does old auditor provide information relevant to new appointment?

3 False

4 False

5 False. It should be re-issued if there is a change in circumstances.

6 (b)

(d) Reference will be made to how the fee is set, but no mention of the actual fee will be made as it will fluctuate over time.

Now try the question below from the Exam Question Bank

Number	Level	Marks	Time
5	Introductory	n/a	30 mins

Part B
Planning

Chapter 6

AUDIT PLANNING

Topic list	Syllabus reference
1 Aims of planning	4
2 Knowledge of the business	4
3 Audit risk	4
4 Materiality	4
5 Analytical procedures	4
6 Audit programme	4
7 Audit approach	4
8 Planning and internal audit	4

Introduction

This chapter covers the aspects of the audit which will be considered at the earliest stages, during planning. It is unlikely that you will have direct experience of planning an audit, but you should acquaint yourself with all the planning documentation on every audit you attend.

Key points this chapter covers which you must understand are:

- The **purposes of planning**

- The importance of **knowledge of the business** and which factors particularly influence the planning process

- The role of **analytical review**, **risk assessment** and **materiality** in planning

- How planning is **documented**; the role of an **audit plan**

You may be asked in the exam to explain various terms such as risk and materiality. This involves not merely learning the definitions but also being able to show how in practice the auditor uses the techniques in planning an audit.

It is also important to know how the audit plan is translated to detail in the form of the audit programme.

Lastly, the issue of planning is looked at from the point of view of the internal auditor.

Study guide

Section 7

- Describe the sources and nature of information gathered in planning audit and review assignments

- Describe the purpose of analytical procedures in planning and illustrate the application of such procedures

- Describe the components of risk and the use of information technology in risk analysis

- Illustrate the application of risk analysis

- Define and illustrate the concepts of materiality and tolerable error

BPP PUBLISHING

---

1 AIMS OF PLANNING

1.1 An effective and efficient audit relies on proper planning procedures. The planning process is covered in general terms by SAS 200 *Planning*. Other more detailed areas are covered in SAS 210 *Knowledge of the business* and the other SASs covered in this chapter.

> **SAS 200.1**
>
> Auditors should plan the audit work so as to perform the audit in an effective manner.

1.2 The SAS distinguishes between the general audit strategy and the detailed audit approach which must be formulated.

> **KEY TERMS**
>
> An **audit plan** is the formulation of the general strategy for the audit, which sets the direction for the audit, describes the expected scope and conduct of the audit and provides guidance for the development of the audit programme.
>
> An **audit programme** is a set of instructions to the audit team that sets out the audit procedures the auditors intend to adopt and may include references to other matters such as the audit objectives, timing, sample size and basis of selection for each area. It also serves as a means to control and record the proper execution of the work.

1.3 The objectives of planning work include:

- Ensuring that **appropriate attention is devoted** to the different areas of the audit
- Ensuring that **potential problems** are **identified**
- **Facilitating review**

1.4 Good planning also helps in assigning the proper tasks to the members of the audit team.

1.5 Audit procedures should be discussed with the client's management, staff and/or audit committee in order to co-ordinate audit work, including that of internal audit. However, all audit procedures remain the responsibility of the external auditors.

1.6 A structured approach to planning will include the following stages:

- **Updating knowledge of the client**
- **Preparing** the **detailed audit approach**
- Making **administrative decisions** such as staffing and budgets

> **SAS 200.2**
>
> Auditors should develop and document an overall audit plan describing the expected scope and conduct of the audit.

1.7 The following table shows the key contents of any audit plan.

OVERALL AUDIT PLAN	
Knowledge of the entity's business	General economic factors and industry conditions
	Important characteristics of the client, (a) business, (b) principal business strategies, (c) financial performance, (d) reporting requirements, including changes since the previous audit
	The operating style and control consciousness of directors and management
	The auditors' cumulative knowledge of the accounting and control systems and any expected changes in the period
Risk and materiality	The setting of materiality for audit planning purposes
	The expected assessments of risks or error and identification of significant audit areas
	Any indication that misstatements that could have a material effect on the financial statements might arise because of fraud or for any other reason
	The identification of complex accounting areas including those involving estimates
Nature, timing and extent of procedures	The relative importance and timing of tests of control and substantive procedures
	The use of information technology by the client or the auditors
	The use made of work of any internal audit function
	Procedures which need to be carried out at or before the year end
	The timing of significant phases of the preparation of the financial statements
	The audit evidence required to reduce detection risk to an acceptably low level
Co-ordination, direction, supervision and review	The involvement of other auditors
	The involvement of experts, other third parties and internal auditors
	The number of locations
	Staffing requirements
Other matters	Any regulatory requirements arising from the decision to retain the engagement
	The possibility that the going concern basis may be inappropriate
	The terms of the engagement and any statutory responsibilities
	The nature and timing of reports or other communication with the entity that are expected under the engagement

2 KNOWLEDGE OF THE BUSINESS

2.1 SAS 210 *Knowledge of the business* covers this area.

SAS 210.1

Auditors should have or obtain a knowledge of the business of the entity to be audited which is sufficient to enable them to identify and understand the events, transactions and practices that may have a significant effect on the financial statements or the audit thereof.

Obtaining the knowledge

2.2 This is discussed in three stages:

- Prior to acceptance of an engagement

BPP PUBLISHING

- Following acceptance of an engagement
- Updating knowledge for succeeding periods

However the SAS stresses that knowledge should be continuously updated throughout the audit.

Sources of knowledge

2.3   The sources mentioned by the SAS are as follows.

- **Previous experience** of the client and its industry

- **Visits** to the client's premises and plant facilities

- **Discussion with** the client's **staff** and **directors**

- **Discussion with other auditors** and with legal and other advisors who have provided services to the client or within the industry

- **Discussion with knowledgeable people outside the client** (for example, economists, industry regulators)

- **Publications** related to the industry (for example, government statistics, surveys, texts, trade journals, reports prepared by banks and securities dealers, financial newspapers)

- **Legislation and regulations** that significantly affect the client

- **Documents produced** by the client

- **Professional literature** giving industry-specific guidance

Matters to consider in relation to knowledge of the business

2.4   This appendix to the SAS provides a useful list of matters to consider. However, the SAS points out that the list is 'not exhaustive, not is it intended that all matters listed will be relevant to every engagement'.

2.5   The following list is given in the appendix to the SAS.

Knowledge of the business	
General economic factors	General level of economic activity (for example, recession, growth)
	Interest rates and availability of financing
	Inflation
	Government policies
	Foreign currency rates and controls
The industry: conditions affecting the client's business	The market and competition
	Cyclical or seasonal activity
	Changes in product technology
	Business risk (for example, high technology, high fashion, ease of entry for competition)
	Declining or expanding operations
	Adverse conditions (for example, declining demand, excess capacity, serious price competition)
	Key ratios and operating statistics
	Specific accounting practices and problems
	Environmental requirements and problems
	Regulatory framework
	Specific or unique practices (for example, relating to labour contracts, financing methods, accounting methods)

Knowledge of the business

The entity: directors, management and ownership	Corporate structure: private, public, government (including any recent or planned changes)
	Beneficial owners, important stakeholders and related parties (local, foreign, business reputation and experience) and any impact on the entity's transactions
	The relationships between owners, directors and management
	Attitudes and policies of owners
	Capital structure (including any recent or planned changes)
	Organisational structure
	Group structure
	Subsidiaries' audit arrangements
	Directors' objectives, philosophy, strategic plans
	Acquisitions, mergers or disposals of business activities (planned or recently executed)
	Sources and methods of financing (current, historical)
	Board of directors: <ul><li>Composition</li><li>Business reputation and experience of individuals</li><li>Independence from and control over operating management</li><li>Frequency of meetings</li><li>Existence and membership of audit committee and scope of its activities</li><li>Existence of policy on corporate conduct</li><li>Changes in professional advisors (for example, lawyers)</li></ul>
	Operating management: <ul><li>Experience and reputation</li><li>Turnover</li><li>Key financial personnel and their status in the organisation</li><li>Staffing of accounting department</li><li>Incentive or bonus plans as part of remuneration (for example, based on profit)</li><li>Use of forecasts and budgets</li><li>Pressures on management (for example, over-extended, dominance by one individual, support for share price, unreasonable deadlines for announcing results)</li><li>Management information systems</li></ul>
	Internal audit function (existence, quality)
	Attitude to internal control environment
The entity's business: products, markets, suppliers, expenses, operations	Nature of business(es) (for example, manufacturer, wholesaler, financial services, import/export)
	Location of production facilities, warehouses, offices
	Employment (for example, by location, supply, wage levels, union contracts, pension commitments, government regulations)
	Products or services and markets (for example, major customers and contracts, terms of payment, profit margins, market share, competitors, exports, pricing policies, reputation of products, warranties, order book, trends, marketing strategy and objectives, manufacturing processes)
	Important suppliers of goods and services (for example, long-term contracts, stability of supply, terms of payment, imports, methods of delivery such as 'just in time')
	Stocks (for example, locations, quantities)
	Franchises, licences, patents
	Important expense categories

BPP PUBLISHING

Knowledge of the business	
	Research and development
	Foreign currency assets, liabilities and transactions by currency, hedging
	Legislation and regulations that significantly affect the entity
	Information systems: current, plans to change
	Debt structure, including covenants and restrictions
Financial performance: factors concerning the entity's financial condition and profitability	Accounting policies
	Earnings and cash flow trends and forecasts
	Leasing and other financial commitments
	Availability of lines of credit
	Off balance sheet finance issues
	Foreign exchange and interest rate exposures
	Comparison with industry trends
Information technology	The significance and complexity of computer processing in each significant accounting application (consider the volume of transactions, complexity of computations, electronic data interchange)
	Organisational structure of information technology activities (especially segregation of duties)
	Availability of data
Reporting environment: external influences which affect the directors in the preparation of the financial statements	Legislation
	Regulatory environment and requirements
	Taxation
	Accounting requirements
	Measurement and disclosure issues peculiar to the business
	Audit reporting requirements
	Users of the financial statements

Using the knowledge

2.6   Having obtained the knowledge relating to the entity discussed above (and below in the appendix to the SAS), the auditors must use it to:

- **Assess risks** and **identify problems**
- **Plan and perform** the audit **effectively** and **efficiently**
- **Evaluate audit evidence**

2.7   The audit areas subject to judgement which may be affected by knowledge of the business are given by the SAS as follows.

- **Developing the overall audit plan** and the **audit programme**

- **Considering risks**

- Assessing **inherent risk** and **control risk**

- Determining a **materiality** level remains appropriate

- Considering the complexity of the entity's **information systems**

- Identifying areas where **special audit considerations and skills** may be necessary

- Assessing **audit evidence** to establish its appropriateness and the validity of the related financial statement assertions

- Evaluating **accounting estimates** and **representations** by the directors

- **Recognising conflicting information** (for example, contradictory representations)

- **Recognising unusual circumstances** (for example, undisclosed related party transactions, possible fraud or non-compliance with law or regulations

- **Making informed enquiries** and assessing the reasonableness of answers

- **Considering the appropriateness of accounting policies** and accounts disclosures

Communication of knowledge

2.8 Knowledge of the entity can only be used effectively if it is communicated to members of the audit team.

SAS 210.2

The audit engagement partner should ensure that the audit team obtains such knowledge of the business of the entity being audited as may reasonably be expected to be sufficient to enable it to carry out the audit work effectively.

2.9 The information will usually be provided in the planning documentation.

3 AUDIT RISK   Pilot paper, Dec 01

KEY TERMS

Audit risk is the risk that auditors may give an inappropriate opinion on the financial statements. Audit risk has three components; inherent risk, control risk and detection risk.

Inherent risk is the susceptibility of an account balance or class of transactions to material misstatement, either individually or when aggregated with misstatements in other balances or classes, irrespective of related internal controls.

Control risk is the risk that a misstatement:

- Could occur in an account balance or class of transactions;

- Could be material, either individually or when aggregated with misstatements in other balances or classes, and

- Would not be prevented, or detected and corrected on a timely basis, by the accounting and internal control systems.

Detection risk is the risk that the auditors' substantive procedures do not detect a misstatement that exists in an account balance or class of transactions that could be material, either individually or when aggregated with misstatements in other balances or classes.

3.1 Audit risk is the risk that the auditors give an unqualified opinion on the accounts when they should have given a qualified opinion **or** they give an opinion qualified for a particular reason where that reason was not justified. SAS 300 *Accounting and internal control and audit risk assessments* covers audit risk.

> ## SAS 300.1
>
> Auditors should:
>
> (a) obtain an understanding of the accounting and internal control system sufficient to plan the audit and develop an effective audit approach; and
>
> (b) use professional judgement to assess the components of audit risk and to design audit procedures to ensure it is reduced to an acceptably low level.

3.2 **Audit risk can never be completely eliminated.** The auditors are called upon to make subjective judgements in the course of forming an opinion and so fraud or error may possibly go undetected.

3.3 A **risk-centred approach** gives the auditors an overall measure of risk, but at the same time it provides a quantification of each stage of the audit. The extent of detailed testing required is determined by a purely risk-based perspective. A diagrammatic view of the risk-based approach is given below.

3.4 Remember that materiality and audit risk are closely connected.

Inherent risk

3.5 Inherent risk is the risk that items will be misstated due to characteristics of those items, such as the fact they are **estimates** or that they are **important** items in the accounts. The auditors must use their professional judgement and all available knowledge to assess inherent risk. If no such information or knowledge is available then the inherent risk is **high**.

3.6 The results of the assessment must be properly documented and, where inherent risk is assessed as not high, then audit work may be reduced. The SAS lists the relevant factors to be considered under two headings.

> ## SAS 300.2
>
> In developing their audit approach and detailed procedures, auditors should assess inherent risk in relation to financial statement assertions about material account balances and classes of transactions, taking account of factors relevant both to the entity as a whole and to the specific assertions.

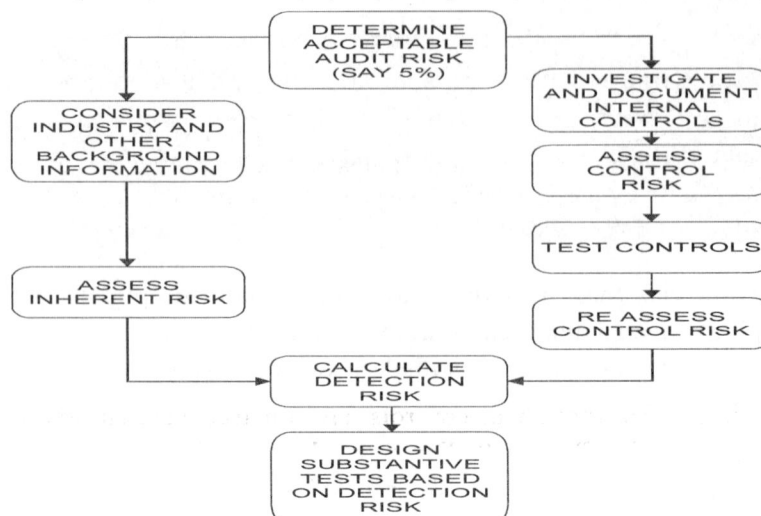

```
                        ┌──────────────────┐
                        │    DETERMINE     │
                        │   ACCEPTABLE     │
                        │   AUDIT RISK     │
                        │    (SAY 5%)      │
                        └──────────────────┘
              ┌───────────────┘        └───────────────┐
              │                              ┌──────────────────┐
    ┌──────────────────┐                     │   INVESTIGATE    │
    │    CONSIDER      │                     │  AND DOCUMENT    │
    │  INDUSTRY AND    │                     │    INTERNAL      │
    │     OTHER        │                     │    CONTROLS      │
    │  BACKGROUND      │                     └──────────────────┘
    │  INFORMATION     │                              │
    └──────────────────┘                     ┌──────────────────┐
              │                              │     ASSESS       │
              │                              │    CONTROL       │
              │                              │      RISK        │
              │                              └──────────────────┘
              │                                       │
    ┌──────────────────┐                     ┌──────────────────┐
    │     ASSESS       │                     │  TEST CONTROLS   │
    │  INHERENT RISK   │                     └──────────────────┘
    └──────────────────┘                              │
              │                              ┌──────────────────┐
              │                              │    RE ASSESS     │
              │                              │    CONTROL       │
              │                              │      RISK        │
              │                              └──────────────────┘
              │        ┌──────────────────┐          │
              └────────│    CALCULATE     │◄─────────┘
                       │    DETECTION     │
                       │      RISK        │
                       └──────────────────┘
                                │
                       ┌──────────────────┐
                       │     DESIGN       │
                       │   SUBSTANTIVE    │
                       │   TESTS BASED    │
                       │  ON DETECTION    │
                       │      RISK        │
                       └──────────────────┘
```

FACTORS AFFECTING CLIENT AS A WHOLE	
Integrity and **attitude to risk** of directors and management	Domination by a single individual can cause problems
Management experience and **knowledge**	Changes in management and quality of financial management
Unusual pressures on management	Examples include tight reporting deadlines, or market or financing expectations
Nature of business	Potential problems include technological obsolescence or over-dependence on single product
Industry factors	Competitive conditions, regulatory requirements, technology developments, changes in customer demand
Information technology	Problems include lack of supporting documentation, concentration of expertise in a few people, potential for unauthorised access

FACTORS AFFECTING INDIVIDUAL ACCOUNT BALANCES OR TRANSACTIONS	
Financial statement **accounts prone to misstatement**	Accounts which require adjustment in previous period, require high degree of estimation or judgement, or which may significantly affect profitability or liquidity
Complex accounts	Accounts which require expert valuations or are subjects of current professional discussion
Assets at risk of being **lost or stolen**	Cash, (consider opportunities for unauthorised payments), stock, portable fixed assets (computers)
High volume of **transactions**	Accounting system may have problems coping
Quality of **accounting systems**	Strength of individual departments (sales, purchases, cash etc)
Unusual transactions	Transactions for large amounts, with unusual names, not settled promptly (particularly important if they occur at period-end)
	Transactions that do not go through the system, that relate to specific clients or processed by certain individuals
Staff	Staff changes or areas of low morale

Exam focus point

The above lists are important. You should remember them when we consider substantive testing of individual audit areas in later chapters, since the factors listed affect the choice of audit tests and also the extent of testing. Audit questions often indicate problems in particular audit areas, and ask for an assessment of the risks involved.

Control risk

3.7 Control risk is the risk that client controls fail to detect material misstatements. We shall discuss control risk in Chapter 9. For now, the most important point is that SAS 300 requires a **preliminary assessment** of **control risk** at the planning stage of the audit if the

BPP PUBLISHING

auditors intend to rely on their assessment to reduce the extent of their substantive procedures. This assessment should be supported subsequently by tests of control.

Detection risk

SAS 300.7

Auditors should consider the assessed levels of inherent and control risk in determining the nature, timing and extent of substantive procedures required to reduce audit risk to an acceptable level.

3.8 Detection risk is the risk that audit procedures will fail to detect material errors. Detection risk relates to the inability of the auditors to examine all evidence. Audit evidence is usually persuasive rather than conclusive so some detection risk is usually present, allowing the auditors to seek 'reasonable confidence'.

3.9 The auditors' **inherent and control risk assessments** influence the **nature, timing and extent of substantive procedures** required to reduce detection risk and thereby audit risk.

(a) Auditors need to be careful when relying on their **assessment** of **control risk,** as good controls may impact upon some but not other aspects of audit areas. For example, good controls over the recording of sales and debtors would not reduce audit testing on bad debts, as the amounts recorded may represent amounts that will not be collected.

(b) To design an efficient audit strategy, auditors should not just consider reducing the number of items they test substantively, **extent** of testing, if inherent and control risks are low. They may also alter the tests they do, **design** of testing, by placing for instance more reliance on analytical procedures. They may also change the **timing** of tests, for example carrying out certain procedures such as circularisation at a date that is not the year-end, and placing reliance upon internal controls functioning at the year-end.

3.10 Misstatements discovered in substantive procedures may cause the auditors to modify their previous assessment of control risk.

SAS 300.8

Regardless of the assessed levels of inherent and control risks, auditors should perform some substantive procedures for financial statement assertions of material account balances and transaction classes.

3.11 **Substantive procedures can never be abandoned entirely** because control and inherent risk can never be assessed at a low enough level, although substantive procedures may be restricted to analytical procedures if appropriate.

3.12 Where the auditors' assessment of the components of audit risk changes during the audit, they should modify the planned substantive procedures based on the revised risk levels.

3.13 When both inherent and control risks are assessed as high, the auditors should consider whether substantive procedures can provide sufficient appropriate audit evidence to reduce detection risk, and therefore audit risk, to an acceptably low level. For example, they may not be able to obtain sufficient evidence about the completeness of income in the absence of some internal controls. If sufficient evidence cannot be obtained, auditors may have to qualify their audit report.

4 MATERIALITY

4.1 We discussed materiality briefly in Chapter 1. Remember it relates to the level of error that affects the decisions of users of the accounts.

> **SAS 220.2**
>
> Auditors should consider materiality when determining the nature, timing and extent of audit procedures.

4.2 Materiality considerations during **audit planning** are extremely important. The assessment of materiality at this stage should be based on the most recent and reliable financial information and will help to determine an effective and efficient audit approach. Materiality assessment will help the auditors to decide:

- **How many** and **what items** to examine
- Whether to use **sampling techniques**
- What **level of error** is likely to lead to a qualified audit opinion

4.3 The resulting combination of audit procedures should help to reduce audit risk to an appropriately low level.

4.4 The effect of planning materiality on the audit process is shown in the diagram below.

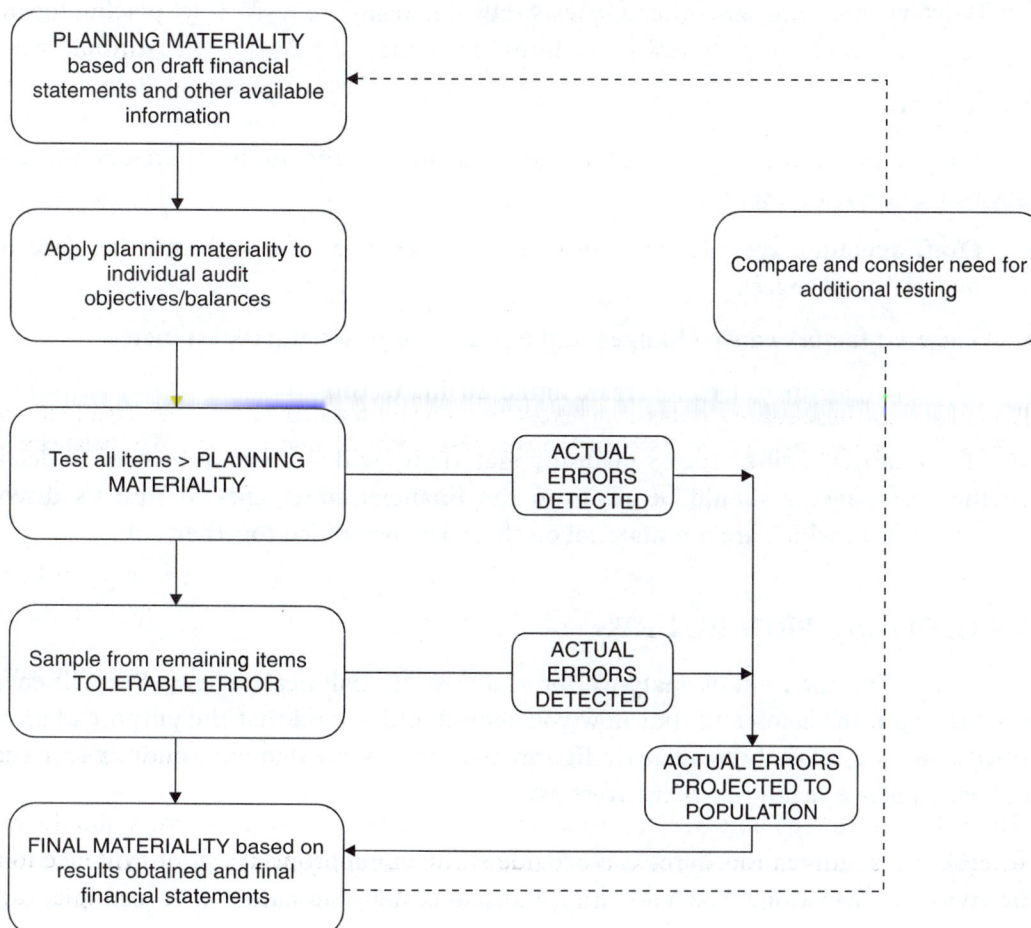

BPP PUBLISHING

4.5   **Tolerable error** may be set at planning materiality, but it is usually reduced to, say 75% or even 50% of planning materiality so as to take account of sampling risk (see Chapter 8). The tolerable error is used to determine sample size.

Practical implications

4.6   To set the materiality level the auditors need to decide the level of error which would distort the view given by the accounts. Because many users of accounts are primarily interested in the profitability of the company, the level is often expressed as a proportion of its **profits**.

4.7   Some argue, however, that materiality should be thought of in terms of the **size** of the business. Hence, if the company remains a fairly constant size, the materiality level should not change; similarly if the business is growing, the level of materiality will increase from year to year.

4.8   The size of a company can be measured in terms of turnover and total assets before deducting any liabilities (sometimes referred to in legislation as 'the balance sheet total') both of which tend not to be subject to the fluctuations which may affect profit. Note that the auditors will often calculate a range of values, such as those shown below, and then take an average or weighted average of all the figures produced as the materiality level.

Value	%
Profit before tax	5
Gross profit	½ - 1
Turnover	½ - 1
Total assets	1 - 2
Net assets	2 - 5
Profit after tax	5 – 10

Audit evaluation

4.9   The level of materiality must be reviewed constantly as the audit progresses and changes may be required because:

- **Draft accounts** are **altered** (due to material error and so on) and therefore overall materiality changes.

- **External factors cause changes** in the control or inherent risk estimates.

- Such changes are caused by errors found during testing.

4.10   At the end of the testing process planning materiality will once again be used to determine whether adjustments should be made to the financial statements. All errors discovered during the audit which are not material on their own are added together.

5   ANALYTICAL PROCEDURES

5.1   This is our first mention of analytical procedures (or analytical review). We will cover the topic in depth in Chapter 12. For now you should understand that the purpose of analytical procedures is essentially to identify figures that are not in line with auditor expectations, and which hence require further investigation.

5.2   Analytical procedures can involve comparisons of current year financial information with past year information, budgets and predictions by the auditor. It can also involve comparisons between different elements of the current year financial information which are expected to have a predictable relationship with each other.

5.3 SAS 410 *Analytical procedures* deals with the subject of analytical review. The SAS requires auditors to carry out analytical procedures at the planning stage of each audit, to **identify areas of potential audit risk** and **helping in planning** the **nature, timing and extent** of other audit **procedures.**

5.4 Auditors can now use **software packages** to perform analytical procedures. These packages are most useful when information can be input directly from the client's computer system. This information can be added to year after year, building up cumulative data.

6 AUDIT PROGRAMME

SAS 200.3

Auditors should develop and document the nature, timing and extent of planned audit procedures required to implement the overall audit plan.

6.1 The audit programme may contain references to other matters such as the audit **objectives, timing, sample size** and **basis of selection** for each area. The audit programme's main use is highlighted by SAS 200.

'It serves as a set of instructions to the audit team and as a means to control and record the proper execution of the work.'

Changes to the audit work planned

SAS 200.4

The audit work planned should be reviewed and, if necessary, revised during the course of the audit.

6.2 An accurate record of changes to the audit plan must be maintained in order to explain the general strategy finally adopted for the audit.

6.3 The following is an example of a audit programme. We shall discuss the testing it outlines in more detail in Section D of this text.

6.4 Remember that that audit programme is not a standardised document, the matters contained within it will be driven by details in the audit plan.

BPP PUBLISHING

EXAMPLE AUDIT PROGRAMME — Audit area: Tangible fixed assets

Test	Objective	Sample size	Reference	Sample selection	Staff	Timing	Completed
Verify additions							
Trace sample of purchases to invoices	Confirm existence and valuation	2 High value 8 Lower value	Plan 2 Plan 2b	- Haphazard	Semi Semi	Day 1 Day 1	
Verify disposals							
Trace disposed item to sales documentation	Confirm valuation and ownership	1 High value	Plan 2	-	Semi	Day 1	
Confirm existence							
(a) Agree sample of physical assets to register	Confirm existence	2 High value 9 Lower value	Plan 2 Plan 2b	- Random	Junior	Day 1	
(b) Agree sample of register asset to physical	Confirm existence	2 High value 8 Lower value	Plan 2 Plan 2b	- Random	Junior	Day 1	
Repairs							
If material, review repairs expenses for capital items	Confirm completeness	-	-	-	Semi	Day 1	
Title							
Obtain title documents for sample of assets	Confirm ownership	4 High value 17 Lower value	Plan 2 Plan 2b	- Random	Semi	Day 1	
- Registration documents							
- Title deeds							
- Purchase documentation							

7 AUDIT APPROACH

7.1 Auditing is an evolving art. There is no one way of obtaining the evidence to support an opinion whether a certain set of financial statements gives a true and fair view.

7.2 Therefore, if you work in an audit department, some of the terms in the following diagram may be familiar to you.

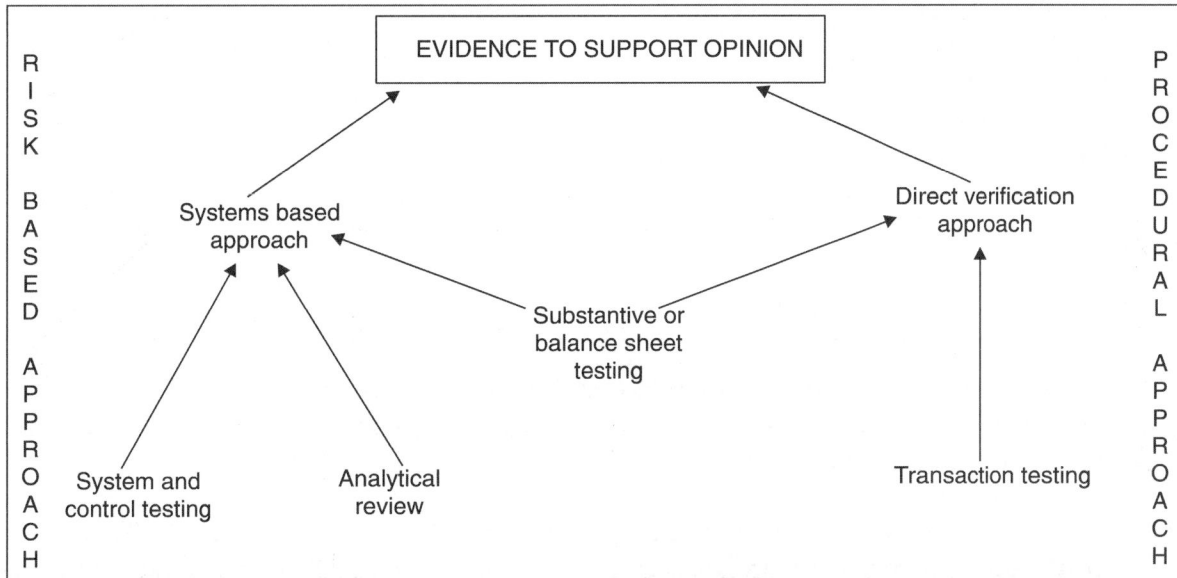

KEY TERMS

A **systems-based approach** is an approach to audit which seeks to place reliance on the accounting systems of an entity and verify the end result of those systems, the financial statements.

A **direct verification approach** is an approach which seeks to audit the amounts more directly, by verifying more individual transactions and balances.

7.3 The chronology of an audit given in Chapter 1 and the basic processes of an audit referred to throughout this text are more relevant to systems-based audits, the most common types of audit, generally being considered to be most cost effective.

7.4 The '**risk-based approach**' was also outlined in Chapter 1. Auditors analyse the risks associated with the client's business, transactions and systems and direct their testing to risky areas. It is a development of the systems-based approach – relying on the systems whose risk is being assessed.

7.5 A **procedural approach** is likely to contain a higher level of testing as it does not take account of the risk attaching to specific areas. It is therefore often less cost-effective than a risk based approach and rarely used.

Audit timing

7.6 There are two relevant questions with regard to audit timing:

- Does all the audit work need to be completed after the year end?
- When, after the year end, should the audit take place?

7.7 The following box shows a number of considerations to take into account when giving answers to the questions.

> - Audit approach
> - Prior practice
> - Client expectations
> - Preparation timetable for financial statements
> - Availability of evidence
> - Cost-effectiveness
> - Staffing
> - Audits of other clients

7.8 We shall consider the second question first, briefly. Generally, the timing of the audit is a matter of negotiation between the client and the audit engagement partner. The client will have to have prepared financial statements for the audit team to audit.

7.9 However, the audit engagement partner must ensure that the timing is suitable. This means that it must allow the appropriate staff for the audit to be available, and allow a sufficient post-balance sheet period for evidence (for example, cash receipts for debtors) to become available.

7.10 Possibly the more important question is whether all the work needs to be done after the year end. This will depend to an extent on audit approach.

7.11 It might be more cost of staff effective to undertake an **interim audit**, during the year under review.

> ### KEY TERMS
>
> The **final audit** is the main period of audit testing, when work if focused on the final financial statements.
>
> The **interim audit** is an audit undertaken prior to the final audit, often during the period under review.

7.12 If a system-based approach is being used, an interim audit can be used as an opportunity to assess the system, as the controls need to be operating effectively throughout the year for the auditors to be able to rely on them. This is discussed further in Chapter 9.

8 PLANNING AND INTERNAL AUDIT

8.1 Planning is also important to the internal auditor. For the internal auditor, planning needs to be at two levels:

- An overall department level (this could be thought of as a '**master plan**' for the aims of the department for a year)

- A plan for each individual engagement or '**project**' in which internal audit are involved

Overall department level

8.2 The overall master plan for the internal audit department should be **consistent** with the **goals** of the organisation and the **objectives** of the department.

8.3 It is likely that it will be linked with any **risk assessment** which the company has participated in, for example, risk assessments undertaken in line with the Turnbull guidance.

Individual assignment

8.4 Each individual assignment should also be planned. Several issues should be considered:

- The **objectives** of the function being reviewed
- How the **performance** of that function is **controlled**
- The risks attaching to the function for the entity and the risk management framework
- Opportunities for improving that function

8.5 A work programme should be developed with these factors in mind.

Question 1

You are the manager in charge of the audit of Ruddington Furniture plc for the year ended 31 July 20X2, and you have been asked to describe the work which should be carried out in planning the statutory audit and in monitoring its progress.

Ruddington Furniture plc buys domestic furniture from manufacturers and sells it to the general public. The company's head office and main warehouse are on the same site, and there are sales branches with associated warehouses in different parts of the country.

Your firm has been auditor of the company for a number of years. All the company's accounting records are maintained on the computer at head office. When a sale takes place at the branch, the salesman checks that the furniture the customer requires is in stock, and if it is, the customer pays for the items by cash, cheque or credit card (or charge card) and collects them from the warehouse. Where the items are not in stock, it is possible to find whether they are available at another local branch, or an order can be placed for the stock.

In previous years' audits there have been problems at branches of the actual stock being less than the computer book stock quantities. Also, problems have been experienced in identifying and valuing damaged stock and goods returned by customers. The company has a small internal audit department and their work includes periodic visits to branches.

The company was subject to a management buy-out in February 20X0 which resulted in high gearing. You understand that because of a recession in the furniture trade the company has liquidity problems and that currently it is negotiating with the bank to obtain additional finance.

Required

List and describe the matters you will consider and the work you will carry out in planning the audit.

Answer

In planning the audit the following matters should be taken into consideration.

(a) The audit files for the previous year should be examined in detail and any important matters should be considered which arise therefrom which might have a bearing on the current year's audit.

(b) Any recent changes in legislation or accounting standards which might affect the financial statements of Ruddington Furniture plc should be considered.

(c) If possible, the management accounts for the year should be obtained from the company. These should be examined to gain information about the trading performance of the company, perhaps in comparison with any budget which is available. Any significant changes in the management or key employees of the company, as well as in the accounting system and procedures, should be noted.

(d) The management of the company should be consulted in advance and the timing of the audit should be agreed. In particular:

    (i) The timing of the stocktake and the level of attendance by the auditors
    (ii) The timing of significant phases of the preparation of the financial statements
    (iii) The extent to which analyses and summaries can be prepared by the company's employees
    (iv) The relevance of any work to be carried out by the enterprise's internal auditors

(e) In terms of the stocktaking procedures, these should be reviewed in detail. In addition, it would be useful to obtain the results of any stock counts during the year, to consider whether problems still exist in the comparison between book and actual stock levels.

(f) In the light of the known liquidity problems of the company, it would be prudent to obtain any forecasts and budgets for the following year or years. This may be useful in performing any post balance sheet review, particularly if there is any considerable period between the end of the audit and the date the directors plan to sign the accounts (and the AGM).

(g) The internal auditors may be of use in the performance of the external audit. Their work should be examined to determine whether it is reliable and relevant, and some of the tests they have performed should be reperformed for this purpose. If it is decided that their work can be relied upon, this may reduce some of the testing the external auditors can perform. The internal audit work should highlight problem areas within the company and reduce the risks of the external auditor missing any fraud or errors.

(h) It should be possible at this stage to decide what the general audit approach is to be. It should be the case that a company of the size of Ruddington Furniture will have a strong system of internal control, as is indicated to some extent by the presence of the internal audit department. A risk-based audit approach is therefore most likely.

(i) It will be necessary to determine which audit staff are to be used. The staff chosen should be suitably qualified and experienced. The number of staff needs to be determined, particularly in relation to the number of stocktake visits the auditors will undertake. Larger branches should be visited and smaller branches in rotation over a few years.

(j) A timetable should be prepared for the audit, including the items for the principal phases of the audit, the date the audit report will be signed and an estimate of fees, costs and profit.

Exam focus point

Exam questions on planning an audit commonly give the circumstances of a particular client, and ask you to consider what factors would influence planning and what the auditors need to do in response to those factors.

Chapter roundup

- This chapter has covered some very important areas of the planning process.

- The auditors will formulate an **overall audit plan** which will be translated into a **detailed audit programme** for audit staff to follow.

- In formulating the audit plan the auditors will consider:

  ° Knowledge of the entity's business
  ° Risk and materiality
  ° Nature, timing and extent of procedures
  ° Co-ordination, direction, supervision and review

- Important aspects of **knowledge of the business** are:

  ° The industry
  ° Directors, managers and ownership
  ° Products, markets, suppliers, expenses and operations
  ° Financial performance
  ° Reporting environment

- **Audit risk** is the risk that the auditors may give an inappropriate opinion on the financial statements. A risk-based audit will make use of the risk model to determine the amount and extent of audit testing. Audit risk comprises **inherent, control** and **detection risk**.

- **Materiality** should be calculated at the planning stages of all audits. The calculation or estimation of materiality should be based on experience and judgement. The materiality level chosen should be reviewed during the audit.

- **Analytical procedures** are very useful at the planning stage, allowing risk areas to be identified.

- An **audit programme** is developed from the overall audit plan. It documents the nature, timing and extent of planned audit procedures.

- There is **no single accepted approach** to audit

- The most commonly used approach is the **systems-based audit**, which has evolved into a risk-based approach

- Some audit work may be completed prior to the end of the period under review, in an **interim audit**.

- An audit should be timed to ensure:

  ° Appropriate staff are available
  ° Audit evidence will be available
  ° Client staff will be prepared

- Internal audit departments need to plan also, both on an **annual department level**, which should focus on the objectives of the entity and the department, and on an **individual assignment level**, which should focus on the objectives and risks of the function being reviewed.

Quick quiz

1   Fill in the **blanks.**

The three objectives of planning are:

- Ensuring that appropriate .... is devoted to key .... of the audit.

- Ensuring that .... are identified.

- Facilitating ....

2   Complete the table, giving three examples from each source of knowledge of the business.

Knowledge of the business	
General economic factors	1
	2
	3
The industry	1
	2
	3
The entity	1
	2
	3
The entity's business	1
	2
	3
Financial performance	1
	2
	3
Information technology	1
	2
	3
Reporting environment	1
	2
	3

3   If control and inherent risk as assessed as sufficiently low, substantive procedures can be abandoned completely.

    True   ☐

    False   ☐

4   Match the percentages to the values for a correct calculation of materiality

	%
Profit before tax	5
Gross profit	5-10
Turnover	1-2
Total assets	$^{1}/_{2}$-1
Net assets	2-5
Profit after tax	$^{1}/_{2}$-1

5   Give two reasons for using analytical procedures at the audit planning stage.

    1   ....

    2   ....

6   Complete the definitions.

    .... risk is the risk that .... may give an ....opinion on the financial statements. It has three components.

    .... risk is the .... of an account balance or .... to material ....

7   Complete the definition

    A .... - .... is an approach to audit which seeks to place reliance on the .... of an entity and verify the end result of those ....

8   The audit programme is a standardised document.

True   ☐

False   ☐

Answers to quick quiz

1   attention, areas
potential problems
review

2   Turn to the complete table at para 2.5.

3   False.

4

	%
Profit before tax	5
Gross profit	$^1/_2$-1
Turnover	$^1/_2$-1
Total assets	1-2
Net assets	2-5
Profit after tax	5-10

5   1   To identify areas of potential audit risk
       2   To help in planning the nature, timing and extent of other audit procedures

6   Audit, auditors, inappropriate
Inherent, susceptibility, class of transactions, misstatement

7   Systems-based approach, accounting systems, systems

8   False

Now try the question below from the Exam Question Bank

Number	Level	Marks	Time
6	Exam	20	36 mins

Chapter 7

USING THE WORK OF OTHERS

Topic list	Syllabus reference
1 Using the work of internal audit	4
2 Using the work of an expert	4
3 Service organisations	4
4 Reporting	4
5 Audit staffing	4

Introduction

In this chapter we explore the various groups of people that can have an impact on the statutory audit and what the auditor's attitude to them should be.

As we saw detail in Chapter 3, internal auditors can, and often do, carry out similar audit tests to external auditors. In fact, some companies maintained internal audit departments to seek to reduce the audit fee.

Section 1 of this chapter looks at the extent to which external auditors can use and rely on the work of internal auditors. It outlines the APB's guidance in this matter, which is found in SAS 500.

While auditors are highly trained individuals, it is possible that when conducting an audit they encounter issues which are outside the scope of their expertise, for example, valuation of buildings. In such circumstances an auditor will have to consult an expert. SAS 520, *Using the work of an expert*, outlines the factors an auditor should bear in mind, as we seen in section 2.

It is increasingly common for companies to outsource specific functions to service organisations who have more expertise than the business. If functions relevant to the audit have been outsourced, the auditor must consider how to obtain the audit evidence he requires to come to his opinion. In section 3, we look at the guidance in SAS 480, *Service Organisations*.

Finally, we consider the staffing of the audit.

Study guide

Section 9

Describe the:

- Extent to which external auditors are able to rely on the work of:

    - Internal audit
    - Experts
    - Service organisations

- Extent to which internal auditors are able to rely on the work of:

    - Experts
    - Service organisations

- Conditions that must be met before reliance can be placed on the work of others and the planning considerations in co-ordinating the work of others

- Extent to which reference to the work of others can be made in audit and review reports.

Exam guide

The relationship between internal and external auditors could be examined as they are both important syllabus areas. Using the work of experts or auditing areas which have been outsourced could be examined in conjunction with a balance sheet area, for example, fixed assets.

1 USING THE WORK OF INTERNAL AUDIT

1.1 The objectives of internal audit will differ from those of the external auditors. However, some of the means of achieving their respective objectives are often similar, and so some of the internal auditors' work may be used by the external auditors.

1.2 Guidance about using the work of internal audit is given to external auditors in SAS 500, *Considering the work of internal audit*.

SAS 500.1

External auditors should consider the activities of internal audit and their effect, if any, on external audit procedures.

Understanding and assessment of the role and scope of internal audit

SAS 500.2

The external auditors should obtain sufficient understanding of internal audit activities to assist in planning the audit and developing an effective audit approach

1.3 An effective IA function may reduce, modify or alter the timing of external audit procedures, but it can **never** eliminate them entirely. Where the IA function is deemed ineffective, it may still be useful to be aware of the IA conclusions.

1.4 The effectiveness of IA will have a great impact on how the external auditors' assess the whole control system and the assessment of audit risk.

SAS 500.3

During the course of their planning the external auditors should perform an assessment of the internal audit function if they consider that it may be possible and desirable to rely on certain internal audit work in specific audit areas for the purpose of the external audit of the financial statements.

BPP PUBLISHING

1.5 The following important criteria will be considered by the external auditors.

ASSESSMENT OF INTERNAL AUDIT	
Organisational status	Consider **to whom** internal audit **reports** (should be board), whether internal audit has any **operating responsibilities** and constraints or restrictions on the function
Scope of function	Consider **extent** and **nature** of **assignments** performed and the action taken by management as a result of internal audit reports.
Technical competence	Consider whether internal auditors have adequate **technical training** and proficiency
Due professional care	Consider whether internal audit is **properly planned**, **supervised**, **reviewed** and **documented**

Timing of liaison and co-ordination

1.6 All timing of IA work should be agreed as early as possible, and in particular how it co-ordinates with the external auditors' work. Liaison with the internal auditors should take place at regular intervals throughout the audit. Information on tests and conclusions should be passed both to and from IA.

Evaluating specific internal audit work

SAS 500.4

When the external auditors use specific internal audit work to reduce the extent of their audit procedures, they should evaluate that work to confirm its adequacy for their purposes.

1.7 The evaluation here will consider the scope of work and related audit programmes **and** whether the assessment of the IA function remains appropriate. This may include the considerations in the table below.

Evaluation	
Training and proficiency	Have the internal auditors had sufficient and adequate technological training to carry out the work?
	Are the internal auditors proficient?
Supervision	Is the work of assistants properly supervised, reviewed and documented?
Evidence	Has sufficient, appropriate audit evidence been obtained to afford a reasonable basis for the conclusions reached?
Conclusions	Are the conclusions reached appropriate, given the circumstances?
Reports	Are any reports produced by internal audit consistent with the result of the work performed?
Unusual matters	Have any unusual matters or exceptions arising and disclosed by internal audit been resolved properly?
Plan	Are any amendments to the external audit programme required as a result of the matters identified by internal audit?
Testing	Has the work of internal audit been sufficiently tested by the external auditor to confirm its adequacy?

1.8 If the external auditors decide that the IA work is not adequate, they should extend their procedures in order to obtain appropriate evidence.

Internal audit using the work of others

1.9 There is no comparable regulation for internal auditors to the above guidelines in SAS 500.

1.10 The situation where internal auditors use the work of experts or service organisations is different to when external auditors use them. The experts etc are **contracted** to provide the service to the organisation (of which the IA function is part).

1.11 This gives the company contractual rights when they rely on the work. If the directors permit the internal auditors to use the services of an expert (for example, the external auditors), the internal auditors may seek to rely on them.

2 USING THE WORK OF AN EXPERT

> **KEY TERM**
>
> An **expert** is a person or firm possessing special skill, knowledge and experience in a particular field other than auditing.

2.1 Professional audit staff are highly trained and educated, but their experience and training is limited to accountancy and audit matters. In certain situations it will therefore be necessary to employ someone else with different expert knowledge.

2.2 Auditors have **sole responsibility** for their opinion, but may use the work of an expert. An expert may be engaged by:

- A **client** to provide **specialist advice** on a particular matter which affects the financial statements

- **The auditors** in order to obtain **sufficient audit evidence** regarding certain financial statement assertions

2.3 SAS 520 Using the work of an expert covers this area.

Determining the need to use the work of an expert

> **SAS 520.1**
>
> When using the work performed by an expert, auditors should obtain sufficient appropriate audit evidence that such work is adequate for the purposes of an audit.

2.4 The following list of examples is given by the SAS of the audit evidence which might be obtained from the opinion, valuation etc of an expert.

- **Valuations of certain types of assets**, for example, land and buildings, plant and machinery

- **Determination of quantities or physical condition of assets**

- **Determination of amounts** using specialised techniques, for example, actuarial valuations

- **The measurement of work completed** and **work in progress** on contracts

- **Legal opinions**

2.5 When considering whether to use the work of an expert, the auditors should review:

- The **importance** of the matter being considered in the context of the accounts
- The **risk of misstatement** based on the nature and complexity of the matter
- The **quantity** and **quality** of other available **relevant audit evidence**

2.6 Once it is decided that an expert is required, the approach should be discussed with the management of the entity. Where the management is unwilling or unable to engage an expert, the auditors should consider engaging an expert themselves unless sufficient alternative audit evidence can be obtained.

Competence and objectivity of the expert

SAS 520.2

When planning to use the work of an expert the auditors should assess the objectivity and professional qualifications, experience and resources of the expert.

2.7 This will involve considering:

- The expert's **professional certification**, or licensing by, or membership of, an appropriate professional body
- The expert's **experience and reputation** in the field in which the auditors are seeking audit evidence

2.8 The risk that an expert's **objectivity is impaired** increases when the expert is:

- **Employed** by the entity
- **Related** in some other manner to the entity, for example, by being financially dependent upon, or having an investment in, the entity

2.9 If the auditors have **reservations** about the competence or objectivity of the expert they may need to carry out other procedures to obtain evidence from another expert.

The expert's scope of work

SAS 520.3

The auditors should obtain sufficient appropriate audit evidence that the expert's scope of work is adequate for the purposes of their audit.

2.10 Written instructions usually cover the expert's terms of reference and such instructions may cover such matters as follows.

- The **objectives** and **scope** of the expert's work
- A **general outline** as to the specific matters the expert's report is to cover
- The **intended use** of the expert's work including the possible communication to third parties of the expert's identity and extent of involvement
- The **extent** of the **expert's access** to appropriate records and files

- Information regarding the **assumptions and methods intended** to be used by the expert and their consistency with those used in prior periods

Assessing the work of the expert

> ### SAS 520.4
>
> The auditors should assess the appropriateness of the expert's work as audit evidence regarding the financial statement assertions being considered.

2.11 Auditors should assess whether the substance of the expert's findings is properly reflected in the financial statements or supports the financial statement assertions. It will also require consideration of:

- The **source data used**

- The **assumptions and methods used**

- **When** the expert carried out the work

- The reasons for any **changes in assumptions and methods**

- The **results** of the expert's work in the light of the auditors' overall knowledge of the business and the results of other audit procedures

2.12 The auditors do **not** have the expertise to judge the assumptions and methods used; these are the responsibility of the expert. However, the auditors should seek to obtain an understanding of these assumptions etc, to consider their reasonableness based on other audit evidence, knowledge of the business and so on.

2.13 Where inconsistencies arise between the expert's work and other audit evidence, then the auditors should attempt to resolve them by discussion with both the entity and the expert. Additional procedures (including use of another expert) may be necessary.

2.14 Where the audit evidence from the expert is insufficient, and there is no satisfactory alternative source of evidence, then the auditors should consider the implications for their audit report.

3   SERVICE ORGANISATIONS

> ### KEY TERM
>
> A **service organisation** is an organisation that provides services to another organisation.

3.1 Some companies choose to outsource activities necessary to the running of their business to service organisations. SAS 480 gives examples of such activities that may be outsourced:

- Information processing
- Maintenance of accounting records
- Facilities management
- Asset management (for example, investments)
- Initiation or execution of transactions on behalf of the other entity

3.2　Some outsourced activities may be directly relevant to the audit. The most obvious example above is the maintenance of accounting records, but most of them actually could impact on the audit.

3.3　Auditors need to obtain sufficient, appropriate audit evidence to express an opinion on financial statements. They therefore need to consider an approach towards the parts of the audit affected by the service organisation.

3.4　SAS 480, *Service organisations* gives guidance in this area.

Audit planning

3.5　As part of their audit planning, auditors need to obtain a knowledge of the business. Understanding what functions are outsourced is a part of that.

> **SAS 480.2**
>
> In planning the audit, user entity auditors should determine whether activities undertaken by service organisations are relevant to the audit.

> **KEY TERM**
>
> The **user entity** is the organisation which is outsourcing any of its activities to the service organisation.

3.6　The SAS lists the following activities as relevant activities. (This is not an exclusive list.)

- Maintenance of accounting records
- Other finance functions
- Management of assets
- Undertaking or making arrangements for transactions as agent of the user entity.

3.7　It is important for the auditor to understand the terms of the agreement between the service organisation and the user entity.

> **SAS 480.3**
>
> User entity and auditors should obtain and document an understanding of:
>
> (a)　the contractual terms which apply to relevant activities undertaken by service organisations; and
>
> (b)　the way that the user entity monitors those activities so as to ensure that it meets its fiduciary and other legal responsibilities.

3.8　The SAS gives a list of things the auditor should consider.

- Whether the terms contain an adequate specification of the information to be provided to the user entity and responsibilities for initiating transactions relating to the activity undertaken by the service organisation.

- The way that accounting records relating to relevant activities are maintained.

- Whether the user entity has right to access to accounting records prepared by the service organisation concerning the activities undertaken, and relevant underlying information held by it, and the conditions in which such access may be sought.

- Whether the terms take proper account of any applicable requirements of regulatory bodies concerning the form of records to be maintained, or access to them.

- The nature of relevant performance standards.

- The way in which the use entity monitors performance of relevant activities and the extent to which its monitoring process relies on controls operated by the service organisation.

- Whether the service organisation has agreed to indemnify the user entity in the event of a performance failure.

- Whether the contractual terms permit the user entity auditors access to source of audit evidence including accounting records of the user entity and the information necessary for the conduct of the audit.

Assessing audit risk and designing audit procedures

3.9 It is important that the auditor considers the impact that the client's use of a service organisation has on the risk of the audit.

> **SAS 480.4**
>
> User entity auditors should determine the effect of relevant activities on their assessment of inherent risk and the user entity's control environment.

3.10 The auditor should consider:

- The nature of the service
- The degree of authority delegated
- The arrangements for ensuring quality
- Whether assets prone to loss or misappropriation are involved
- The reputation of the service organisation

3.11 In relation to control risk, the auditor should consider the monitoring that the user entity has in place over the service organisation's activities. The appendix to the SAS outlines a number of control considerations.

3.12 Having considered the risk attached to the use of the service organisation, the auditor should design audit procedures to obtain sufficient, appropriate audit evidence.

Accounting records

> **SAS 480.5**
>
> If a service organisation maintains all or part of user entity's accounting records, user entity auditors should assess whether the arrangements affect their reporting responsibilities in relation to accounting records arising from law or regulations.

3.13 This is because it is a legal requirement (under the Companies Act 1985) that directors are responsible for maintaining accounting records.

Obtaining audit evidence

SAS 480.6

Based on their understanding of the aspects of the user entity's accounting system and control environment relating to relevant activities, user entity auditors should:

(a) assess whether sufficient appropriate audit evidenced concerning the relevant financial statement assessment is available from records held at the user entity; and if not

(b) determine effective procedures to obtain evidence necessary for the audit, either by direct access to records kept by service organisations or through information obtained from the service organisations or their auditors.

3.14 The SAS outlines a series of procedures which the auditors should evaluate for efficiency and effectiveness:

- Inspecting records and documents held by the user entity

- Establishing the effectiveness of controls

- Obtaining representations to confirm balance and transactions from the service organisation

- Performing analytical review on

    - The records maintained by the user entity, or
    - The returns received from the service organisation

- Inspecting records and documents held by the service organisation

- Requesting specified procedures re performed by

    - The service organisation
    - The user entity's internal audit department

- Reviewing information from the service organisation or its auditors concerning the design and operation of its control systems.

SAS 480.7

When using a report issued by the service organisation's auditors, the user entity's auditors should consider the scope of the work performed and assess whether the report is sufficient and appropriate for its intended use.

3.15 The new entity's auditors should consider whether the information contained in the report is:

- Relevant
- Adequate
- Covers the right time period

4   REPORTING

4.1   The auditor is always **solely responsible** for the audit opinion. He must be assured that he has gained sufficient, appropriate advice to have an opinion on the financial statements, he must then express his opinion.

4.2   It would therefore be inappropriate to refer to the work of others in his final report. His thoughts on the work of others should, however, be adequately documented in the audit file.

4.3   The advice given about reporting having used the work of others is laid out below.

Internal audit

4.4   SAS 500 states (our bold)

'The external auditors have **sole responsibility** for the audit opinion expressed and for determining the nature, timing and extent of external audit procedures. **All judgements** relating to the audit of the financial statements **are those of the external auditors**. That responsibility is not reduced by any use made of internal audit work. However, internal audit work may serve to provide external auditors with audit evidence.'

Experts

4.5   SAS 520 refers more to the auditors report (our bold).

'When the auditors are satisfied that the work of an expert provides appropriate audit evidence, **reference is not made to the work of the expert in their report.**'

Service organisations

SAS 480.8

If user entity auditors conclude that evidence from records held by a service organisation is necessary in order to form an opinion on the user entity's financial statements and they are unable to obtain such evidence, they should:

(a)   include a description of the factors leading to the lack of evidence in the basis of opinion section of their report; and

(b)   qualify their opinion or issue a disclaimer of opinion on the financial statements.

4.6   If the user entity auditor judges that insufficient audit evidence concerning the activity undertaken by the service organisation, then he will mention the service organisation in his reasoning for qualifying the audit report.

4.7   Qualified audit reports will be discussed in detail in Chapter 19.

5   AUDIT STAFFING

5.1   When planning the audit the partner or manager must decide how many staff are to be allocated to the assignment, how experienced (which grade) and whether any of them will require special knowledge, skills or experience.

5.2 EXAMPLE

The client may undertake complicated leasing transactions, so an auditor with some experience of leasing would be required.

5.3 The partner will look at the staffing of the audit in previous years and he will need to decide whether that level of staffing was acceptable. He might judge this by looking at the amount of overtime worked last year and whether the budgeted cost was over or under run. This must be gauged with reference to any unexpected problems which arose in the previous year and whether they are likely to recur.

5.4 The audit partner is in charge of the audit and it is his opinion that will be given in the audit report.

5.5 Audit engagement partners should ensure that audit work is directed, supervised and reviewed in a manner that provides reasonable assurance that the work has been performed competently. This can be achieved by:

- Good audit planning which is communicated properly to audit staff
- Allocating work to appropriate members of staff
- Supervising work done by keeping in contact with the audit team
- Reviewing the audit file prior to expressing an opinion

Chapter roundup

- External auditors may use the work of a variety of other people in forming their opinion on financial statements.

- SAS 500 governs using the work of internal audit. The main provisions are:
  - Obtain sufficient understanding
  - Evaluate internal audit function
  - Evaluate specific work

- SAS 520 governs using the work of an expert. The main provisions are:
  - Obtain sufficient, appropriate evidence
  - Assess objectivity and qualifications of expert
  - Assess appropriateness of expert's work

- SAS 480 governs the approach to audits of entities that use service organisations. The main provisions are:
  - Determine if service organisation's activities are relevant to the audit
  - Obtain understanding of the service and assess risk arising from it
  - Design audit procedures to obtain a sufficient, appropriate evidence

- The auditor's report is the sole responsibility of the auditor.

- Audit partners should use appropriate audit staff for each assignment. They should also undertake direction, supervision and review.

Quick quiz

1   An effective internal audit function may eliminate the need for external audit procedures.

   True ☐

   False ☐

2   Name **four** things the external audit function may consider when evaluating the work of internal audit.

   1   ....

   2   ....

   3   ....

   4   ....

3   Complete the definitions using the words given below.

   An .... is a person or firm possessing ...., knowledge and .... in a particular field other than auditing.

   A .... is an organisation that provides .... to another organisation.

   | services, special, expert, experience, service, skills, organisation |

4   The auditor may not use the work of an expert employed by the organisation being audited.

   True ☐

   False ☐

5   Give two examples of services which may be outsourced.

   1   ....

   2   ....

6   If the auditor relies on the work of an expert or service organisation, he may refer to that person/organisation in his report and share responsibility with them.

   True ☐

   False ☐

7   Complete the guidance given in SAS 240, using the words given below.

   Audit engagement .... should ensure that work is ...., ... and .... in a manner that provides .... assurance that the work has been performed ....

   | competently, partners, reviewed, supervised, reasonable, directed |

8   There are four criteria for assessing the internal audit function. Name two.

   1   2   ....

BPP PUBLISHING

Answers to quick quiz

1   False

2   Refer to the table at para 1.7

3   expert, special skill, experience
    service organisation, services

4   False

5   See the list at para 3.1

6   False

7   Partners, directed, supervised, reviewed, reasonable, competently

8   See the table at para 1.5

Now try the question below from the Exam Question Bank

Number	Level	Marks	Time
7	Exam	20	36 mins

Chapter 8

AUDIT EVIDENCE AND SAMPLING

Topic list	Syllabus reference
1 Audit evidence	6
2 Audit sampling	6
3 Computer Assisted Audit Techniques (CAATs)	6
4 Audit documents	4

Introduction

Before we can start the audit, we must determine what kind of **evidence** we are looking for; particularly what kinds of evidence would satisfy an auditor and what kinds would not. In the exam you might be asked to make judgements on the strengths of particular types of evidence.

We also introduce the **financial statement assertions**. These will be particularly important when we consider balance sheet testing in Part D, since the balance sheet tests are designed to obtain **sufficient, appropriate** evidence about the assertions in each area.

Whatever type of test is chosen, the auditors need to decide **how they will select the items to be tested** from the whole population.

This is not as simple as it sounds. The auditors will want to **select a sample** which reflects, as closely as possible, the characteristics of the population from which the sample has been selected. If this is not the case, then the auditors cannot draw valid conclusions from the tests carried out on the sample.

The auditing standard on audit sampling is discussed in Section 2. Practical sampling methods range from the very simple to the very complex. The more sophisticated sampling techniques involve the use of probabilities and statistics. We will explain these practical aspects of sampling as simply as possible as you are not expected to understand the more complicated aspects of sampling theory.

Sampling theory is closely associated with the definition of **audit risk** and you should refer back to Chapter 6 to remind yourself of the relevant definitions.

When studying this chapter, you should particularly note how sample sizes are determined, methods of **sample selection** and the advantages and disadvantages of **statistical sampling**. You should also remember that sampling is only one type of audit test, and other tests, for example testing all high-value items, may be more appropriate in certain circumstances.

Once we have established what to test, we must determine **how to test the sample** we have chosen. **CAATs** are a way of carrying out a variety of audit tests using computer-assisted techniques.

Lastly in this Chapter we shall look at **why and how** the **evidence** obtained is **documented** on the audit files.

1 AUDIT EVIDENCE

> **KEY TERM**
>
> **Audit evidence** is the information auditors obtain in arriving at the conclusions on which their report is based.

1.1 In order to reach a position in which they can express a professional opinion, the auditors need to gather evidence from various sources. SAS 400 *Audit evidence* covers this area.

> **SAS 400.1**
>
> Auditors should obtain sufficient appropriate audit evidence to be able to draw reasonable conclusions on which to base the audit opinion.

Sufficient appropriate audit evidence

1.2 'Sufficiency' and 'appropriateness' are interrelated and apply to both tests of controls and substantive procedures.

- **Sufficiency** is the measure of the **quantity** of audit evidence.
- **Appropriateness** is the measure of the **quality** or **reliability** of the audit evidence.

1.3 Auditors are essentially looking for enough reliable audit evidence. Audit evidence usually indicates what is probable rather than what is definite (is usually persuasive rather than conclusive) so different sources are examined by the auditors. However, auditors can only give reasonable assurance that the financial statements are free from misstatement, so not **all** sources of evidence will be examined.

Sufficiency of audit evidence

1.4 The auditors' judgement as to what is sufficient appropriate audit evidence is influenced by a number of factors.

- **Risk assessment**
- The **nature** of the **accounting and internal control systems**
- The **materiality** of the item being examined
- The **experience gained during previous audits**
- The auditors' **knowledge of the business** and **industry**
- The **results of audit procedures**
- The **source** and **reliability of information** available

1.5 If they are unable to obtain sufficient appropriate audit evidence, the auditors should consider the implications for their report.

Tests of control

> **SAS 400.2**
>
> In seeking to obtain audit evidence from tests of control, auditors should consider the sufficiency and appropriateness of the audit evidence to support the assessed level of control risk.

1.6 There are two aspects of the relevant parts of the accounting and internal control systems about which auditors should seek to obtain audit evidence.

- **Design**: the accounting and internal control systems are capable of preventing or detecting material misstatements.

- **Operation**: the systems exist and have operated effectively throughout the relevant period.

Substantive procedures

> **SAS 400.3**
>
> In seeking to obtain audit evidence from substantive procedures, auditors should consider the extent to which that evidence together with any evidence from tests of controls supports the relevant financial statement assertions.

1.7 Substantive procedures are designed to obtain evidence about the financial statement assertions.

> **KEY TERMS**
>
> **Financial statement assertions** are the representations of the directors that are embodied in the financial statements. By approving the financial statements, the directors are making representations about the information therein. These representations or assertions may be described in general terms in a number of ways, one of which is as follows.

BPP PUBLISHING

Existence An asset or liability exists at a given date

Rights and obligations An asset or liability pertains to the entity at a given date

Occurrence A transaction or event took place which pertains to the entity during the relevant period

Completeness There are no unrecorded assets, liabilities, transactions or events, or undisclosed items

Valuation An asset or liability is recorded at an appropriate carrying value

Measurement A transaction or event is recorded in the proper amount and revenue or expense is allocated to the proper period

Presentation and disclosure An item is disclosed, classified and described in accordance with the applicable reporting framework (for example, relevant legislation and applicable accounting standards)

1.8 An eighth assertion, **accuracy** that all assets, liabilities, transactions and events are **recorded accurately** is sometimes added.

Exam focus point

When designing audit programmes, focus on the financial statement assertions listed above.

1.9 Audit evidence is usually obtained to support each financial statement assertion and evidence from one does not compensate for failure to obtain evidence for another. However, tests may provide audit evidence of more than one assertion.

Reliability of evidence

1.10 The following generalisations may help in assessing the reliability of audit evidence.

QUALITY OF EVIDENCE	
External	Audit evidence from **external sources** is more reliable than that obtained from the entity's records.
Auditor	Evidence obtained **directly by auditors** is more reliable than that obtained by or from the entity
Entity	Evidence obtained from the entity's records is more reliable when accounting and internal **control system operates effectively**
Written	Evidence in the form of **documents** or **written representations** are more reliable than oral representations
Originals	Original documents are more realistic than photocopies, or facsimiles

1.11 **Consistency** of audit evidence from different sources will have a **corroborating effect**, making the evidence more persuasive. Where such evidence is **inconsistent**, the auditors must determine what additional procedures are necessary to resolve the inconsistency.

1.12 Auditors must consider the cost-benefit relationship of obtaining evidence but any difficulty or expense is not in itself a valid basis for omitting a necessary procedure.

Exam focus point

You may be asked to consider how strong certain evidence is from the auditor's viewpoint, for example debtors' circularisation or third party valuation of assets.

1.13 Auditors obtain evidence by one or more of the following procedures.

PROCEDURES	
Inspection of assets	Inspection of assets that are recorded in the accounting records confirms **existence**, gives evidence of **valuation**, but does not confirm **rights and obligations**
	Confirmation that assets seen are recorded in accounting records gives evidence of **completeness**
Inspection of documentation	Confirmation to documentation of items recorded in accounting records confirms that an asset **exists** or a transaction **occurred**. Confirmation that items recorded in supporting documentation are recorded in accounting records tests **completeness**
	Cut-off can be verified by inspecting reverse population ie checking transactions recorded **after** the balance sheet date to supporting documentation to confirm that they occurred after the balance sheet date
	Inspection also provides evidence of **valuation/measurement**, **rights and obligations** and the nature of items (**presentation and disclosure**). It can also be used to **compare** documents (and hence test **consistency** of audit evidence) and confirm **authorisation**
Observation	Involves watching a procedure being performed (for example, post opening)
	Of limited use, as only confirms procedure took place when auditor watching
Enquiries	Seeking information from **client staff** or **external sources**
	Strength of evidence depends on knowledge and integrity of source of information
Confirmation	Seeking confirmation from another source of details in client's accounting records for example, confirmation from bank of bank balances
Computations	Checking arithmetic of client's records for example, adding up ledger account
Analytical procedures	See Chapter 12

Question 1

The examination of evidence is fundamental to the audit process. SAS 400 *Audit evidence* states that: 'the auditors should obtain sufficient appropriate audit evidence to be able to draw reasonable conclusions on which to base the audit opinion'. Evidence is available to the auditors from sources under their own control, from the management of the company and from third parties. Each of these sources presents the auditors with differing considerations as to the quality of the evidence so produced.

Required

(a) Discuss the quality of the following types of audit evidence, giving two examples of each form of evidence.

(i) Evidence originated by the auditors
(ii) Evidence created by third parties

BPP PUBLISHING

(iii) Evidence created by the management of the client

(b) Describe the general considerations which the auditors must bear in mind when evaluating audit evidence.

Answer

(a) (i) There is little risk that evidence originated by the auditors can be manipulated by management. It is therefore, in general, the most reliable type of audit evidence. Examples include the following.

(1) Analytical procedures, such as the calculation of ratios and trends in order to examine unusual variations

(2) Physical inspection or observation, such as attendance at physical stocktakes or inspection of a fixed asset

(3) Re-performance of calculations making up figures in the accounts, such as the computation of total stock values

(ii) Third party evidence is more reliable than client-produced evidence to the extent that it is obtained from sources independent of the client. Its reliability will be reduced if it is obtained from sources which are not independent, or if there is a risk that client personnel may be able to and have reason to suppress or manipulate it. This, for instance, is an argument against having replies to circularisations sent to the client instead of the auditors.

Examples of third party evidence include the following.

(1) Circularisation of debtors or creditors and other requests from the auditors for confirming evidence, such as requests for confirmation of bank balances.

(2) Reports produced by experts, such as property valuations, actuarial valuations, legal opinions. In evaluating such evidence, the auditors need to take into account the qualifications of the expert, his or her independence of the client and the terms of reference under which the work was carried out.

(3) Documents held by the client which were issued by third parties, such as invoices, price lists and statements. These may sometimes be manipulated by the client, to the extent that items may be suppressed or altered, and to this extent they are less reliable than confirmations received direct.

(iii) The auditors cannot place the same degree of reliance on evidence produced by client management as on that produced outside the client organisation. It will, however, often be necessary to place some reliance on the client's evidence. The auditors will need to apply judgement in doing so, taking into account previous experience of the client's reliability and the extent to which the client's representations appear compatible with other audit findings, as well as the materiality of the item under discussion. Examples of evidence originating from client management include the following.

(1) The company's accounting records and supporting schedules. Although these are prepared by management, the auditors have a statutory right to examine such records in full: this right enhances the quality of this information.

(2) The client's explanations of, for instance, apparently unusual fluctuations in results. Such evidence requires interpretation by the auditors and, being oral evidence, only limited reliance can be placed upon it.

(3) Information provided to the auditors about the internal control system. The auditors need to check that this information is accurate and up-to-date, and that it does not simply describe an idealised system which is not adhered to in practice.

(b) Audit evidence will often not be wholly conclusive. The auditors must obtain evidence which is sufficient and appropriate to form the basis for their audit conclusions. The evidence gathered should also be relevant to those conclusions, and sufficiently reliable ultimately to form the basis for the audit opinion. The auditors must exercise skill and judgement to ensure that evidence is correctly interpreted and that only valid inferences are drawn from it.

Certain general principles can be stated. Written evidence is preferable to oral evidence; independent evidence obtained from outside the organisation is more reliable than that obtained internally; and that evidence generated by the auditors is more reliable than that obtained from others.

2   AUDIT SAMPLING

SAS 430.1

When using either statistical or non-statistical sampling methods, auditors should design and select an audit sample, perform audit procedures thereon and evaluate sample results **so as to obtain appropriate audit evidence.**

2.1   SAS 430 *Audit sampling* is based on the premise that auditors do not normally examine all the information available to them. It would be impractical to do so. Using audit sampling will produce valid conclusions.

KEY TERMS

Audit sampling is the application of audit procedures to less than 100% of the items within an account balance or class of transactions. It enables auditors to obtain and evaluate evidence about some characteristic of the items selected in order to form a conclusion about the population sampled.

Sampling units are the individual items that make up the population.

Error is an unintentional mistake in the financial statements.

Tolerable error is the maximum error in the population that the auditors are willing to accept and still conclude that the audit objective has been achieved.

Sampling risk is the risk that the auditors' conclusion, based on a sample, may be different from the conclusion that would be reached if the entire population was subject to the same audit procedure.

Non-sampling risk is the risk that the auditors might use inappropriate procedures or might misinterpret evidence and thus fail to recognise an error.

2.2   The SAS points out that some testing procedures do not involve sampling, such as:

- Testing 100% of items in a population (this should be obvious)

- Testing all items with a certain characteristic (for example, over a certain value) as selection is not representative

2.3   The SAS distinguishes between **statistically based sampling**, which involves the use of random selection techniques from which mathematically constructed conclusions about the population can be drawn, and **non-statistical sampling methods**, from which auditors draw a judgemental opinion about the population. However the principles of the SAS apply to both methods.

Design of the sample

SAS 430.2

When designing the size and structure of an audit sample, auditors should consider the specific audit objectives, the nature of the population from which they wish to sample, and the sampling and selection methods.

Audit objectives

2.4 Auditors must consider the **specific audit objectives** to be achieved and the audit procedures which are most likely to achieve them. The auditors also need to consider the **nature and characteristics of the audit evidence** sought and **possible error conditions**. This will help them to define what constitutes an error and what population to use for sampling.

Population

2.5 The population from which the sample is drawn must be **appropriate** and **complete** for the specific audit objectives. The population may be divided into **sampling units** in a variety of ways, for example, an individual debtors balance or, in monetary unit sampling, £1 of the total debtors balance. Auditors must define the sampling unit in order to obtain an efficient and effective sample to achieve the particular audit objectives.

Sample size

SAS 430.3

When determining sample sizes, auditors should consider sampling risk, the amount of error that would be acceptable and the extent to which they expect to find errors.

2.6 Examples of some factors affecting sample size are given in an appendix to the SAS, reproduced here.

Table 1: Some factors influencing sample size for tests of controls

Factor	Impact on sample size
Sampling risk	• The greater the reliance on the results of a test of control using audit sampling, the lower the sampling risk the auditors are willing to accept and, consequently, the larger the sample size. • The lower the assessment of control risk, the more likely the auditors are to place reliance on audit evidence from tests of control. • A high control risk assessment may result in a decision not to perform tests of control and rely entirely on substantive procedures.
Tolerable error rate	The higher the tolerable error rate the lower the sample size and vice versa.
Expected error rate	• If errors are expected, a larger sample ordinarily needs to be examined to confirm that the actual error rate is less than the tolerable error rate. • High expected error rates may result in a decision not to perform tests of control.
Number of items in population	Virtually no effect on sample size unless population is small.

Table 2: Some factors influencing sample size for substantive tests

Factor	Impact on sample size
Inherent risk*	• The higher the assessment of inherent risk, the more audit evidence is required to support the auditors' conclusion.
Control risk*	• The higher the assessment of control risk, the greater the reliance on audit evidence obtained from substantive procedures.
Detection risk*	• Sampling risk for substantive tests is one form of detection risk. The lower the sampling risk the auditors are willing to accept, the larger the sample size. • Other substantive procedures may provide audit evidence regarding the same financial statement assertions and reduce detection risk. This may reduce the extent of the auditors' reliance on the results of a substantive procedure using audit sampling. • The lower the reliance on the results of a substantive procedure using audit sampling, the higher the sampling risk the auditors are willing to accept and, consequently, the smaller the sample size.
Tolerable error rate	The higher the monetary value of the tolerable error rate the smaller the sample size and vice versa.
Expected error rate	If errors are expected, a larger sample ordinarily needs to be examined to confirm that the actual error rate is less than the tolerable error rate.
Population value	The less material the monetary value of the population to the financial statements, the smaller the sample size that may be required.
Numbers of items in population	Virtually no effect on sample size unless population is small.
Stratification	If it is appropriate to stratify the population this may lead to a smaller sample size.

Sampling risk

2.7 Sampling risk is encountered by the auditors in both tests of control and substantive procedures. It is the risk of drawing a wrong conclusion from audit sampling. **It is part of detection risk.** It affects different types of tests as follows:

(a) **Tests of control**

(i) The risk of placing a **higher than necessary assessment** on control risk, because the error in the sample is greater than the error in the total population (alpha risk)

(ii) The risk of placing a **lower than required assessment** on control risk, because the error in the sample is less than the error in the population as a whole (beta risk)

(b) **Substantive tests**

(i) The risk of concluding that a recorded account balance or class of transactions is **materially misstated when** it is **not**, because the error in the sample is greater than the error in the population as a whole (alpha risk)

(ii)   The risk of concluding that a recorded account balance or class of transactions is **acceptable when** it is **materially misstated,** because the error in the sample is less than the error in the population as a whole (beta risk)

2.8   The **greater** their reliance on the results of the procedure in question, the **lower** the sampling risk auditors will be willing to accept and the **larger** the sample size needs to be. Sample size will therefore be considered in the context of overall risk assessment (see SAS 300 *Accounting and internal control systems and audit risk assessments* in Chapter 9).

2.9   The SAS also adds the following note regarding **non-sampling risk.**

> 'Sampling risk can be contrasted with non-sampling risk which arises when auditors use any audit procedures. Non-sampling risk arises because, for example, most audit evidence is persuasive rather than conclusive, or auditors might use inappropriate procedures or might misinterpret evidence and thus fail to recognise an error. Auditors attempt to reduce non-sampling risk to a negligible level by appropriate planning, direction, supervision and review.'

Tolerable error

2.10   This will still be considered during the planning stage.

(a)   In tests of control, the **tolerable error** is the **maximum rate of deviation from a prescribed control procedure** that auditors are willing to accept in the population and still conclude that the preliminary assessment of control risk is valid. Often this rate will be very low since the auditor is likely to be concentrating on testing important controls.

(b)   In substantive procedures, the **tolerable error** is the **maximum monetary error** in an account balance or class of transactions that auditors are willing to accept so that, when the results of all audit procedures are considered, they are able to conclude, with reasonable assurance, that the financial statements are not materially misstated. Sometimes the tolerable error for substantive tests will be the materiality rate. Some accountancy firms set tolerable error as being a fixed percentage of materiality, say 50% or 70%, for reasons of safety.

Expected error

2.11   Larger samples will be required when errors are expected than would be required if none were expected, in order to conclude that the **actual** error is **less** than the **tolerable** error. If the expected error rate is high then sampling may not be appropriate and auditors may have to examine 100% of the population.

Setting the sample size

2.12   The sample size can be calculated as follows:

$$\text{Sample size} = \frac{\text{Reliability factor}}{\text{Precision}}$$

where the **reliability factor** (R factor), taken from tables based on the Poisson distribution, is associated with the level of assurance the auditors want or need to obtain from the test. Such a table is given below and it shows the relationship between risk levels, and the reliability factor.

Risk level	Confidence level	Reliability factor (R factor)	
		No errors expected	*One error expected*
1%	99%	4.6	6.61
5%	95%	3.0	4.75
10%	90%	2.3	3.89
15%	85%	1.9	3.38
20%	80%	1.6	3.00
30%	70%	1.2	2.44

2.13 The **precision level** is the number of errors the auditors are willing to accept in a population to be assured that the population is correct. For example, if the auditors decide that the population could be accepted as correct with no more than a 10% (say) risk that two or more out of every 100 items was incorrect, then the precision level would be 0.03 (in other words, less than three are incorrect).

2.14 Many auditing firms (particularly large firms) will standardise their approach to sampling by giving set sample sizes for given planned levels of reliance or applying R factors to the audit risk model.

								Detection risk	
	Audit risk		Inherent risk		Control risk		Sampling risk		Non-sampling risk
Risk levels	5%	=	80%	×	35%	×	18%	×	100%

Selection of the sample

> ### SAS 430.4
>
> Auditors should select sample items in such a way that the sample can be expected to be representative of the population in respect of the characteristics being tested.

2.15 The SAS makes a very important point.

> 'For a sample to be representative of the population, all items in the population are required to have an equal or known probability of being selected.'

2.16 There are a number of selection methods available, but the SAS identifies three that are commonly used.

(a) **Random selection** ensures that all items in the population have an equal chance of selection, for example, by use of random number tables.

(b) **Systematic selection** involves selecting items using a constant interval between selections, the first interval having a random start. When using systematic selection auditors must ensure that the population is not structured in such a manner that the sampling interval corresponds with a particular pattern in the population.

(c) **Haphazard selection** may be an acceptable alternative to random selection provided auditors are satisfied that the sample is representative of the entire population. This method requires care to guard against making a selection which is biased, for example towards items which are easily located, as they may not be representative.

2.17 In addition the auditors may also consider for certain tests:

(a) **Stratification.** This means dividing the population being sampled into sub-populations of items with similar characteristics. By stratifying, auditors can concentrate on particular sections of the population which they feel may be vulnerable to error (for example the transactions processed by a new purchase ledger clerk).

(b) **Sequence or block sampling.** Sequence sampling may be used to check whether certain items have particular characteristics. For example an auditor may use a sample of 50 consecutive cheques to check whether cheques are signed by authorised signatories rather than picking 50 single cheques throughout the year. Sequence sampling may however produce samples that are not representative of the population as a whole particularly if errors occurred only during a certain part of the period.

Evaluation of sample results

SAS 430.5

Having carried out, on each sample item, those audit procedures which are appropriate to the particular audit objective, auditors should:

(a) analyse any errors detected in the sample; and

(b) draw inferences for the population as a whole.

Analysis of errors in the sample

2.18 To begin with, the auditors must consider whether the items in question are **true errors**, as they defined them before the test, for example, a misposting between customer accounts will not affect the total debtors. When the expected audit evidence regarding a specific sample item cannot be found, the auditors may be able to obtain sufficient appropriate audit evidence by performing alternative procedures. In such cases, the item is not treated as an error.

2.19 The **qualitative** aspects of errors should also be considered, including the nature and cause of the error and any possible effects the error might have on other parts of the audit.

2.20 Where common features are discovered in errors, the auditors may decide to identify all items in the population which possess the common feature (for example, location), thereby producing a sub-population. Audit procedures could then be extended in this area and separate analysis could then be performed based on the items examined for each sub-population.

Inferences to be drawn from the population as a whole

2.21 The auditors should project the error results from the sample on to the relevant population. The projection method should be consistent with the method used to select the sampling unit. The auditors will **estimate the probable error** in the population by extrapolating the errors found in the sample. Two methods can be used.

2.22 The **ratio method** should be used when the amount of error in an item relates to the size of the item. As the monetary value of the item increases, so does the monetary value of the error. The projected error is found by the formula:

$$\text{Most likely error in population} = \text{Error found in sample} \times \frac{\text{Population value}}{\text{Sample value}}$$

For example

Total value	£1,000,000
Sample value	£200,000
Errors found in sample	£9,000

Most likely error in population $= \dfrac{1,000,000}{200,000} \times £9,000$

$= \underline{£45,000}$

2.23 The **difference method** should be used where the error does not have a direct relationship to the monetary value of the item. It is relatively constant for all items, and so will increase in proportion to the number of items in the population. Here the most likely error is found by the formula:

$$\text{Most likely error in population} = \text{Error found in sample} \times \frac{\text{Number of items in population}}{\text{Number of items in sample}}$$

For example

Total number of items	400
Number of items in sample	20
Errors found in sample	£9,000

Most likely error in population $= \dfrac{400}{20} \times £9,000$

$= \underline{£180,000}$

2.24 In both cases allowance should be made when calculating the most likely error in the population for the actual error in items taken out of the population and tested automatically because of certain characteristics they have for example, being over a certain value.

2.25 The auditors can then **estimate any further error** that might not have been detected because of the imprecision of the technique (in addition to consideration of the qualitative aspects of the errors).

2.26 The auditors should then compare the projected population error (net of adjustments made by the entity in the case of substantive procedures) to the tolerable error, taking account of other audit procedures relevant to the specific control or financial statement assertion.

2.27 If the projected population error **exceeds** tolerable error, then the auditors should re-assess sampling risk. If it is unacceptable, they should consider extending auditing procedures or performing alternative procedures, either of which may result in a proposed adjustment to the financial statements.

2.28 **Summary**

Key stages in the sampling process are as follows.

- Determining **objectives** and **population**
- Determining **sample size**
- **Choosing method** of **sample selection**
- **Analysing** the **results** and **projecting errors**

Question 2

You are required to present the arguments for and against the use of statistical sampling in auditing and reach a conclusion on the subject.

BPP PUBLISHING

Answer

An inevitable characteristic of audit testing is that a sample only of transactions or items can be examined. The auditors examine a sample of items and thereby seek to obtain assurance that the whole group is acceptable.

Provided that conditions are appropriate for its use, a statistical approach to sampling is likely to have many advantages over the alternative of judgement sampling.

Conditions favouring the use of statistical sampling are:

(a)   Existence of large and homogeneous groups of items
(b)   Low expected error rate and clear definition of error
(c)   Reasonable ease of identifying and obtaining access to items selected

If these conditions are present, statistical sampling is likely to have the following advantages.

(a)   At the conclusion of a test the auditors are able to state a definite level of confidence they may have that the whole population conforms to the sample result, within a stated precision limit.

(b)   Sample size is objectively determined, having regard to the degree of risk the auditors are prepared to accept for each application.

(c)   It may be possible to use smaller sample sizes, thus saving time and money.

(d)   The process of fixing required precision and confidence levels compels the auditors to consider and clarify their audit objectives.

(e)   The results of tests can be expressed in precise mathematical terms.

(f)   Bias is eliminated.

Statistical sampling is not without disadvantages.

(a)   The technique may be applied blindly without prior consideration of the suitability of the statistical sampling for the audit task to be performed. This disadvantage may be overcome by establishing soundly-based procedures for use in the firm, incorporating standards on sampling in the firm's audit manual, instituting training programmes for audit staff and proper supervision.

(b)   Unsuspected patterns or bias in sample selection may invalidate the conclusions. The probability of these factors arising must be carefully judged by the auditor before they decide to adopt statistical sampling.

(c)   It frequently needs back-up by further tests within the population reviewed: large items, non-routine items, sensitive items like directors' transactions.

(d)   At the conclusion of a statistical sampling-based test the auditors may fail to appreciate the further action necessary based on the results obtained. This potential disadvantage may be overcome by adequate training and supervision, and by requiring careful evaluation of all statistical sampling tests.

(e)   Statistical sampling may be applied carelessly, without due confirmation that the sample selected is acceptably random.

(f)   The selection exercise can be time consuming.

(g)   The degree of tolerance of acceptable error must be predetermined.

The disadvantages listed above can all be overcome if the technique is applied sensibly and competently.

Provided that the conditions favouring its use are present, statistical sampling is a useful technique for several auditing tasks.

(a)   Tests of controls
(b)   Substantive procedures
(c)   Debtor and creditor circularisation
(d)   Fraud investigation using discovery sampling

Statistical techniques should be used when they are convenient and of positive use to the auditors in achieving a level of reliability in their results. If they are used selectively, in cases where their advantages are conspicuous and their disadvantages can be reduced to a minimum, they can make a significant contribution towards greater quality control on an audit

Monetary unit sampling (MUS)

2.29 MUS has two main characteristics: items are selected for testing by weighting the items in proportion to their value and inferences are drawn based on 'attribute sampling' concepts.

2.30 MUS produces conclusions based on monetary amounts, **not** occurrence rates, by defining each £1 of a population as a separate sampling unit. Thus, a purchase ledger of £3.6m is described as a population of 3.6m sampling units of £1; an individual balance of £4,000 merely represents 4,000 £1 sampling units.

2.31 We saw in Section 1 above that the sample size was calculated as:

$$\text{Sample size} = \frac{\text{Reliability factor}}{\text{Precision}}$$

2.32 This formula is restated in monetary terms for MUS.

$$\text{Precision (as above)} = \frac{\text{Tolerable error}}{\text{Population value}}$$

Thus:

$$\text{Sample size} = \frac{\text{Reliability factor} \times \text{Population value}}{\text{Tolerable error}}$$

2.33 Having calculated the sample size, the auditors can then select the sample items. Firstly, the sampling interval must be calculated using either:

$$\text{Sampling interval} = \frac{\text{Population value}}{\text{Sample size}}$$

or

$$\text{Sampling interval} = \frac{\text{Tolerable error}}{\text{Reliability factor}}$$

2.34 Given a sample size of £X, the auditors will then select every X sampling unit in the population, starting from zero and added cumulatively (0, X, 2X etc), starting from a random point in the population.

Question 3

Show the selection of sample items, given that:

(a) Tolerable error = £200,000

(b) Reliability factor = 3.0

(c) Population value = £5m

(d) Random start at item 10,000

(e) The first ten ledger balances on the ledger in question are: £25,000; £27,250; £75,100; £8,450; £9,900; £1,720; £98,210; £227,190; £3,590; £48,620

Answer

$$\text{Sample size} = \frac{\text{Reliability factor} \times \text{Population value}}{\text{Tolerable error}}$$

$$= \frac{3.0 \times 5,000,000}{200,000} = 75$$

$$\text{Sampling interval} = \frac{\text{Population value}}{\text{Sample size}}$$

$$= \frac{£5,000,000}{75} = £66,666$$

The sample will be selected as follows.

Ledger balance £	Value £	Cumulative value £	Select pound £
1	25,000	25,000	10,000
2	27,250	52,250	
3	75,100	127,350	76,666
4	8,450	135,800	
5	9,900	145,700	143,332
6	1,720	147,420	
7	98,210	245,630	209,998

Ledger balance £	Value £	Cumulative value £	Select pound £
8	227,190	472,820	276,664
			343,330
			409,996
9	3,590	476,410	
10	48,620	525,030	476,662
etc	etc	etc	etc

2.35 The sample in the above exercise will not be as great as 75 because of item 8 on the ledger (and other balances of a similar value will have the same effect). This demonstrates one of the advantages of MUS in that all items larger than the sampling interval will be selected. This selection of larger items gives a weighting which makes the reduction in the sample size acceptable.

Evaluation of MUS results

2.36 Where no errors are found in the sample, then the 'precision' achieved will be that predicted in terms of 'tolerable error' by the auditors before the test was carried out. The conclusion can then be drawn that the population from which the sample is drawn is not overstated by more than the monetary precision specified here (usually materiality).

2.37 This conclusion cannot be drawn when errors are found. It is then necessary to differentiate between two different types of error.

2.38 Where an error is in an item **larger** than the sampling interval, the auditors will be assured that the absolute amount of error in this top 'strata' of balances is known, because **all** such items have been examined in the test.

2.39 Where an error is found in an item which is **smaller** than the sampling interval, then it will be necessary to **project** the level of error on to the rest of the population.

2.40 This projection has two aspects.

(a) Estimating the probable error in the population

(b) Adjusting the value of each error by a precision gap widening factor to arrive at the upper error limit (the purpose of this is to estimate the error that may not have been found because of the imprecision of the estimation technique)

2.41 If the upper error limit is greater than the tolerable error, the old audit brief recommended the following actions.

- Ask the client to **adjust** for any **specific errors** identified

- **Reconsider** such aspects of the process as **risk levels, tolerable error** and **sample size**. Great care should be taken before original audit judgements are revised

- **Consider** the need for **further adjustments** of the **account balances** concerned, for example additional debt provision

- **Consider** the **eventual form** of the **audit report** - is a qualification or a disclaimer required?

Advantages and disadvantages of MUS

2.42 **MUS** has the following advantages and disadvantages.

Advantages

(a) The auditors can design and evaluate the sample manually with little difficulty. They can also select samples in a relatively straightforward way, either manually or by computer.

(b) MUS will **stratify items by monetary value** (so that the probability with which each item may be selected will be proportional to its monetary value). In addition, it will automatically stratify the population to ensure that the auditor selects all items over a certain size (the sampling interval), even though they do not form part of the sample but are separately evaluated.

Disadvantages

(a) MUS **does not cope** easily with **errors of understatement** or where there are negative-valued items in the population. There are two reasons for this. Firstly, items that are omitted completely from the population will have no probability at all of being selected. Secondly, items whose monetary amount is understated will have too low a probability of being selected, so that the chances of selecting a £1,000 item recorded as £1 will be negligible.

(b) MUS sampling can be **over-conservative** in evaluating errors. This may cause the auditors to reject an acceptable population.

(c) Where the auditors cannot use computerised sample selection, adding cumulatively through the population (the most common means of sample selection for MUS) by hand can be **time-consuming**. This disadvantage will be offset where the auditors decide they wish to check the addition of the population anyway.

(d) Where there are likely to be **numerous errors**, a **large sample size** may be required in order to obtain an acceptable result.

Exam focus point

In the exam, you may be asked to describe sampling in general terms or how it will be used in a specific situation.

---

3 COMPUTER ASSISTED AUDIT TECHNIQUES (CAATS)

3.1 There is no mystique about using a computer to help with auditing. You probably use common computer assisted audit techniques all the time in your daily work without realising it.

(a) Most modern accounting systems allow data to be manipulated in various ways and extracted into a **report**.

(b) Even if reporting capabilities are limited, the data can often be exported directly into a **spreadsheet** package (sometimes using simple Windows-type cut and paste facilities in very modern systems) and then analysed.

(c) Most systems have **searching** facilities that are much quicker to use than searching through print-outs by hand.

3.2 There are a variety of packages specially designed either to ease the auditing task itself or to carry out audit **interrogations** of computerised data automatically.

3.3 Auditors can use PC's such as laptops that are independent of the organisation's systems when performing CAATs.

Using the right files

3.4 Before any audit software is run, the auditors should check the identity and version of the data files and programs used, whether they are taken from the company's records and systems or supplied by themselves.

Audit software

3.5 Audit software performs the sort of checks on data that auditors might otherwise have to perform by hand. Examples of uses of audit software are:

- Interrogation software, which accesses the client's data files
- Comparison programs which compare versions of a program
- Interactive software for interrogation of on-line systems
- Resident code software to review transactions as they are processed

3.6 The case example below will give you a clear idea of what interrogation software can achieve.

Case example: ACL for Windows

Here are some extracts (from some marketing blurb) about one of the leading CAAT products, ACL for Windows.

'ACL for Windows is PC software that allows users to independently and interactively read, analyse, interrogate and report on data from virtually any mainframe, mini or microcomputer. ACL for Windows is the industry standard and is specifically designed for the non-technical user.

Here are just a few of the many uses of ACL.

Identify trends, pinpoint exceptions and potential areas of concern

Locate errors and potential fraud by comparing and analysing files according to end user criteria

Recalculate and verify balances

Identify control issues and ensure compliance with standards

Age and analyse accounts receivable, payables or any other time-sensitive transactions

Recover expenses or lost revenues by testing for duplicate payments, gaps in invoice numbers or unbilled services

Test for unauthorised employee/supplier relationships

Automate repetitive tasks by creating custom ACL applications or batches

3.7 Although audit interrogation software may be used during many tests of controls and substantive procedures, its use is particularly appropriate during substantive testing of transactions and especially balances. By using audit software, the auditors may **scrutinise large volumes of data** and concentrate skilled manual resources on the investigation of results, rather than on the extraction of information and **selection** of **samples**.

3.8 Major considerations when deciding whether to use file interrogation software are as follows.

(a) As a minimum auditors will require a **basic understanding** of data processing and the enterprise's computer application, together with a detailed knowledge of the audit software and the computer files to be used.

(b) Depending on the complexity of the application, the auditors may need to have a sound appreciation of **systems analysis**, operating systems and, where program code is used, experience of the programming language to be utilised.

(c) Auditors will need to consider how easy it is to **transfer** the **client's data** onto the auditors' PC.

(d) The client may **lack full knowledge** of the **computer system**, and hence may not be able to explain fully all the information it produces.

Test data

3.9 An obvious way of seeing whether a system is **processing** data in the way that it should be is to input some valid test data and see what happens. The expected results can be calculated in advance and then compared with the results that actually arise.

3.10 Test data can also be used to check the controls that prevent processing of **invalid data** by entering data with say a non-existent customer code or worth an unreasonable amount, or transactions which may if processed breach limits such as customer credit limits.

3.11 A significant problem with test data is that any resulting corruption of the data files has to be corrected. This is difficult with modern real-time systems, which often have built in (and highly desirable) controls to ensure that data entered **cannot** easily be removed without leaving a mark.

3.12 Other problems with **test data** are that it only tests the operation of the system at a **single point of time,** and auditors are only testing controls in the programs being run and controls which they know about. The problems involved mean that test data is being used less as a CAAT.

Embedded audit facilities

3.13 The results of using test data would, in any case, be completely distorted if the programs used to process it were not the ones **normally** used for processing. For example a fraudulent member of the IT department might substitute a version of the program that gave the correct results, purely for the duration of the test, and then replace it with a version that syphoned off the company's funds into his own bank account.

3.14 To allow a **continuous** review of the data recorded and the manner in which it is treated by the system, it may be possible to use CAATs referred to as 'embedded audit facilities'.

3.15 An embedded facility consists of audit modules that are incorporated into the computer element of the enterprise's accounting system. Two frequently encountered examples are Integrated Test Facility (ITF) and Systems Control and Review File (SCARF).

EXAMPLES OF EMBEDDED AUDIT FACILITIES	
Integrated test facility (ITF)	Creates a **fictitious entity** within the company application, where transactions are posted to it alongside regular transactions, and actual results of fictitious entity compared with what it should have produced
Systems control and review file (SCARF)	Allows auditors to have transactions above a **certain amount** from **specific ledger account** posted to a file for later auditor review

Simulation

3.16 Simulation (or 'parallel simulation') entails the preparation of a separate program that simulates the processing of the organisation's real system. Real data can then be passed not only through the system proper but also through the simulated program. For example the simulation program may be used to re-perform controls such as those used to identify any missing items from a sequence.

Knowledge-based systems

3.17 Decision support systems' and expert systems can be used to assist with the auditors' own judgement and decisions.

Question 4

When auditing a computer based accounting system, it is possible for most of the audit to be completed using conventional audit techniques. In some computer based systems, however, it is necessary for the auditors to employ computer assisted audit techniques (CAATs).

Required

(a) Outline the major types of CAATs and describe the potential benefits that might be derived from using them.

(b) Briefly explain the use that the auditors could make of such a test pack when examining a sales ledger system maintained on a computer system.

Answer

(a) Audit techniques that involve, directly or indirectly, the use of a client's computer are referred to as Computer Assisted Audit Techniques (CAATs), of which the following are two principal categories.

(i) *Audit software*: computer programs used for audit purposes to examine the contents of the client's computer files.

(ii) *Test data*: data used by the auditors for computer processing to test the operation of the enterprise's computer programs.

The benefits of using CAATs are as follows.

(i) By using computer audit programs, the auditors can scrutinise large volumes of data and concentrate skilled manual resources on the investigation of results, rather than on the extraction of information.

(ii) Once the programs have been written and tested, the costs of operation are relatively low, indeed the auditors do not necessarily have to be present during its use (though there are frequently practical advantages in the auditors attending).

(b) The auditors could use a test pack to test the sales ledger system by including data in the pack which would normally be processed through the system, such as:

(i) Sales
(ii) Credits allowed
(iii) Cash receipts
(iv) Discounts allowed

The processing of the input would involve:

(i) Production of sales invoices (with correct discounts)

(ii) Production of credit notes

(iii) Posting of cash received, invoices and credit notes to individual debtor's accounts to appear on statements

(iv) Posting all transactions to the sales ledger control account and producing balances

The result produced would be compared with those predicted in the test pack. Errors should appear on exception reports produced by the computer, for example, a customer credit limit being breached.

---

4   AUDIT DOCUMENTS

4.1 All audit work must be documented: the working papers are the tangible evidence of the work done in support of the audit opinion. SAS 230 *Working papers* covers this area.

> ## SAS 230.1
>
> Auditors should document in their working papers matters which are important in supporting their report.

> ## KEY TERM
>
> **Working papers** are the material the auditors prepare or obtain, and retain in connection with the performance of the audit.
>
> Working papers may be in the form of data stored on paper, film, electronic media or other media.
>
> Working papers support, amongst other things, the statement in the auditors' report as to the auditors' compliance or otherwise with Auditing Standards to the extent that this is important in supporting their report.

Form and content of working papers

SAS 230.2

Working papers should record the auditors' planning, the nature, timing and extent of the audit procedures performed, and the conclusions drawn from the audit evidence obtained.

SAS 230.3

Auditors should record in their working papers their reasoning on all significant matters which require the exercise of judgement, and their conclusions thereon.

4.2 The reasons why auditors use working papers to record their work, and why it is necessary for auditors to record all their work, are as follows.

(a) The **reporting partner** needs **to be able to satisfy himself that work delegated** by him has been **properly performed**. The reporting partner can generally only do this by having available detailed working papers prepared by the audit staff who performed the work.

(b) **Working papers** will **provide**, for future reference, **details of audit problems** encountered, together with evidence of work performed and conclusions drawn in arriving at the audit opinion. This can be invaluable if, at some future date, the adequacy of the auditors' work is called into question in the event of litigation against them by either the client or some third party.

(c) Good working papers will not only **assist** in the **control** of the **current audit**, but will also be invaluable in the **planning** and **control** of **future audits**.

(d) The preparation of working papers **encourages** the auditors to adopt a **methodical approach** to their audit work, which in turn is likely to improve the quality of that work.

4.3 Auditors cannot record everything they consider. Therefore judgement must be used as to the extent of working papers, based on:

General rule for documenting the audit process
'What would be necessary to provide an experienced auditor, with no previous connection with the audit, with an understanding of the work performed and the basis of the decisions taken.'

4.4 The form and content of working papers are affected by matters such as:

- The nature of the engagement

- The form of the auditors' report

- The nature and complexity of the entity's business

- The nature and condition of the entity's accounting and internal control systems

- The needs in the particular circumstances for direction, supervision and review of the work of members of the audit team

- The specific methodology and technology the auditors use

4.5 The SAS warns on the use of **standardised** working papers, for example, checklists, specimen letters, because they:

'may improve the efficiency with which such working papers are prepared and reviewed. While they facilitate the delegation of work and provide a means to control its quality, it is never appropriate to follow mechanically a standard approach to the conduct and documentation of the audit without regard to the need to exercise professional judgement.'

4.6 While auditors utilise schedules and analyses prepared by the entity, they require evidence that such information is properly prepared.

Examples of working papers

4.7 These include the following.

- Information concerning the legal and organisational structure of the client
- Information concerning the client's industry, economic and legal environment
- Evidence of the planning process and any changes thereto
- Evidence of the auditors' understanding of the accounting and internal control systems
- Evidence of inherent and control risk assessments and any revisions
- Analyses of transactions and balances
- Analyses of significant ratios and trends
- A record of the nature, timing, extent and results of auditing procedures
- Copies of communications with other auditors, experts and other third parties
- Copies of correspondence with the client
- Reports to directors or management
- Notes of discussions with the entity's directors or management
- A summary of the significant aspects of the audit
- Copies of the approved financial statements and auditors' reports

4.8 Working papers should show:

- The **name of** the **client**
- The **balance sheet date**
- The **file reference** of the working paper
- The **name of** the **person** preparing the working paper
- The **date the working paper** was **prepared**
- The **subject** of the working paper
- The **name of** the **person reviewing** the working paper
- The **date** of the **review**

4.9 Working papers should also show:

- The **objective** of the work done
- The **source of information**
- How any **sample was selected** and the sample size determined
- The **work done**
- A **key** to any audit ticks or symbols
- Appropriate **cross-referencing**
- The **results obtained**
- **Analysis of errors** or other significant observations
- The **conclusions drawn**
- The **key points highlighted**

4.10 Firms should have standard **referencing** and **filing** procedures for working papers, to facilitate their review.

BPP PUBLISHING

4.11 Working paper files are generally split into sections with a lead schedule at the front showing the value of items in the amounts, and referenced to the working papers showing the work done and how in detail the balance is made up.

4.12 For recurring audits, working papers may be split between permanent and current audit files.

(a) **Permanent audit files** contain information of **continuing importance** to the audit.

- Engagement letters
- New client questionnaire
- The memorandum and articles
- Other legal documents such as prospectuses, leases, sales agreement
- Details of the history of the client's business
- Board minutes of continuing relevance
- Previous years' signed accounts, analytical review and management letters
- Accounting systems notes, previous years' control questionnaires

(b) **Current audit files** contain information of relevance to the current year's audit.

- Financial statements
- Accounts checklists
- Management accounts details
- Reconciliations of management and financial accounts
- A summary of unadjusted errors
- Report to partner including details of significant events and errors
- Review notes
- Audit planning memorandum
- Time budgets and summaries
- Letter of representation
- Management letter
- Notes of board minutes
- Communications with third parties such as experts or other auditors

They also contain working papers covering each audit area. These should include the following.

- A lead schedule including details of the figures to be included in the accounts,
- Problems encountered and conclusions drawn
- Audit programmes
- Risk assessments
- Sampling plans
- Analytical review
- Details of substantive tests and tests of control

4.13 Working papers should be properly referenced. The referencing system used should be **logical, facilitate review** by enabling reviewers to be able to find their way about the audit file easily and help ensure that **audit work** is **completely carried out** and no important tasks are missed.

4.14 **Automated** working paper packages have been developed which can make the documenting of audit work much easier. Such programs will aid preparation of working papers, lead schedules, trial balance and the financial statements themselves. These are automatically cross referenced, adjusted and balanced by the computer.

4.15 The **advantages** of automated working papers are as follows.

- The risk of errors is reduced.

- The working papers will be neater and easier to review.

- The time saved will be substantial as adjustments can be made easily to all working papers, including working papers summarising the key analytical information.

- Standard forms do not have to be carried to audit locations.

- Audit working papers can be transmitted for review via a modem, or fax facilities (if both the sending and receiving computers have fax boards and fax software).

Question 5

The auditing standard SAS 230 *Working Papers* contains the following statement on working papers.

'Auditors base their judgement as to the extent of working papers upon what would be necessary to provide an experienced auditor, with no previous connection with the audit, with an understanding of the work performed and the basis of the decisions taken.'

Describe four benefits that auditors will obtain from working papers that meet the above requirement in SAS 230.

Answer

- The reporting partner can be satisfied that work delegated by him has been completed adequately.

- Working papers are a record of work performed and conclusions drawn which might be necessary in the future, for example, in litigation.

- Good working papers and the planning and control of future audits.

- Preparing working papers encourages auditors to adopt a methodical approach. This is likely to improve quality.

Confidentiality, safe custody and ownership

> **SAS 230.4**
>
> Auditors should adopt appropriate procedures for maintaining the confidentiality and safe custody of their working papers.

4.16 Statute does not set down the period of retention of audit working papers; judgement must be used, and further consideration should be given to the matter before their destruction. The ACCA recommends seven years as a minimum period.

4.17 Working papers are the property of the auditors. They are not a substitute for, nor part of, the entity's accounting records.

4.18 Auditors must follow ethical guidance on the confidentiality of audit working papers. They may, at their discretion, release parts of or whole working papers to the entity, as long as disclosure does not undermine 'the independence or validity of the audit process'. Information should not be made available to third parties without the permission of the entity.

Client: *Woodright Ltd*

Subject: *Creditors*

Year end: *31 December 1993*

Prepared by	Reviewed by
........PC.............	....
Date:.......*16/2/94*.....	Date:..............

$H^3/_1$

Work done							
	Selected a sample of trade creditors as at 31 December and reconciled the supplier's statement to the year						
	end purchase ledger balance. Vouched any reconciling items to source documentation.						
Results							
	See $H^3/_2$						
	One credit note, relating to Woodcutter Ltd, has not been accounted for. An adjustment is required.						
	DEBIT	*Trade creditors*		*£4,975*			
	CREDIT	*Purchases*			*£4,975*	*H 1/2*	
	One other error was found, which was immaterial, and which was the fault of the supplier.						
	In view of the error found, however, we should recommend that the client management checks supplier						
	statement reconciliations, at least on the larger accounts - management letter point.						
Conclusion							
	After making the adjustment noted above, purchase ledger balances are fairly stated as at 31 December 1993.						

Review of audit working papers: practical points

4.19 Throughout the audit, a system of review of all working papers will be used. In the case of a large audit, the work of assistants will be reviewed by the supervisor(s). In turn, the audit manager will review the work of the supervisor and at least some, if not all, of the work performed by the assistants. The overall and final review will be undertaken by the audit engagement partner.

4.20 Each working paper should be initialled (or signed) and dated by the person who prepared it.

Client _ _ _ *ABC plc* _ _ _ _ _ _ _ _ _ _ _ _ _

Period _ _ *Y/E 31 Dec* _ *20X2* _

Subject _ _ _ *Fixed assets* _ _ _ _ _ _ _ _ _

Prepared by *AR* _ _ Date *6/2/X3* _ _
Reviewed by *PW* _ _ Date *9/2/X3* _

F1

4.21 When a review takes place, the reviewer will often use a separate working paper to record queries and their answer.

4.22 The need to sign off all working papers and queries acts as an extra check, helping to ensure that all work has been carried out and completed.

4.23 After the supervisor has reviewed the work of the assistants there will usually be (in larger audit firms):

- A **manager review**, which will cover some of the assistants' work and an overall review of the audit work

- An **engagement partner review**, which will look at the manager's review, any controversial areas of the audit, the auditors' report etc

---

Chapter roundup

- The auditors must be able to evaluate all types of audit evidence in terms of its sufficiency and appropriateness.

- Evidence can be in the form of tests of controls or substantive procedures.

- Tests of control concentrate on the design and operation of controls.

- Substantive testing aims to test all the financial statement assertions.

    ° Existence
    ° Rights and obligations (ownership)
    ° Occurrence
    ° Completeness
    ° Valuation
    ° Measurement
    ° Presentation and disclosure

- The **reliability** of audit evidence is influenced by its **source** and by its **nature.**

- Audit evidence can be obtained by the following techniques.

    ° Inspection
    ° Observation
    ° Enquiry and confirmation
    ° Computation
    ° Analytical procedures

- SAS 430 covers **audit sampling**. The main stages of sampling are:

    ° Design of the sample
    ° Selection of the sample
    ° Evaluation of sample results

- **Sample sizes for tests of control** are influenced by:

    ° Sampling risk
    ° Tolerable error rate
    ° Expected error rate

- **Sample sizes for substantive tests** are influenced by:

    ° Inherent, control and detection risk
    ° Tolerable error rate
    ° Expected error rate
    ° Population value
    ° Stratification

- **Sample sizes** can be chosen by a variety of means including:

BPP PUBLISHING

- °   Random selection
- °   Systematic selection
- °   Haphazard selection

- When evaluating results, auditors should:

  - °   Analyse any errors considering their amount and the reasons why they have occurred
  - °   Draw conclusions for the population as a whole.

- **Monetary unit sampling (MUS)** makes it much easier to test populations substantively, by adopting many of the techniques in attribute sampling.

- Auditors may use a number of computer assisted audit techniques including:

  - °   Audit interrogation software
  - °   Test data
  - °   Embedded audit facilities
  - °   Simulation
  - °   Logical path analysis
  - °   Code comparison programs

- It is important to document audit work performed in working papers. This is to:

  - °   Enable reporting partner to ensure all planned work has been completed adequately
  - °   Provide details of work done for future reference
  - °   Assist is planning and control of future audits
  - °   Encourage a methodical approach and therefore quality

- Working papers should be headed in a certain way and contain certain information. They may be automated.

Quick quiz

1   Define sufficiency and appropriateness of evidence in one line each.

2   Name seven financial statement assertions.

3   Fill in the **blanks**

Audit evidence from external sources is .... than that obtained from the entity's records.

Evidence obtained directly .... is more ....
than that obtained by or from the entity.

4   Match the definitions to the terms

(a) Sampling risk
(b) Non-sampling risk

(i)   The risk that the auditors' conclusion, based on a sample, may be different from the conclusions that would be reached if the entire population was subject to the same audit procedure.

(ii) The risk that the auditors might use inappropriate procedures or might misinterpret evidence and thus fail to recognise an error.

5   Name three methods of sample selection

1   ....
2   ....
3   ....

6   Name two types of audit software

1   ....
2   ....

7   Give two advantages and one disadvantage of standardised working papers.

1   1   ....

2   ....

8   Complete the table, using the working papers given below.

Current audit file	Permanent audit file

engagement letters	new client questionnaire
financial statements	management letter
accounts checklists	audit planning memo
board minutes of continuing relevance	accounting systems notes

Answers to quick quiz

1   Sufficiency is the measure of the quantity of audit evidence.
    Appropriateness is the measure of the quality/reliability of audit evidence.

2   Existence, right and obligations, occurrence, completeness, valuation, measurement, presentation and disclosure.

3   More reliable
    By auditors, reliable

4   (a)   (i)
    (b)   (ii)

5   Random
    Haphazard
    Systematic

6   See the list at para 3.5

7   **Advantages**   **Disadvantage**

    1   Facilitate the delegation of work   1   Detracts from proper exercise of profession
    2   Means to control quality   judgement

8 | **Current audit file** | **Permanent audit file** |
    | --- | --- |
    | financial statements | engagement letters |
    | management letter | new client questionnaire |
    | accounts checklists | board minutes of continuing relevance |
    | audit planning memo | accounting systems notes |

Now try the question below from the Exam Question Bank

Number	Level	Marks	Time
8	Exam	20	36 mins

BPP PUBLISHING

Part C
Internal controls

Chapter 9

INTERNAL CONTROL AND AUDIT RISK EVALUATION

Topic list	Syllabus reference
1 Features of accounting and control systems	5
2 Controls in a computer environment	5
3 Controls in on-line and real-time systems	5
4 Internal controls and their inherent limitations	5
5 Assessment of accounting and control systems	5
6 Acting on assessment of accounting and control systems	5
7 Recording of accounting and control systems	5

Introduction

The modern audit encompasses reliance on internal controls in order to reduce the amount of testing of final balances.

The evaluation of a client's system will generally take place at the planning stage, when it will also be recorded and assessed. If the auditors wish to rely on the **internal controls** within the system, then these controls must be tested.

We shall examine the detailed controls that businesses operate in Chapters 10 and 11. You should bear in mind the principles discussed in this chapter when considering the controls needed over specific accounting and other system areas.

Study guide

Section 10

- Describe the objectives of internal control systems and the responsibility for internal control system in the context of organisational objectives

- Describe the importance of internal control to auditors

- Describe and illustrate the limitations of internal control systems in the context of fraud and error

- Explain the need to modify the audit plan in the light of the results of tests of control

Exam Guide

There is likely to be a question on internal controls in the exam, as there was on the pilot paper. Remember exam questions can cover the controls that ought to be operating, or how auditors should test the controls that are in place.

BPP
PUBLISHING

1   FEATURES OF ACCOUNTING AND CONTROL SYSTEMS

> ### KEY TERM
>
> An **internal control system** comprises the control environment and control procedures. It includes all the policies and procedures (internal controls) adopted by the directors and management of an entity to ensure, as far as practicable, the orderly and efficient conduct of its business, including adherence to internal policies, the safeguarding of assets, the prevention and detection of fraud and error, the accuracy and completeness of the accounting records, and the timely preparation of reliable financial information. Internal controls may be incorporated within computerised accounting systems. However the internal control system extends beyond those matters which relate directly to the accounting system.

1.1   SAS 300 *Accounting and internal control systems and audit risk assessments* covers the whole area of controls.

Control environment

1.2   Control environment is the framework within which controls operate. The control environment is very much determined by the management of a business.

> ### KEY TERM
>
> **Control environment** is the overall attitude, awareness and actions of directors and managers regarding internal controls and their importance in the entity. The control environment encompasses the management style, and corporate culture and values shared by all employees. It provides the background against which the various other controls are operated.

1.3   The SAS adds to the definition of the control environment that a strong control environment does not, by itself, ensure the effectiveness of the overall internal control system. However, aspects of the control environment (such as management attitudes towards control) will be a significant factor in determining **how controls operate**.

1.4   Controls are more likely to operate well in an environment where they are treated as being important. In addition consideration of the control environment will, as shown above, mean considering whether certain controls (internal audits, budgets) actually exist.

1.5   The following factors will be reflected in the control environment.

CONTROL ENVIRONMENT	
Philosophy and **operating style** of management	Consider attitude towards controls - do management override controls? Do they neglect controls? Do they concentrate solely on results and targets and encourage employees to do likewise?
	Examine attitudes to financial reporting and how these are manifest, for example in choice of accounting policies and view of accounting function

	Consider also attitudes to business risk and ethics – does management set a clear example? Is there a formal code of ethics?
	Does management have a clear commitment to maintaining and enhancing competence of all employees?
Organisation structure and segregation of duties	Consider delegation of authority and accountability. Segregation of duties - the principle that no single person should record and process all stages of a transaction - is vital
Directors' methods of imposing controls	Consider extent to which management supervise operations and how control is exercised (whether management solely use informal methods or have formal procedures such as budgets, management accounts, audit committee and internal audit)
	Personnel policies including recruitment, training, appraisal, rewards and discipline are also important

Segregation of duties

1.6 **Segregation of duties** is a vital aspect of the control environment. Segregation of duties implies a **number of people** being involved in the accounting process.

1.7 This makes it more difficult for fraudulent transactions to be processed (since a number of people would have to collude in the fraud), and it is also more difficult for accidental errors to be processed (since the more people are involved, the more checking there can be). Segregation should take place in various ways:

(a) **Segregation of function.** The key functions that should be segregated are the **carrying out** of a transaction, **recording** that transaction in the accounting records and **maintaining custody** of assets that arise from the transaction.

(b) The various **steps** in carrying out the transaction should also be segregated. We shall see how this works in practice when we look at the major control cycles in Chapters 10 and 11.

(c) The **carrying out** of various **accounting operations** should be segregated. For example the same staff should not record transactions and carry out the reconciliations at the period-end.

Control procedures

KEY TERM

Control procedures are those policies and procedures in addition to the control environment which are established to achieve the entity's specific objectives.

1.8 The definition of control procedures is extended in the SAS. Control procedures include those designed to **prevent** or to **detect** and **correct** errors. We have already discussed the importance of segregation of duties, and the SAS lists some other specific control procedures.

Approval and control of documents

1.9 Transactions should be **approved** by an appropriate person (for example, overtime being approved by departmental managers). Important aspects of documentation are:

(a) **Multi-part documents**. Copies are sent to everyone who needs to know about the event recorded in the document.

(b) **Pre-numbering of documents**. Missing numbers in a sequence may indicate that operations have not been **recorded** or have **not** been **processed** further, for example outstanding orders.

(c) **Standardisation of documents**. Each document should be in a standard format showing clearly the required information.

Checking the arithmetical accuracy of records

1.10 An example of this type of control would be checking to see individual invoices have been added up correctly.

Maintaining and reviewing individual accounts, control accounts and trial balances

1.11 Control accounts bring together transactions in individual ledgers, trial balances bring together transactions for the organisation as a whole. Preparing these can highlight unusual transactions or accounts. Review of individual expense accounts can highlight whether certain regular expenses are unreasonable (for example, electrical and telephone).

Reconciliations

1.12 Reconciliations involve comparison of a specific balance in the accounting records with what another source says that balance should be. Differences between the two figures should only be due to valid reconciling items. A good example is a bank reconciliation.

Comparing the results of cash, security and stock counts with accounting records

1.13 An example of this is a physical count of petty cash where the balance shown in the cash book should be the amount of cash in the petty cash box.

Comparing internal data with external sources of information

1.14 An example would be comparing records of goods despatched to customers with customer acknowledgement of goods that have been received.

Limiting direct physical access to assets and records

1.15 Authorised personnel alone should have access to certain assets, particularly those which are valuable or portable. An example would be ensuring the stock store is only open when the stores personnel are there, and is locked at other times.

1.16 Restricting access to records can be a particular problem in computerised systems.

Small companies – the problem of control

1.17 Many of the controls which would be relevant to a large enterprise are neither practical nor appropriate for the small enterprise. For these the most important form of internal control is generally the **close involvement** of the **directors or proprietors**. However, that very involvement will enable them to **override controls** and, if they wish, to **exclude transactions** from the records.

1.18 Auditors can have difficulties not because there is a general lack of controls but because the evidence available as to their operation and the completeness of the records is insufficient.

1.19 **Segregation of duties** will often appear inadequate in enterprises having a small number of staff. Similarly, because of the scale of the operation, organisation and management controls are likely to be rudimentary at best.

1.20 The onus is on the proprietor, by virtue of his day-to-day involvement, to compensate for this lack. This involvement should encompass physical, authorisation, arithmetical and accounting checks as well as supervision.

1.21 However it is important to stress that in a well run small company there will be a system of internal control. In any case, all companies must comply with the provisions of the Companies Act concerning the maintenance of a proper accounting system.

1.22 Where the manager of a small business is not himself the owner, he may not possess the same degree of commitment to the running of it as an owner-manager would. In such cases, the auditors will have to consider the adequacy of controls exercised by the shareholders over the manager in assessing internal control.

2   CONTROLS IN A COMPUTER ENVIRONMENT

2.1 The expansion in the use of computers for accounting purposes will certainly continue. Auditors must therefore be able to cope with the special problems that arise when auditing in a computer environment.

2.2 First we look in a rather general way at the nature of controls in a computer environment. Broad guidance is provided for the auditor in the form of the old APC operational guideline *Auditing in a computer environment*.

> 'Computer systems record and process transactions in a manner which is significantly different from manual systems, giving rise to such possibilities as a lack of visible evidence and systematic errors. As a result, when auditing in a computer environment, the auditor will need to take into account additional considerations relating to the techniques available to him, the timing of his work, the form in which the accounting records are maintained, the internal controls which exist, the availability of the data and the length of time it is retained in readily usable form.'

KEY TERMS

Application controls relate to the transactions and standing data appertaining to each computer-based accounting system and are therefore specific to each such application.

The objectives of application controls, which may be manual or programmed, are to ensure the completeness and accuracy of the accounting records and the validity of the entries made in these records resulting from both manual and programmed processing.

General controls are controls, other than application controls, which relate to the environment within which computer based accounting systems are developed, maintained and operated, and which are therefore applicable to all the applications. The objectives of general controls are to ensure the proper development and implementation of applications and the integrity of program and data files and of computer operations. Like application controls, general controls may be either manual or programmed.

2.3 Application controls and general controls are inter-related. Strong general controls contribute to the assurance which may be obtained by an auditor in relation to application controls. On the other hand, unsatisfactory general controls may **undermine strong application** controls or exacerbate unsatisfactory application controls.

2.4 The following points will particularly influence the auditors' approach.

(a) Before auditors place reliance on application controls which involve computer programs, they need to obtain reasonable assurance that the programs have **operated properly**.

(b) Often transactions will be generated automatically without the need for human agency. Sometimes a programmed accounting procedure may not be subject to effective application controls. In such circumstances, in order to put themselves in a position to limit the extent of substantive procedures, the auditors may choose to perform tests of controls by **testing** the **relevant general controls**.

(c) Computer systems are generally more reliable than manual systems, but in a computer environment there is the possibility of **systematic errors**. This may take place because of program faults or hardware malfunction in computer operations. However, many such potential recurrent errors should be prevented or detected by general controls over the development and implementation of applications and the integrity of the program and data files.

(d) The extent to which the auditors can rely on general controls may be **limited** because many of these controls might not be evidenced, or because they could have been performed inconsistently.

(e) There may be a lack of **segregation of duties**, with users authorised to perform various accounting functions. This particularly applies in on-line and real-time systems (see Section 3).

(f) Detailed knowledge of computer **operations, programs** and **files** may be confined to a few people or even a single person. This may increase the opportunity to commit an undiscovered fraud by changing **programs** or **data**.

Management policy

2.5 It is important for management to have a clear overall policy on the use of computers. A policy statement should include the following:

- Commitment to information security
- Procedures including passwords, data protection and information distribution
- Legal requirements (data protection legislation) and licensing agreements
- Overall supervision by senior management
- Consequences of disobeying the rules

2.6 A policy statement is of particular importance if users are operating on personal computers. Instructions should include policies on:

- Environmental protection
- Security
- Anti-virus checks
- Training
- Documentation standards
- Error correction procedures
- Back-up procedures

Examples of application controls

2.7 To achieve the overall objectives of application controls identified above, the specific requirements are controls over:

- **Completeness, accuracy** and **authorisation** of **input**
- **Completeness** and **accuracy** of **processing**
- **Maintenance** of **master files** and the **standing data contained therein**.

Standing data is data that will be used over and over again eg staff grades, or rates of pay. Master files use this data and store an accumulation of transactions.

Controls over input

2.8 Control techniques for ensuring the **completeness** of input in a timely fashion include:

- **Manual** or **programmed agreement** of control totals
- **Document counts**
- **One for one checking** of **processed output** to source documents
- **Manual** or **programmed sequence checking**
- **Programmed matching** of **input** to a **control file**, containing details of expected input
- **Procedures** over **resubmission** of **rejected controls**

2.9 Controls over the **accuracy** of input are concerned with the data fields on input transactions. Control should be exercised not only over **value** fields, such as invoice amounts, but also important **reference** fields, such as account number or date of payment.

2.10 Techniques to ensure accuracy include:

- **Programmed check digit verification** (a digit included in a reference number which is arithmetically checked for having the required relationship to the rest of the number)

- **Programmed reasonableness checks,** including checking the logical relationship between two or more files

- **Programmed existence checks** of customer name, code against valid lists of customers, codes etc

- **Programmed checks** that **characters** are of **correct type**

- **Programmed checks** that **number** and **format** of characters are **correct**

- **Programmed checks** that **all necessary information** is present

- **Programmed checks** that **input** is within **permitted range**

- **Manual scrutiny of output** and checking to **source documents**

- **Manual** or **programmed agreement** of **control totals**

2.11 Controls over **authorisation** involve checking:

- All transactions are authorised.
- The individual who authorised each transaction was empowered to do so.

This will generally involve a clerical review of input transactions, although a programmed check to detect transactions that exceed authorisation limits may be possible.

Controls over processing

2.12 Controls are required to ensure that:

- All **input** data is **processed**.

- The **correct master** files and **standing data** files are used.

- The **processing** of each transaction is **accurate**.

- The **updating of data**, and any new data generated during processing, is **accurate and authorised**.

- **Output reports** are **complete** and **accurate**.

- The **user does not log out** before processing is complete.

2.13 The control techniques used to ensure the completeness and accuracy of input may also be used to ensure the completeness and accuracy of processing. The techniques must be applied to the results of processing, such as a batch reconciliation produced after the update and not the one produced after the initial edit. **Screen warnings** (do you wish to save your work) can ensure that users do not log out before completing all the necessary routines.

Controls over master files and standing data

2.14 Techniques for ensuring the completeness, accuracy and authorisation of amendments to master files and standing data files and for ensuring the completeness and accuracy of the processing of these amendments are similar to the techniques for transaction input.

2.15 The following controls may be particularly important.

(a) **One to one checking** may be used extensively because of the greater importance of master files and standing data.

(b) All **master files** and **standing data** may be reviewed cyclically.

(c) **Record counts** and **hash totals** may be used every time master files are used. (Record counts are counts of the total number of documents processed. Hash totals are the totals of, for example, the payroll numbers of all staff members on a payroll. That total can be used as a check that all records have been processed, but is otherwise of no significance.)

(d) **Controls** may be exercised over the **deletion** of accounts which contain a current balance.

Examples of general controls

2.16 To achieve the overall objectives of general controls identified above, controls may be needed in the following areas.

GENERAL CONTROLS	
Development of computer applications	Standards over **systems design, programming and documentation**
	Full **testing procedures** using test data
	Approval by **computer users** and **management**
	Segregation of duties so that those responsible for design are not responsible for testing
	Installation procedures so that data is not corrupted in transition
	Training of staff in new procedures and availability of adequate documentation

GENERAL CONTROLS	
Prevention of unauthorised changes to programs	**Segregation of duties**
	Full records of program **changes**
	Password protection of programs so that access is limited to computer operations staff
	Restricting access to **central computer** by locked doors, keypads and other access controls
	Maintenance of programs logs
	Virus checks on software, use of anti-virus software and policy prohibiting use of non-authorised programs or files
	Back-up copies of programs being taken and stored in other locations
	Control copies of programs being preserved and regularly **compared** with **actual programs**
	Stricter controls over certain programs (utility programs) by use of **read only memory** and file **libraries**
Testing and documentation of program changes	Complete **testing procedures**
	Documentation standards
	Approval of changes by computer users and management
	Training of staff using programs
Prevention of use of wrong programs or files being used	**Operation controls** over programs
	Libraries of programs
	Proper job scheduling
Prevention of unauthorised changes to data files	See section below on real-time systems
Controls to ensure continuity of operation	**Storing extra copies** of programs and data files off site
	Protection of equipment against fire and other hazards
	Back-up power sources
	Emergency procedures
	Disaster recovery procedures eg availability of back-up computer facilities.
	Maintenance agreements and **insurance**

3 CONTROLS IN ON-LINE AND REAL-TIME SYSTEMS

Nature of on-line and real-time systems

3.1 Whilst traditional batch processing is still a common method of using a computer to process accounting data there is a rapid increase in the use of an on-line system, including those in real-time.

3.2 **On-line** systems provide the facilities for data to be passed to and from the central computer via remote terminals. **Real-time** systems are a further development of on-line systems and permit immediate updating of computer held files. The data input and file update phases are therefore merged and the system accepts individual transactions rather than batches of data.

Controls in real-time systems

3.3 There are certain control problems associated with most real-time systems. The main points to remember are as follows. We are concerned primarily with larger, multi-user systems. By **terminals** we mean either dumb terminals or networked PCs.

Segregation of duties

3.4 The same person is often responsible for producing **and** processing the same information. To compensate for the reduction in internal check, supervisory controls should be strengthened.

3.5 The role of the systems administrator is particularly important; he should be responsible for backing up files, authorising users, controlling the file server and investigating problems.

Data file security

3.6 The ability of a person using a remote terminal to gain access to databases at will results in the need for special controls to ensure that files are neither read nor written to (nor destroyed), either accidentally or deliberately, without proper authority.

(a) The controls may be partly **physical**. For example:

    (i) **Access to terminals** is **restricted** to authorised personnel.

    (ii) The **terminals** and the **rooms** in which they are kept are **locked** when not in use or have entry restricted to authorised cardholders, or by keypad codes.

(b) They may be partly controlled by the **operating system**, including the following.

    (i) The use of **passwords** (or lockwords), or **special badges** or keys, sometimes linked to a user's personal identification code which must be used before the terminal operator can gain access to the computer/particular files.

    In some systems one password or other identification is required before it is possible to read a file, a second before it is possible to write new data and yet a third if both operations are permitted. Obviously, the code given to a particular individual will depend on his job function and status within the organisation.

    More sophisticated controls might include voice and fingerprint recognition.

    (ii) **Restriction** by the operating system of **certain users** to **certain files**. For example, the PC in the wages department may only be given access to the wages files.

    (iii) **Logging** of all **attempted violations** of the above controls possibly accompanied by the automatic shut down of the PC or terminal used. Obviously all violations should be speedily and thoroughly investigated.

    (iv) **Reviews** of **systems records** of entries made to system and files accessed.

    (v) **Internet controls**. Unauthorised users may be able to access businesses' internal systems to obtain confidential information, or to launch a virus that disrupts internal systems. Controls include **firewalls** which disable part of the communication technology that normally allows two-way communication, so that external contacts are denied access to part of the system. Other possibilities are **encryption** of data, and **callback** to external customers who wish to access the system.

(c) **Application controls** may include validity checks on input and reporting of unusual transactions.

3.7 Passwords are particularly important and there are various procedures that can be implemented to prevent unauthorised use of passwords.

• Passwords should be changed regularly, for example, every month and if possible changed by the user.

- Passwords should be of a reasonable length, and possibly mix numbers and words to minimise the possibility of their being guessed.

- Passwords should not be displayed when being input.

- Re-use of old passwords should not be permitted.

- The system should automatically 'log-off' if a terminal is not used for a certain time.

- If someone tries to log on with the wrong password, the terminal should be disabled after two or three wrong attempts.

Server security

3.8 Access controls on the server are particularly important, since interference here can damage the whole system. The server should not also be used as a normal terminal, and it should be in secure accommodation.

Back-ups

3.9 Back-ups must be taken at least **daily**, and separately on a weekly basis. In a real time system it may be necessary to have a cut off time after which no further transactions are ever posted. Attempts to open a file when a back-up is in progress can sometimes corrupt the process. Stray transactions posted after the back-up has been done could be lost if there is some sort of accident and the back-up data has to be restored in full the next day.

3.10 On the other hand, immediate access to files allows more sophisticated checks to be performed. For example it allows more extensive use of computer matching, where the information input may be checked for accuracy against that held on file. Moreover, in spite of the potential for abuse, there is a distinct advantage to enabling users to correct certain types of error immediately.

Database management systems (DBMS)

3.11 DBMS are normally designed for use in real-time environments. They enable elements of data to be accessed by different programs. This avoids the duplication of data which inevitably occurs in a traditional system.

3.12 As data is normally only stored once, and may be accessible to all users that require it, the principal control problems raised concern the authorisation of data amendments and restriction of access to data. Any data amendments must take into account the requirements of all the users.

3.13 An **administration function** should be set up to run and control the day to day operation of the database, thereby enhancing segregation of duties (this function will be independent of the systems development personnel and programmers and data processing manager).

3.14 The audit of DBMS creates particular problems as the two principal CAATs, test data and audit software, tend to work unsatisfactorily in these systems. The auditors may, however, be able to use **embedded audit facilities**. The auditors should if possible be involved at the evaluation, design and development stages so that they are able to determine their audit requirements and identify control problems.

Electronic Data Interchange systems

3.15 Electronic Data Interchange (EDI) systems allow businesses to **transmit** standard business documents such as sales invoices or purchase orders **electronically**.

3.16 EDI systems pose a number of problems for auditors.

(a) **Originating documents** may be **eliminated,** and there may be a **lack of evidence** of the operation of controls.

(b) The **consequences** of **problems** may be **enhanced**. Greater integration between the various aspects of an entity's accounting system is likely, and problems with one business may have a serious impact upon its suppliers or competitors. Computer failures may rapidly lead to material losses.

(c) The **risk of unauthorised access** to data may be **increased**. Not only will a business have to have its own controls, but it will have to rely as well on the controls operated by its business partners.

3.17 Controls over transmission including **acknowledgements, agreements** by both parties of amounts transmitted, **authentication codes** and **encryption** are particularly important. Transactions should be monitored continuously by **checking** the **sequence** of transaction numbers and **integrated test facilities** within the computer. **Limitation controls,** such as only allowing transactions with certain businesses, can be built into the organisation's computer system. There should also be **virus protection** and appropriate **insurance,** and **contingency plans** and **back-up arrangements**.

3.18 Auditors are likely to have to place significant reliance on controls and may be able to **test compliance** with agreed **best practice**. Auditors may also be able to obtain assurance on the working of controls of business partners by obtaining a certificate from their auditors.

4 INTERNAL CONTROLS AND THEIR INHERENT LIMITATIONS

4.1 SAS 300 states that the directors of an entity will set up internal controls in the accounting system to assess the following.

- **Transactions** are executed in accordance with **proper authorisation**.

- All transactions and other events are **promptly recorded** at the **correct amount,** in the **appropriate accounts** and in the **proper accounting period**.

- **Access to assets** is permitted only in accordance with proper authorisation.

- **Recorded assets** are **compared** with the **existing assets** at reasonable intervals and appropriate action is taken with regard to any differences.

4.2 However, any internal control system can only provide the directors with **reasonable assurance** that their objectives are reached, because of **inherent limitations**. These include

- The **costs** of control **not outweighing** their **benefits**
- The **potential** for **human error**

- **Collusion** between employees
- The possibility of **controls** being **by-passed** or **overridden** by management
- Controls being **designed to cope** with **routine** and **not non-routine transactions**

4.3 These factors show why auditors cannot obtain all their evidence from tests of the systems of internal control.

4.4 The key factors in the limitations of controls system are:

- Human error
- Potential for fraud

4.5 We have seen above that computer systems can detect and guard against logical errors. However, other simple errors such as incorrect amounts cannot be detected.

4.6 The safeguard of segregation of duties can help deter fraud. However, if employees decide to perpetrate frauds in harness, or management commit fraud by overriding systems, the accounting system will not be able to prevent such frauds.

4.7 This is one of the reasons that auditors need to be alert to the possibility of fraud and error, the subject of SAS 110, which was discussed in Chapter 5.

5   ASSESSMENT OF ACCOUNTING AND CONTROL SYSTEMS

5.1 Auditors are only concerned with assessing policies and procedures which are relevant to financial statement assertions. Auditors try to:

- **Assess the adequacy** of the accounting system as a basis for preparing the accounts
- **Identify** the types of **potential misstatements** that could occur in the accounts
- **Consider factors** that affect the **risk of misstatements**
- **Design appropriate audit procedures**

Accounting system and control environment

> ### SAS 300.3
>
> In planning the audit, auditors should obtain and document an understanding of the accounting system and control environment sufficient to determine their audit approach.

5.2 Auditors must obtain an **understanding** of the accounting system to enable them to identify and understand:

- **Major classes of transactions** in the entity's operations
- **How such transactions** are initiated
- **Significant accounting records**, supporting documents and accounts
- The **accounting and financial reporting process**

5.3 The factors affecting the **nature, timing and extent** of the **procedures** performed in order to understand the systems include:

- **Materiality** considerations
- The **size and complexity** of the entity
- Their **assessment** of **inherent risk**

BPP PUBLISHING

- The **complexity** of the entity's computer systems
- The **type of internal controls** involved
- The **nature of the entity's documentation** of specific internal controls

5.4 The auditors will normally update previous knowledge of the systems in the following ways.

- **Enquiries** of appropriate supervisory and other personnel
- **Inspection** of relevant documents and records produced by the systems
- **Observation** of the entity's activities and operations

5.5 Auditors must also make an assessment of whether accounting records fulfil Companies Act requirements.

Accounting records: statutory requirements

5.6 The **responsibility for installing and maintaining** a satisfactory **accounting system** rests, in the case of a company, with the **directors**. The Companies Act 1985 requires that companies shall keep accounting records which are sufficient to show and explain the company's transactions and are such that they:

- Disclose with reasonable accuracy, at any time, the financial position of the company at that time

- Enable the directors to ensure that any balance sheet and profit and loss account prepared under this Part complies with the requirements of this Act

5.7 S 221 goes on to state that the accounting records should show how **monies** have been **received** and **expended** and **record** the **assets** and **liabilities** of the company. If the company deals in goods, records should show **statements** of **stock held** at the **year end** and also **stocktake records** that form the basis of statements of stock held.

5.8 Officers of a company are liable to imprisonment or a fine (or both) if found guilty of knowingly failing to comply with the above sections.

5.9 During their assessment of the systems, the auditors will obtain knowledge of the design and operation of the systems. To confirm this knowledge, 'walk-through tests' are often performed.

> **KEY TERM**
>
> **Walk-through tests** involve tracing one or more transactions through the accounting system and observing the application of relevant aspects of the control system on these transactions.

5.10 Having assessed the accounting system and control environment, the auditors can make a **preliminary assessment** of whether the system is capable of producing reliable financial statements and of the likely mix of tests of control and substantive procedures.

Control risk

SAS 300.4

If auditors, after obtaining an understanding of the accounting system and control environment, expect to be able to rely on their assessment of control risk to reduce the extent of their substantive procedures, they should make a preliminary assessment of control risk for material financial statement assertions, and should plan and perform tests of control to support that assessment.

5.11 Assessment of control risk is not necessary when the auditors decide it is likely to be **impossible** to rely on any assessment to reduce their substantive testing. In such cases control risk is assumed to be **high**. It may also be inefficient to test controls if for example the population consists of a few large items which can be tested quickly by substantive tests.

Preliminary assessment of control risk

5.12 This evaluation of the accounting and control systems' effectiveness in correcting material misstatements will entail consideration of the design of the systems. Auditors should remember that some control risk will always exist as internal controls have inherent limitations (as we have seen above).

Relationship between the assessments of inherent and control risks

5.13 Where inherent risk is high, management may institute a more rigorous accounting and control systems to prevent and detect material misstatements. This interrelationship means that inherent and control risks should often be assessed in combination.

6 ACTING ON ASSESSMENT OF ACCOUNTING AND CONTROL SYSTEMS

Tests of control

6.1 Tests of controls are used to confirm auditors' assessments of the operation of control systems.

KEY TERM

Tests of control are tests to obtain audit evidence about the effective operation of the accounting and internal control systems, that is, that properly designed controls identified in the preliminary assessment of control risk exist in fact and have operated effectively throughout the relevant period.

6.2 Tests of control may include the following.

Enquiries about, and observation of, internal control functions
Inspection of documents supporting controls or events to gain audit evidence that internal controls have operated properly, for example verifying that a transaction has been authorised or a reconciliation approved
Examination of evidence of **management views**, for example minutes of management meetings

BPP PUBLISHING

Reperformance of control procedures, for example reconciliation of bank accounts, to ensure they were correctly performed by the entity
Testing of the internal controls operating on **specific computerised systems**
Observation of controls. Auditors will consider the manner in which the control is being operated.

6.3 Auditors should consider:

- **How** controls were **applied**
- The **consistency** with which they were applied during the period
- **By whom** they were applied

6.4 **Changes** in the **operation** of **controls** (caused by change of staff etc) may increase control risk and tests of control may need to be modified to confirm effective operation during and after any change.

6.5 Radical changes in controls, including a periodic breakdown in controls, should be considered as **separate periods** by the auditors.

Interim testing

6.6 In relation to tests before the period end, the SAS states:

> **SAS 300.5**
>
> If intending to rely on tests of control performed in advance of the period end, auditors should obtain sufficient appropriate audit evidence as to the nature and extent of any changes in design or operation of the entity's accounting and internal control systems within the accounting period since such procedures were performed.

6.7 Further evidence must be obtained to augment the results of tests carried out at an interim audit, that is, before the period end.

Final assessment of control risk

> **SAS 300.6**
>
> Having undertaken tests of control, auditors should evaluate whether the preliminary assessment of control risk is supported.

6.8 Failures of controls to operate should be investigated, but in such cases the preliminary assessment may still be supported if the failure is isolated. More frequent failures may require the level of control risk to be revised.

6.9 When control risk assessment is revised, the nature, timing and extent of the auditors' planned substantive procedures should be modified.

Communication of weaknesses

6.10 The auditors may become aware of weaknesses in the system as a result of obtaining an understanding of those systems. Such weaknesses should be reported to management, as shall be discussed in Chapter 20. The issues which might arise to be reported are discussed in Chapters 10 and 11.

Question 1

An internal control system has been described as comprising 'the control environment and control procedures. It includes all the policies and procedures (internal controls) adopted by the directors and management of an entity to assist in achieving their objective of ensuring, as far as practicable, the orderly and efficient conduct of its business, including adherence to internal policies, the safeguarding of assets, the prevention and detection of fraud and error, the accuracy and completeness of the accounting records, and the timely preparation of reliable financial information'.

Explain the meaning and relevance to the auditors giving an opinion on financial statements of each of the management objectives above.

Answer

The auditors' objective in evaluating and testing internal controls is to determine the degree of reliance which they may place on the information contained in the accounting records. If they obtain reasonable assurance by means of tests of controls that the internal control system is effective in ensuring the completeness and accuracy of the accounting records and the validity of the entries therein, they may limit the extent of their substantive procedures.

(a)   *'the orderly and efficient conduct of its business'*

An organisation which is efficient and conducts its affairs in an orderly manner is much more likely to be able to supply the auditors with sufficient appropriate audit evidence on which to base their audit opinion. More importantly, the level of inherent and control risk will be lower, giving extra assurance that the financial statements do not contain material errors.

(b)   *'adherence to internal policies'*

Management is responsible for setting up an effective system of internal control and management policy provides the broad framework within which internal controls have to operate. Unless management does have a pre-determined set of policies, then it is very difficult to imagine how the company could be expected to operate efficiently. Management policy will cover all aspects of the company's activities and will range from broad corporate objectives to specific areas such as determining selling prices and wage rates.

Given that the auditors must have a sound understanding of the company's affairs generally, and of specific areas of control in particular, then the fact that management policies are followed will make the task of the auditors easier in that they will be able to rely more readily on the information produced by the systems established by management.

(c)   *'safeguarding of assets'*

This objective may relate to the physical protection of assets (for example locking monies in a safe at night) or to less direct safeguarding (for example ensuring that there is adequate insurance cover for all assets). It can also be seen as relating to the maintenance of proper records in respect of all assets.

The auditors will be concerned to ensure that the company has properly safeguarded its assets so that they can form an opinion on the existence of specific assets and, more generally, on whether the company's records can be taken as a reliable basis for the preparation of financial statements. Reliance on the underlying records will be particularly significant where the figures in the financial statements are derived from such records rather than as the result of physical inspection.

(d)   *'prevention and detection of fraud and error'*

The directors are responsible for taking reasonable steps to prevent and detect fraud. They are also responsible for preparing financial statements which give a true and fair view of the entity's affairs. However, the auditors must plan and perform their audit procedures and evaluate and report the results thereof, recognising that fraud or error may materially affect the financial statements. A strong system of internal control will give the auditors some assurance that frauds and errors are not occurring, unless management are colluding to overcome that system.

(e)   *'accuracy and completeness of the accounting records'/timely preparation of reliable financial information'*

This objective is most clearly related to statutory requirements relating to both management and auditors. The company has an obligation under the Companies Act 1985 to maintain proper accounting records. The auditors must form an opinion on whether the company has fulfilled this obligation and also conclude whether the financial statements are in agreement with the underlying records.

7 RECORDING OF ACCOUNTING AND CONTROL SYSTEMS

7.1 As mentioned above, there are several techniques for recording the assessment of control risk, that is, the system. One or more may be used depending on the complexity of the system.

- Narrative notes
- Questionnaires
- Checklists
- Flowcharts

7.2 Whatever method of recording the system is used, the record will usually be retained on the permanent file and updated each year.

Narrative notes

7.3 Narrative notes have the advantage of being simple to record. However they are awkward to change if written manually. Editing in future years will be easier if they are computerised. The purpose of the notes is to **describe** and **explain** the **system,** at the same time making any comments or criticisms which will help to demonstrate an intelligent understanding of the system.

7.4 For each system notes need to deal with the following questions.

- What functions are performed and by whom?
- What documents are used?
- Where do the documents originate and what is their destination?
- What sequence are retained documents filed in?
- What books are kept and where?

Narrative notes can be used to support flowcharts.

Flowcharts

7.5 There are two methods of flowcharting in regular use:

- Document flowcharts
- Information flowcharts

Document flowcharts

7.6 Document flowcharts are more commonly used because they are relatively easy to prepare.

- All documents are followed through from 'cradle to grave'.
- *All* operations and controls are shown.

We shall concentrate on document flowcharts.

Information flowcharts

7.7 Information flowcharts are prepared in the reverse direction from the flow: they start with the entry in the general/nominal ledger and work back to the actual transaction. They concentrate on significant information flows and key controls and ignore any unimportant documents or copies of documents.

Advantages of flowcharts

7.8 These are as follows.

(a) After a little experience they can be **prepared quickly**.

(b) As the information is presented in a standard form, they are fairly **easy to follow** and to review.

(c) They generally ensure that the system is **recorded in its entirety,** as all document flows have to be traced from beginning to end. Any 'loose ends' will be apparent from a cursory examination.

(d) They **eliminate** the need for **extensive narrative** and can be of considerable help in highlighting the salient points of control and any weaknesses in the system.

Disadvantages of flowcharts

7.9 These include the following.

(a) They are **only really suitable for describing standard systems**. Procedures for dealing with unusual transactions will normally have to be recorded using narrative notes.

(b) They are useful for recording the flow of documents, but once the **records** or the assets to which they relate have **become static** they **can no longer be used for describing the controls** (for example over fixed assets).

(c) Major **amendment is difficult** without redrawing.

(d) **Time** can be **wasted** by **charting areas** that are of no **audit significance** (a criticism of **document** not information flowcharts).

Questionnaires

7.10 We can look at two types of questionnaire here, each with a different purpose.

- **Internal Control Questionnaires (ICQs)** are used to ask whether controls exist which meet specific control objectives.

- **Internal Control Evaluation Questionnaires (ICEQs)** are used to determine whether there are controls which prevent or detect specified errors or omissions.

Internal Control Questionnaires (ICQs)

7.11 The major question which internal control questionnaires are designed to answer is 'How good is the system of controls?'

7.12 Where strengths are identified, the auditors will perform work in the relevant areas. If, however, weaknesses are discovered they should then ask:

- What errors or irregularities could be made possible by these weaknesses?

- Could such errors or irregularities be material to the accounts?

- What substantive procedures will enable such errors or irregularities to be discovered and quantified?

7.13 Although there are many different forms of ICQ in practice, they all conform to the following basic principles:

(a) They comprise a list of questions designed to determine whether desirable controls are present.

(b) They are formulated so that there is one to cover each of the major transaction cycles.

7.14 Since it is the primary purpose of an ICQ to evaluate the system rather than describe it, one of the most effective ways of designing the questionnaire is to phrase the questions so that all the answers can be given as 'YES' or 'NO' and a 'NO' answer indicates a weakness in the system. An example would be:

Are purchase invoices checked to goods received notes before being passed for payment?	YES/NO/Comments

A 'NO' answer to that question clearly indicates a weakness in the company's payment procedures.

7.15 The ICQ questions below dealing with goods inward provide additional illustrations of the ICQ approach.

Goods inward

(a) Are supplies examined on arrival as to quantity and quality?

(b) Is such an examination evidenced in some way?

(c) Is the receipt of supplies recorded, perhaps by means of goods inwards notes?

(d) Are receipt records prepared by a person independent of those responsible for:

    (i) Ordering functions

    (ii) The processing and recording of invoices

(e) Are goods inwards records controlled to ensure that invoices are obtained for all goods received and to enable the liability for unbilled goods to be determined (by pre-numbering the records and accounting for all serial numbers)?

(f) (i) Are goods inward records regularly reviewed for items for which no invoices have been received?

    (ii) Are any such items investigated?

(g) Are these records reviewed by a person independent of those responsible for the receipt and control of goods?

Internal Control Evaluation Questionnaires (ICEQs)

7.16 In recent years many auditing firms have developed and implemented an evaluation technique more concerned with assessing whether specific errors (or frauds) are possible rather than establishing whether certain desirable controls are present.

7.17 This is achieved by reducing the control criteria for each transaction stream down to a handful of key questions (or control questions). The characteristic of these questions is that they concentrate on the significant errors or omissions that could occur at each phase of the appropriate cycle if controls are weak.

7.18 The nature of the key questions may best be understood by reference to the examples on the following pages.

Internal control evaluation questionnaire: control questions

The sales (revenue) cycle

Is there reasonable assurance that:

(a) Sales are properly authorised?
(b) Sales are made to reliable payers?
(c) All goods despatched are invoiced?
(d) All invoices are properly prepared?
(e) All invoices are recorded?
(f) Invoices are properly supported?
(g) All credits to customers' accounts are valid?
(h) Cash and cheques received are properly recorded and deposited?
(i) Slow payers will be chased and that bad and doubtful debts will be provided against?
(j) All transactions are properly accounted for?
(k) Cash sales are properly dealt with?
(l) Sundry sales are controlled?
(m) At the period end the system will neither overstate nor understate debtors?

The purchases (expenditure) cycle

Is there reasonable assurance that:

(a) Goods or services could not be received without a liability being recorded?
(b) Receipt of goods or services is required in order to establish a liability?
(c) A liability will be recorded:
    (i) Only for authorised items
    (ii) At the proper amount?
(d) All payments are properly authorised?
(e) All credits due from suppliers are received?
(f) All transactions are properly accounted for?
(g) At the period end liabilities are neither overstated nor understated by the system?
(h) The balance at the bank is properly recorded at all times?
(i) Unauthorised cash payments could not be made and that the balance of petty cash is correctly stated at all times?

Wages and salaries

Is there reasonable assurance that:

(a) Employees are only paid for work done?
(b) Employees are paid the correct amount (gross and net)?
(c) The right employees actually receive the right amount?
(d) Accounting for payroll costs and deductions is accurate?

Stock

Is there reasonable assurance that:

(a) Stock is safeguarded from physical loss (eg fire, theft, deterioration)?
(b) Stock records are accurate and up to date?
(c) The recorded stock exists?
(d) The recorded stock is owned by the company?
(e) The cut off is reliable?
(f) The costing system is reliable?
(g) The stock sheets are accurately compiled?
(h) The stock valuation is fair?

Fixed tangible assets

Is there reasonable assurance that:

(a) Recorded assets actually exist and belong to the company?
(b) Capital expenditure is authorised and reported?
(c) Disposals of fixed assets are authorised and reported?

(d)   Depreciation is realistic?
(e)   Fixed assets are correctly accounted for?
(f)   Income derived from fixed assets is accounted for?

Investments

Is there reasonable assurance that:

(a)   Recorded investments belong to the company and are safeguarded from loss?
(b)   All income, rights or bonus issues are properly received and accounted for?
(c)   Investment transactions are made only in accordance with company policy and are appropriately authorised and documented?
(d)   The carrying values of investments are reasonably stated?

Management information and general controls

Is the nominal ledger satisfactorily controlled?
Are journal entries adequately controlled?
Does the organisation structure provide a clear definition of the extent and limitation of authority?
Are the systems operated by competent employees, who are adequately supported?
If there is an internal audit function, is it adequate?
Are financial planning procedures adequate?
Are periodic internal reporting procedures adequate?

7.19   Each key control question is supported by detailed control points to be considered. For example, the detailed control points to be considered in relation to key control question (b) for the expenditure cycle (Is there reasonable assurance that receipt of goods or services is required to establish a liability?) are as follows.

(1)   Is segregation of duties satisfactory?

(2)   Are controls over relevant master files satisfactory?

(3)   Is there a record that all goods received have been checked for:

   •   Weight or number?
   •   Quality and damage?

(4)   Are all goods received taken on charge in the detailed stock ledgers:

   •   By means of the goods received note?

   •   Or by means of purchase invoices?

   •   Are there, in a computerised system, sensible control totals (hash totals, money values and so on) to reconcile the stock system input with the creditors system?

(5)   Are all invoices initialled to show that:

   •   Receipt of goods has been checked against the goods received records?
   •   Receipt of services has been verified by the person using it?
   •   Quality of goods has been checked against the inspection?

(6)   In a computerised invoice approval system are there print-outs (examined by a responsible person) of:

   •   Cases where order, GRN and invoice are present but they are not equal ('equal' within predetermined tolerances of minor discrepancies)?

   •   Cases where invoices have been input but there is no corresponding GRN?

(7)   Is there adequate control over direct purchases?

(8)   Are receiving documents effectively cancelled (for example cross-referenced) to prevent their supporting two invoices?

7.20   Alternatively, ICEQ questions can be phrased so that the weakness which should be prevented by a key control is highlighted, such as the following.

Question	Answer	Comments or explanation of 'yes' answer
Can goods be sent to unauthorised suppliers?		

7.21 In these cases a 'yes' answer would require an explanation, rather than a 'no' answer.

Advantages and disadvantages of ICQs and ICEQs

7.22 ICQs have various advantages:

(a) If drafted thoroughly, they can ensure **all controls** are **considered.**

(b) They are **quick** to **prepare.**

(c) They are **easy** to **use** and **control.**

7.23 However they also have some disadvantages.

(a) The client may be able to **overstate controls.**

(b) They may contain a large number of **irrelevant controls.**

(c) They may not include **unusual controls,** which are nevertheless effective in particular circumstances.

(d) They can give the impression that all controls are of **equal** weight. In many systems one NO answer (for example lack of segregation of duties) will cancel out a string of YES answers.

7.24 ICEQs have the following advantages:

(a) Because they are drafted in terms of **objectives** rather than specific controls, they are easier to apply to a variety of systems than **ICQs.**

(b) Answering ICEQs should enable auditors to **identify the key controls** which they are most likely to test during control testing.

(c) ICEQs can **highlight areas of weakness** where extensive substantive testing will be required.

7.25 The principal disadvantage is that they can be **drafted vaguely,** hence **misunderstood** and important controls not identified.

Question 2

Explain the importance of the following control procedures.

(a) Segregation of duties
(b) Bank reconciliation
(c) Comparing the results of stock counts with accounting records.

Answer

(a) Segregation of duties is important because the more people that are involved in all the stages of processing a transaction, the more likely it is that fraud or error by a single person will be identified. In addition the more people that are involved, the less the changes of fraudulent collusion between them.

(b) A bank reconciliation is important because it reconciles the business's records of cash held at bank with the bank's records of cash held at bank. Written confirmation from the bank is strong evidence since it arises from an independent source and is in writing. Generally the only differences on the reconciliation should be timing differences on unpresented cheques or uncleared bankings. For large unpresented cheques and for all uncleared bankings the timing differences involved should be small.

(c) Stock is an important figure in the accounts often materially affecting both the profit and loss account and balance sheet. In addition the stock of many businesses is highly portable, and it is thus subject to a high risk of theft.

A main comparison of stock as recorded in the accounting records with actual stock held may identify differences which have to be investigated. The differences may be due to theft of stock but may also be due to failure to record stock movements properly. This may also mean that purchases or sales have been recorded incorrectly.

Chapter roundup

- There are always inherent limitations to internal controls.

- Specific **control procedures** include the following.

  ° Approval and control of documents
  ° Controls over computerised applications and the information technology environment
  ° Checking the arithmetical accuracy of the records
  ° Maintaining and reviewing control accounts and trial balances
  ° Reconciliations
  ° Comparing the results of cash, security and stock counts with accounting records
  ° Comparing internal data with external sources of information
  ° Limiting direct physical access to assets and records

- **Application controls** should ensure:

  ° The completeness, accuracy and authorisation of input
  ° The completeness and accuracy of processing
  ° The proper maintenance of master files and standing data

- **General controls** are required to:

  ° Ensure proper application development
  ° Prevent or detect unauthorised changes to programs
  ° Ensure that all program changes are adequately tested and documented
  ° Prevent or detect errors during program execution
  ° Prevent unauthorised amendments to data files
  ° Ensure that systems software is properly installed and maintained
  ° Ensure that proper documentation is kept
  ° Ensure continuity of operations

- The majority of modern systems are **real-time systems**, where users have instant and direct access to data. Important real-time controls are:

  ° Segregation of duties
  ° Data file security
  ° Program security
  ° Back-ups

- The auditors must **understand** the **accounting system** and **control environment** in order to determine the audit approach.

- Learn the CA 1985 requirements relating to the **accounting records**.

- Both **ICQs** and **ICEQs** are used to evaluate control systems.

- ICQs consist of a list of questions asking if various internal controls exist.

- ICEQs consist of a list of questions which are used to establish whether the system has internal controls that fulfil the important control objectives.

> • A report to directors or management may be sent after both the interim and final audits, or combined in one letter or report at the end. The primary purpose of the report is to inform the management of **weaknesses** in the system of **internal controls** but the letter can also be used for other purposes.

Quick quiz

1   Complete the definition taking the words given below.

.... is the overall ...., ... and actions of directors and managers regarding internal .... and their .... in the entity. The .... encompasses the management style and corporate culture and values shared by all .... It provides the background against which various other controls are operated.

> employees, controls, attitude, environment, control, awareness, importance, environment, control

2   Name two **key** inherent limitations of an internal control system

   1   ....

   2   ....

3   Put the controls below in the correct category

Application controls	General controls

one to one checking	virus checks	hash totals
segregation of duties	passwords	program libraries
review of master files	training	controls over account deletions
back-up copies	record counts	back-up power source

4   Which of the following is not a test of control.

   A   Inspection of documents
   B   Reperformance of control procedures
   C   Observation of controls
   D   Verification of value to invoice

5   Flowcharts are suitable for describing unusual systems

   True   ☐

   False   ☐

6   After the controls have been assessed, the audit plan may be modified.

   True   ☐

   False   ☐

Answers to quick quiz

1   Control environment, attitude, awareness, controls, importance, control environment, employees.

2   Human error
    Possibility of staff colluding in fraud

3	Application controls	General controls
	one to one checking	virus checks
	hash totals	program libraries
	review of master files	segregation of duties
	record counts	passwords
		controls over account deletion
		training
		back-up power source
		back-up copies

4   D

5   False

6   True

Now try the question below from the Exam Question Bank

Number	Level	Marks	Time
9	Exam	20	36 mins

Chapter 10

TESTS OF CONTROLS: INCOME CYCLES

Topic list	Syllabus reference
1 The sales system	5
2 The purchases and expenses system	5
3 The wages system	5
4 Smaller entities	5

Introduction

We have mentioned tests of controls in the last chapter and have considered methods of sample selection and evaluation. In this chapter we will look at **how tests of controls** might be **applied in practice**. We will examine each major component of an average accounting system.

In Chapter 9 we stated that the auditors must ascertain the accounting system and the system of internal control. The auditors will then decide which controls, if any, they wish to rely on and plan **tests of controls** to obtain the audit evidence as to whether such reliance can be warranted. For each of the systems listed above we will look at the system **objectives** the auditors will bear in mind while assessing the internal controls and give examples of common controls. We shall then go on to look at a 'standard' programme of tests of controls.

In this chapter we deal with **sales, purchases** and **wages and salaries**. These areas are the areas that are most commonly tested in auditing exams.

For **sales**, businesses want to give credit only to customers who will **pay their debts**. In addition there are various stages of the selling process- **ordering, despatch and charging**, all of which should be **documented** and **matched** so that customers receive what they ordered and are appropriately billed. In order to keep track of who owes what and to be able to identify slow-paying customers, a **sales ledger** should be maintained.

Similarly **purchases** must be controlled. Businesses should ensure that only **properly authorised purchases** which are necessary for the business are made. Again all stages of the purchase process, ordering, receiving goods and being charged for them should be **documented and matched** so that the business gets what it ordered and only pays for what it ordered and received. Businesses also need to keep track of what they owe to each supplier by maintaining a purchase ledger.

For **wages and salaries** businesses are trying to ensure that they only pay for **hours worked** and that they pay the **right staff** the **right amount**. Controls should also be in place to ensure **PAYE and VAT liabilities** are calculated correctly otherwise penalties may be imposed by the tax authorities.

Study guide

Section 11

- Describe, illustrate and analyse how internal control system over sales and purchase transaction cycles operate in both large and small entities.

BPP
PUBLISHING

- Describe and illustrate the use by auditors of internal control checklists for sales and purchase transaction cycles.

- Describe and tabulate tests of control of sales and purchases for inclusion in a work programme

Section 12

- Describe, illustrate and analyse how internal control systems over the payroll transaction cycle operate in both large and small entities

- Describe and illustrate the use by auditors of internal control checklists for the payroll transaction cycle

- Describe and tabulate tests of control of payroll for inclusion in a work program

Exam guide

The controls relating to receipts from sales were tested in the pilot paper. You should be aware of the links between the transaction cycles and the balance sheet - in the pilot paper, sales systems and debtors. In December 2001, controls in the purchases cycle were examined.

---

1   THE SALES SYSTEM   **Pilot paper**

Aims of controls

1.1   The most important aims of the control system relating to debtors and sales are:

Ordering and granting of credit

- **Goods** and **services** are **only supplied** to **customers** with **good credit ratings**
- **Customers** are encouraged to **pay promptly**
- **Orders** are **recorded correctly**
- **Orders** are **fulfilled**

Despatch and invoicing

- All **despatches** of goods are **recorded**
- All **goods and services** sold are **correctly invoiced**
- All **invoices** raised **relate to goods and services supplied** by the business
- **Credit notes** are only given for **valid reasons**

Recording, accounting and credit control

- All sales that have been **invoiced** are **recorded** in the general and sales ledgers
- All **credit notes** that have been **issued** are **recorded** in the general and sales ledgers
- All **entries** in the sales ledger are **made** to the **correct** sales ledger **accounts**
- **Cut-off** is applied correctly to the sales ledger
- Potentially **doubtful debts** are **identified**

Controls

1.2   The following controls relate to the **ordering and granting of credit** process.

- **Segregation** of duties; credit control, invoicing and stock despatch

- **Authorisation** of **credit terms** to customers

  - References/credit checks obtained
  - Authorisation by senior staff
  - Regular review

- **Authorisation** for changes in **other customer data**
  - ° Change of address supported by letterhead
  - ° Deletion requests supported by evidence balances cleared/customer in liquidation
- **Orders** only **accepted** from **customers** who have no credit problems
- **Sequential numbering** of blank pre-printed order documents
- **Correct prices quoted** to **customers**
- **Matching** of **customer orders** with production orders and despatch notes and querying of orders not matched
- **Dealing** with **customer queries**

1.3 The following checks relate to **despatches** and **invoice preparation**.

- **Authorisation** of **despatch** of **goods**
  - ° Despatch only on sales order
  - ° Despatch only to authorised customers
  - ° Special authorisation of despatches of goods free of charge or on special terms
- **Examination** of **goods outwards** as to quantity, quality and condition
- **Recording** of **goods outwards**
- **Agreement** of **goods outwards records** to **customer orders, despatch notes** and **invoices**
- **Prenumbering** of despatch notes and delivery notes and regular checks on sequence
- **Condition** of **returns checked**
- Recording of goods returned on **goods returned notes**
- **Signature** of **delivery notes** by customers
- Preparation of invoices and credit notes
  - ° **Authorisation** of **selling prices**/use of **price lists**
  - ° **Authorisation** of **credit notes**
  - ° **Checks on prices, quantities, extensions** and totals on invoices and credit notes
  - ° **Sequential numbering** of blank invoices/credit notes and regular sequence checks
- **Stock records updated**
- **Matching** of sales **invoices** with **despatch** and **delivery notes** and sales orders
- **Regular review** for **despatch notes** not matched by invoices

1.4 The following controls relate to **accounting, recording and credit problems.**

- **Segregation of duties:** recording sales, maintaining customer accounts and preparing statements
- **Recording** of **sales invoices** sequence and **control** over **spoilt invoices**
- **Matching** of **cash receipts** with **invoices**
- **Retention** of **customer remittance advices**
- **Separate recording** of **sales returns, price adjustments** etc
- **Cut-off procedures** to ensure goods despatched and not invoiced (or vice versa) are properly dealt with the correct period

BPP PUBLISHING

- Regular **preparation** of **debtor statements**
- **Checking** of **debtors' statements**
- **Safeguarding** of **debtor statements** so that they cannot be altered before despatch
- **Review** and **follow-up** of **overdue accounts**
- **Authorisation** of **writing off** of **bad debts**
- **Reconciliation** of **sales ledger control account**
- Analytical review of sales ledger and profit margins

Tests of controls

1.5 Auditors should carry out the following tests on **ordering** and **granting of credit** procedures.

- **Check** that **references** are being **obtained** for **all new customers**
- **Check** that all **new accounts** on the sales ledger have been **authorised** by senior staff
- **Check** that **orders** are only **accepted** from customers who are **within** their **credit terms** and **credit limits**
- **Check** that **customer orders** are being **matched** with **production orders** and **despatch notes**

1.6 The following tests should be carried out over **despatches** and **invoices.**

- Verify details of **trade sales** or goods despatched notes with **sales invoices** **checking**
    - **Quantities**
    - **Prices** charged with official price lists
    - **Trade discounts** have been properly dealt with
    - **Calculations** and **additions**
    - **Entries** in sales day book are correctly **analysed**
    - **VAT,** where chargeable, has been properly **dealt with**
    - **Postings** to sales ledger
- Verify details of trade sales with **entries in stock records**
- Verify **non-routine** sales (scrap, fixed assets etc) with:
    - **Appropriate supporting evidence**
    - **Approval** by authorised officials
    - **Entries** in **plant register**
- Verify **credit notes** with:
    - **Correspondence** or other supporting evidence
    - **Approval** by authorised officials
    - **Entries** in **stock records**
    - **Entries** in **goods returned records**
    - **Calculations** and **additions**
    - **Entries** in **day book**, checking these are correctly analysed
    - **Postings** to **sales ledger**
- **Test numerical sequence** of **despatch notes** and **enquire** into **missing numbers**

- Test numerical **sequence** of **invoices** and **credit notes, enquire** into **missing numbers** and **inspect copies** of those cancelled

- Test numerical **sequence** of **order forms** and enquire into missing numbers

- **Check** that **despatches** of **goods free of charge** or on **special terms** have been **authorised** by management

1.7 The following tests should be carried out over **recording** of and **accounting** for **sales,** and **problems control.**

Sales day book

- **Check entries** with **invoices** and **credit notes** respectively
- **Check additions** and **cross casts**
- **Check postings** to **sales ledger control account**
- **Check postings** to **sales ledger**

Sales ledger

- **Check** entries in a **sample of accounts** to sales day book
- **Check additions** and **balances** carried down
- **Note** and **enquire** into **contra entries**
- Check that **control accounts** have been **regularly reconciled** to total of sales ledger balances
- **Scrutinise accounts** to see if credit limits have been observed
- Check that **debtor statements** are **prepared** and **sent out regularly**
- Check that **overdue accounts** have been **followed up**
- Check that **all bad debts written off** have been **authorised** by management

Question 1

What tests of control can give auditors assurance that the company's system of control ensures that sales are completely recorded?

Answer

Tests of control over completeness of recording of sales include:

(a) Sequence tests on sales orders, despatch notes, invoices and credit notes to ensure that there are no missing numbers or two documents with the same number

(b) Comparisons of despatch notes with order and invoices, checking documents are cross-referenced to each other

(c) Checking posting of sales day book to sales ledger control account and sales ledger

(d) Checking control account reconciliations have been carried out and have been reviewed by senior staff

(e) Controls over computerised input including:

    (i) Control totals
    (ii) Checking of output to source documents
    (iii) Procedure over resubmisson of rejected inputs

Question 2

You are the auditor of Arcidiacono Stationery Ltd, and you have been asked to suggest how audit work should be carried out on the sales system.

Arcidiacono Stationery Ltd sells stationery to shops. Most sales are to small customers who do not have a sales ledger account. They can collect their purchases and pay by cash. For cash sales:

(a) The customer orders the stationery from the sales department, which raises a pre-numbered multi-copy order form.

(b) The dispatch department make up the order and give it to the customer with a copy of the order form.

(c) The customer gives the order form to the cashier who prepares a hand-written sales invoice.

(d) The customer pays the cashier for the goods by cheque or in cash.

(e) The cashier records and banks the cash.

Required

(a) State the weaknesses in the cash sales system.
(b) Describe the systems based tests you would carry out to check the controls over the system.

Answer

(a) The weaknesses in the cash system are as follows.

    (i) The physical location of the dispatch department and the cashier are not mentioned here, but there is a risk of the customer taking the goods without paying. The customer should pay the cashier on the advice note and return for the goods, which should only be released on sight of the paid invoice.

    (ii) There is a failure in segregation of duties in allowing the cashier to both complete the sales invoice and receive the cash as he could perpetrate a fraud by replacing the original invoice with one of lower value and keeping the difference.

    (iii) No-one checks the invoices to make sure that the cashier has completed them correctly, for example by using the correct prices and performing calculations correctly.

    (iv) The completeness of the sequence of sales invoices cannot be checked unless they are pre-numbered sequentially and the presence of all the invoices is checked by another person. The order forms should also be pre-numbered sequentially.

    (v) There is also no check that the cashier banks all cash received, ie this is a further failure of segregation of duties.

If the sales department prepared and posted the invoices and also posted the cash for cash sales to a sundry sales account, this would solve some of the internal control problems mentioned above. In addition, the sales department could run a weekly check on the account to look for invoices for which no cash had been received. These could then be investigated.

All of these weaknesses, and possible remedies, should be reported to management.

(b) After confirming the cash sales system was operating as described (by walk-through test) I would carry out the following tests.

    (i) Select a sample of order forms issued to customers during the year. Trace the related sales invoice and check that the details correlate (date, unit amounts etc). The customer should have signed for the goods and this copy should be retained by the despatch department.

    (ii) For the sales invoices discovered in the above test, I would check that the correct order form number is recorded on the invoice, that the prices used are correct (by reference to the prevailing price list) and that the castings and cross-castings (ie arithmetic) is correct.

    (iii) I will then trace the value of the sales invoices to the cash book and from the cash book that the total receipts for the day have been banked and appear promptly on the bank statement.

    (iv) I would check that the sales invoices have been correctly posted to a cash or sundry sales account. For any sales invoices missing from this account (assuming they are sequentially numbered), I will trace the cancelled invoice and check that the cancelled invoice was initialled by the customer and replaced by the next invoice in sequence.

    (v) Because of the weaknesses in the system I would carry out the following sequence checks on large blocks of order forms/invoices, eg four blocks of 100 order forms/invoices.

        (1) Check all order forms present; investigate those missing.
        (2) Check sales invoices raised for all order forms.
        (3) Check all sales invoices in a sequence have been used; investigate any missing.
        (4) Cash for each sales invoice has been entered into the cash book.

Using the results of the above tests I would decide whether the system for cash sales has operated without material fraud or error. If I am not satisfied that it has then I will consider qualifying my audit report on the grounds of limitation of scope.

---

2 THE PURCHASES AND EXPENSES SYSTEM   Dec 01

2.1   We will follow much the same procedure for the purchases and expenses system.

Aims of controls

2.2   The most important aims of the control system relating to creditors and purchases are:

Ordering

- All **orders for goods and services** are properly **authorised**, and are for **goods and services** that are actually **received** and are for the company
- Orders are only made to **authorised suppliers**
- Orders are made at **competitive prices**

Receipt and invoices

- All goods and services received are used for the **organisation's purposes**, and not private purposes
- Goods and services are **only accepted if** they have been **ordered**, and the **order** has been **authorised**
- All **goods** and **services received** are accurately **recorded**
- **Liabilities** are **recognised** for all **goods and services** that have been **received**
- All **credits** to which business is due are **claimed** and **received**
- **Receipt** of **goods** and **services** is **necessary** to establish a **liability to be recorded**

BPP PUBLISHING

Accounting

- All **expenditure** is for goods that are **received**
- **All expenditure** is **authorised**
- All **expenditure** that is made is **recorded** correctly in the general and purchase ledger
- All **credit notes** that are received are **recorded** in the general and purchase ledger
- All **entries** in the **purchase ledger** are **made** to the **correct purchase ledger accounts**
- **Cut-off** is **applied correctly** to the purchase ledger

Controls

2.3 The following controls should be in place over **ordering**.

- **Segregation** of duties; requisition and ordering
- **Central policy** for choice of suppliers
- Evidence required of **requirements** for purchase before purchase authorised (re-order quantities and re-order levels)
- **Order forms** prepared only when a **pre-numbered purchase requisition** has been **received**
- **Authorisation** of order forms
- **Prenumbered order forms**
- **Safeguarding** of **blank order forms**
- **Review** for **orders not received** or invoiced
- **Monitoring** of **supplier terms** and taking advantage of favourable conditions (bulk order, discount)

2.4 The client should carry out the following checks on **goods received** and invoices from suppliers.

• **Examination** of goods inwards
○ Quality
○ Quantity
○ Condition
• **Recording arrival** and **acceptance** of goods (prenumbered goods received notes)
• **Comparison** of **goods received notes** with **purchase orders**
• **Referencing** of supplier invoices; numerical sequence and supplier reference
• **Checking** of **suppliers' invoices**
○ Prices, quantities, accuracy of calculation
○ Comparison with order and goods received note
• **Recording return of goods** (pre-numbered goods returned notes)
• Procedures for **obtaining credit notes** from suppliers

2.5 The following controls should be in place over **accounting** for purchases.

- **Segregation** of **duties:** accounting and checking functions
- Prompt **recording of purchases** and **purchase returns** in day books and ledgers
- **Regular maintenance** of **purchase ledger**
- **Comparison** of **supplier statements** with **purchase ledger balances**
- **Authorisation** of **payments**
  - Authority limits

        ○   Confirmation that goods have been received, accord with purchase order, and are properly priced and invoiced

- **Review** of **allocation** of expenditure
- **Reconciliation** of **purchase ledger** control account to total of purchase ledger balances
- **Cut-off** accrual of goods received notes not matched by purchases at year-end

Tests of controls

2.6   A most important test of controls is for auditors to check that all **invoices** are **supported** by authorised **purchase invoices** and **purchase orders**. The officials who approve the invoices should be operating within laid-down **authority limits.**

2.7   Auditors should carry out the following tests on **receipts of goods** and **invoices.**

- Check invoices for goods, raw materials are:
    - **Supported** by **goods received notes** and **inspection notes**
    - **Entered** in **stock records**
    - **Priced correctly** by checking to **quotations, price lists** to see the price is in order
    - **Properly referenced** with a number and supplier code
    - **Correctly coded** by type of expenditure

    Trace entry in **record of goods returned** etc and see credit note duly received from the supplier, for invoices not passed due to defects or discrepancy

- For invoices of all types:
    - **Check calculations** and **additions**
    - **Check entries in purchase day book** and verify that they are correctly **analysed**
    - **Check posting** to **purchase ledger**

- For credit notes:
    - **Verify** the **correctness** of credit received with correspondence
    - **Check entries** in **stock records**
    - **Check entries** in **record of returns**
    - **Check entries** in **purchase day book** and verify that they are correctly analysed
    - **Check postings** to **purchase ledger**

- Check for returns that **credit notes** are duly **received** from the suppliers

- Test **numerical sequence** and enquire into missing numbers of:
    - Purchase requisitions
    - Purchase orders
    - Goods received notes
    - Goods returned notes
    - Suppliers' invoices

- **Obtain explanations** for **items** which have been **outstanding** for a long time:
    - Unmatched purchase requisitions
    - Purchase orders
    - Goods received notes (if invoices not received)
    - Unprocessed invoices

BPP PUBLISHING

Purchase day book

2.8 The following tests should be carried out over the recording of purchases.

- Verify that invoices and credit notes recorded in the purchase day book are:

    ° **Initialled** for prices, calculations and extensions
    ° **Cross-referenced** to purchase orders, goods received notes etc
    ° **Authorised** for payment

- **Check additions**

- **Check postings** to general ledger accounts and control account

- **Check postings** of entries to purchase ledger

Purchase ledger

- For a sample of accounts recorded in the purchase ledger

    ° **Test check entries** back into books of prime entry
    ° **Test check additions** and **balances** forward
    ° **Note** and **enquire** into all contra entries

- Confirm **control account balancing** has been regularly carried out during the year

- **Examine control account** for unusual entries

2.9 Once again the following question should help you to apply these 'standard' tests in an exam.

Question 3

Derek Limited operates a computerised purchase system. Invoices and credit notes are posted to the bought ledger by the bought ledger department. The computer subsequently raises a cheque when the invoice has to be paid.

Required

List the controls that should be in operation:

(a) Over the addition, amendment and deletion of suppliers, ensuring that the standing data only includes suppliers from the company's list of authorised suppliers

(b) Over purchase invoices and credit notes, to ensure only authorised purchase invoices and credit notes are posted to the purchase ledger

Answer

(a) Controls over the standing data file containing suppliers' details will include the following. These should prevent fraud by the creation of a fictitious supplier.

   (i) All amendments/additions/deletions to the data should be authorised by a responsible official. A standard form should be used for such changes.

   (ii) The amendment forms should be input in batches (with different types of change in different batches), sequentially numbered and recorded in a batch control book so that any gaps in the batch numbers can be investigated. The output produced by the computer should be checked to the input.

   (iii) A listing of all such adjustments should automatically be produced by the computer and reviewed by a responsible official, who should also check authorisation.

   (iv) A listing of suppliers' accounts on which there has been no movement for a specified period (6 months, 12 months) should be produced to allow decisions to be made about possible deletions, thus ensuring that the standing data is current. The buying department manager might also recommend account closures on a periodic basis.

(v) Users should be controlled by use of passwords. This can also be used as a method of controlling those who can amend data.

(vi) Periodic listings of standing data should be produced in order to verify details (for example addresses) with suppliers' documents (invoices/ statements).

(b) The input of authorised purchase invoices and credit notes should be controlled in the following ways.

(i) Authorisation should be evidenced by the signature of the responsible official (say the Chief Accountant). In addition, the invoice or credit note should show initials to demonstrate that the details have been agreed: to a signed GRN; to a purchase order; to a price list; for additions and extensions.

(ii) There should be adequate segregation of responsibilities between the posting function, stock custody and receipt, payment of suppliers and changes to standing data.

(iii) Input should be restricted by use of passwords linked to the relevant site number.

(iv) A batch control book should be maintained, recording batches in number sequence. Invoices should be input in batches using pre-numbered batch control sheets. The manually produced invoice total on the batch control sheet should be agreed to the computer generated total. Credit notes and invoices should be input in separate batches to avoid one being posted as the other.

(v) A program should check calculation of VAT at standard rate and total (net + VAT = gross) of invoice. Non-standard VAT rates should be highlighted.

(vi) The input of the supplier code should bring up the supplier name for checking by the operator against the invoice.

(vii) Invoices for suppliers which do not have an account should be prevented from being input. Any sundry suppliers account should be very tightly controlled and all entries reviewed in full each month.

(viii) An exception report showing unusual expense allocation (by size or account) should be produced and reviewed by a responsible official. Expenses should be compared to budget and previous years.

(ix) There should be monthly reconciliations of purchase ledger balances to suppliers' statements by someone outside the purchasing (accounting) function.

Question 4

You have recently been appointed auditor of Dryden Manufacturing Ltd and are commencing the audit of the purchases system for the year ended 31 December 20X6. The company has about 200 employees and generally has sufficient staff for there to be a proper division of duties for internal control purposes.

Required

For the audit of the company's purchases system:

(a) Describe how you would evaluate the controls, and how your audit tests would be affected by the results of this evaluation;

(b) List the audit tests you would perform (your answer should include consideration of:

(i) The number of items you would select for testing

(ii) The basis of selecting the items

(iii) What action you would take if errors are found, and you should consider the effect of the size and frequency of errors)

(c) Describe the general form of your conclusions on the results of testing the purchase system and how these conclusions may influence your work at the final audit.

Answer

(a) Many large audit firms now use a standard method of internal control evaluation questionnaire (ICEQ) based on key control questions. The characteristics of this system are usually as follows.

   (i) It is concerned only with the primary or key controls.

   (ii) The format of the questionnaires leads to a detailed assessment of each of the primary control areas.

   (iii) The ICEQ schedules can normally be linked and cross-referenced to the flowcharts, ICQs or other systems records.

   (iv) It encourages the audit staff to design their tests to suit the particular needs of each client's systems. In other words, it ensures that time is not wasted in performing 'standard' audit programme tests that are not relevant to the circumstances, and that there is a direct link between the evaluation of the system of internal control and the tests carried out.

   One method of constructing an ICEQ could be by listing under each major control question the answers of the detailed questions relating to that control which appear in the ICQ and then answering the major question on the basis of the subsidiary questions.

   It is also important that against each major control question in the ICEQ there should be space for the auditors to cross-reference their answer to the action they have taken (eg modifying the audit programme or advising the client of weaknesses). An ICEQ will be useless unless the appropriate action is taken as a result of the evaluation.

(b) The audit tests necessary in relation to the purchases system will depend very much upon the auditors' evaluation of the strengths of the system. Assuming there to be a sound system of internal control in operation, then it will be necessary to carry out a programme of both tests of controls and substantive procedures and these will be spread over the interim and final audit visits. The sample size will depend on:

   (i) The level of tolerable error, the error that the auditor is prepared to tolerate and still conclude that the objectives of the tests have been achieved. For tests of control the level is likely to be low.

   (ii) The level of sampling risk. The more I am relying on the tests, the lower will be the level of sampling risk I am prepared to tolerate, and the higher the sample size will be.

   (iii) The level of control risk. The lower the level, the lower will be the sample size.

   Samples should be selected using a method that ensures samples chosen are representative of the population. Random sampling would be one such method.

   Typically the majority of the tests of control will be carried out on the occasion of the interim audit and should cover tests on the following.

   (i) Sequence of purchase orders
   (ii) Approval of purchase orders
   (iii) Adherence to authority limits
   (iv) Sequence of goods received records
   (v) Sequence of goods returned records
   (vi) Authorisation of adjustments to purchase ledger balances
   (vii) Serial numbering of purchase orders
   (viii) Sequence of purchase invoices
   (ix) Correlation of purchase invoices with purchase orders and goods received records
   (x) Correlation of credit notes with goods returned records
   (xi) Checking of castings and extensions on purchase invoices
   (xii) Coding of purchase invoices for accounting classification purposes
   (xiii) Correct segregation of VAT
   (xiv) Initialling of purchase invoice 'grid' for work done
   (xv) Approval of purchase invoices for processing into accounting system

   Since the main aim of the testing at the interim stage is to ensure that the company's laid down procedures are being properly applied, it will be necessary to follow up an error on a transaction of £5 in the same way as an error in a transaction of £50,000. Where errors are found further testing will usually be necessary in the area of weakness to confirm whether the error is isolated or recurring. If the errors persist, then management should be informed of the facts and the matters should be noted in the interim comments letter sent by the auditors to the client.

(c) If the results of the auditors' tests on the purchases system are satisfactory they may conclude that it will produce reliable accounting records and this in turn will mean that they may keep substantive testing at the year end to a minimum. If, however, the tests of control reveal weaknesses in the system then at the final audit, the auditors will have to carry out a more extensive programme of substantive tests.

3 THE WAGES SYSTEM

Aims of controls

3.1 The most important aims of the control system relating to wages and salaries are:

Setting of wages and salaries

- **Employees** are **only paid** for **work** that they have **done**
- **Gross pay** has been **calculated correctly** and **authorised**

Recording of wages and salaries

- **Gross** and **net pay** and **deductions** are **accurately recorded** on the payroll
- **Wages and salaries paid** are **recorded correctly** in the **bank** and **cash records**
- **Wages and salaries** are **correctly recorded** in the **general ledger**

Payment of wages and salaries

- The **correct employees** are **paid**

Deductions

- All **deductions** have been **calculated correctly** and are **authorised**
- The **correct amounts** are **paid** to the **taxation authorities**

3.2 While in practice separate arrangements are generally made for dealing with wages and salaries, the considerations involved are broadly similar and for convenience the two aspects are here treated together.

Controls

General arrangements

3.3 Responsibility for the preparation of pay sheets should be delegated to a suitable person, and adequate staff appointed to assist him. The extent to which the staff responsible for preparing wages and salaries may perform other duties should be clearly defined. In this connection full advantage should be taken where possible of the division of duties, and checks available where automatic wage-accounting systems are in use.

3.4 Setting of wages and salaries

- **Staffing** and **segregation of duties**
- **Maintenance of personnel records** and regular checking of wages and salaries to details in personnel records
- **Authorisation**
  - ° Engagement and discharge of employees
  - ° Changes in pay rates
  - ° Overtime
  - ° Non-statutory deductions (for example pension contributions)
  - ° Advances of pay
- **Recording** of **changes** in **personnel** and **pay rates**
- **Recording** of hours worked by **timesheets, clocking** in and out arrangements
- **Review** of hours worked
- **Recording** of **advances** of **pay**
- **Holiday pay** arrangements
- **Answering queries**

BPP PUBLISHING

- **Review** of **wages** against **budget**

3.5   Payment of cash wages

- **Segregation of duties**
  - ° Cash sheet preparation
  - ° Filling of pay packets
  - ° Distribution of wages
- **Authorisation** of **wage cheque** cashed
- **Custody** of cash
  - ° Encashment of cheque
  - ° Security of pay packets
  - ° Security of transit
  - ° Security and prompt banking of unclaimed wages
- **Verification of identity**
- **Recording** of distribution

3.6   Payment of salaries

- **Preparation** and **authorisation** of cheques and bank transfer lists
- Comparison of **cheques** and **bank transfer list** with **payroll**
- **Maintenance** and **reconciliation** of wages and salaries bank account

3.7   Recording of wages and salaries

- **Bases** for **compilation** of payroll
- **Preparation, checking** and **approval** of payroll
- Dealing with **non-routine matters**

3.8   Deductions from pay

- **Maintenance** of **separate employees' records,** with which pay lists may be compared as necessary
- **Reconciliation** of **total pay** and **deductions** between one pay day and the next
- **Surprise cash counts**
- **Comparison** of actual pay totals with **budget estimates** or standard costs and the investigation of variances
- **Agreement** of **gross earnings** and **total tax deducted** with PAYE returns to the Inland Revenue

3.9   Appropriate arrangements should be made for dealing with statutory and other authorised deductions from pay, such as national insurance, PAYE, pension fund contributions, and savings held in trust. A primary consideration is the establishment of adequate controls over the **records** and **authorising** deductions.

Tests of controls

Setting of wages and salaries

3.10   Auditors should check that the **wages** and **salary summary** is approved for payment. They should confirm that procedures are operating for **authorising changes** in **rates of pay,** overtime, and holiday pay.

3.11   A particular concern will be joiners and leavers. Auditors will need to obtain evidence that staff only start being paid when they join the company, and are removed from the payroll when they leave the company. They should check that the **engagement** of **new employees** and **discharges** have been **confirmed in writing**.

3.12 Auditors will also wish to check calculations of wages and salaries. This test should be designed to check that the client is carrying out **checks** on **calculations** and also to provide substantive assurance that **wages** and **salaries** are being **calculated correctly**.

3.13 For wages, this will involve checking **calculation** of **gross pay** with:

> • Authorised rates of pay
>
> • Production records. See that production bonuses have been authorised and properly calculated
>
> • Clock cards, time sheets or other evidence of hours worked. Verify that overtime has been authorised

3.14 For salaries, auditors should **verify that gross salaries and bonuses are in accordance with personnel records, letters of engagement** etc and that increases in pay have been properly authorised.

Payment of wages and salaries

3.15 If wages are paid in cash, auditors should carry out the following procedures.

> • **Arrange to attend** the **pay-out** of wages to confirm that the official procedures are being followed
>
> • Before the wages are paid **compare payroll** with **wage packets** to ensure all employees have a wage packet
>
> • **Examine receipts** given by employees; **check unclaimed wages** are recorded in unclaimed wages book
>
> • **Check** that **no employee receives more than one wage packet**
>
> • **Check entries** in the **unclaimed wages book** with the entries on the payroll
>
> • **Check that unclaimed wages** are **banked regularly**
>
> • **Check** that unclaimed wages books shows **reasons** why wages are unclaimed
>
> • **Check pattern** of **unclaimed wages** in unclaimed wages book; variations may indicate failure to record
>
> Holiday pay
>
> • Verify a sample of payments with the underlying records and check the calculation of the amounts paid

3.16 For salaries, auditors should check that comparisons are being made between payment records and they should themselves **examine paid cheques** or a **certified copy** of the **bank list f**or employees paid by cheque of banks transfer.

Recording of wages and salaries

3.17 A key control auditors will be concerned with will be the reconciliation of wages and salaries.

BPP PUBLISHING

3.18   For wages, there should have been reconciliations with:

> * The **previous week's payroll**
> * **Clock cards/time sheets/job cards**
> * **Costing analyses, production budgets**

3.19   The total of **salaries** should be **reconciled** with the **previous week/month** or the **standard payroll.**

3.20   In addition auditors should confirm that important calculations have been checked by the clients and re-perform those calculations.

3.21   These include checking for wages for a number of weeks:

> * **Additions** of **payroll sheets**
> * **Totals** of **wages sheets** selected to summary
> * **Additions** and **cross-casts** of summary
> * **Postings** of **summary** to **general ledger** (including control accounts)
> * **Casts** of **net cash column** to cash book

3.22   For salaries they include checking for a number of weeks/months:

> * **Additions of payroll sheets**
> * **Totals of salaries sheets** to **summary**
> * **Additions** and **cross-casts** of **summary**
> * **Postings** of **summary** to **general ledger** (including control accounts)
> * **Total** of **net pay column** to cash book

Deductions

3.23   Auditors should **check** the **calculations** of **PAYE, National Insurance** and **non-statutory deductions.** For PAYE and NI they should carry out the following tests:

> * **Scrutinise** the **control accounts** maintained to see **appropriate deductions** have been **made**
> * **Check** to see that the **employer's contribution** for national insurance has been **correctly calculated**
> * **Check** that the **payments** to the **Inland Revenue** and other bodies are **correct**
>
> They should check other deductions to appropriate records. For voluntary deductions, they should see the authority completed by the relevant employees.

Question 5

The following questions have been selected from an internal control questionnaire for wages and salaries.

Internal control questionnaire - wages and salaries

		Yes	No
1	Does an appropriate official authorise rates of pay?		
2	Are written notices required for employing and terminating employment?		
3	Are formal records such as time cards used for time keeping?		

4   Does anyone verify rates of pay, overtime hours and computations of gross pay before the wage payments are made?

5   Does the accounting system ensure the proper recording of payroll costs in the financial records?

Required

(a)   Describe the internal control objective being fulfilled if the controls set out in the above questions are in effect.

(b)   Describe the audit tests which would test the effectiveness of each control and help determine any potential material error.

(c)   Identify the potential consequences for the company if the above controls were not in place.

You may answer in columnar form under the headings:

ICQ question	Internal control objective	Audit tests	Consequences

Answer

	ICQ question	Internal control objective	Audit tests	Consequences
1	Does an appropriate official authorise rates of pay?	Employees are paid amounts authorised	Test rates of pay from payroll to schedule of authorised pay rates (personnel files, board minutes etc)	Incorrect rates of pay could lead to over/under statement of profit
2	Are written notices required for employing and terminating employment?	All employees paid through payroll exist	Check a sample of employees from payroll files for authorisation of employment or termination. Check details for cheque or credit transfer salary payments to personnel files	Payroll may include fictitious employees
3	Are formal records such as time cards used for time keeping?	Employees are only paid for work done	Review time records to ensure they are properly completed and controlled. Observe procedures for time recording	Overstatement of payroll costs. Employees over/under paid
			Check time records where absences are recorded to payroll to ensure they have been accounted for. Review the wages account and investigate any large or unusual amounts	
4	Does anyone verify rates of pay, overtime hours and computation of gross pay before wage payments are made?	Employees are paid the correct amount	Examine payroll for evidence of verification. Recompute gross pay (including overtime). Check wage rates to authorised schedule	Misstatement of payroll costs

BPP PUBLISHING

	ICQ question	Internal control objective	Audit tests	Consequences
5	Does the accounting system ensure the proper recording of payroll costs in the financial records?	Payroll costs are properly recorded	Check posting of payroll costs to the nominal ledger	Misstatement of payroll costs

4 SMALLER ENTITIES

4.1 Remember, the control systems in smaller entities are often not as sophisticated as those in larger entities. The particular area that can be a concern for smaller entities with few staff is **segregation of duties**. It can be impossible to adequately share duties between staff when there are only one or two staff.

4.2 Having established in Chapter 9 that proprietor involvement is the key to internal control in the small enterprise, we need next to be rather more precise and identify the types of control relevant to each principal accounting area. These controls can be referred to as '**minimum business controls**'.

4.3 It is important to appreciate that such controls will not, and **cannot, be evaluated and relied on** by the auditors as in a 'systems' audit approach, but they do **provide overall comfort** to the auditors, particularly when determining whether to seek to rely on management assurances as to the completeness of the accounting records.

4.4 The following checklist provides illustrative examples of minimum control standards.

Mail

- Is all mail received and opened by the proprietor?
- If the proprietor does not himself open the mail, is it opened by a person not connected with the accounts and read by him before it is distributed to the staff?

Receipts

- Are all cheques and postal orders received by post counted by the proprietor before they are passed to the cashier?
- Are all cheques and postal orders crossed to the company's branch of its bankers 'Not negotiable - account payee only'.
- Are cash sales and credit sale receipts over the counter controlled by locked cash register tapes which only the proprietor can open?
- Does the proprietor reconcile the cash register totals with the cash sales receipts daily?
- Is the person performing the duties of cashier barred any responsibility concerning the sales, purchase or nominal ledgers?

Banking

- Is all cash received banked intact at intervals of not more than three days?
- Does the proprietor reconcile all monies received with the copy paying-in slips at regular intervals?

Payments

- Are all payments except sundry expenses made by cheques?
- Does the proprietor sign all cheques?

- Are cheques signed by the proprietor only after he has satisfied himself that:
  - He has approved and cancelled all vouchers supporting the payment?
  - All cheques are crossed not negotiable and account payee only?
  - All cheque numbers are accounted for?
- Are petty cash expenses controlled by the imprest system?
- Does the proprietor review all expenses and initial the petty cash book before reimbursing the cashier?

Bank statements

- Are bank statements and paid cheques sent direct to the proprietor and opened only by him?
- Does the proprietor scrutinise all paid cheques to ensure that he has signed them all before he passes them to the cashier?
- Does the proprietor:
  - Prepare a bank reconciliation each month? or
  - Review in detail a reconciliation produced by the cashier?

Orders

- Are all purchase orders issued:
  - Serially numbered by the printer?
  - Pre-printed duplicate order forms?
- Does the proprietor approve all orders?

Receipt of goods

Are delivery notes:
- Checked with goods?
- Compared with the copy order?
- Compared with the invoice?

Wages

- Is a separate cheque drawn for the exact amount to pay wages and PAYE/National Insurance?
- Does the proprietor either prepare or examine the wages records before signing the cheque?
- Does the proprietor initial the wages records after his examination?
- Does the proprietor oversee the distribution of the wages packets or does he distribute them himself?

Debtors

- If credit is granted to customers does the proprietor:
  - Authorise every extension of credit to a customer?
  - Approve credit limits for each customer?
- Does the proprietor authorise all:
  - Write offs of bad debts?
  - Sales returns and allowances?
  - Discounts other than routine cash discounts?
- Does the proprietor receive a monthly list of debtors, showing the age of the debts?
- Are all authorisations by the proprietor evidenced by his initials?

Goods outwards

- Are pre-numbered despatch notes prepared for all goods leaving the premises?
- Are all despatch notes:
  - Accounted for?
  - Cross referenced with invoices and credit notes?
- Is the proprietor satisfied that all goods leaving the premises have been accounted for?

Stock

Does the proprietor scrutinise the stocks regularly to:

- Keep abreast of what is in stock?
- Discover obsolete items?
- Discover damaged articles?
- Ensure that stock levels are kept under control?

4.5 Although the above types of control are desirable and feasible, they are nevertheless relatively informal. Consequently evidence of their performance tends to be lacking and they may indeed be overridden as there is no check on the proprietor himself.

Exam focus point

In the exam, run the following checklist through your mind when approaching questions about controls in smaller entities.

Are you being logical?

- Consider the number of staff the entity is likely to employ.
- Remember, top management or the owners are likely to be involved on a day to day level
- Bear in mind a general rule: The smaller the entity, the fewer the daybooks and ledgers...

Chapter roundup

- The sales and purchases systems will be the most important components of most company accounting systems.

- The tests of controls of the **sales system** will be based around:

  - **Selling** (authorisation)
  - **Goods outwards** (custody)
  - **Accounting** (recording)

- Similarly, the **purchases systems** tests will be based around:

  - **Buying** (authorisation)
  - **Goods** inwards (custody)
  - **Accounting** (recording)

- Important **tests of control** by auditors include:

  - Checking documentation for correct details, authorisation and calculations
  - Comparing documents
  - Checking completeness of documentation series

- Note that all weaknesses discovered in these tests will be included in a **report to management**. Management reports will be discussed in Chapter ??.

- Obviously, most manufacturing companies will have a large payroll. Wages and salaries are usually dealt with in very different ways, but they are often grouped together for audit testing purposes.

- Key controls over **wages** cover:

  - **Documentation** and **authorisation** of staff changes
  - **Calculation** of wages and salaries
  - **Payment** of wages
  - **Authorisation** of **deductions**

- These three systems are those most likely to come up in the exam, as you can see by how often they have been examined recently.

Quick quiz

1   Complete the table, putting the sales system control considerations under the correct headings.

Ordering/granting of credit	Despatch/invoicing	Recording/accounting

- (a)   All sales that have been invoiced have been put in the general ledger
- (b)   Orders are fulfilled
- (c)   Cut off is correct
- (d)   Goods are only supplied to good credit risks
- (e)   Goods are correctly invoiced
- (f)   Customers are encouraged to pay promptly

2 Name five controls relating to the ordering and granting of credit process.

    1 ....

    2 ....

    3 ....

    4 ....

    5 ....

3 When checking sales invoicing the auditor should verify ...., ..., ... and ...., ..., correct analysis in the sales ledger and correct posting and that VAT has been dealt with.

4 Complete the table, putting the purchase system control considerations under the correct headings.

Ordering	Receipt/invoices	Accounting

    (a) Orders are only made to authorised suppliers
    (b) Liabilities are recognised for all goods and services received
    (c) Orders made at competitive prices
    (d) All expenditure is authorised
    (e) Cut off is correctly applied
    (f) Goods and services are only accepted if there is an authorised order

5 (a) Name four examples of purchase documentation on which numerical sequence should be checked

    1 ....

    2 ....

    3 ....

    4 ....

    (b) Why is numerical sequence checked?

6 Name 6 procedures auditors should carry out if wages are paid in cash.

    1 ....

    2 ....

    3 ....

    4 ....

    5 ....

    6 ....

Answers to quick quiz

1	Ordering/granting of credit	Despatch/invoicing	Recording/accounting
	(b)	(e)	(a)
	(d)		(c)
	(f)		

2   See para 1.2

3   quantities, prices, calculations, additions, discounts

4	OrderingReceipt/invoices	Accounting	
	(a)	(b)	(d)
	(c)	(f)	(e)

5   (a)   (1) purchase requisitions, (2) purchase orders, (3) goods received notes, (4) goods returned notes, (5) suppliers invoices

       (b)   Sequence provides a control that sales are complete. Missing documents should be explained, or cancelled copies available.

6   See para 3.15

Now try the question below from the Exam Question Bank

Number	Level	Marks	Time
10	Exam	20	36 mins

Chapter 11

TESTS OF CONTROLS: OTHER CYCLES

Topic list		Syllabus reference
1	The cash system	5
2	The stock system	5
3	Revenue and capital expenditure	5
4	Providing assurance on internal controls	1
5	Internal audit: relevant cycles	2

Introduction

This chapter completes the tests of controls topic begun in Chapter 10. Other 'specialised' companies may have different systems, for example a share dealing system in a bank.

Controls over **cash and bank balances** cannot be seen in complete isolation from controls over the sales, purchases and wages cycle. In this chapter we concentrate on controls over and testing of the safe **custody and recording** of cash. You should note in particular the emphasis on prompt recording of receipts and payments, and prompt banking of cash and cheques received. Bear in mind also when you work through the section on bank and cash that controlling cheque receipts and payments is significantly easier than controlling cash receipts and payments.

For **stock**, there should be **proper security arrangements** and **prompt recording**. You should note however the other aspects of control of stock, particularly reviews of the condition of stock, and stockholding policies designed to ensure that the business is not holding too much or too little stock. These controls interest auditors since they may impact upon how stock is valued. We shall discuss valuation of stock further in Chapter 14.

For **fixed assets,** it is vital that there are controls in place to ensure that capital items are capitalised as assets and revenue items are charged to the profit and loss account.

In a number of areas discussed in this chapter, auditors will be considering controls at the same time as they are carrying out substantive tests. Thus for example when receiving cash at bank, auditors will be interested in the clients' bank reconciliations as an important control over the custody of cash; they will also re-perform one (or more) reconciliations to gain substantive assurance. Similarly with stock auditors will review stock counts held by the client over the year, and also attend one or more stocktakes themselves to gain the necessary substantive assurance.

Note that weakness reporting is covered in the section on management letters in Chapter 20.

The APB have recently issued guidance about **providing assurance** on **the effectiveness of internal controls**. We shall consider this guidance briefly in section 4.

Lastly in this chapter we shall look at some of the **operational cycles** which were touched on in Chapter 3, and the aims and operations of controls in these cycles. We shall also consider tests of control which **internal auditors** might carry out on them.

Study guide

Section 4

Describe the:

- Nature and purpose of operational internal audit and review assignments including:

  ° procurement
  ° marketing
  ° treasury
  ° HR

Section 13

- Describe, illustrate and analyse how internal control systems over the stock transaction cycle operate in both large and small entities

- Describe and illustrate the use by auditors of internal control checklists for the stock transaction cycle

- Describe and tabulate tests of control of stock for inclusion in a work program

Section 15

- Describe, illustrate and analyse how internal control system over the bank and cash transaction cycle operate in both large and small entities

- Describe and illustrate the use by auditors of internal control checklists for the bank and cash transaction cycle

- Describe and tabulate tests of control of bank and cash for inclusion in a work program

Section 14

- Describe, illustrate and analyse how internal control systems over revenue and capital expenditure transaction cycles operate in both large and small entities

- Describe and illustrate the use by auditors of internal control checklists for revenue and capital expenditure transaction cycles

- Describe and tabulate tests of control of revenue and capital expenditure for inclusion in a work program

Exam guide

Controls testing and substantive testing could both be examined in a question on a specific balance sheet area.

1 THE CASH SYSTEM

Aims of controls

1.1 The most important aims of the control system relating to cash receipts and payments are:

- **All monies received** are **recorded**
- **All monies received** are **banked**
- **Cash and cheques** are **safeguarded** against loss or theft
- **All payments** are **authorised, made** to the **correct payees** and **recorded**
- **Payments** are **not made twice** for the same liability

1.2 Controls over the **completeness** of **recording** of cash receipts are particularly important. If these controls are inadequate, there may be insufficient audit evidence available when the auditor carries out substantive procedures.

1.3   Segregation of duties is also important. The person responsible for receiving and recording cash when it arrives in the post should not be the same as the person responsible for banking it. Ideally the cash book should be written up by a further staff member, and a fourth staff member should reconcile the various records of amounts received.

1.4   Records of cash are obviously also at the heart of a company's accounting records; therefore if these accounting records are to fulfil Companies Act requirements, cash must be recorded **promptly.**

1.5   The following matters should be considered.

Controls

Cash at bank and in hand - receipts

1.6   **Segregation of duties** between the various functions listed below is particularly important.

1.7   Recording of receipts by post

- **Safeguards** to **prevent interception of mail** between receipt and opening
- Appointment of **responsible person** to supervise mail
- **Protection** of **cash and cheques** (restrictive crossing)
- **Amounts received listed** when post opened
- **Post stamped** with date of receipt

1.8   Recording of cash sales and collections

- **Restrictions** on **receipt of cash** (by cashiers only, or by salesmen etc)
- **Evidencing** of receipt of cash

     ○   Serially numbered receipt forms
     ○   Cash registers incorporating sealed till rolls

- **Clearance** of cash offices and registers
- **Agreement of cash collections with till rolls**
- **Agreement of cash collections with bankings and** cash and sales **records**
- **Investigation** of cash shortages and surpluses

1.9   General controls over recording

- Prompt **maintenance of records** (cash book, ledger accounts)
- **Limitation** of **duties** of receiving cashiers
- **Holiday arrangements**
- **Giving** and **recording** of **receipts**

     ○   Retained copies
     ○   Serially numbered receipts books
     ○   Custody of receipt books
     ○   Comparisons with cash records and bank paying in slips

1.10   Banking

- **Daily bankings**
- **Make-up** and **comparison** of **paying-in** slips against initial receipt records and cash book
- **Banking** of receipts **intact**/control of disbursements

1.11   Safeguarding of cash and bank accounts

- **Restrictions** on **opening new bank accounts**
- **Limitations** on **cash floats** held
- **Restrictions** on **payments** out of **cash received**
- **Restrictions** on **access** to cash registers and offices
- **Independent checks** on cash floats
- **Surprise cash counts**
- **Custody** of **cash** outside **office hours**
- **Custody** over **supply** and issue of cheques
- **Preparation** of **cheques** restricted
- **Safeguards** over **mechanically signed cheques**/cheques carrying printed signatures
- **Restrictions** on issue of **blank** or **bearer** cheques
- **Safeguarding** of **IOUs**, cash in transit
- **Insurance arrangements**
- **Control of funds** held in trust for employees
- **Bank reconciliations**
    - ○ Issue of bank statements
    - ○ Frequency of reconciliations by independent person
    - ○ Reconciliation procedures
    - ○ Treatment of longstanding unpresented cheques
    - ○ Stop payment notice
    - ○ Sequence of cheque numbers
    - ○ Comparison with cash books

Cash at bank and in hand - payments

1.12   The arrangements for controlling payments will depend to a great extent on the nature of business transacted, the volume of payments involved and the size of the company.

Cheque and cash payments generally

1.13   The cashier should generally not be concerned with keeping or writing-up books of account other than those recording disbursements nor should he have access to, or be responsible for the custody of, securities, title deeds or negotiable instruments belonging to the company.

1.14   The person responsible for preparing cheques or traders' credit lists should not himself be a cheque signatory. Cheque signatories in turn should not be responsible for recording payments.

1.15   Cheque payments

- **Cheque requisitions**
    - ○ Appropriate supporting documentation
    - ○ Approval by appropriate staff
    - ○ Presentation to cheque signatories
    - ○ Cancellation (crossing/recording cheque number on requisition)

- **Authority** to sign cheques
    - ○ Signatories should not also approve cheque requisitions
    - ○ Limitations on authority to specific amounts
    - ○ Number of signatories
    - ○ Prohibitions over signing of blank cheques

- **Prompt despatch** of signed **cheques**

- **Obtaining** of paid **cheques** from **banks**
- Payments **recorded promptly** in **cash book** and **general** and **purchase ledger**

1.16 Cash payments

- **Authorisation** of **expenditure**
- **Cancellation** of **vouchers** to ensure cannot be paid
- **Limits** on **disbursements**
- **Rules** on **cash advances** to employees, IOUs and cheque cashing

Tests of controls

1.17 Note that as well as testing controls over receipts, auditors are also obtaining evidence to support the assertion that sales and receipts are **completely recorded.**

1.18 Receipts received by post

- **Observe procedures** for **post opening** are being followed

- **Observe** that **cheques** received by post are immediately **crossed** in the company's favour of the company

- For items entered in the rough cash book (or other record of cash, cheques etc received by post), **trace entries** to:
  - **Cash book**
  - **Paying-in book**
  - **Counterfoil** or carbon copy receipts

- **Verify amounts entered** as **received** with remittance advices or other supporting evidence

---

1.19 Cash sales, branch takings

- For a sample of cash sales summaries/branch summaries from different locations:
  - **Verify with till rolls** or copy cash sale notes
  - **Check to paying-in slip** date-stamped and initialled by the bank
  - **Verify that takings** are banked intact daily
  - **Vouch expenditure** out of takings

1.20 Collections

- For a sample of items from the original collection records:
  - **Trace amounts** to **cash book** via collectors' cash sheets or other collection records
  - **Check entries** on **cash sheets** or collection records with collectors' receipt books
  - **Verify** that **goods delivered** to travellers/salesmen have been regularly **reconciled** with sales and stocks in hand
  - **Check numerical sequence** of collection records

1.21 Receipts cash book

> - For cash receipts for several days throughout the period:
>   - **Check to entries in rough cash book**, receipts, branch returns or other records
>   - **Check to paying-in slips** obtained direct from the bank, observing that there is no delay in banking monies received
>   - **Check additions** of **paying-in slips**
>   - **Check additions** of **cash book**
>   - **Check postings to the sales ledger**
>   - **Check postings** to the **general ledger**, including control accounts
> - **Scrutinise the cash book** and **investigate items** of a **special** or **unusual nature.**

1.22 Auditors will be concerned with whether cash payments have been **authorised** and are to the **correct payee**. The following tests may be performed on the payment cash book.

> - For a sample of payments:
>   - **Compare** with paid cheques to ensure payee agrees
>   - **Note** that **cheques** are **signed** by the **persons authorised** to do so within their authority limits
>   - **Check** to **suppliers' invoices** for goods and services. Verify that supporting documents are signed as having been **checked** and **passed for payment** and have been stamped 'paid'
>   - **Check** to **suppliers' statements**
>   - **Check** to **other documentary evidence**, as appropriate (agreements, authorised expense vouchers, wages/salaries records, petty cash books etc)

1.23 When checking the **recording** of payments, auditors will carry out the following tests on the payments cash book.

> - For a sample of weeks:
>   - **Check the sequence of cheque numbers** and enquire into missing numbers
>   - **Trace transfers** to other bank accounts, petty cash books or other records, as appropriate
>   - **Check additions**, including extensions, and balances forward at the beginning and end of the months covering the periods chosen
>   - **Check postings** to the **purchase ledger**
>   - **Check postings** to the **general ledger**, including the control accounts

1.24 When checking that bank and cash are **secured**, auditors should consider the security arrangements over blank cheques. Bank reconciliations are also a very important control and auditors should carry out the following tests on these.

> - For a period which includes a reconciliation date **reperform reconciliation** (see Chapter 18)
> - **Verify** that **reconciliations have been prepared** at **regular intervals** throughout the year
> - **Scrutinise reconciliations for unusual items**

1.25 The following tests should be carried out for petty cash

> - For a sample of payments:
>   - **Check** to supporting vouchers
>   - **Check** whether they are properly **approved**
>   - **See** that **vouchers** have been **marked and initialled** by the cashier to prevent their re-use
> - For a sample of weeks:
>   - **Trace amounts** received to **cash books**
>   - **Check additions** and **balances carried** forward
>   - **Check postings** to the **nominal ledger**

Exam focus point

Questions about the sales or purchases systems may also require consideration of controls over receipts or payments.

2 THE STOCK SYSTEM

2.1 The stock system can be very important in an audit because of the high value of stock or the complexity of its audit. It is closely connected with the sales and purchases systems covered in Chapter 10.

Aims of controls

2.2 The most important aims of the control system relating to stock are:

Recording

- All **stock movements** are **authorised** and **recorded**
- **Stock records** only **include items** that **belong** to the client
- **Stock records** include stock that **exists** and is **held** by the client
- **Stock quantities** have been **recorded correctly**
- **Cut-off procedures** are **properly applied** to stock

Protection of stock

- **Stock** is **safeguarded** against loss, pilferage or damage

Valuation of stock

- The **costing system values stock correctly**
- **Allowance** is **made** for **slow-moving, obsolete** or **damaged stock**

Stock-holding

- **Levels** of **stock held** are **reasonable**

Controls

2.3 Significant controls are as follows.

Recording of stock

- **Segregation** of duties; custody and recording of stocks

- **Reception, checking** and **recording** of goods inwards
- **Stock issues supported** by **appropriate documentation**
- **Maintenance** of **stock records**
  - ° Stock ledgers
  - ° Bin cards
  - ° Transfer records

Protection of stock

- **Precautions** against **theft, misuse** and **deterioration**
  - ° Restriction of access to stores
  - ° Controls on stores environment (right temperature, precautions against damp etc).
- **Security** over **stock** held by third parties, and third party stock held by entity
- **Stock-taking** (see also Chapter 14).
  - ° Regular stock-taking
  - ° Fair coverage so that all stock is counted at least once a year
  - ° Counts by independent persons
  - ° Recording
  - ° Cut-off for goods in transit and time differences
  - ° Reconciliation of stock count to book records and control accounts

Valuation of stock

- **Computation** of **stock valuation**
  - ° Accords with SSAP 9
  - ° Checking of calculations
- **Review** of **condition** of stock
  - ° Treatment of slow-moving, damaged and obsolete stock
  - ° Authorisation of write-offs
- **Accounting** for **scrap** and **waste**

Stockholding

- **Control** of **stock levels**
  - ° Maximum stock limits
  - ° Minimum stock limits
  - ° Re-order quantities and levels
- Arrangements for dealing with **returnable containers**

Tests of controls

2.4 Most of the testing relating to stock has been covered in the purchase and sales testing outlined in Chapter 10. Auditors will primarily be concerned at this stage with ensuring that the business keeps track of stock. To confirm this, checks must be made on how stock **movements** are **recorded** and how **stock** is **secured**.

- **Select** a sample of **stock movements records** and **agree** to **goods received** and **goods despatched notes**
- **Confirm** that **movements** have been **authorised** as **appropriate**
- **Select** a sample of **goods received** and **goods despatched** notes and agree to **stock movement records**
- **Check sequence** of stock records

2.5 Other tests that auditors are likely to perform include:

- **Test** check **stock counts** carried out from time to time (eg monthly) during the period and confirm:
    ◦ **All discrepancies** between **book** and **actual** figures have been fully investigated
    ◦ **All discrepancies** have been **signed off** by a senior manager
    ◦ **Obsolete, damaged or slow-moving goods** have been **marked accordingly** and written down to net realisable value
- **Observe security arrangements** for stocks
- **Consider environment** in which stocks are held

Auditors will carry out extensive tests on the **valuation** of stock at the substantive testing stage (see Chapter 14).

Question 1

Jonathan is the sole shareholder of Furry Lion Stores Ltd, a company which owns five stores in the west of England. The stores mainly stock food and groceries, and four of the stores have an off-licence as well.

Each store is run by a full-time manager and three or four part-time assistants. Jonathan spends on average ½ a day a week at each store, and spends the rest of his time at home, dealing with his other business interests.

All sales are for cash and are recorded on till rolls which the manager retains. Shop manager wages are paid monthly by cheque by Jonathan. Wages of shop assistants are paid in cash out of the takings.

Most purchases are made from local wholesalers and are paid for in cash out of the takings. Large purchases (over £250) must be made by cheques signed by the shop manager and countersigned by Jonathan.

Shop managers bank surplus cash once a week, apart from a float in the till.

All accounting records including the cash book, wages and VAT records are maintained by the manager. Jonathan reviews the weekly bank statements when he visits the shops. He also has a look at stocks to see if stock levels appear to be about right. All invoices are also kept in a drawer by a manager and marked with a cash book reference, and where appropriate a cheque number when paid.

Required

Discuss the weaknesses in the control systems of Furry Lion Ltd, and how the weaknesses can be remedied.

Answer

Weaknesses in the system, and their remedies are as follows.

Stock

The shops do not appear to have any stock movement records. This would appear to breach the Companies Act s 221 requirement for the company to maintain proper accounting records. Jonathan has also only a very approximate indication of stock levels. Hence it will be difficult to detect whether stock levels are too high, or too low with a risk of running out of stock. Theft of stock would also be difficult to detect. The company should therefore introduce stock movement records, detailing values and volumes.

In addition regular stock counts should be made either by Jonathan or by staff from another shop. Discrepancies between the stock records and the actual stock counted should be investigated.

Cash controls

Too much cash appears to be held on site. In addition the fact that most payments appear to be for cash may mean inadequate documentation is kept. The level of cash on site can be decreased by daily rather than weekly bankings. In addition the need for cash on site can be decreased by paying wages by cheque, and by paying all but the smallest payments by cheque.

The cash book should obviously still be maintained but cheque stubs should also show details of amounts paid. The cash book should be supported by invoices and other supporting documentation, and should be cross-referenced to the general ledger (see below).

Cash reconciliations

There is no indication of the till-rolls that are kept being reconciled to cash takings.

There should be a daily reconciliation of cash takings and till rolls; this should be reviewed if not performed by the shop manager.

Bank reconciliations

There is no mention of bank reconciliations taking place.

Bank reconciliations should be carried out at least monthly by the shop manager, and reviewed by the owner.

Purchases

There is no formal system for recording purchases. Invoices do not appear to be filed in any particular way. It would be difficult to see whether accounting records were complete, and hence it would be difficult to prepare a set of accounts from the accounting records available.

In addition the way records are maintained means that accounts would have to be prepared on a cash basis, and not on an accruals basis, as required by the Companies Act.

A purchase day book should be introduced. Invoices should be recorded in the purchase day book, and filed in a logical order, either by date received or by supplier.

General ledger

There is no general ledger, and again this means that annual accounts cannot easily be prepared (and also management accounts).

A general ledger should be maintained with entries made from the cash book, wages records and purchase day book. This will enable accounts to be prepared on an accruals basis.

Supervision

Jonathan does not take a very active part in the business, only signing cheques over £250, and visiting the shops only half a day each week. This may mean that assets can easily go missing, and Jonathan cannot readily see whether the business is performing as he would wish.

Jonathan should review wage/VAT/cash book reconciliations. Management accounts should also be prepared by shop managers for Jonathan.

Tutorial note. This question deals with controls that are possible given the circumstances of the business. Greater segregation of duties does not appear to be possible as the shops are small, and Jonathan cannot spend more time at the shops (although he can use his time more productively by reviewing reconciliations).

---

3   REVENUE AND CAPITAL EXPENDITURE   Dec 01

3.1   The nature of a balance sheet and profit and loss account means that it is important to classify capital and revenue expenditure correctly, or profit will be over or understated. You should know the distinction between them from your 2.5 studies.

BPP PUBLISHING

3.2   The controls and tests outlined below are often considered and performed when during the audit of fixed assets (see Chapter 13) as this is where the main issue of capitalisation occurs.

Aims of control

3.3   The most important aims of the control system relating to expenditure are:

Authorisation

- All expenditure is authorised

Recording

- All expenditure is classified correctly in the financial statements as capital or revenue expenditure

3.4   The issue of authorisation was considered in Chapter 10 as part of the controls surrounding purchases and expenses. We shall consider the issue of recording briefly here.

Controls

3.5   Significant controls are as follows.

Ordering

- Orders for capital items should be authorised
- Order should be requisitioned on appropriate (different to revenue) documentation

Invoices

- Invoices should be approved by the person who authorised the order
- They should be marked with the appropriate general ledger code

Recording

- All the standard controls over purchases are relevant here
- Capital items should be written up in the fixed asset register
- The fixed asset register should be reconciled regularly to the general ledger

Tests of controls

3.6   If the ordering documentation is different for capital purchases, all the standard purchase control tests should be carried out.

3.7   If the documentation is not different, the auditor should enquire as to the client's system for recording and filing capital invoices

3.8   It is likely that capital purchases in the year will be fewer than standard purchases in the year and if the invoices are not segregated it may not be cost efficient to test the controls over this area.

3.9   Alternative substantive procedures include:

> **Analytical review**
> - General review between current and prior year figures to ascertain any unexplained differences
> - Review of sensitive codes in the general ledger such as repairs or maintenance
> - Review of the movements on the fixed asset codes
> - Compare budgeted capital purchases with actual capital purchases
>
> **Enquiry and review**
> - Discuss the level of capital purchases in the year with the purchasing manager
> - Review the board minutes for authorisation of capital purchases

3.10   These substantive tests are often carried out as part of the substantive audit of fixed assets.

3.11   The auditor should be aware of the risks attaching to the audit of this area. As test of controls might be cost-ineffective, control risk in this area is higher than would have been if they were tested.

3.12   Inherent risk can also be high in this area. Capital and revenue expenditure is treated differently for the purposes of tax, and if the client is sensitive to their tax bill, there may be motivation to creatively account.

4   PROVIDING ASSURANCE ON INTERNAL CONTROLS

4.1   In July 2001, the APB issued a briefing paper on the issue of providing assurance in the effectiveness of internal control. This was issued in the light of previous consultation documents by the APB, but particularly, in the context of the recent publication by the IPAC, ISA 100, *Assurance Engagements*.

4.2   The briefing paper outlines the **APB's thinking in relation to assurance engagements. Internal controls** are an area of particular importance in the UK, having been given prominence by the investigations in to **corporate governance** in the 1990s, notably the **Turnbull report**, which concentrated on the risks facing companies, and the need for directors to manage that risk. This was discussed in Chapter 3 in the context of internal audit.

Providing assurance on internal control

4.3   The APB draw a clear distinction between two areas of assurance:

- Assurance on the **design** of internal control systems
- Assurance on the **operation** of the internal control system, in accordance with the design

These are two very distinct issues, and the two assignments should be approached very differently.

Process of internal control

4.4   The APB recognise the following process in relation to internal controls:

| Identify **BUSINESS OBJECTIVES** | → | Assess **RISKS** that will threaten those objectives | → | **DESIGN INTERNAL CONTROLS** to manage those risks | → | **OPERATE** the internal controls in accordance with their design |

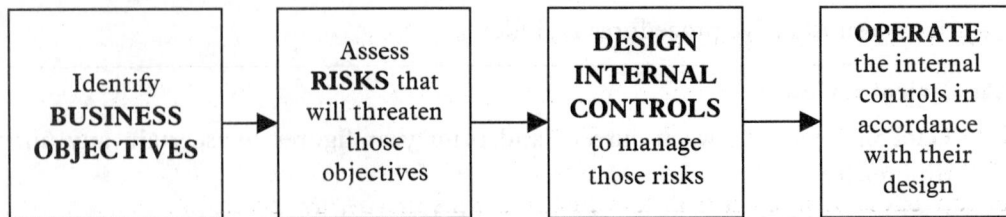

4.5   The diagram above also illustrates the points of the process where assurance services can be given:

- Risk identification
- Design of system
- Operation of system

4.6   In order to carry out an engagement in relation to the internal controls, the practitioners will require sufficient **knowledge of the business** that they can **identify and understand** the events, transactions and practices which will impact on the system of internal control.

Providing assurance on the operation of the system

4.7   The practitioner should establish whether the engagement relates to a period of time or a point of time. The practitioner will only be able to provide a **high level of assurance** on this point if the entity has a detailed description of the design of their system of internal control.

4.8   The **report** arising from such an assignment need not be extensive, but is likely to be narrative. This is because practitioners are likely to include such issues as:

- Isolated control failures
- Observation about the abilities of staff involved in operating the system of control
- Potential weaknesses observed which were not contemplated within the design

Providing assurance on the design and operation of the system

4.9   In such an engagement practitioners will consider two issues:

- The design of the system in addressing a set of identified risks
- The operation of the system (discussed above)

4.10   Such an engagement will involve significant **discussions with management** at the outset, to establish matters such as:

- The desired balance between prevention and detection controls
- The balance between costs and benefits
- The importance of specific control objectives

4.11   The outcome of these discussions will necessarily be included in the assurance **report,** to provide a context for their conclusions. The following things will also be included in the report:

- The applicable risks
- Any framework for design used by either the directors or the practitioners
- A description of the design of the system of internal control.

4.12   The **level of assurance** given by the practitioners will **depend on several factors,** including the nature of the entity, the knowledge of the business the practitioner possesses and the scope of the engagement. It is likely that the report in this instance would be quite long.

Providing assurance on applicable risks and design and operation of the system

4.13 This engagement would include consideration of all the three stages of the internal controls process identified above. The identification of risks is likely to involve a **high degree of judgement** as there are no universally recognised criteria suitable for evaluating the effectiveness of an entity's risk evaluation. This means that practitioners are **unlikely to be** able to provide a **high level of assurance** in this area.

4.14 The starting point for the practitioner would be the entity's business objectives. The key considerations will include:

- The completeness of the applicable identified risks
- The probability of a risk crystallising
- The materiality of the likely impact of the risk
- The time period over which crystallisation is anticipated

4.15 In their **report**, the practitioners would have to outline the business objectives of the entity, a description of the risk identification process and the applicable risks.

Inherent limitations

4.16 Internal control systems have inherent limitations, a key one of which is the chance of staff colluding in fraud to override the system. **Any assurance report on internal controls** systems should **include a mention of these inherent limitations**, in order to prevent an unnecessary expectations gap.

Reports

4.17 The nature of the individual reports has been touched on above. The discussion paper also includes an example report. However, as the APB make the key point that it is difficult to issue a standard report for assurance services, which are largely dependent on the scope and nature of the individual assignment, this has not been reproduced here.

5 INTERNAL AUDIT: RELEVANT CYCLES

5.1 In Chapter 3 we discussed some of the operational cycles that internal auditors might be interested in. These are likely to be of lesser interest to the external auditor, particularly where the cycle does not directly impact on the financial statements.

5.2 In this section we shall consider some of the matters which will affect the work of the internal auditors, in particular, aims of controls in the cycles, the controls themselves, and how the auditor will test those controls.

Procurement

5.3 We have already noted that many of the controls will in this cycles will be the same as in the purchases cycle which the external auditor is interested in. However, as the scope of the internal auditor goes beyond the financial statements, consider these additional factors which he will be interested in.

5.4 A procurement system is likely to have many systems within it (for example, tendering, placing orders, checking goods inwards), which the internal auditor would probably approach separately.

Aims of control

5.5   The following might be aims of a procurement system:

- The business has goods and services when it needs them

- The business does not pay too much for those goods and services

- The business does not make short-term savings on goods and services which lead to longer term inflated costs

- Employees or suppliers do not defraud the company

Controls

5.6   Controls such as the following could be instituted:

- The business always invites tenders for goods and services

- Research is conducted on potential suppliers before they are invited to tender

- Requirements for goods and services are always put in writing

- Use is made of discounting and calculations of long term costs where service is for a prolonged period

- No transactions are carried out with employees and connected persons

Tests of control

5.7   The following related tests of the above controls could be carried out.

> - A sample of contracts can be reviewed to confirm research and tender process
> - A sample of invoices checked back to written requisition
> - For a sample of long term contracts, check long term calculations exist and are correct
> - Review central database of suppliers to ensure that none are connected parties

Exam focus point

As usual, there could be various tests of these controls. If required in an exam to suggest tests of controls, you should consider what the objective of the control is, and how you could prove that that objective is being met.

Remember however, that only internal audit would be interested in some of these controls features. In principle, for example, the external auditors are not too concerned if the company pays more than it should do for its goods and services, so long as what it does pay is recorded properly in the financial statements.

Marketing

5.8   Similarly to procurement, 'marketing' covers a wide range of systems, including research, advertising, promotions, sales, after-sales.

Aims of controls

5.9   The objectives of a marketing system might include the following:

- Customer demand should be understood and met
- Customers should be made aware of products
- Products are competitive, not hampered by pricing or promotion tactics
- Goods are sold for valuable consideration

Controls

5.10   Some of the controls will be similar to those discussed in the sales cycle in Chapter 10. However, think again that the internal auditor is interested in objectives beyond the scope of the financial systems. The following controls might be used to meet the above objectives:

- Market research should be commissioned or carried out
- Actual sales should be compared to budgets
- Advertising is targeted
- Promotions are timed to coincide with periods historically linked with sales, eg Christmas
- Competitor prices are monitored
- Terms and conditions are made known to customers
- Credit checks are made

Tests of control

5.11   Some of the tests, particularly those in relation to credit, will be the same as those discussed in the sales system in Chapter 10.

Question 2

Try to think up some ways of testing the controls listed in paragraph 5.10.

Answer

Potential tests of control include:

- Review company policy on commissioning market research
- For a sample of major promotions, check that research was commissioned and used
- Check that actual sales are compared to budget sales and that variances are investigated
- For a sample of major promotions, ensure that timing has been considered and documented
- Ensure that records are maintained of competitor pricing policy
- Review terms and conditions to ensure that they comply with company policy
- Check as sample of contracts/sales to ensure terms and conditions were highlighted

You may have thought of other tests of controls, this list is not definitive. Check that your answers prove that the objective you had in mind is being tested.

Treasury

Aims of controls

5.12   The following will be objectives of the treasury department:

- Money is available to the company when it is required
- Risks in relation to foreign currency and interest rates are managed effectively
- Transactions do not lose the company money over time
- Exposures are highlighted and reported on, on a timely basis

Controls

5.13   These objectives will be met the following controls:

- Cash flow forecasting
- Arrangements with the bank in the event of cash emergencies
- Contingency plans available
- Clear policy on tolerated risk
- Regular review of investment

- Frequent two-way communication

Tests of controls

5.14 The internal auditor may carry out the following tests

> - Reviewing cash flow forecasts
> - Reading correspondence with the bank
> - Reading contingency plans and assessing them for realism
> - Discuss review of investments with investment managers
> - Seek evidence of such reviews being made (reports, memos)
> - Seek evidence of communication

Human resources

Aims of controls

5.15 The objectives of a human resources department will be as follows:

- Sufficiently qualified and capable staff are available when required
- There is no significant over-reliance on key personnel
- Staff are paid the correct remuneration on a timely basis
- Staff are contented and not prone to industrial action or seeking alternative employment
- Employment laws are complied with
- The human resource is handled considerately

Controls

5.16 The following controls will be put into place to meet these objectives:

- The business has a long term human requirement plan
- Salary is benchmarked against the market
- Performance of staff is regularly and formally appraised
- Staff are given adequate training
- Key personnel are not put at risk together
- Long term succession planning is undertaken
- Payroll controls as discussed in Chapter 10
- Relationships with trade unions are well maintained
- Human resources managers receive training in employment law

Tests of control

5.17 The internal auditors may use the following tests:

> - Obtain a copy of the long term human resource plan and review it
> - Obtain evidence that the HR department monitors pay levels in the market
> - Review of appraisal procedure, check that a sample of employees have had appraisals
> - Review training records to ensure that training is in accordance with company policy
> - Review long term succession plan and any 'apprenticing' schemes are in operation
> - Review training procedures within department by discussion with staff

Exam focus point

As you considered each of these cycles more carefully, you will have seen the strong links that they have with the income and asset cycles that the external auditor is interested in. You will also have seen that the internal auditor is interested in risks arising to the company, whereas the external auditor is more interested in risks of errors in the financial statements.

In the exam, you could be asked the difference between the internal and external auditors interest in internal controls. Remember that the difference is in the objectives each is interested in, and the controls and the tests follow on from that.

You might want to re-read the following sections in conjunction with one another, to see how the objectives of the internal auditors (or the company) extend further than the external auditors in each case:

- Purchases/procurement
- Sales/marketing
- Cash/treasury
- Payroll/human resources

Chapter roundup

- Controls over cash receipts and payments should prevent fraud or theft.

- Key controls over **receipts** include:

    ○ Proper **post-opening** arrangements
    ○ **Prompt recording**
    ○ **Prompt banking**
    ○ **Reconciliation** of records of cash received and banked

- Key controls over **payments** include:

    ○ **Restriction of access** to cash and cheques
    ○ Procedures for **preparation and authorisation** of payments

- A further important control is **regular independent bank reconciliations**

- **Stock controls** are designed to ensure safe custody. These include:

    ○ **Restriction of access** to stock
    ○ **Documentation** and **authorisation** of movements

- Other important controls over stock include regular **independent stock-taking** and **review of stock condition**.

- Most of the key controls over capital and revenue expenditure are the general purchase controls, covered in Chapter 10.

- It is also important that they are recorded correctly, so that profit/loss and assets are not misstated.

- It may not be cost-effective to test controls in this area. Alternative substantive procedures include:

    ○ Analytical review
    ○ Enquiry of purchasing personnel
    ○ Review of board minutes

- The APB has issued guidance on **providing assurance** on the effectiveness of internal controls. Such assurance can be related to the identification of risks, but is more likely to relate to the **design and operation of controls**.

- The **internal auditors are interested in the risks arising to the company in certain cycles**, not simply the risks of errors arising in the financial statements

---

- The objectives and controls they are interested in are more extensive. However, the following links can be seen:
  - ○ Purchases/procurement
  - ○ Sales/marketing
  - ○ Cash/treasury
  - ○ Payroll/human resources

Quick quiz

1   Name the five key aims of controls of the cash system.

 1   ....

 2   ....

 3   ....

 4   ....

 5   ....

2   Give five examples of tests to be performed on the cash payments book.

 1   ....

 2   ....

 3   ....

 4   ....

 5   ....

3   Three important controls over the protection of stocks are:

- Restriction of access to stores
- Regular stocktaking
- Reconciliation of book stock to physical stock

 True   ☐

 False ☐

4   Give two examples of **substantive procedures** that can be used to test capital and revenue expenditure.

Answers to quick quiz

1   See para 1.1

2   See para 1.22

3   True

4   See para 3.9

Now try the questions below from the Exam Question Bank

Number	Level	Marks	Time
11	Exam	20	36 mins

Part D
Balance sheet audit

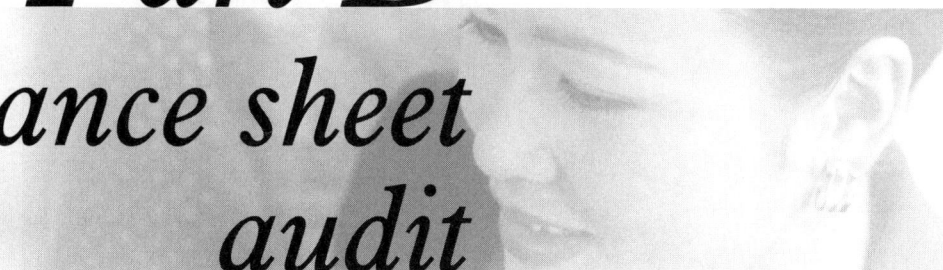

Chapter 12

THE SUBSTANTIVE AUDIT

Topic list	Syllabus reference
1 Substantive testing	6
2 Directional testing	6
3 Analytical procedures	6
4 Accounting estimates	6
5 Opening balances and comparatives	6

Introduction

Having looked at tests of control in detail, we now move onto substantive testing. In the following chapters we shall consider substantive testing in each of the major audit areas. In this chapter however we consider general auditing issues that affect substantive tests generally, directional testing, analytical review and the audit of estimates.

Analytical review impacts upon the whole audit process. We mentioned briefly in Chapter 6 that auditors are required to carry out analytical procedures when **planning** an audit; this chapter goes into more detail.

We then go on to discuss how substantive analytical review can provide **audit evidence**.

Lastly analytical review is required at the final stage of the audit, as a key part of the **overall review** of the final accounts. The purpose of analytical review at this stage is to answer the question 'Do the figures make sense?'

In the second part of this chapter we examine **accounting estimates**. We have mentioned in previous chapters that judgement has to be used in accounting for several figures in the accounts. Often these judgements depend on uncertain future events - what percentage of outstanding debtors will fail to pay their debts, or for how much will stock which has been in the warehouse eventually sell.

Since there may be a range of plausible answers to questions such as these, estimates can cause problems for auditors. We shall see that there are a number of possible ways in which estimates can be tested, and auditors will often wish to use a combination of procedures to obtain the required assurance.

Lastly, we look at the work that the auditor has to do on **opening balances and comparatives**. Substantiating the opening position is a key feature of any substantive audit.

Study guide

Section 16

- Describe and illustrate how analytical procedures are used as substantive procedures
- Explain the problems associated with the audit and review of accounting estimates

---

Exam guide

This chapter forms a basis for the rest of the chapters in this Part of the Text, so the topics covered here are likely to be examined in that context.

---

1 SUBSTANTIVE TESTING

1.1 As discussed in Chapter 8, the auditors need to obtain **sufficient and appropriate audit evidence** to support the financial statement assertions. Substantive procedures aim to obtain that evidence.

KEY TERM

Substantive procedures are tests to obtain audit evidence to detect material misstatements in the financial statements. They are generally of two types:

(a) Analytical procedures

(b) Other substantive procedures such as tests of detail of transactions and balances, review of minutes of directors' meetings and enquiry.

Question 1

Complete the following table showing standard audit tests for each balance sheet objective.

Audit objective	Typical audit tests
Completeness	
Rights and obligations	
Valuation	
Existence	
Occurrence	

Measurement	
Disclosure	

Answer

Audit objective	Typical audit tests
Completeness	(a) Review of post balance sheet items (b) Cut off (c) Analytical review (d) Confirmations (e) Reconciliations to control account (f) Sequence checks (g) Review of reciprocal populations
Rights and obligations	(a) Checking invoices for proof that item belongs to the company (b) Confirmations with third parties
Valuation	(a) Checking to invoices (b) Recalculation (c) Confirming accounting policy consistent and reasonable (d) Review of post balance sheet payments and invoices
Existence	(a) Physical verification (b) Third party confirmations (c) Cut off testing
Occurrence	(a) Inspection of supporting documentation (b) Confirmation from directors that transactions relate to business (c) Inspection of items purchased
Measurement	(a) Re-calculation of correct amounts (b) Third party confirmation (c) Expert valuation (d) Analytical review
Disclosure	(a) Check compliance with CA 1985 and SSAPs and FRSs (b) True and fair override invoked

1.2 The following model for drawing up an audit programme should be borne in mind.

- **Agree opening balances** with **previous year's working papers** (see section 5)
- **Review general ledger** for unusual records
- **Check schedules** provided by client **to and from accounting records** to ensure completeness

BPP PUBLISHING

- Carry out **analytical review**
- **Test transactions in detail**
- **Test balances in detail**
- **Review presentation** and **disclosure** in accounts.

1.3 Auditing exams require a good knowledge of how the **financial statement assertions** determine audit objectives, and the procedures for obtaining audit evidence. Students should be aiming to produce a description of procedures that could be followed by an inexperienced staff member.

2 DIRECTIONAL TESTING

2.1 Broadly speaking, substantive procedures can be said to fall into two categories:

- Tests to discover **errors** (resulting in over- or under-statement)
- Tests to discover **omissions** (resulting in under-statement)

We have already mentioned over- and under-statement in previous chapters, but such matters are particularly relevant in the next few chapters.

Tests designed to discover errors

2.2 These tests will start with the **accounting records** in which the transactions are recorded and check from the entries to supporting documents or other evidence. Such tests should detect any over-statement and also any under-statement through causes other than omission.

Case example: test for errors

If the test is designed to ensure that sales are priced correctly, the test would begin with a sales invoice selected from the sales ledger. Prices would then be checked to the official price list.

Tests designed to discover omissions

2.3 These tests must start from **outside the accounting records** and then check back to those records. Understatements through omission will never be revealed by starting with the account itself as there is clearly no chance of selecting items that have been omitted from the account.

Case example: tests for omission

If the test is designed to discover whether all raw material purchases have been properly processed, the test would start, say, with goods received notes, to be checked to the stock records or purchase ledger.

Directional testing

2.4 For most systems auditors would include tests designed to discover both errors and omissions. The type of test, and direction of the test, should be recognised before selecting the test sample. If the sample which tested the accuracy and validity of the sales ledger were chosen from a file of sales invoices then it would not substantiate the fact that there were no errors in the sales ledger. The approach known as 'directional testing' applies this testing discipline.

2.5 Directional testing is particularly appropriate when testing the financial statement assertions of existence, completeness, rights and obligations, and valuation.

Directional testing and double entry

2.6 The concept of directional testing derives from the principle of double-entry bookkeeping, in that for every **debit** there is a **corresponding credit**, (assuming that the double entry is complete and that the accounting records balance). Therefore, any **misstatement** of a **debit entry** will result in either a corresponding **misstatement** of a **credit entry** or a **misstatement** in the opposite direction, of **another debit entry**.

2.7 By designing audit tests carefully the auditors are able to use this principle in drawing audit conclusions, not only about the debit or credit entries that they have directly tested, but also about the corresponding credit or debit entries that are necessary to balance the books.

2.8 Tests are therefore designed in the following way.

Test item	Example
Test **debit items** (expenditure or assets) for overstatement by selecting debit entries recorded in the nominal ledger and checking value, existence and ownership	If a fixed asset entry in the nominal ledger of £1,000 is selected, it would be overstated if it should have been recorded at anything less than £1,000 or if the company did not own it, or indeed if it did not exist (eg it had been sold or the amount of £1,000 in fact represented a revenue expense)
Test **credit items** (income or liabilities) for understatement by selecting items from appropriate sources independent of the nominal ledger and ensuring that they result in the correct nominal ledger entry	Select a goods despatched note and check that the resultant sale has been recorded in the nominal ledger sales account. Sales would be understated if the nominal ledger did not reflect the transaction at all (completeness) or reflected it at less than full value (say if goods valued at £1,000 were recorded in the sales account at £900, there would be an understatement of £100).

2.9 The matrix set out below demonstrates how directional testing is applied to give assurance on all account areas in the financial statements.

| Type of account | Purpose of primary test | Primary test also gives comfort on | | | |
		Assets	Liabilities	Income	Expenses
Assets	Overstatement (O)	U	O	O	U
Liabilities	Understatement (U)	U	O	O	U
Income	Understatement (U)	U	O	O	U
Expense	Overstatement (O)	U	O	O	U

2.10 Thus, a test for the overstatement of an asset simultaneously gives comfort on understatement of other assets, overstatement of liabilities, overstatement of income and understatement of expenses.

Question 2

Fill in the blank spaces.

(a) Based on double-entry bookkeeping, it can be seen from the matrix that assets can only be *understated* by virtue of:

    (i) Other assets being _____; or
    (ii) Liabilities being _____; or
    (iii) Income being _____; or
    (iv) Expenses being _____.

(b) Similarly, liabilities can only be *overstated* by virtue of:

    (i) Assets being _____; or
    (ii) Other liabilities being _____; or
    (iii) Income being _____; or
    (iv) Expenses being _____.

Answer

(a)	(i)	Overstated	(b)	(i)	Overstated
	(ii)	Understated		(ii)	Understated
	(iii)	Understated		(iii)	Understated
	(iv)	Overstated		(iv)	Overstated

2.11 So, by performing the primary tests shown in the matrix, the auditors obtain audit assurance in other audit areas. Successful completion of the primary tests will therefore result in them having tested all account areas both for overstatement and understatement.

2.12 The **major advantage** of the directional audit approach is its **cost-effectiveness.**

(a) Assets and expenses are tested for overstatement only, and liabilities and income for understatement only, that is, items are not tested for both overstatement and understatement.

(b) It audits directly the more likely types of transactional misstatement, that is, unrecorded income and improper expense (arising intentionally or unintentionally).

3 ANALYTICAL PROCEDURES

3.1 We defined analytical procedures briefly in Chapter 6. SAS 410 *Analytical procedures* deals with the subject.

> **KEY TERM**
>
> **Analytical procedures** are the analysis of relationships:
>
> (a) Between items of financial data, or between items of financial and non-financial data, deriving from the same period, or
>
> (b) Between comparable financial information deriving from different periods to identify consistencies and predicted patterns or significant fluctuations and unexpected relationships, and the results of investigation thereof

Nature and purpose of analytical procedures

3.2 The SAS states that analytical procedures include:

(a) The **consideration of comparisons** of this year's financial information with:

- **Similar information** for prior periods
- **Anticipated results** of the client
- **Predictions prepared** by the auditors, such as an estimation of the depreciation charge for the year
- **Industry information,** such as a comparison of the client's ratio of sales to trade debtors with industry averages, or with the ratios relating to other entities of comparable size in the same industry.

(b) Those between **elements of financial information** that are **expected to conform** to a predicted pattern based on experience, such as the relationship of gross profit to sales

(c) Those between **financial information** and **relevant non-financial information,** such as the relationship of payroll costs to number of employees

3.3 A variety of methods can be used to perform the procedures discussed above, ranging from **simple comparisons** to **complex analysis** using statistics, on a company level, branch level or individual account level. The choice of procedures is a matter for the auditors' professional judgement.

Analytical procedures in planning the audit

SAS 410.2

Auditors should apply analytical procedures at the planning stage to assist in understanding the entity's business, in identifying areas of potential audit risk and in planning the nature, timing and extent of other audit procedures.

3.4 Analytical procedures at the planning stage have to be seen in conjunction with risk analysis and materiality as means of identifying key audit areas.

3.5 Possible **sources of information** about the client include:

- Interim financial information
- Budgets
- Management accounts
- Non-financial information
- Bank and cash records
- VAT returns
- Board minutes
- Discussions or correspondence with the client at the year-end.

Auditors may also use specific industry information or general knowledge of current industry conditions to assess the client's performance.

3.6 As well as helping to determine the nature, timing and extent of other audit procedures, such analytical procedures may also indicate aspects of the business of which the auditors were previously unaware.

3.7 Auditors are looking to see if developments in the client's business have had the expected effects. They will be particularly interested in changes in audit areas where problems have occurred in the past.

BPP PUBLISHING

3.8 SAS 410 *Analytical procedures* states that auditors must decide whether using available analytical procedures as substantive procedures will be effective and efficient in reducing **detection risk** for specific financial statement assertions.

3.9 Auditors may efficiently use analytical data produced by the entity itself, provided they are satisfied that it has been properly prepared.

3.10 The SAS lists a number of factors which the auditors should consider when deciding whether to use analytical procedures as substantive procedures.

Factors to consider	Example
The **plausibility and predictability** of the relationships identified for comparison and evaluation	The strong relationship between certain selling expenses and turnover in businesses where the sales force is paid by commission
The **objectives** of the analytical procedures and the extent to which their results are reliable	
The **detail** to which information can be **analysed**	Analytical procedures may be more effective when applied to financial information on individual sections of an operation such as individual factories or shops
The **availability of information**	Financial: budgets or forecasts
	Non-financial: eg the number of units produced or sold
The **relevance of the information** available	Whether budgets are established as results to be expected rather than as tough targets (which may well not be achieved)
The **comparability of the information** available	Comparisons with average performance in an industry may be of little value if a large number of companies differ significantly from the average.
The **knowledge gained during previous audits**	The effectiveness of the accounting and internal control systems
	The types of problems giving rise to accounting adjustments in prior periods

Reliance on analytical procedures

3.11 From our earlier coverage of audit evidence we can see that the information used in analytical procedures will be more reliable if it comes from sources independent from, rather than internal to, the client. Information produced independently outside the accounting function is more reliable than that originating from within it.

3.12 The results of **other audit procedures** will help to determine the reliability of the information used in analytical procedures, as will the importance of the results of the procedure for the auditors' opinion.

3.13 The SAS identifies other factors which should be considered when determining the reliance that the auditors should place on the results of substantive analytical procedures.

Reliability factors	Example
Other audit procedures directed towards the same financial statements assertions	Other procedures auditors undertake in reviewing the collectability of debtors, such as the review of subsequent cash receipts, may confirm or dispel questions arising from the application of analytical procedures to a profile of customers' accounts which lists for how long monies have been owed
The **accuracy** with which the expected results of analytical procedures can be predicted	Auditors normally expect greater consistency in comparing the relationship of gross profit to sales from one period to another than in comparing expenditure which may or may not be made within a period, such as research or advertising
The **frequency** with which a relationship is observed	A pattern repeated monthly as opposed to annually

3.14 Reliance on the results of analytical procedures depends on the auditors' assessment of the **risk** that the procedures may identify relationships (between data) do exist, whereas a material misstatement exists (that is, the relationships, in fact, do not exist).

3.15 It depends also on the results of investigations that auditors have made if substantive analytical procedures have highlighted significant fluctuations or unexpected relationships (see below).

Analytical review at the final stage

3.16 SAS 410 goes on to look at analytical procedures as part of the overall review when completing the audit. The key aim of procedures is to see whether the overall accounts appear reasonable. The final review procedures are considered in Chapter 18.

> ### SAS 410.3
>
> When completing the audit, auditors should apply analytical procedures in forming an overall conclusion as to whether the financial statements as a whole are consistent with their knowledge of the entity's business.

3.17 The conclusions from these analytical procedures should be consistent with the conclusions formed from other audit procedures on parts of the financial statements. However, these analytical procedures may highlight areas which require further investigation and audit.

Investigating significant fluctuations or unexpected relationships

> ### SAS 410.4
>
> When significant fluctuations or unexpected relationships are identified that are inconsistent with other relevant information or that deviate from predicted patterns, auditors should investigate and obtain adequate explanations and appropriate corroborative evidence.

3.18 Investigations will start with **enquiries** to management and then confirmation of management's responses by:

- **Comparing them** with the auditors' knowledge of the entity's business and with other evidence obtained during the course of the audit, or

- **Carrying out additional audit procedures** where appropriate to confirm the explanations received

3.19 If explanations cannot be given by management, or if they are insufficient, the auditors must determine which further audit procedures to undertake to explain the fluctuation or relationship.

Practical techniques

3.20 When carrying out analytical procedures, auditors should remember that every industry is different and each company within an industry differs in certain respects.

Important accounting ratios

$$\text{Gross profit margin} = \frac{\text{Gross profit}}{\text{Turnover}} \times 100\%$$

This should be calculated in total and by product, area and month/quarter if possible.

$$\text{Debtors turnover period} = \frac{\text{Debtors}}{\text{Sales}} \times 365$$

$$\text{Stock turnover ratio} = \frac{\text{Cost of sales}}{\text{Stock}}$$

$$\text{Current ratio} = \frac{\text{Current assets}}{\text{Current liabilities}}$$

$$\text{Quick or acid test ratio} = \frac{\text{Current assets (excluding stock)}}{\text{Current liabilities}}$$

$$\text{Gearing ratio} = \frac{\text{Loans}}{\text{Share capital and reserves}} \times 100\%$$

$$\text{Return on capital employed} = \frac{\text{Profit before tax}}{\text{Total assets - current - liabilities}}$$

Significant items

Creditors and purchases

Stocks and cost of sales

Fixed assets and depreciation, repairs and maintenance expense

Intangible assets and amortisation

Loans and interest expense

Investments and investment income

Debtors and bad debt expense

Debtors and sales

3.21 Ratios mean very little when used in isolation. They should be calculated for **previous periods** and for **comparable companies**. The permanent file should contain a section with summarised accounts and the chosen ratios for prior years.

3.22 In addition to looking at the more usual ratios the auditors should consider examining **other ratios** that may be **relevant** to the particular **clients' business,** such as revenue per passenger mile for an airline operator client, or fees per partner for a professional office.

3.23 Other analytical techniques include:

(a) **Examining related accounts** in conjunction with each other. Often revenue and expense accounts are related to balance sheet accounts and comparisons should be made to ensure relationships are reasonable.

(b) **Trend analysis**. Sophisticated statistical techniques (beyond the scope of this paper) can be used to compare this period with previous periods.

(c) **Reasonableness tests**. These involve calculating **expected value** of an item and comparing it with its actual value, for example, for straight-line depreciation.

$$(Cost + Additions - Disposals) \times Depreciation \% = Charge \ in \ P\&L \ A/C$$

3.24 Other areas that might be investigated as part of the analytical procedures include the following.

- **Examine changes** in **products, customers and levels** of **returns**
- **Assess** the effect of **price and mix changes** on the cost of sales
- **Consider** the effect of **inflation, industrial disputes, changes in production methods** and **changes in activity** on the charge for wages
- **Obtain explanations** for all **major variances** analysed using a standard costing system. Particular attention should be paid to those relating to the over or under absorption of overheads since these may, inter alia, affect stock valuations
- **Compare trends in production and sales** and assess the effect on any provisions for obsolete stocks
- **Ensure** that **changes in the percentage labour or overhead content** of production costs are also reflected in the stock valuation
- **Review other profit and loss expenditure**, comparing:
  ◦ Rent with annual rent per rental agreement
  ◦ Rates with previous year and known rates increases
  ◦ Interest payable on loans with outstanding balance and interest rate per loan agreement
  ◦ Hire or leasing charges with annual rate per agreements
  ◦ Vehicle running expenses to vehicles
  ◦ Other items related to activity level with general price increase and change in relevant level of activity (for example telephone expenditure will increase disproportionately if export or import business increases)
  ◦ Other items not related to activity level with general price increases (or specific increases if known)
- **Review** profit and loss account for **items** which may have been **omitted** (eg scrap sales, training levy, special contributions to pension fund, provisions for dilapidation etc)
- **Ensure expected variations** arising from the following have occurred:
  ◦ Industry or local trends
  ◦ Known disturbances of the trading pattern (for example strikes, depot closures, failure of suppliers)

3.25 Certain of the comparisons and ratios measuring liquidity and longer-term capital structure will assist in evaluating whether the company is a **going concern**, in addition to contributing to the overall view of the accounts. We shall see in Chapter 18, however, that there are factors other than declining ratios that may indicate going concern problems.

3.26 The working papers must contain the completed results of analytical procedures. They should include:

- The **outline programme** of the work
- The **summary of significant figures** and relationships for the period
- A **summary** of **comparisons made** with budgets and with previous years
- Details of all **significant fluctuations** or **unexpected relationships** considered
- Details of the **results of investigations** into such fluctuations/relationships
- The **audit conclusions** reached
- **Information considered necessary** for assisting in the planning of subsequent audits

Exam focus point

In the exam you may be given a set of figures and:

(a) Asked to calculate changes, key ratios etc and hence identify significant areas of the accounts
(b) Asked what audit work will be required on these significant areas

When analysing figures, make sure that the points which you make are consistent with each other.

Factors that indicate possible going concern problems are particularly important.

Mention of analytical procedures will generally be worth a couple of marks in any question on substantive testing.

However you will not get any marks just for saying 'perform analytical procedures'; you will need to give details of the procedures that should be performed.

4 ACCOUNTING ESTIMATES

4.1 SAS 420 *Audit of accounting estimates* provides guidance on the audit of accounting estimates contained in financial statements.

SAS 420.1

Auditors should obtain sufficient appropriate audit evidence regarding accounting estimates.

KEY TERM

An **accounting estimate** is an approximation of the amount of an item in the absence of a precise means of measurement.

4.2 SAS 420 gives these examples.

- Allowances to reduce stocks and debtors to their estimated realisable value
- Depreciation provisions
- Accrued revenue
- Provision for a loss from a lawsuit
- Profits or losses on construction contracts in progress
- Provision to meet warranty claims

4.3   **Directors and management** are responsible for making accounting estimates included in the financial statements. These estimates are often made in conditions of uncertainty regarding the outcome of events and involve the use of judgement. The risk of a material misstatement therefore increases when accounting estimates are involved.

4.4   **Audit evidence** supporting accounting estimates is **generally less than conclusive** and so auditors need to exercise **significant judgement**.

The nature of accounting estimates

4.5   Accounting estimates may be produced as part of the routine operations of the accounting system, or may be a non-routine procedure at the period end. Where, as is frequently the case, a **formula** based on past experience is used to calculate the estimate, it should be reviewed regularly by management (for example, actual vs estimate in prior periods).

Audit procedures

> **SAS 420.2**
>
> Auditors should obtain sufficient appropriate evidence as to whether an accounting estimate is reasonable in the circumstances and, when required, is appropriately disclosed.

4.6   The auditors should gain an understanding of the procedures and methods used by management to make accounting estimates. This will aid the auditors' planning of their own procedures.

> **SAS 420.3**
>
> Auditors should adopt one or a combination of the following approaches in the audit of an accounting estimate:
>
> (a)   review and test the process used by management or the directors to develop the estimate;
>
> (b)   use an independent estimate for comparison with that prepared by management or the directors; or
>
> (c)   review subsequent events.

Review and testing the process

4.7   The auditors will carry out the following steps.

- **Consider whether data is accurate, complete and reliable**
- **Seek appropriate evidence from outside client** (for example, industry sales projections to confirm internal estimates of future sales orders)
- **Check** whether **data is appropriately analysed** and **projected** (for example, age analysis of accounts receivable)
- **Evaluate** whether **base used** for assumptions is **appropriate**
- **Evaluate** whether **assumptions** are **reasonable** in light of **prior period results**
- **Consider** whether **formulae** used remain **appropriate** in the light of current conditions
- Consider whether **assumptions** are **consistent**
  - With those used for other accounting estimates

> ○ With management's plans
>
> - **Consider** whether **expert opinion** is required if estimates are complex
>
> - **Test calculations** involved in the estimate considering:
>   ○ Complexity of calculation
>   ○ Procedures and methods used by the client
>   ○ Materiality of estimate
>
> - **Compare previous estimates** with actual results, aiming to obtain evidence about:
>   ○ General reliability of the client's estimating procedures
>   ○ Whether adjustments to estimating formulae will be required
>   ○ Whether differences between previous estimates and actual figures ought to be disclosed
>
> - Consider management's approval procedures, confirming it is performed by the **appropriate level of management** and **evidenced**

Use of an independent estimate

4.8 Such an estimate (made or obtained by the auditors) may be compared with the accounting estimate. The auditors should **evaluate the data, consider the assumptions** and **test** the **calculation procedures** used to develop the independent estimate. Prior period independent assessments and actual results could also be compared.

Review of subsequent events

4.9 The auditors should review transactions or events after the period end which may reduce or even remove the need to test accounting estimates (as described above).

Evaluation of results of audit procedures

SAS 420.4

Auditors should make a final assessment of the reasonableness of the accounting estimate based on their knowledge of the business and whether the estimate is consistent with other audit evidence obtained during the audit.

4.10 Auditors must assess the difference between the amount of an estimate supported by evidence and the estimate calculated by management.

- If the auditors believe that the difference is unreasonable then an adjustment should be made.

- If the directors or management refuse to revise the estimate, then the difference is considered a misstatement and will be treated as such.

5   OPENING BALANCES AND COMPARATIVES

KEY TERMS

Opening balances are those account balances that exist at the beginning of the period. Opening balances are based upon the closing balances of the preceding period and reflect the effect of transactions of preceding periods and accounting policies applied in the preceding period.

Comparatives are the corresponding amounts and other related disclosures from the preceding period which are part of the current period's financial statements as required by relevant legislation and applicable accounting standards. Such comparatives are intended to be read in relation to the amounts and other disclosures related to the current period.

5.1   SAS 450 *Opening balances and comparatives* covers this area. It is appropriate to consider such matters at the planning stage and early in the audit process as the **outcome of the relevant audit procedures could have a substantial impact on the audit of current year transactions and balances**.

SAS 450.1

Auditors should obtain sufficient appropriate audit evidence that amounts derived from the preceding period's financial statements are free from material misstatements and are appropriately incorporated in the financial statements for the current period.

5.2   Note that the preceding period accounts, when new auditors are appointed, may have been reported on by the predecessor auditors or they may have been **unaudited**.

Opening balances

SAS 450.2

Auditors should obtain sufficient appropriate audit evidence that:

(a)   opening balances have been appropriately brought forward;

(b)   opening balances do not contain errors or misstatements which materially affect the current period's financial statements; and

(c)   appropriate accounting policies are consistently applied or changes in accounting policies have been properly accounted for and adequately disclosed.

5.3   If the auditors are unable to obtain sufficient appropriate audit evidence, then they should consider the implications for their audit report. The reporting implications of this are discussed in Chapter 19.

5.4   The SAS goes on to look at opening balances from the point of view of both **continuing auditors** and **incoming auditors**.

> **KEY TERMS**
>
> **Continuing auditors** are the auditors who audited and reported on the preceding period's financial statements and continue as the auditors for the current period.
>
> **Predecessor auditors** are the auditors who previously audited and reported on the financial statements of an entity, and who have been replaced by the incoming auditors.
>
> **Incoming auditors** are the auditors who are auditing and reporting on the current period's financial statements, not having audited and reported on those for the preceding period.

Continuing auditors

5.5 Audit procedures need not extend beyond ensuring that opening balances have been **appropriately brought forward** and the current accounting policies have been consistently applied, **if:**

- The continuing auditors issued an unqualified report on the preceding periods' financial statements.

- The audit of the current period does not reveal any matters which cast doubt on those financial statements.

5.6 If a **qualified audit report** was issued on the preceding period's financial statements then the auditors should consider whether the matter which gave rise to the qualification has been **adequately resolved** and properly dealt with in the **current period's financial statements**. This is in addition to the procedures above.

Incoming auditors

5.7 This situation is obviously more difficult. Appropriate and sufficient audit evidence is required on the opening balances and this depends on matters such as the following.

- The **accounting policies** followed by the entity
- Whether the **preceding period's financial statements were audited** and, if so, whether the auditors' report was **qualified**
- The **nature of the opening balances**, including the risk of their misstatement
- The **materiality of the opening balances** relative to the current period's financial statements

5.8 The **procedures given** for continuing auditors should be carried out. Other procedures suggested by the SAS are as follows.

- **Consultations with management** and review of records, working papers and accounting and control procedures for the preceding period

- **Substantive testing of any opening balances** in respect of which the results of other procedures are considered unsatisfactory

5.9 Consultations with predecessor auditors will not normally be necessary as the above procedures will be sufficient. Predecessor auditors have no legal or ethical duty to provide information and would not normally be expected to release relevant working papers. However:

'they are expected to cooperate with incoming auditors to provide clarification of, or information on, specific accounting matters where this is necessary to resolve any particular difficulties.'

Comparatives

5.10 Opening balances will, in the current year's financial statements, become comparative figures which must be disclosed.

SAS 450.3

Auditors should obtain sufficient appropriate audit evidence that:

(a) the accounting policies used for the comparatives are consistent with those of the current period and appropriate adjustments and disclosures have been made where this is not the case;

(b) the comparatives agree with the amounts and other disclosures presented in the preceding period and are free from errors in the context of the financial statements of the current period; and

(c) where comparatives have been adjusted as required by relevant legislation and accounting standards, appropriate disclosures have been made.

5.11 The SAS then goes on to discuss the status of comparatives from an audit perspective.

'The comparatives form part of the financial statements on which the auditors express an opinion, although they are not required to express an opinion on the comparatives as such. Their responsibility is to establish whether the comparatives are the amounts which appeared in the preceding period's financial statements or, where appropriate, have been restated.'

5.12 Where the auditors are unable to obtain sufficient appropriate audit evidence to support the comparatives they must consider the implications for their report. The SAS then discusses these implications in various situations.

Continuing auditors

5.13 The extent of audit procedures for comparatives will be significantly less then those for current year balances; normally they will be limited to a **check that balances have been brought forward correctly**. Materiality of any misstatements should be considered in relationship to **current** period figures.

5.14 The auditors' report on the previous period financial statements may have been qualified. Where the qualification matter is still **unresolved**, two situations may apply.

(a) If the matter is material in the context of the current period's opening balances as well as comparatives, the report on the current period's financial statements should be **qualified regarding opening balances and comparatives**.

(b) If the matter does not affect opening balances but is material in the context of the current period's financial statements, the report on the current period's financial statements should **refer to the comparatives**.

   (i) If comparatives are **required by law or regulation**, the reference will be in the form of a **qualification on the grounds of non-compliance** with that requirement.

   (ii) If comparatives are presented solely as **good practice**, the reference should be in the form of an **explanatory paragraph**.

5.15 Where a previous qualification has been resolved and dealt with properly in the financial statements then no mention of the qualification needs to be made in the current audit report.

5.16 If, however, the matter was material to the current period, then it should be mentioned in the current report, including an explanation of how it has been resolved. It is also possible that a qualification will still be necessary, for example, if a provision has been made in the current year which should have been made in the previous period.

Incoming auditors: audited comparatives

5.17 In this situation, the preceding period's financial statements have been audited by other auditors. The **incoming auditors only bear audit responsibility for the comparatives in the context of the financial statements as a whole**.

5.18 The incoming auditors will use the knowledge gained in the current audit to decide whether the previous period's financial statements have been properly reflected as comparatives in the current period's financial statements.

5.19 The procedures described above should be considered should such a situation arise.

Incoming auditors: unaudited comparatives

5.20 In this situation (for example, where the company took advantage of the small company audit exemption in the previous period) the auditors should check that there is clear **disclosure** in the current financial statements that the **comparatives are unaudited**. They must still undertake the duties mentioned above as far as is appropriate.

5.21 If there is not sufficient appropriate evidence, or if disclosure is inadequate, the auditors should consider the implications for their reports.

Question 3

An auditing standard has been issued on *Opening balances and comparatives*, and one of the matters it considers is where one firm of auditors takes over from another firm. You have recently been appointed auditor of Lowdham Castings Ltd, a company which has been trading for about thirty years, and are carrying out the audit for the year ended 30 September 20X6. The company's turnover is about £500,000 and its normal profit before tax is about £30,000.

Required

Discuss your responsibilities in relation to the comparatives included in the accounts for the year ended 30 September 20X6. You should also consider the information you would require from the retiring auditors.

Answer

Consideration of the financial statements of the preceding period is necessary in the audit of the current period's financial statements in relation to three main aspects.

(a) *Opening position:* obtaining satisfaction that those amounts which have a direct effect on the current period's results or closing position have been properly brought forward

(b) *Accounting policies:* determining whether the accounting policies adopted for the current period are consistent with those of the previous period

(c) *Comparatives:* determining that the comparatives are properly shown in the current period's financial statements

The auditors' main concern will therefore be to satisfy themselves that there were no material misstatements in the previous year's financial statements which may have a bearing upon their work in the current year.

The new auditors do not have to 're-audit' the previous year's financial statements, but they will have to pay more attention to them than would normally be the case where they had themselves been the auditors in the earlier period. A useful source of audit evidence will clearly be the previous auditors, and, with the client's permission, they should be contacted to see if they are prepared to co-operate. Certainly, any known areas of weakness should be discussed with the previous auditors and it is also possible that they might be prepared to provide copies of their working papers (although there is no legal or ethical provision which requires the previous auditors to co-operate in this way).

Chapter roundup

- **Analytical procedures** cover comparisons of financial data with other financial or non-financial data of the same or previous periods, also comparisons of financial data with expected data.

- Analytical procedures aim to **identify inconsistencies** or **significant fluctuations**.

- Analytical procedures must be undertaken at the **planning** stage of audits.

- Analytical procedures can be used as substantive procedures, depending on the **available information** and the plausibility and predictability of the relationships.

- Analytical review should be undertaken at the **final stage** of an audit on the final accounts.

- **Significant fluctuations** and **unexpected variations** should be investigated by enquiries of management, comparisons with other evidence and further audit procedures as required.

- Accounts may contain **accounting estimates** in a number of areas.

- Auditors can test accounting estimates by:

  ○ **Reviewing** and **testing** the management process
  ○ **Using an independent estimate**
  ○ **Reviewing subsequent events**

- Specific procedures must be applied to **opening balances** at a new audit client.

- The auditors' responsibilities for **comparatives** relate mainly to **consistency**, although comparatives and opening balances can have an impact on current results.

Quick quiz

1   Link the type of account with the purpose of the primary test in directional testing.

(a)	Assets	(i)	Overstatement
(b)	Liabilities	(ii)	Overstatement
(c)	Income	(iii)	Understatement
(d)	Expense	(iv)	Understatement

2   Name four sources of analytical information which can be used at the planning stage of the audit.

1   ....

2   ....

3   ....

4   ....

3   Identify the significant relationships in the list of items below

(a) creditors	(b) interest	(c) purchases	(d) sales
(e) amortisation	(f) loans	(g) debtors	(h) intangibles

4   Complete the definition.

An accounting estimate is an .... of the .... of an item in the absence of a .... of measurement.

5   Give three examples of an accounting estimate.

1   ....

2   ....

3   ....

6   Auditors are responsible for making accounting estimates to be used in the accounts.

True   ☐

False ☐

7   Give three steps in the review and test the stage of auditing accounting estimates.

1   ....

2   ....

3   ....

8   The audit report covers the comparatives as well as the current year figures

True   ☐

False ☐

Answers to quick quiz

1   (a)   (i)
(b)   (iii)
(c)   (ii)
(d)   (iv)

2   See para 3.5

3   (a)   (c)
(b)   (f)
(d)   (g)
(e)   (h)

4   approximation, amount, precise means

5   See para 4.2

6   False

7   Any from para 4.7

8   True

Now try the question below from the Exam Question Bank

Number	Level	Marks	Time
12	Introductory	n/a	20 mins

Chapter 13

FIXED ASSETS

Topic list	Syllabus reference
1 Tangible fixed assets	6
2 Audit procedures	6
3 Other fixed assets	6

Introduction

The final audit will concentrate on the balance sheet to a great extent. The following chapters cover the audit of the key balance sheet areas.

Although each audit client is different, most of the assets in this and the next two chapters will be present in the final accounts. The importance of each balance sheet component will vary from client to client.

The chapter highlights the key objectives for each major component. You must understand what **objectives** the various audit tests are designed to achieve. Objectives of particular significance for tangible fixed assets are **rights and obligations** (that is ownership), **existence and valuation**. You should note it is generally necessary to carry out different tests on ownership and existence.

Valuation is the other important assertion. The auditors will concentrate on testing any valuations made during the year, and also whether other values appear reasonable given asset usage and condition. A very important aspect of testing valuation is reviewing depreciation rates.

A topic which we covered in an earlier chapter may well be important in the audit of fixed assets, using the work of an expert (which we covered in Chapter 7). You should refer back to your notes in this subject.

Study guide

Section 21

- Describe and tabulate for inclusion in a work program the substantive procedures used in obtaining evidence in relation to tangible fixed assets and the related income statement entries.

- Explain the purpose of substantive procedures in relation to financial statement assertions concerning tangible fixed assets.

Exam guide

Exam questions on any balance sheet area may either focus on:

- Audit work required
- Accounting treatment problems
- Both the above

Tangible fixed assets are often financed by long term loans (for instance a mortgage or lease). Therefore these areas could be examined together. Fixed assets were examined on the pilot paper.

BPP PUBLISHING

1 TANGIBLE FIXED ASSETS

1.1 The auditors' substantive work in respect of tangible fixed assets may involve an important technique highlighted earlier in this text: using the work of an expert. However, the subjective area of depreciation may cause the greatest audit headache.

Internal control considerations

1.2 The **fixed asset register** is a very important aspect of the internal control systems. It enables assets to be identified, and comparisons between the general ledger, fixed asset register and the assets themselves provide **evidence** that the assets are **completely recorded**.

1.3 Another significant control is procedures over acquisitions and disposals, that acquisitions are properly **authorised**, and **disposals** are **authorised** and **proceeds accounted for**.

1.4 Other significant aspects are:

- **Security arrangements** over fixed assets are **sufficient**.
- **Fixed assets** are **maintained properly**.
- **Depreciation** is **reviewed every year**.
- **All income** is **collected** from **income-yielding assets**.

Ownership and existence: freehold and leasehold properties

1.5 The verification of the client's title to property shown in the accounts is strictly a matter for a solicitor, although for normal audit purposes *prima facie* evidence of title is acceptable.

1.6 If the deeds are held on the client's premises the auditors should inspect them at or near the balance sheet date; if held by an independent third party, and that third party is a bank, solicitor, insurance company or another recognised depository, auditors will normally obtain a certificate stating whether or not the deeds are held in safe custody or as security. Where there is doubt about the status of the third party, auditors should seek to inspect the deeds themselves at the party's premises.

1.7 If the certificate is couched in unsatisfactory terms, such as '... an envelope purporting to contain ...' the auditors should arrange to inspect the deeds physically. In future years they should request confirmation that the deeds examined have not been withdrawn from the depository during the year; if they have, a further inspection will be necessary.

1.8 The examination of title deeds verifies **rights and obligations**; it does not itself verify the actual existence of buildings, even if the deeds refer to them. The auditors should consider a physical inspection of any buildings whose existence may be in doubt.

2 AUDIT PROCEDURES   Pilot paper

Exam focus point

In the exam you may be asked generally how to audit certain aspects of tangible fixed assets (such as valuation) or you may be given a specific example and asked what audit work you would carry out. (For example, X Limited has revalued its properties by £40,000 this year using a valuation by a director.)

Completeness

2.1

- **Obtain** or **prepare** a **summary** of tangible fixed assets showing how:
  - ° **Gross book value**
  - ° **Accumulated depreciation**
  - ° **Net book value**

  reconcile with the **opening position**.

- **Compare fixed assets** in the general ledger with the **fixed assets register** and **obtain explanations** for **differences**

- **Check** whether **assets** which **physically exist** are **recorded** in **fixed asset register**

- If a fixed asset register is not kept, **obtain** a **schedule** showing the original costs and present depreciated value of major fixed assets

- **Reconcile** the **schedule** of fixed assets with the **general ledger**

Existence

2.2

- **Confirm** that the **company physically inspects** all items in the fixed asset register each year

- **Inspect assets,** concentrating on high value items and additions in year. Confirm items inspected:
  - ° Exist
  - ° Are in use
  - ° Are in good condition
  - ° Have correct serial numbers

- **Review records** of **income yielding assets**

- **Reconcile** opening and closing **vehicles** by numbers as well as amounts

Valuation

2.3

- **Verify valuation** to valuation certificate

- **Consider reasonableness** of **valuation**, reviewing:
  - ° Experience of valuer
  - ° Scope of work
  - ° Methods and assumptions used
  - ° Valuation bases are in line with FRS 15

- **Check revaluation** surplus has been **correctly calculated**

- Check valuations of all assets that have been revalued have been **updated regularly** (full valuation every five years and an interim valuation in year three generally)

- Check that client has **recognised** in the **profit and loss account** revaluation losses which relate to clear consumption of economic benefits or which take the valuation below depreciated historical cost, and client has **recognised all other gains and losses** in **statement of total recognised gains and losses**

Rights and obligations

2.4
- **Verify title** to land and buildings by inspection of:
  - ° Title deeds
  - ° Land registry certificates
  - ° Leases
- Obtain a certificate from solicitors/bankers:
  - ° **Stating purpose** for which the deeds are being held (custody only)
  - ° **Stating deeds** are **free** from **mortgage** or **lien**
- **Inspect registration documents** for vehicles held, checking that they are in client's name
- **Confirm** all vehicles used for the **client's business**
- **Examine documents** of **title** for other assets (including purchase invoices, architects' certificates, contracts, hire purchase or lease agreements)

Additions

2.5 These tests are to confirm **rights and obligations**, **valuation** and **completeness**

- **Verify additions** by inspection of architects' certificates, solicitors' completion statements, suppliers' invoices etc.
- **Check capitalisation** of **expenditure** is correct by considering for fixed assets additions and items in relevant expense categories (repairs, motor expenses, sundry expenses) whether:
  - ° Capital/revenue distinction is correctly drawn
  - ° Capitalisation is in line with consistently applied company policy
- **Check purchases** have been **properly allocated** to correct fixed asset accounts
- **Check purchases** have been **authorised** by directors/senior management
- **Ensure** that appropriate **claims** have been made for **grants,** and grants received and receivable have been received
- **Check additions** have been **recorded** in fixed asset register and general ledger

Self-constructed assets

2.6 These tests are to confirm **valuation** and **completeness**

- **Verify material** and **labour** costs and **overheads** to invoices, wage records etc
- **Ensure expenditure** has been **analysed correctly** and **properly charged** to capital
- **Check no profit element** has been included in costs
- Check **finance costs** have been **capitalised** (or not) on a consistent basis and costs capitalised in period do not exceed total finance costs

Disposals

2.7 These tests are to confirm **rights and obligations, completeness, occurrence** and **measurement.**

- **Verify disposals** with supporting documentation, checking transfer of title, sales price and dates of completion and payment
- **Check calculation** of profit or loss is accurate and is in **accordance** with FRS 3
- **Check** that **disposals** have been **authorised**
- **Consider** whether **proceeds** are **reasonable**
- If the asset was **used as security,** ensure **release from security** has been correctly made

Depreciation

2.8   These tests are to confirm **valuation**

- **Review depreciation rates** applied in relation to:
  - Asset lives
  - Residual values
  - Replacement policy
  - Past experience of gains and losses on disposal
  - Consistency with prior years and accounting policy
  - Possible obsolescence
- **Check depreciation** has been **charged on all assets** with a limited useful life
- For **revalued assets,** ensure that the charge for **depreciation** is **based** on the **revalued amount**
- **Check calculation** of depreciation rates
- **Compare ratios** of depreciation to fixed assets (by category) with:
  - Previous years
  - Depreciation policy rates
- **Ensure no further depreciation** provided on **fully depreciated assets**
- **Check** that **depreciation policies and rates are disclosed** in the accounts

Charges and commitments

2.9   These tests are to confirm **rights and obligations**

- **Review for evidence** of charges in statutory books and by company search
- **Review leases** of leasehold properties to ensure that company has fulfilled covenants therein
- **Examine invoices received after year-end, orders and minutes** for evidence of capital commitments

Insurance

2.10   This test is to confirm **valuation**

- **Review insurance policies** in force for all categories of tangible fixed assets and consider the adequacy of their insured values and check expiry dates

Question 1

You are the manager in charge of the audit of Maurice plc, a building and construction company, and you are reviewing the fixed asset section of the current audit file for the year ended 30 September 20X5. You find the following five matters which the audit senior has identified as problem areas. He is reviewing the company's proposed treatment of the five transactions in the accounts and is not sure that he has yet carried out sufficient audit work.

The five matters are as follows.

(a) During the year Maurice plc built a new canteen for its own staff at a cost of £450,000. This amount has been included in buildings as at 30 September 20X5.

(b) Loose tools included in the financial statements at a total cost of £166,000 are tools used on two of the construction sites on which Maurice operates. They are classified as fixed assets and depreciated over two years.

(c) A dumper truck, previously written off in the company's accounting records has been refurbished at a cost of £46,000 and this amount included in plant and machinery as at 30 September 20X5.

(d) The company's main office block has been revalued from £216,000 to £266,000 and this amount included in the balance sheet as at 30 September 20X5.

(e) A deposit of £20,000 for new equipment has been included under the heading plant and machinery although the final instalment of £35,000 was not paid over until 31 October 20X5 which was the date of delivery of the plant.

You are required, for each of the above matters to:

(a) Comment on the acceptability of the accounting treatment and disclosure as indicated above.
(b) Outline the audit work and evidence required to substantiate the assets.

Answer

(a) *Acceptability of accounting treatment and disclosure*

(i) *New staff canteen.* The costs of building a new staff canteen can quite properly be capitalised and treated as part of buildings in the balance sheet. The company's normal depreciation policy should be applied, subject only to the canteen being completed and in use at the year end.

(ii) *Loose tools.* Loose tools tend to have a very limited life and individually not to be material in value. For these reasons any capitalisation policy must be extremely prudent. The acceptability of this accounting treatment would depend on the policy in previous years and normal practice within the industry.

(iii) *Dumper truck.* The refurbishment costs have obviously extended the useful life of this asset and it therefore seems reasonable to capitalise the expenditure. Depreciation should be charged on the refurbishment costs over the estimated remaining useful life.

(iv) *Revaluation of office block.* The revaluation of property is acceptable, but the auditors will need to ensure that the company complies with a number of disclosure requirements. A note to the accounts should give details of the revaluation and the name of the valuer. The surplus on revaluation should be transferred to a separate non-distributable reserve in the balance sheet as part of shareholders' funds. In addition, the audit report will make reference to this modification of the use of the historical cost convention used in the preparation of the financial statements.

(v) *Deposit for new equipment.* As the equipment was not actually in the company's possession and use at the year end, the deposit should not have been shown as plant and machinery, but rather as a payment on account. If the amount was considered to be material a note to the accounts should give details of this prepayment.

(b) The audit work and evidence required to substantiate each of the assets referred to in (a) above would be as follows.

(i) *New staff canteen*

(1) Physically confirm existence of the asset.

(2) Confirm title to building by reference to Land Registry Certificate.

(3) Ascertain and confirm the details of any security granted over the asset, ensuring that this is properly recorded and disclosed.

    (4)   Test the detailed costings of the building and obtain explanations for any material variances from the original budget. Particular care should be taken in assessing the reasonableness of any overheads included as an element of cost.

    (5)   Review the depreciation policy for adequacy and consistency.

(ii)   *Loose tools*

    (1)   Visit the two sites where the loose tools are used to confirm the existence and condition of a sample of them.

    (2)   Vouch the cost and ownership of the loose tools to purchase invoices and the company's asset register.

    (3)   Confirm the company's estimate of a two year life for these assets.

    (4)   Review control procedures for safe custody of the loose tools.

    (5)   Review the company's policy with regard to scrapping and/or sale of tools no longer required to ensure that any proceeds are properly recorded and the assets register appropriately updated and tools are completely recorded.

(iii)   *Dumper truck*

    (1)   Inspect the truck to confirm its existence and to gain evidence of its valuation by reviewing its condition and the fact that it is still being used.

    (2)   If the vehicle is used at all on public roads then the vehicle registration document should be inspected as some evidence of title.

    (3)   Inspect the insurance policy for the truck as evidence of valuation.

    (4)   Vouch the expenditure on refurbishment to suppliers' invoices or company's payroll records where any of the work has been done by the client's own staff.

    (5)   Review the depreciation policy and assess for reasonableness by discussion with management and past experience of similar vehicles.

(iv)   *Revaluation of office block*

    (1)   Inspect the building to confirm its existence and state of repair.

    (2)   Examine documents of title to confirm ownership.

    (3)   Enquire about any charges on the building and confirm that these have been properly recorded and disclosed.

    (4)   Review the valuer's certificate and agree to the amount used in the financial statements, with consideration also being given to his qualifications, experience and reputation.

    (5)   Assess the reasonableness of the valuation by comparison with any similar properties which may have recently changed hands on the open market.

(v)   *Deposit for new equipment*

    (1)   Agree the payment of the deposit to the contract for purchase of the equipment.

    (2)   Confirm the existence of the plant following its delivery on 31 October 20X5 as it is unlikely that the audit work will have been completed by that date.

3   OTHER FIXED ASSETS

Exam focus point

The study guide for paper 2.6 refers to tangible fixed assets only. However, the accounting knowledge relevant to this paper includes FRS 10 *Goodwill and intangible assets* and SSAP 13 *Accounting for research and development costs*. You should work through the following issues, therefore, to prepare you if a question on intangible assets came up.

3.1   The key assertions relating to intangibles are **existence** (not so much 'do they exist?', but, 'are they genuinely assets?') and **valuation**. They will therefore be audited with reference to criteria laid down in the financial reporting standards. As only purchased goodwill or intangibles or intangibles with a readily ascertainable market value can be capitalised, **audit evidence should be available** (purchase invoices or specialist valuations). Audit of **amortisation** will be similar to the audit of depreciation.

Goodwill

3.2 The following procedures should be carried out.

> - Agree the consideration to sales agreement
> - Check that asset valuation is reasonable
> - Agree that the calculation is correct
> - Review the amortisation calculation and check it is correct
> - Ensure valuation of goodwill is reasonable/there has been no impairment

Intangibles

3.3 The following procedures should be carried out.

> - Agree purchased intangibles to purchase documentation
> - Review specialist valuation of intangibles and ensure they are reasonable
> - Review amortisation calculations and ensure they are correct

Research and development costs

3.4 The following procedures should be carried out.

> - Check that capitalised development costs conform to SSAP 13 criteria
> - Confirm feasibility and viability by reference to budgets
> - Check amortisation calculation, to ensure it commences with production/is reasonable

Chapter roundup

- The disclosure and valuation requirements for all fixed assets under CA 1985 are relevant here.
- Key areas when testing **tangible fixed assets** are:
    - **Confirmation** of ownership
    - **Inspection** of fixed assets
    - **Valuation** by third parties
    - **Adequacy** of **depreciation** rates

Quick quiz

1 Complete the control procedures.

(a) Acquisitions are properly ....

(b) Disposals are .... and proceeds ....

(c) Security .... over fixed assets are ....

(d) .... is reviewed ....

2 Complete the table, showing which tests are designed to provide evidence about which financial statement assertion.

Completeness	Existence
Valuation	Rights and obligations

(a) Inspect assets

(b) Verify to valuation certificate

(c) Refer to title deeds

(d) Compare assets in ledger to fixed asset register

(e) Review depreciation rates

(f) Verify material on self-constructed asset to invoices

(g) Examine invoices after the year end

(h) Review repairs in general ledger

3 Name two tests to confirm rights and obligations concerning charges and commitments.

1 ....

2 ....

Answers to quick quiz

1 (a) authorised
   (b) authorised, accounted for
   (c) arrangements, sufficient
   (d) depreciation, every year

2
Completeness	Existence
(d) Compare assets in ledger to register	(a) Inspect assets
(h) Review repairs in general ledger	
Valuation	**Rights and obligations**
(b) Verify to valuation certificate	(c) Refer to title deeds
(e) Review valuation rates	(g) Examine invoices after the year end
(f) Verify material on self-constructed assets to invoice	

3 See para 2.9

Now try the question below from the Exam Question Bank

Number	Level	Marks	Time
13	Exam	20	36 mins

BPP PUBLISHING

Chapter 14

STOCKS AND WORK IN PROGRESS

Topic list		Syllabus reference
1	Regulatory aspects of stock	6
2	The stocktake	6
3	The main stocktaking procedures	6
4	Cut-off	6
5	Audit procedures on cut-off	6
6	Stock valuation procedures	6

Introduction

No balance sheet audit area creates more potential problems for the auditors than that of stock.

Closing stock does not normally form an integrated part of the double entry bookkeeping system and hence a misstatement (under or overstatement) may not be detected from tests in other audit areas. This is a summary of why stocks and work in progress is often the most difficult and time consuming part of the audit.

(a) Stock and work in progress often represent a significant asset on the balance sheet.

(b) The value of closing stock and work in progress has a direct impact on profit.

(c) Stock is often made up of a large number of diverse items with different unit values.

(d) The valuation of work in progress is often a subjective process as the decision as to the stage which work in progress has reached and the costs to be included is often subjective. This also applies to the allocation of overheads to stock.

(e) Verification of the existence of stock and work in progress involves attendance at the stock-take and extensive follow-up procedures.

(f) The provision for slow-moving and obsolete stock is another subjective area.

(g) The physical control of stock is often difficult because of multiple locations, stock held by third parties and so on.

(h) Different valuation methods are allowed under SSAP 9 *Stocks and long-term contracts*, although they must be applied consistently.

The four main elements of the audit of stocks (completeness, existence, rights and obligations (ownership) and valuation) require careful consideration. Typically, the auditors will adopt the following broad approach.

(a) **Existence** and **apparent ownership** will be verified by observing the stocktake (whether year-end or continuous).

(b) Raw material **costs** and further comfort on ownership will be verified by checking invoice prices (cost ascertainment may require evaluation of a standard costing system). Cost in the case of work in progress and finished goods will involve consideration of overhead absorption bases.

(c) **Completeness** is checked by observing the stocktake, checking that stocktaking records are correctly processed, applying analytical procedures and occasionally relying on stock records where internal control has been evaluated and tested as strong.

(d)   **Valuation** is checked by comparing cost with net realisable value. A working knowledge of SSAP 9 *Stocks and long-term contracts* is necessary here.

Study guide

Section 18

*   Describe and tabulate for inclusion in a work program the substantive procedures used in obtaining evidence in relation to stock

*   Explain the purpose of substantive procedures in relation to financial statement assertions concerning stock

Exam guide

As stock is often the most difficult area in practice for auditors it is also very important in exams. Questions could be on any area covered in this chapter, or a combination of them. The stocktake and valuation were examined in the pilot paper.

Exam focus point

You need to ensure that you understand what an exam question is asking for. A question on valuation may ask about absorption of overheads, or the valuation of stock at the lower of cost and net realisable value.

1   REGULATORY ASPECTS OF STOCK

1.1   The rules surrounding the audit of stocks and the related reporting requirements come from three sources:

*   Companies Act 1985 (disclosure, basis of valuation)

*   SSAP 9 *Stocks and long-term contracts* (departure, disclosure and valuation)

*   The auditing standards and guidelines relating to the audit of stock (audit approach, valuation)

Companies Act 1985

1.2   In terms of valuation, CA 1985 states that all current assets should be stated at the lower of their **purchase price** and their **net realisable value**. 'Purchase price' can be interpreted as 'fair value'. 'Production cost' is determined according to the provision of SSAP 9.

1.3   CA 1985 allows certain methods of identifying cost, because it recognises that it is impossible to identify cost for each item individually. The methods allowed are:

*   First in first out (FIFO)
*   Last in first out (LIFO)
*   Weighted average cost
*   Other similar methods, such as standard cost

SSAP 9 does **not** allow LIFO as a method of valuation.

SSAP 9 *Stocks and long-term contracts*

KEY TERMS

Cost is defined by SSAP 9 as that expenditure which has been incurred in the normal course of business in bringing the product or service to its present location and condition. This includes the purchase price plus production costs (costs of conversion) appropriate to the location and condition of the stock.

Net realisable value as the estimated or actual selling price, (net of trade discounts but before settlement discounts,) less all further costs to completion and all cost to be incurred in marketing, selling and distributing the good or service.

1.4 Production costs (costs of conversion) include:

- Costs specifically attributable to units of production
- Production overheads
- Other overheads attributable to bringing the product or service to its present location and condition

---

Question 1

Give some of the main reasons why stock and work in progress is one of the most difficult areas of the audit.

Answer

See Introduction.

Exam focus point

You **must** have a thorough knowledge of audit procedures before, during and after the stocktake

---

2   THE STOCKTAKE   Pilot paper

Responsibilities in relation to stock	
Management	Ensure stock figure in accounts • Represents stock that **exists** • Includes all stock **owned** Ensure accounting records include **stocktaking statements.**
Auditors	**Obtain sufficient audit evidence** about stock figure from • Stock records • Stock control systems • Results of stocktaking • Test counts by auditors **Attend stocktaking if** stock is material and evidence of existence is provided by management stocktake.

Methods of stocktaking

2.1 A business may take stock by one or a combination of the following methods.

(a) **Stocktaking** at the **year-end**

From the viewpoint of the auditor, this is often the best method.

(b) **Stocktaking before** or **after** the **year-end**

This will provide audit evidence of varying reliability depending on:

- The **length of time** between the stocktake and the year-end; the greater the time period, the less the value of audit evidence

- The **business's system** of **internal controls**

- The **quality of records** of stock movements in the period between the stocktake and the year-end

(c) **Continuous stocktaking** where management has a programme of stock-counting throughout the year

2.2 If continuous stocktaking is used, auditors will check that management:

(a) Ensures that **all stock lines** are **counted at least once a year.**

(b) Maintains **adequate stock records** that are kept up-to-date. Auditors may compare sales and purchase transactions with stock movements, and carry out other tests on the stock records, for example checking casts and classification of stock.

(c) Has **satisfactory procedures** for **stocktaking** and **test-counting**. Auditors should confirm the stocktaking arrangements and instructions are as rigorous as those for a year-end stocktake by reviewing instructions and observing counts. Auditors will be particularly concerned with **cut-off**, that there are no stock movements whilst the count is taking place, and stock records are updated up until the time of the stocktakes.

(d) **Investigates** and **corrects** all **material differences**. Reasons for differences should be recorded and any necessary corrective action taken. All corrections to stock movements should be **authorised** by a manager who has not been involved in the detailed work; these procedures are necessary to guard against the possibility that stock records may be adjusted to conceal shortages. Auditors should check that the procedures are being operated.

2.3 Auditors should:

> **Attend one** of the stock counts (to observe and confirm that instructions are being adhered to)
>
> **Follow up** the **stock counts attended** to compare quantities counted by the auditors with the stock records, obtaining and verifying explanations for any differences, and checking that the client has reconciled count records with book stock records
>
> **Review** the **year's stock counts** to confirm the extent of counting, the treatment of discrepancies and the overall accuracy of records, if matters are not satisfactory, auditors will only be able to gain sufficient assurance by a full count at the year-end
>
> Assuming a full count is not necessary at the year-end, **compare** the **listing of stock with** the **detailed stock records**, and carry out other procedures (**cut-off, analytical review**) to gain further comfort

Work-in-progress

2.4   Evidence of the existence of work-in-progress should be obtained by:

(a)   **Attending** a **stocktake**

(b)   **Reviewing management controls** over completeness and accuracy of accounting records and inspection of work-in-progress (these procedures will be required if the nature of work-in-progress means that a stocktake is impractical)

2.5   The auditors need to do this to gain assurance that the stock-checking system as a whole is effective in maintaining accurate stock records from which the amount of stocks in the financial statements can be derived.

3   THE MAIN STOCKTAKING PROCEDURES

3.1   The following paragraphs set out the principal procedures which may be carried out by an auditors when attending a stocktake, but are not intended to provide a comprehensive list of the audit procedures which the auditors may find it necessary to perform during their attendance.

PLANNING STOCKTAKE	
Gain knowledge	**Review** previous year's **arrangements** **Discuss** with **management stock-taking arrangements** and **significant changes**
Assess key factors	The **nature** and **volume** of the **stocks** The **identification** of **high value items** **Method of accounting for stocks** **Location** of stock and how it affects stock control and recording **Internal control** and **accounting systems** to identify potential areas of difficulty
Plan procedures	**Ensure** a **representative selection** of **locations, stocks** and **procedures** are covered Ensure sufficient attention is given to **high value items** **Arrange to obtain** from **third parties confirmation** of stocks they hold Consider the need for **expert help**

Review of stock-taking instructions

REVIEW OF STOCK-TAKING INSTRUCTIONS	
Organisation of count	**Supervision** by senior staff including senior staff not normally involved with stock **Tidying** and **marking** stock to help counting **Restriction** and **control** of the production process and stock movements during the count **Identification of damaged, obsolete, slow-moving, third party** and **returnable** stock
Counting	**Systematic counting** to ensure all stock is counted Teams of **two counters,** with one counting and the other checking or two **independent counts**

Recording	**Serial numbering, control** and **return** of all stock sheets
	Stock sheets being **completed** in **ink** and **signed**
	Information to be recorded on the **count records** (location and identity, count units, quantity counted, conditions of items, stage reached in production process)
	Recording of **quantity, conditions** and **stage of production** of **work-in-progress**
	Recording of last numbers of **goods inwards** and **outwards** records and of internal transfer records
	Reconciliation with **stock records** and **investigation** and correction of any **differences**

During the stocktaking

3.2 Key tasks during the stocktake are:

> - **Check** the **client's staff** are following instructions
>
> - **Make test counts** to ensure procedures and internal controls are working properly, if the results of the test counts are not satisfactory, the auditors may request stock be recounted
>
> - **Ensure** that the **procedures** for **identifying damaged, obsolete** and **slow-moving** stock **operate** properly; the auditors should obtain information about the stocks' condition, age, usage and in the case of work in progress, its stage of completion
>
> - **Confirm** that **stock held** on behalf of **third parties** is separately identified and accounted for
>
> - **Conclude** whether the **stocktaking** has been **properly carried out** and is sufficiently reliable as a basis for determining the existence of stocks
>
> - **Consider** whether any **amendment** is **necessary** to subsequent **audit procedures**
>
> - **Gain** an **overall impression** of the levels and values of stocks held so that the auditors may, in due course, judge whether the figure for stocks appearing in the financial statements is reasonable

3.3 When carrying out test counts the auditors should select items from the count records and from the physical stocks and check one to the other, to confirm the accuracy of the count records. The auditors should concentrate on high value stock.

3.4 The auditors' working papers should include:

- Details of their **observations** and **tests**

- The manner in which **points** that are **relevant** and **material** to the stocks being counted or measured have been dealt with by the client

- Instances where the **client's procedures** have **not been satisfactorily carried out**

- **Items for subsequent testing,** such as photocopies of (or extracts from) rough stocksheets

- **Details** of the **sequence** of **stocksheets**

- The **auditors' conclusions**

After the stocktaking

3.5   After the stocktaking, the matters recorded in the auditors' working papers at the time of the count or measurement should be followed up. Key tests include the following.

> *   **Trace items** that were **test counted** during the stocktake to final stocksheets
> *   **Check all count** records have been **included** in final stocksheets
> *   **Check final stocksheets** are **supported by** count records
> *   **Ensure** that **continuous stock records** have been **adjusted** to the amounts physically counted or measured, and that differences have been investigated
> *   **Confirm cut-off** by using details of the last serial number of goods inward and outwards notes; and of movements during the stocktake
> *   **Check replies** from **third parties** about stock held by or for them
> *   **Confirm** the client's final **valuation** of stock has been calculated correctly
> *   **Follow up queries** and **notifying problems** to management

Question 2

In connection with your examination of the financial statements of Camry Products Ltd for the year ended 31 March 20X9, you are reviewing the plans for a physical stock count at the company's warehouse on 31 March 20X9. The company assembles domestic appliances, and stocks of finished appliances, unassembled parts and sundry stocks are stored in the warehouse which is adjacent to the company's assembly plant. The plant will continue to produce goods during the stock count until 5pm on 31 March 20X9. On 30 March 20X9, the warehouse staff will deliver the estimated quantities of unassembled parts and sundry stocks which will be required for production for 31 March 20X9; however, emergency requisitions by the factory will be filled on 31 March. During the stock count, the warehouse staff will continue to receive parts and sundry stocks, and to despatch finished appliances. Appliances which are completed on 31 March 20X9 will remain in the assembly plant until after the physical stock count has been completed.

Required

(a)   List the principal procedures which the auditors should carry out when planning attendance at a company's stocktake.

(b)   Describe the procedures which Camry Products Ltd should establish in order to ensure that all stock items are counted and that no item of stock is counted twice.

Answer

(a)   In planning attendance at a stocktake the auditors should:

(i)   Review previous year's audit working papers and discuss any developments in the year with management.

(ii)   Obtain and review a copy of the company's stocktaking instructions.

(iii)   Arrange attendance at stockcount planning meetings, with the consent of management.

(iv)   Gain an understanding of the nature of the stock and of any special stocktaking problems this is likely to present, for example liquid in tanks, scrap in piles.

(v)   Consider whether expert involvement is likely to be required as a result of any circumstances noted in (iv) above.

(vi)   Obtain a full list of all locations at which stock is held, including an estimate of the amount and value of stock held at different locations.

(vii) Using the results of the above steps, plan for audit attendance by appropriately experienced audit staff at all locations where material stocks are held, subject to other factors (for example rotational auditing, reliance on internal controls).

(viii) Consider the impact of internal controls upon the nature and timing of the stocktaking attendance.

(ix) Ascertain whether stocks are held by third parties and if so make arrangements to obtain written confirmation of them or, if necessary, to attend the stocktake of them.

(b) Procedures to ensure a complete count and to prevent double-counting are particularly important in this case because stock movements will continue throughout the stocktake.

    (i) Clear instructions should be given as to stocktaking procedures, and an official, preferably not someone normally responsible for stock, should be given responsibility for organising the count and dealing with queries.

    (ii) Before the count, all locations should be tidied and stock should be laid out in an orderly manner.

    (iii) All stock should be clearly identified and should be marked after being counted by a tag or indelible mark, so that it is evident that it has been counted.

    (iv) Prenumbered stock sheets should be issued to counters and should be accounted for at the end of the stocktake.

    (v) Counters should be given responsibility for specific areas of the warehouse. Each area should be subject to a recount.

    (vi) A separate record should be kept of all goods received or issued during the day (for example by noting the GRN or despatch note numbers involved).

    (vii) Goods received on the day should be physically segregated until the count has been completed.

    (viii) Similarly, goods due to be despatched on the day should be identified in advance and moved to a special area or clearly marked so that they are not inadvertently counted in stock as well as being included in sales.

4   CUT-OFF

4.1 The auditors should consider whether management has instituted adequate cut-off procedures: procedures intended to ensure that movements into, within and out of stocks are properly identified and reflected in the accounting records.

4.2 Cut-off is most critical to the accurate recording of transactions in a manufacturing enterprise at particular point in the accounting cycle as follows:

- The **point of purchase** and **receipt of goods and services**
- The **requisitioning of raw materials** for production
- The **transfer of completed work-in-progress** to finished goods stocks
- The **sale and despatch of finished goods**

4.3 **Purchase invoices** should be recorded as liabilities only if the goods were received prior to the stock count. A schedule of 'goods received not invoiced' should be prepared, and items on the list should be accrued for in the accounts.

4.4 **Sales cut-off** is generally more straightforward to achieve correctly than purchases cut-off. Invoices for goods despatched after the stock count should not appear in the profit and loss accounts for the period.

4.5 Prior to the stock-take management should make arrangements for cut-off to be properly applied.

(a) Appropriate systems of recording of receipts and despatches of goods are in place, and also a system for documenting materials requisitions. Goods received notes (GRNs) and goods despatched notes (GDNs) should be sequentially pre-numbered.

(b) Final GRN and GDN and materials requisition numbers are noted. These numbers can then be used to check subsequently that purchases and sales have been recorded in the current period.

    (c)   Arrangements should be made to ensure that the cut-off arrangement for stock held by third parties are satisfactory.

4.6   There should ideally be no movement of stocks during the stock count. Preferably, receipts and despatches should be suspended for the full period of the count. It may not be practicable to suspend all deliveries, in which case any deliveries which are received during the count should be segregated from other stocks and carefully documented.

5   AUDIT PROCEDURES ON CUT-OFF

Stocktake

5.1   At the **stocktake,** therefore, the auditors should carry out the following procedures.

- Record **all movement notes** relating to the period, including:
  - All interdepartmental requisition numbers
  - The last goods received notes(s) and despatch note(s) prior to the count
  - The first goods received notes(s) and despatch note(s) after the count

- **Observe** whether **correct cut-off procedures** are being **followed** in the despatch and receiving areas

- **Discuss procedures** with **company staff** performing the count to ensure they are understood

- **Ensure** that **no goods finished** on the day of the count are **transferred** to the warehouse

---

Final audit

5.2   During the final audit, the auditors will use the cut-off information from the stocktake to perform the following tests.

- **Match up** the **goods received notes** with **purchase invoices** and ensure the **liability** has been **recorded** in the **correct period** (only goods received before the year end should be recorded as purchases)

- **Match up** the **goods despatched notes** to **sales invoices** and ensure the **income** has been **recorded** in the **correct period** (only stocks despatched before the year end should be recorded as sales)

- **Match up** the **requisition notes** to the **work in progress** figures for the receiving department to ensure correctly recorded

---

Question 3

Using the information in Question 2 above, describe the audit procedures you would carry out at the time of the stocktake in order to ensure that cut-off is correct.

Answer

In order to ensure that stock cut-off is correct, the following procedures should be carried out.

    (a)   Make a record during the stocktaking attendance of all movement notes relating to the period, including:

- All interdepartmental requisition numbers
- The last goods received note and despatch note prior to the count

- The first goods received note and despatch note after the count. This information can be used for subsequent cut-off tests

(b) Observe whether correct cut-off procedures are being followed in the despatch and receiving areas. Discuss procedures with company staff performing the count to ensure they are understood.

(c) Ensure that no goods finished on the day of the count are transferred to the warehouse.

6 STOCK VALUATION PROCEDURES   Pilot paper

Assessment of cost and net realisable value

Exam focus point

Valuation of stock has always been a very popular exam topic. You must know the audit work needed to confirm valuation of stock when overheads have been absorbed, and to confirm stock is stated at the lower of cost and net realisable value.

Knowledge of the requirements of SSAP 9 is essential when considering absorption of overheads, hence we have gone into detail about these provisions. You should refer back to your Paper 2.5 notes if you are still unsure about this area.

6.1 Auditors must understand how the company determines the cost of an item for stock valuation purposes. Cost should include an appropriate proportion of overheads, in accordance with SSAP 9.

6.2 There are several ways of determining cost. Auditors must ensure that the company is **applying** the method **consistently** and that each year the method used **gives** a **fair approximation** to cost. They may need to support this by additional procedures such as:

- **Reviewing price** changes near the year end
- **Ageing the stock** held
- **Checking gross profit** margins to reliable management accounts

Valuation of raw materials and brought in components

6.3 The auditors should check that the correct prices have been used to value raw materials and brought in components valued at actual costs by **referring to suppliers' invoices.** The stock valuation may include unrealised profit if stock is valued at the latest invoice price. Reference to suppliers' invoice will also provide the auditors with assurance as regards ownership.

6.4 If standard costs are used, auditors should **check the basis of the standards, compare standard costs** with **actual costs** and **confirm** that **variances** are being **treated appropriately**.

Valuation of work in progress and finished goods
(other than long-term contract work in progress)

6.5 As we saw above, SSAP 9 defines 'cost' as comprising the cost of purchase plus the costs of conversion (production costs).

BPP PUBLISHING

Audit procedures

6.6 The audit procedures will depend on the methods used by the client to value work in progress and finished goods, and on the adequacy of the system of internal control.

6.7 The auditors should consider what tests they can carry out to check the reasonableness of the valuation of finished goods and work in progress. **Analytical procedures** may assist comparisons being made with stock items and stock categories from the previous year's stock summaries.

Costs attributable to production

6.8 The auditors should carry out the following tests.

> * For materials:
>   * **Check** the **valuation** of raw materials to **invoices** and **price lists**
>   * **Confirm appropriate basis** of **valuation** (for example, FIFO) is being used
>   * **Confirm correct quantities** are being used when calculating raw material value in work in progress and finished goods
> * For labour costs:
>   * **Check labour costs** to **wage records**
>   * **Review standard labour costs** in the light of actual costs and production
>   * **Check labour hours** to **time summaries**

Overhead allocation

6.9 The auditors should ensure that the client includes a proportion of overheads **appropriate** to **bringing the stock to its present location and condition**. The basis of overhead allocation should be:

* **Consistent with prior years**
* **Calculated on the normal level of production activity**

6.10 Thus, overheads arising from **reduced levels** of **activity, idle time** or **inefficient production** should be written off to the profit and loss account, rather than being included in stock.

6.11 In an appendix to SSAP 9 there is general guidance on the allocation of overheads which the auditors should follow.

> (a) All **abnormal conversion** costs (such as idle capacity) must be **excluded**.
>
> (b) Where **firm sales contracts** have been entered into for the provision of goods or services to customer's specification, **design, marketing and selling costs** incurred before manufacture may be **included**.
>
> (c) Overheads are **classified by function** when being allocated (eg whether they are a function of production, marketing, selling or administration).
>
> (d) The **costs of general management**, as distinct from functional management, are not directly related to current production and are, therefore, **excluded**.
>
> (e) The allocation of costs of **central service departments** should depend on the function or functions that the department is serving. **Only** those costs that can reasonably be allocated to the **production function** should be **included**.

(f) In determining what constitutes **'normal' activity** the following factors need to be considered:

- The volume of production which the production facilities are **designed to achieve**

- The **budgeted level** of **activity** for the year under review and for the ensuing year

- The **level of activity achieved** both in the **year under review** and in **previous years**

Although temporary changes in the level of activity may be ignored, persistent variation should lead to revision of the previous norm.

Question 4

Give a brief list of general procedures the auditors might undertake to determine whether a company is operating at a normal level of activity.

Answer

The procedures, in brief, are likely to be as follows.

(a) Compare the level of production with previous years.

(b) Compare production/sales with budget.

(c) Investigate overtime levels of production staff, compared to previous years.

(d) Enquire of management about any changes in production during the year, and investigate:

    (i) Board/management minutes
    (ii) New machinery/production space

6.12 Difficulty may be experienced if the client operates a system of total overhead absorption. It will be necessary for those overheads that are of a general, non-productive nature to be identified and excluded from the stock valuation.

Cost vs NRV

6.13 Auditors should **compare cost and net realisable value** for each item of stock. Where this is impracticable, the comparison may be done by stock group or category.

6.14 Net realisable value is likely to be less than cost when there has been:

- An **increase in costs** or a fall in selling price
- **Physical deterioration** of stocks
- **Obsolescence** of products
- A **decision** as part of **marketing strategy** to manufacture and sell products at a loss
- **Errors in production or purchasing**

6.15 The following audit tests are important.

- **Review and test the client's system** for **identifying slow-moving**, obsolete or damaged stock

- **Follow up** any such **items** that were **identified** at the **stocktaking**, ensuring that the client has made adequate provision to write down the items to net realisable value

> - **Examine stock records** to identify slow-moving items (it may be possible to incorporate into a computer audit program certain tests and checks such as listing items whose value or quantity has not moved over the previous year)
>
> - **Examine the prices** at which finished goods have been sold after the year-end and ascertain whether any finished goods items need to be reduced below cost
>
> - **Review quantities of goods sold after the year end** to determine that year end stock has, or will be, realised
>
> - If significant quantities of finished goods stock remain unsold for an unusual time after the year-end, **consider** the **need** to **make appropriate provision**

6.16   For work in progress, the **ultimate selling price** should be **compared** with the **carrying value** at the year end plus **costs** to be **incurred** after the year end to bring work in progress to a finished state.

Question 5

Your firm is the auditor of Arnold Electrical Ltd and you have been asked to audit the valuation of the company's stock at 31 May 20X1 in accordance with SSAP 9 *Stocks and long-term contracts*. Arnold Electrical Ltd operates from a single store and purchases domestic electrical equipment from wholesalers and manufacturers and sells them to the general public. These products include video and audio equipment, washing machines, refrigerators and freezers. In addition, it sells small items such as electrical plugs, magnetic tape for video and audio recorders, records and compact discs.

A full stocktake was carried out at the year end, and you are satisfied that the stock was counted accurately and there are no cut-off errors. Because of the limited time available between the year end and the completion of the audit, the company has valued the stock at cost by recording the selling price and deducting the normal gross profit margin. Stock which the company believes to be worth less than cost has been valued at net realisable value. The selling price used is that on the item in the store when it was counted.

The stock has been divided into three categories.

(a)   Video and audio equipment: televisions, video recorders, video cameras and audio equipment
(b)   Domestic equipment: washing machines, refrigerators and freezers
(c)   Sundry stocks: electrical plugs, magnetic tapes and compact discs

The normal gross profit margin for each of these categories has been determined and this figure has been used to calculate the cost of the stock (by deducting the gross profit margin from the selling price). In answering the question you should assume there are no sales taxes (for example, value added tax in the UK).

Required

(a)   List and describe the audit work you will carry out to check that the stock has been correctly valued at cost.

(b)   List and describe the audit work you will carry out to:

(i)   To find stock which should be valued at net realisable value
(ii)   To check that net realisable value for this stock is correct

(c)   List and describe the other work you will perform to check that the stock value is accurate.

Note. In answering the question you are only required to check that the price per unit of the stock is correct. You should assume that the stock quantities are accurate and there are no purchases or sales cut-off errors.

Answer

(a)   This method of valuation at cost is permitted by SSAP 9, but it is usually applied to large retail concerns which stock thousands of low value items, for example supermarket chains. This method is only permitted when it can be shown that it gives a reasonable approximation of the actual cost.

The following tests should be performed to ensure that the stock is correctly valued at cost.

(i) Obtain a schedule of the client calculations of the gross profit margins. Check the mathematical accuracy and consider the reliability of all sources of information used in the calculation.

(ii) Where the normal overall gross margin has been used, check the reasonableness of the figure by comparing it to the monthly management accounts for the year and last year's published accounts.

Test a sample of items to make sure that gross profit does not vary too much across all items of stock (which is unlikely for Arnold Electrical). The test will compare selling price to purchase price.

(iii) If a weighted average gross margin has been used, check that the weighting is correct in terms of the proportion of each type of product in closing stock.

(iv) Select a sample of high value stock lines and check the reasonableness of the gross profit estimate by calculating the gross profit for each of those lines. Sales price will be compared to stock sheets and to sale prices in the shop at the year end. Cost will be checked by examining purchase invoices. The weighted average profit margin for the selected lines can then be calculated and compared to the gross margin applied to the whole stock. *(Note.* High value stock lines may consist of individual items with a high selling price, or a large number of low value items.)

(v) Overvaluation of slow moving stock is possible when the prices of those items are affected by inflation. To check this, examine the stock sheets for any slow moving items (or ask the management of the company or use my own observation). Compare the value of the stock at the end of the accounting period to cost according to purchase invoices. If an overvaluation has occurred it should be quantified.

(vi) Check whether any goods were being offered for sale at reduced prices at the year end. If the reduced price is greater than cost, the use of an average gross profit percentage will cause stock to be undervalued. This undervaluation must be quantified. If full selling price was used in the calculation then the problem will not arise. Check a sample of stock items to sales invoices issued around the year end to make sure that the correct price was used in the stock costing calculation.

(b) (i) Stock which may be worth less than cost will include:

(1) Slow moving stock
(2) Obsolete or superseded stock
(3) Seconds stock and items that have been damaged
(4) Stock which is being, or is soon likely to be, sold at reduced prices
(5) Discontinued stock lines

Finished goods where the selling price is less than cost will be valued at net realisable value. This is defined as the actual or estimated selling price less costs to completion and marketing, selling and distribution expenses.

To identify stock which may be worth less than cost the following work will be carried out.

(1) Examine the computerised stock control system and list items showing an unacceptably low turnover rate. An unacceptable rate of turnover may be different for different items, but stock representing more than six months' sales is likely to qualify.

(2) Check the stock printout for items already described as seconds or recorded as damaged.

(3) Discuss with management the current position regarding slow moving stock and their plans and expectations in respect of products that may be discontinued. The standard system must be carefully considered and estimates obtained of the likely selling price of existing stock. The most likely outcome regarding the use and value of discontinued components must be decided.

(4) At the stocktake, look for stock which is dusty, inaccessible and in general not moving and mark on the stock sheets.

(5) Find out whether any lines are unreliable and therefore frequently returned for repairs as these may be unpopular.

(6) Check with the trade press or other sources to see whether any of the equipment is out of date.

(ii) Determining the net realisable value of stock is a difficult task and involves management in judging how much stock can be sold and at what price, together with deciding whether to sell off raw materials and components separately or to assemble them into finished products. Each separate type of stock item should be considered separately in deciding on the level of prudent provision.

To determine the net realisable value of the stock the following tests should be carried out.

(1) Find the actual selling prices from the latest sales invoice. For items still selling, invoices will be very recent, but for slow moving and obsolete items the invoiced prices will be out of date and allowance will have to be made for this (probably a reduction in estimating the most likely sale price of the stock concerned).

(2) Estimate the value of marketing, selling and distribution expenses using past figures for the types of finished goods concerned as a base. I would update and check for reasonableness against the most recent accounting records.

(3) Discuss with management what selling prices are likely to be where there is little past evidence. Costs to completion will be questioned where these are difficult to estimate and where there are any unusual assembly, selling or distribution problems.

(c) The following procedures would also be performed to check the value of stock at the year end.

(i) Compare current results with prior year(s). This would include gross profit margins, sales and stock turnover. Marked variations from the current year's results should be investigated.

(ii) Consider the effects of new technology and new fashions. The electrical appliance business will be exposed to obsolescence problems. Quantify any necessary write down.

(iii) Compare selling prices to those charged elsewhere. If the prices elsewhere are lower, than the distortion in selling price might affect the value of the stock of Arnold Electrical. Alternatively, if prices elsewhere are higher, then the company's prices may occasionally fall below cost. Again, any adjustment discovered to be necessary must be quantified.

(iv) Compare the valuation of stock this year to that at the end of last year. This will be particularly useful for lines held at both dates. If the values are comparable, taking account of inflation, then the current valuation is more likely to be correct.

(v) Sale prices should be checked as long after the year end as possible, to make sure that prices were not kept artificially high over the year end and then reduced at a later date. Stock turnover should also be examined on this same basis.

Chapter roundup

- The audit of stocks and work in progress is difficult and time consuming, but it is of primary importance.

- The **valuation** and **disclosure** rules for stock are laid down in SSAP 9 and CA 1985.

- An old APC guideline on the auditors' attendance at the stocktake still demonstrates best practice.

- Stocktake procedures are vital as they provide evidence which cannot be obtained elsewhere or at any other time about the quantities and conditions of stocks and work in progress.

  ° Before the stocktake the auditors should ensure audit **coverage** of **stock-taking** is **appropriate**, and that the client's **stock-taking instructions** have been reviewed.

  ° During the stocktake the auditors should **check stock count** is being carried out according to instructions, carry out **test counts**, and watch for **third party, slow moving stock, cut-off problems.**

  ° After the stocktake the auditors should check that **final stock sheets** have been **properly compiled** from stock count records and that **book stock** has been appropriately adjusted.

- Auditors should check **cut-off** by noting the **serial numbers** of items received and despatched just before and after the year-end, and subsequently checking that they have been included in the correct period.

- Auditing the valuation of stock includes:

  ° Checking the **allocation of overheads** is appropriate
  ° Confirming stock is carried at the lower of **cost** and **net realisable value**

Quick quiz

1   Complete the definition, using the words given below.

.... is defined by SSAP ...... as that expenditure which ahs been incurred in the .... in bringing the product or service to its present location and condition. This includes the .... plus .... (costs of conversion) appropriate to bringing the .... to its present location and condition.

stock of business, normal price, purchase cost, cost, 9, course, production

2   Name three methods of stocktaking

   1   ....

   2   ....

   3   ....

3   When should the following stocktaking tests take place?

   (a)   Check client staff are following instructions
   (b)   Review previous year's stocktaking arrangements
   (c)   Assess method of accounting for stocks
   (d)   Trace counted items to final stock sheets
   (e)   Check replies from third parties about stock held for them
   (f)   Conclude as to whether stocktake has been properly carried out
   (g)   Gain an overall impression of levels and values of stocks
   (h)   Consider the need for expert help

BEFORE	DURING	AFTER

4   Name four points in the accounting cycle when cut off is critical.

   1   ....

   2   ....

   3   ....

   4   ....

5   Give four occasions when the net realisable value of stock is likely to fall below cost.

   1   ....

   2   ....

   3   ....

   4   ....

Answers to quick quiz

1   cost, 9, normal course of business, purchase price, production cost, stock

2   • Year end
    • Pre/post year end
    • Continuous

3   (a) DURING   (b) BEFORE   (c) BEFORE   (d) AFTER
    (e) AFTER   (f) DURING   (g) DURING   (h) BEFORE

4   See para 4.2

5   See para 6.4

Now try the questions below from the Exam Question Bank

Number	Level	Marks	Time
14	Exam	20	36 mins

Chapter 15

DEBTORS AND PREPAYMENTS

Topic list	Syllabus reference
1 Debtors	6
2 Bad debts	6
3 Sales	6
4 Prepayments	6

Introduction

Debtors will generally be a material figure on a company's balance sheet, and must therefore be given due weight.

You should make sure that you are fully conversant with the 'standard' procedures such as the **debtors' circularisation**. The debtors' circularisation is primarily designed to test the client's entitlement to receive the debt, not the debtor's ability to pay. Auditors also need to consider **cut-off** for debtors.

Study guide

Section 17

- Describe and tabulate for inclusion in a work program the substantive procedures used in obtaining evidence in relation to debtors and prepayments, and the related income statement entries

- Explain the purpose of substantive procedures in relation to financial statement assertions concerning debtors and prepayments

Exam guide

Debtors were examined in conjunction with sales system controls in the pilot paper. In December 2001, the debtors' circularisation was examined.

1 DEBTORS

Debtors' listing and aged analysis

1.1 Much of the auditors' detailed work will be based on a selection of debtors' balances chosen from a listing of sales ledger balances, prepared by the client or auditors. Ideally the list should be aged, showing the period or periods of time money has been owed. The following substantive procedures to check the **completeness** and **accuracy** of a client-prepared list.

> - **Check** the **balances** from the **individual sales ledger accounts** to the **list of balances** and vice versa
> - **Check** the **total** of the **list** to the **sales ledger control account**
> - **Cast** (that is, add up) the **list of balances** and the **sales ledger control account**
> - **Confirm** whether **list of balances reconciles** with the **sales ledger control account**

The debtors' circularisation   Dec 01

Objectives of circularisation

1.2 The verification of trade debtors by direct circularisation is the normal means of providing audit evidence to satisfy the objective of checking whether debtors exist and owe *bona fide* amounts due to the company (**existence, rights** and **obligations**)

1.3 Circularisation will produce for the current audit file a written statement from each respondent debtor that the amount owed at the date of the circularisation is correct. This is, *prima facie*, reliable audit evidence, being from an independent source and in 'documentary' form.

Timing

1.4 Ideally the circularisation should take place immediately after the year-end and hence cover the year-end balances to be included in the balance sheet. However, time constraints may make it impossible to achieve this ideal.

1.5 In these circumstances it may be acceptable to carry out the circularisation **prior to the year-end** provided that circularisation is no more than three months before the year-end and internal controls are strong.

Client's mandate

1.6 Circularisation is essentially an act of the **client**, who alone can authorise third parties to divulge information to the auditors.

1.7 Should the client refuse to co-operate in the circularisation the auditors will inevitably consider whether they should **qualify** their **audit report**, as they may not be able to satisfy themselves, by means of other audit procedures, as to the validity and accuracy of the debtor balances.

Positive v negative circularisation

1.8 When circularisation is undertaken the method of requesting information from the debtor may be either 'positive' or 'negative'.

   - Under the **positive** method the debtor is requested to confirm the accuracy of the balance shown or state in what respect he is in disagreement.
   - Under the **negative** method the debtor is requested to reply if the amount stated is disputed.

1.9 The positive method is generally preferable as it is designed to encourage definite replies from those circularised.

1.10 The negative method may be used if the client has good internal control, with a large number of small accounts. In some circumstances, say where there is a small number of large accounts and a large number of small accounts, a combination of both methods, as noted above, may be appropriate.

1.11 A specimen 'positive' confirmation letter is shown below.

1.12 The statements will normally be prepared by the client's staff, from which point the auditors, as a safeguard against the possibility of fraudulent manipulation, must maintain strict control over the checking and despatch of the statements.

1.13 Precautions must also be taken to ensure that undelivered items are returned, not to the client, but to the auditors' own office for follow-up by them.

MANUFACTURING CO LIMITED
15 South Street
London

Date

Messrs   (debtor)

In accordance with the request of our auditors, Messrs Arthur Daley & Co, we ask that you kindly confirm to them directly your indebtedness to us at (insert date) which, according to our records, amounted to £.......... as shown by the enclosed statement.

If the above amount is in agreement with your records, please sign in the space provided below and return this letter direct to our auditors in the enclosed stamped addressed envelope.

If the amount is not in agreement with your records, please notify our auditors directly of the amount shown by your records, and if possible detail on the reverse of this letter full particulars of the difference.

Yours faithfully,

For Manufacturing Co Limited

Reference No: ....

....

(Tear off slip)

The amount shown above is/is not * in agreement with our records as at

Account No   ....   Signature   ....

Date   ....   Title or position   ....

* The position according to our records is shown overleaf.

Note:

- The letter is on the client's paper, signed by the client.
- A copy of the statement is attached.
- The reply is sent directly to the auditor in a pre-paid envelope.

Sample selection

1.14 Auditors will normally only circularise a sample of debtors. If this sample is to yield a meaningful result it must be based upon a complete list of all debtor accounts. In addition, when constructing the sample, the following classes of account should receive special attention:

- **Old unpaid accounts**
- **Accounts written off** during the period under review
- **Accounts with credit balances**
- **Accounts settled by round sum payments**

Similarly, the following should not be overlooked:

- **Accounts with nil balances**
- **Accounts which** have been **paid** by the date of the examination

Follow up procedures

1.15 Auditors will have to carry out further work in relation to those debtors who:

- **Disagree** with the **balance stated** (positive and negative circularisation)
- **Do not respond** (positive circularisation only)

1.16 In the case of disagreements, the debtor response should have identified specific amounts which are disputed.

REASONS FOR DISAGREEMENTS
There is a **dispute** between the client and the customer. The reasons for the dispute would have to be identified, and provision made if appropriate against the debt.
Cut-off problems exist, because the client records the following year's sales in the current year or because goods returned by the customer in the current year are not recorded in the current year. Cut-off testing may have to be extended (see below).
The customer may have sent the **monies before** the year-end, but the monies were **not recorded** by the client as receipts until **after** the year-end. Detailed cut-off work may be required on receipts.
Monies received may have been posted to the **wrong account** or a cash-in-transit account. Auditors should check if there is evidence of other mis-posting. If the monies have been posted to a cash-in-transit account, auditors should ensure this account has been cleared promptly.
Customers who are also suppliers may **net off balances** owed and owing. Auditors should check that this is allowed.
Teeming and lading, stealing monies and **incorrectly posting** other receipts so that no particular debtor is seriously in debt is a fraud that can arise in this area. If auditors suspect teeming and lading has occurred, detailed testing will be required on cash receipts, particularly on prompt posting of cash receipts.

1.17 When the positive request method is used the auditors must follow up by all practicable means those debtors who **fail to respond**. Second requests should be sent out in the event of no reply being received within two or three weeks and if necessary this may be followed by telephoning the customer, with the client's permission.

1.18 After two, or even three, attempts to obtain confirmation, a list of the outstanding items will normally be passed to a responsible company official, preferably independent of the sales accounting department, who will arrange for them to be investigated.

1.19 If it proves impossible to get confirmations from individual debtors, alternative procedures include the following.

- **Check receipt of cash** after date
- **Verify valid purchase** orders if any
- **Examine the account** to see if the balance outstanding represents specific invoices and **confirm** their **validity**
- **Obtain explanations** for **invoices remaining unpaid** after subsequent ones have been paid
- **Check** if the **balance** on the account is **growing,** and if so, why
- **Test company's control** over the issue of **credit notes** and the **write-off of bad debts**

Non purchase ledger accounting

1.20 Certain companies, government departments and local authorities operate systems, often computerised, which make it impossible for them to confirm the balance on their account.

1.21 Typically in these circumstances their 'purchase ledger' is merely a list of unpaid invoices in date order.

1.22 However, given sufficient information the debtor will be able to confirm that any given invoice is outstanding. Hence the auditors can circularise such enterprises, but they will need to break down the total on the account into its constituent outstanding invoices.

1.23 Confirmation letters should nevertheless state the full balance so that the debtor has the option of confirming the balance and also has the opportunity to object if he thinks the total appears incorrect.

Additional procedures where circularisation is carried out before year-end

1.24 The auditors will need to carry out the following procedures where their circularisation is carried out before the year-end.

- **Review** and **reconcile entries** on the **sales ledger control account** for the intervening period
- **Verify sales entries** from the control account by checking sales day book entries, copy sales invoices and despatch notes
- **Check** that **appropriate credit entries** have been made for goods returned notes and other evidence of returns/allowances to the sales ledger control account
- Select a sample from the cash received records and **ensure** that **receipts** have been **credited** to the control account
- **Review** the **list of balances** at the **circularisation** date and year end and **investigate** any **unexpected movements** or lack of them (it may be prudent to send further confirmation requests at the year end to material debtors where review results are unsatisfactory)
- **Carry out analytical review** procedures, comparing debtors' ratios at the confirmation date and year-end
- **Carry out** year end **cut-off tests,** in addition to any performed at the date of the confirmation (see below)

Evaluation and conclusions

1.25 All circularisations, regardless of timing, must be properly recorded and evaluated. All **balance disagreements** and **non-replies** must be **followed up** and their effect on total debtors evaluated.

1.26 **Differences** arising that merely represent **invoices** or **cash in transit** (normal timing differences) generally do not require adjustment, but disputed amounts, and errors by the client, may indicate that further substantive work is necessary to determine whether material adjustments are required.

2   BAD DEBTS   Dec 01

Valuation

2.1 A significant test here will be reviewing the **cash received** after date. This will provide evidence of collectability of debts (and hence valuation). It also provides some evidence of correctness of title (rights and obligations), although ideally it should be carried out as well as a debtors' circularisation (which is the main test on rights and obligations).

2.2 The following procedures will be important to check for bad debts, and thus confirm **valuation.**

- **Confirm necessity/adequacy** of provision against **write-off** of specific debts by review of correspondence, solicitors' debt collection, agencies' letters, liquidation statements
- **Examine customer files** on **overdue debts**, and **assess** whether **provision** is required in the circumstances
- **Consider** whether **amounts owed** may be **not recovered** where there has been:
  - Round sum payments on account
  - Invoices unpaid after subsequent invoices paid
- **Review customer files/correspondence** from solicitors and **debtors' circularisation results** for evidence of potential bad debts
- **Confirm general provisions** for bad debts considering:
  - How well previous year's provision predicted actual bad debts
  - Whether calculation correct
  - Whether formula used reasonable and consistent with previous years
  - Exclusion of debtors against whom specific provision is made
- **Examine credit notes** issued after the year-end for **provisions** that should be made against current period balances
- **Check accuracy** of **aged debtor analysis** by comparing analysis with dates on invoices and **matching cash receipts** against outstanding invoices
- **Investigate** and **consider need for provision against unusual features** on aged debtors analysis, such as:
  - Unapplied credits
  - Unallocated cash
- **Investigate** and **consider need for provision against unusual items** in the sales ledger, such as:
  - Journal entries transferring balances from one account to another
  - Journal entries that clear post year-end debtor balances
  - Balances not made up of specific invoices
  - Sales ledger accounts with significant adjustments or credit notes

2.3 Auditors should also consider the collectability of material debtor balances other than those contained in the sales ledger. Auditors should request certificates of loan balances from employees and others, and inspect the authority if necessary.

3 SALES

3.1 Debtors will often be tested in conjunction with sales. Auditors are seeking to obtain evidence that sales are **completely** and **accurately recorded**. This will involve carrying out certain procedures to test for **completeness** of sales and also testing **cut-off.**

Completeness and occurrence of sales

3.2 **Analytical review** is likely to be important when testing completeness. Auditors should consider the following.

> * The **level of sales** over the year, compared on a month-by-month basis with the previous year
>
> * The effect on sales value of **changes in quantities** sold
>
> * The effect on sales value of **changes in products** or **prices**
>
> * The level of **goods returned, sales allowances** and **discounts**
>
> * The **efficiency of labour** as expressed in sales or profit per tax per employee

3.3 In addition auditors must record reasons for changes in the **gross profit margin** ($\frac{\text{Gross profit}}{\text{Turnover}} \times 100\%$). Analysis of the gross profit margin should be as detailed as possible, ideally broken down by **product area** and **month or quarter.**

3.4 As well as analytical review, auditors may feel that they need to test **completeness of recording** of individual sales in the accounting records. To do this, auditors should start with the documents that first record sales (**goods despatched notes** or **till rolls** for example), and trace sales recorded in these through intermediate documents such as sales summaries to the **sales ledger.**

3.5 Auditors must ensure that the population of documents from which the sample is originally taken is itself complete, by checking for example the **completeness** of the **sequence** of goods despatched notes.

Exam focus point

You must remember the direction of this test. Since we are checking the completeness of recording of sales in the sales ledger, we cannot take a sample from the ledger since the sample cannot include what has not been recorded.

3.6 If on the other hand, the auditors suspect that sales may have been **invalidly** recorded, and have not **occurred**, then the sample will be taken from the **sales ledger** and **confirmed** to **supporting documentation** (orders, despatch notes etc).

Measurement of sales

3.7   The following tests may be performed.

- Check the **pricing calculations** and **additions** on invoices
- Check whether **discounts** have been **properly calculated**
- **Check** whether **VAT** has been **added appropriately**

3.8   Other tests that may be carried out on sales include:

- **Trace debits** in the **sales account** to credit notes

- **Check casting** of **sales ledger accounts** and **sales ledger control account**

- **Review reconciliations** of sales ledger control account and other relevant reconciliations (for example till rolls) and investigate unusual items

Sales cut-off

3.9   We can now turn to the requirement to confirm that sales cut-off is satisfactory and hence sales are completely recorded. During the stocktake the auditors will have obtained details of the last serial numbers of goods outward notes issued before the commencement of the stocktaking.

3.10   The following suggested substantive procedures are designed to test that goods taken into stock are not also treated as sales in the year under review and, conversely, goods despatched are treated as sales in the year under review and not also treated as stock.

- **Check goods despatched** and **returns inwards** notes around year-end to ensure:

- **Invoices** and **credit notes** are **dated** in the **correct period**

- **Invoices** and **credit notes** are **posted** to the **sales ledger** and **general ledger** in the correct period

- **Reconcile entries** in the **sales ledger control account** around the **year-end** to daily batch invoice totals ensuring batches are posted in correct year

- **Review sales ledger control account** around year-end for **unusual items**

- **Review material after-date invoices, credit notes** and **adjustments** and ensure that they are properly treated as following year sales

Goods on sale or return

3.11   Care should be exercised to ensure that goods on sale or return are properly treated in the accounts. Except where the client has been notified of the sale of the goods they should be reflected in the accounts as **stock** at cost and not as debtors, otherwise profits may be incorrectly anticipated.

4   PREPAYMENTS

4.1   The extent of audit testing will depend on the materiality of the amounts.

> - **Verify prepayments** by reference to the cash book, expense invoices, correspondence and so on
>
> - **Check calculations** of prepayments
>
> - **Review** the **detailed profit and loss account** to ensure that all likely prepayments have been provided for
>
> - **Review** the **prepayments** for **reasonableness** by comparing with prior years and using analytical procedures where applicable

Question 1

Sherwood Textiles plc manufactures knitted clothes and dyes these clothes and other textiles. You are carrying out the audit of the accounts of the company for the year ended 30 September 20X6 which show a turnover of about £10 million, and a profit before tax of about £800,000.

You are attending the final audit in December 20X6 and are commencing the audit of trade debtors, which are shown in the draft accounts at £2,060,000.

The interim audit (tests of control) was carried out in July 20X6 and it showed that there was a good system of internal control in the sales system and no serious errors were found in the audit tests. The company's sales ledger is maintained on a computer, which produces at the end of each month:

(i)   A list of transactions for the month

(ii)   An aged list of balances

(iii) Open item statements which are sent to customers. (*Note.* Open item statements show all items which are outstanding on each account, irrespective of their age.)

Required

(a)   List and briefly describe the audit tests you would carry out to verify trade debtors at the year end. You are not required to describe how you would carry out a debtors' circularisation.

(b)   Describe the audit work you would carry out on the following replies to a debtors' circularisation:

   (i)   Balance agreed by debtor

   (ii)   Balance not agreed by debtor

   (iii) Debtor is unable to confirm the balance because of the form of records kept by the debtor

   (iv)   Debtor does not reply to the circularisation

Answer

(a)   The auditors will carry out the following tests on the list of balances.

   (i)   Check the balances from the individual sales ledger accounts to the list of balances and vice versa.

   (ii)   Check the total of the list to the sales ledger control account.

   (iii) Cast the list of balances and the sales ledger control account.

   Other general tests auditors will carry out will be:

   (i)   Agree the opening balance on the sales ledger control account to last year's working papers to ensure that last year's audit adjustments were recorded.

   (ii)   Scrutinise ledger balances for unusual entries.

   (iii) Carry out analytical procedures considering particularly changes in debtors' collection period and in age profile of debtors.

   The determination of whether the company has made reasonable provision for bad and doubtful debts, will be facilitated as the company produces an aged listing of balances.

Auditors will carry out the following procedures to check bad debts.

(i)   Debts against which specific provision has been made (and debts written off) should be examined in conjunction with correspondence, solicitors'/debt collection agencies' letters, liquidators' statements and so on, and their necessity or adequacy confirmed.

(ii)   A general review of relevant correspondence may reveal debts where a provision is warranted, but has not been made.

(iii)   Where specific and/or general provisions have been determined using the aged analysis, the auditors should ensure that the analysis has been properly prepared by comparing analysis with dates on invoice and matching cash receipts against outstanding invoices. They should check the reasonableness and consistency of any formula used to calculate general provisions.

(iv)   Additional tests that should be carried out on individual balances will include the ascertainment of the subsequent receipt of cash, paying particular attention to, round sum payments on account, examination of specific invoices and, where appropriate, goods received notes, and enquiry into any invoices that have not been paid when subsequent invoices have been paid.

(v)   Excessive discounts should be examined, as should journal entries transferring balances from one account to another and journal entries that clear debtor balances after the year end.

(vi)   Credit notes issued after the year end should be reviewed and provisions checked where they refer to current period sales.

In order to check cut-off and hence completeness, the auditors should, during the stocktake, have obtained details of the last serial numbers of goods outwards issued before the commencement of stocktaking. The following substantive procedures are designed to test that goods taken into stock are not also treated as sales in the year under review and, conversely, goods despatched are treated as sales in the year under review and not also treated as stock.

(i)   Check goods outwards and returns inwards notes around year end to ensure that:

    (1)   Invoices and credit notes are dated in the correct period.

    (2)   Invoices and credit notes are posted to the sales ledger and nominal ledger in the correct period.

(ii)   Reconcile entries in the sales ledger control around the year end to daily batch invoice totals ensuring batches are posted in correct year.

(iii)   Review sales ledger control account around year end for unusual items.

(iv)   Review material after date invoices and ensure that they are properly treated as following year sales.

(b)   The verification of trade debtors by direct communication is the normal means of providing audit evidence to prove that debtors represent bona fide amounts due to the company (existence and rights and obligations).

The audit work required on the various replies to a debtors' circularisation would be as follows.

(i)   *Balances agreed by debtor*

    Where the balance has been agreed by the debtor all that is required would be to ensure that the debt does appear to be collectable. This would be achieved by reviewing cash received after date or considering the adequacy of any provision made for a long outstanding debt.

(ii)   *Balances not agreed by debtor*

    All balance disagreements must be followed up and their effect on total debtors evaluated. Differences arising that merely represent invoices or cash in transit (which are normal timing differences) generally do not require adjustment, but disputed amounts, and errors by the client, may indicate that further substantive work is necessary to determine whether material adjustments are required.

(iii)   *Debtor is unable to confirm the balance because of the form of records he or she maintains*

    Certain companies, often computerised, operate systems which make it impossible for them to confirm the balance on their account. Typically in these circumstances their purchase ledger is merely a list of unpaid invoices. However, given sufficient information the debtor will be able to confirm that any given invoice is outstanding. Hence the auditors can circularise such enterprises successfully, but they will need to break down the total on the account into its constituent outstanding invoices.

(iv) *Debtor does not reply to circularisation*

When the positive request method is used the auditors must follow up by all practicable means those debtors who fail to respond. Second requests should be sent out in the event of no reply being received within two or three weeks and if necessary this may be followed by telephoning the customer with the client's permission.

After two, or even three attempts to obtain confirmation, a list of the outstanding items will normally be passed to a responsible company official, preferably independent of the sales department, who will arrange for them to be investigated.

This does not, of course, absolve the auditors from satisfying themselves that the clearance procedure is properly carried out and from examining the results. Where there is any limitation in the follow-up procedure it is all the more important to apply other auditing tests to establish that there existed a valid debt from a genuine customer at the date of the verification. Alternative procedures might include the following.

(1) Check receipt of cash after date.

(2) Verify valid purchase orders, if any.

(3) Examine the account to see if the balance represents specific outstanding invoices.

(4) Obtain explanations for invoices remaining unpaid after subsequent ones have been paid.

(5) See if the balance on the account is growing, and if so, why.

(6) Test the company's control over the issue of credit notes and the write-off of bad debts.

Chapter roundup

- A **circularisation** of **trade debtors** is a major procedure. The **choice** and **performance** of the circularisation must be carefully thought out.

- Auditors must follow up **debtor disagreements** and **failure by debtors** to **respond**.

- The **recoverability** of **debts** can be tested by a combination of methods. The provision for bad debts can have a significant impact on profits.

Quick quiz

1   The negative method of debtors' circularisation should only be used if the client has a good internal control and a small number of large debtors accounts.

True ☐

False ☐

2   Name four types of account which should receive special attention when picking a sample for a debtors' circularisation.

1   ....

2   ....

3   ....

4   ....

3   Complete the following tests which aim to confirm the valuation of bad debts.

(a) Confirm adequacy of provision by reviewing correspondence with

   (i)   ....

   (ii) ....

(b) Examine .... issued after the year end for provisions that should be made against current period balances.

4 Name three things that can be considered when undertaking analytical review on sales.

    1 ....

    2 ....

    3 ....

5 Give two examples of tests to verify prepayments

    1 ....

    2 ....

Answers to quick quiz

1 False

2 See para 1.14

3 (a) debtors, solicitors
  (b) credit notes

4 1 level of sales, month by month
  2 price
  3 goods returned

5 1 Verify by reference to invoices, cash book correspondence
  2 Check calculations

Now try the questions below from the Exam Question Bank

Number	Level	Marks	Time
15	Exam	20	36 mins

BPP PUBLISHING

Chapter 16

BANK AND CASH

Topic list	Syllabus reference
1 Bank	6
2 Bank balance procedures	6
3 Cash	6

Introduction

Work on bank and cash will concentrate on completeness and accuracy of balances. The audit of cash book transactions has been considered in the chapters on sales, purchases and wages cycles, and fixed asset additions and disposals.

Study guide

Section 20

- Describe and tabulate for inclusion in a work program the substantive procedures used in obtaining evidence in relation to bank and cash, and the related income statement entries

- Explain the purpose of substantive procedures in relation to financial statement assertions concerning bank and cash

Exam guide

Bank reconciliation testing is often the most important in practice, and so may be where exam questions are focused.

1   BANK

1.1   The audit of bank balances will need to cover **completeness, existence, rights and obligations and valuation**. All of these elements can be audited directly through the device of obtaining third party confirmations from the client's banks and reconciling these with the accounting records, having regard to cut-off.

1.2   As preparation, the auditors should update details of bank accounts held, ensuring the client holds accounts with bona fide banks.

Bank reports

1.3   The Auditing Practices Board issued Practice Note 16 *Bank reports for audit purposes* in August 1998. The note sets out a revised process for auditors when requesting information from the banks. It draws a distinction between standard and supplementary information.

1.4 The standard request consists of information about account and balance details, facilities, securities, and additional banking relationships. The request for supplementary information is concerned with requests for trade finance information, and derivatives and commodity trading information.

1.5 **Bank confirmation request letter - illustration**

[XXXXXX Bank plc
25 XXX Street
Warrington
Cheshire
WA1 1XQ]

Dear Sirs,

In accordance with the agreed practice for provision of information to auditors, please forward information on our mutual client(s) as detailed below on behalf of the bank, its branches and subsidiaries. This request and your response will not create any contractual or other duty with us.

COMPANIES OR OTHER BUSINESS ENTITIES
(attach a separate listing if necessary)

[Parent Company Ltd
Subsidiary 1 Ltd
Subsidiary 2 Ltd]

AUDIT CONFIRMATION DATE (30 APRIL 2000)

Information required	Tick
Standard	
Trade finance	
Derivative and commodity trading	
Custodian arrangements	
Other information (see attached)	

The authority to disclose information signed by your customer is attached / already held by you (delete as appropriate). Please advise us if this authority is insufficient for you to provide full disclosure of the information requested.

The contract name is [John Caller]   Telephone [01 234 5678]

Yours faithfully,
[XXX Accountants]

1.6 The procedure is simple but important.

(a) The banks will require **explicit written authority** from their client to disclose the information requested.

(b) The **auditors' request** must **refer** to the **client's letter** of authority and the date thereof. Alternatively it may be countersigned by the client or it may be accompanied by a specific letter of authority.

(c) In the case of joint accounts, **letters of authority** signed by all **parties** will be necessary.

(d) Such **letters** of **authority** may either **give permission** to the bank to disclose information for a specific request or grant permission for an indeterminate length of time.

(e) The request should **reach** the **branch manager** at least **two weeks in advance** of the client's **year-end** and should state both that year-end date and the previous year-end date.

(f) The **auditors** should themselves **check** that the bank response covers all the information in the standard and other responses.

Standard request for information

1.7   The following information should always be disclosed by banks upon receipt of a request for information for audit purposes. Responses should be given in the order below and if no information is available then this must be stated as 'None' in the response.

---

1   **Account and balance details**

Give full titles of all bank accounts including loans, (whether in sterling or another currency) together with their account numbers and balances. For accounts closed during the 12 months up to the audit confirmation date give the account details and date of closure.

Note. Also give details where your customer's name is joined with that of other parties and where the account is in a trade name.

State if any account or balances are subject to any restriction(s) whatsoever. Indicate the nature and extent of the restriction, eg garnishee order.

2   **Facilities**

Give the following details of all loans, overdrafts and associated guarantees and indemnities:

- Term
- Repayment frequency and/or review date
- Details of period of availability of agreed finance, ie finance remaining undrawn
- Detail the facility limit

3   **Securities**

With reference to the facilities detailed in (2) above give the following details:

- Any security formally charged (date, ownership and type of charge). State whether the security supports facilities granted by the bank to the customer or to another party.

    Note. Give details if a security is limited in amount or to a specific borrowing or if to your knowledge there is a prior, equal or subordinate charge.

- Where there are any arrangements for set-off of balances or compensating balances, eg back to back loans, give particulars (ie date, type of document and accounts covered) of any acknowledgement of set-off, whether given by specific letter of set-off or incorporated in some other document.

4   **Additional banking relationship**

State if you are aware of the customer(s) having any additional relationships with branches or subsidiaries of the bank not covered by the response. Supply a list of branches etc.

Request for supplementary information

1.8 The Practice Note also gives example letters if information about **trade finance**, **derivatives** and **custodian arrangements** is required.

Cut-off

1.9 Care must be taken to ensure that there is no **window dressing**, by checking cut-off carefully. Window dressing in this context is usually manifested as an attempt to overstate the liquidity of the company by:

(a) Keeping the cash book open to take credit for **remittances actually received** after the year end, thus enhancing the balance at bank and reducing debtors

(b) **Recording cheques paid in** the period under review which are not actually despatched until after the year end, thus decreasing the balance at bank and reducing creditors

A combination of (a) and (b) can contrive to present an artificially healthy looking current ratio.

1.10 With the possibility of (a) above in mind, where lodgements have not been cleared by the bank until the new period the auditors should **examine the paying-in slip** to ensure that the amounts were actually paid into the bank on or before the balance sheet date.

1.11 As regards (b) above, where there appears to be a particularly **large number of outstanding cheques** at the year-end, the auditors should check whether these were **cleared** within a **reasonable time** in the new period. If not, this may indicate that despatch occurred after the year-end.

2 BANK BALANCE PROCEDURES

2.1 The following suggested substantive balance sheet tests summarise the principal audit procedures discussed above relevant to cash and bank balances. The procedures apply to all bank accounts.

- **Obtain standard bank confirmations** from each bank with which the client conducted business during the audit period

- **Check arithmetic** of bank reconciliation

- **Trace cheques shown as outstanding** from the bank reconciliation to the cash book prior to the year-end and to the **after date bank statements** and **obtain explanations** for any **large or unusual items** not cleared at the time of the audit

- **Compare cash book(s)** and **bank statements** in detail for the last month of the year, and **check items outstanding** at the reconciliation date to bank reconciliations

- **Review bank reconciliation** previous to the year-end bank reconciliation and check that **all items** are **cleared** in the last period or **taken forward** to the year-end bank reconciliation

- **Obtain satisfactory explanations** for **all items** in the **cash book** for which there are **no corresponding entries** in the **bank statement** and vice versa

- **Verify contra items** appearing in the cash books or bank statements with original entry

---

- **Verify** by checking pay-in slips that **uncleared bankings** are **paid in** prior to the year end

- **Examine all lodgements** in respect of which payment has been refused by the bank; ensure that they are cleared on representation or that other appropriate steps have been taken to effect recovery of the amount due

- **Verify balances** per the **cash book** according to the **bank reconciliation** with **cash book, bank statements and general ledger**

- **Verify** the **bank balances** with reply to **standard bank letter** and with the **bank statements**

- **Scrutinise** the cash book and bank statements before and after the balance sheet date for **exceptional entries** or **transfers** which have a material effect on the balance shown to be in hand

- **Identify** whether any **accounts** are **secured** on the **assets** of the company

- **Consider** whether there is a **legal right** of **set-off** of overdrafts against positive bank balances

- **Determine** whether the **bank accounts** are **subject** to any **restrictions**

Note. Auditors should ensure that all cheques are despatched immediately after signature and entry in the cash book. Examine the interval between dates of certain of the larger cheques in the cash book and payment by the bank since this may indicate that cheques were despatched after the year-end (window dressing).

Exam focus point

Remember that the bank letter contains the balance held by the client at the bank **per the bank's records**. This must be reconciled to the balance held with the bank **per the client's records**.

3 CASH

3.1 Cash balances/floats are often individually immaterial but they may require some audit emphasis because of the opportunities for fraud that could exist where internal control is weak and because in total they may be material.

3.2 However in enterprises such as hotels, the amount of cash in hand at the balance sheet date could be considerable; the same goes for retail organisations. Cash counts may be important for internal auditors, who have a role in fraud **prevention**.

3.3 Where the auditors determine that cash balances are potentially material they may conduct a cash count, ideally at the balance sheet date. Rather like attendance at stocktaking, the conduct of the count falls into three phases: planning, the count itself and follow up procedures.

Planning

3.4 Planning is an essential element, for it is an important principle that all cash balances are counted at the same time as far as possible. Cash in this context may include unbanked cheques received, IOUs and credit card slips, in addition to notes and coins.

3.5 As part of their planning procedures the auditors will hence need to determine the **locations** where cash is held and which of these locations warrant a count.

3.6 Planning decisions will need to be recorded on the current audit file including:

- The **precise time** of the count(s) and location(s)
- The **names** of the **audit staff** conducting the counts
- The **names** of the **client staff** intending to be present at each location

Where a location is not visited it may be expedient to obtain a letter from the client confirming the balance.

Cash count

3.7 The following matters apply to the count itself.

- All cash/petty **cash books** should be **written up** to date in ink (or other permanent form at the time of the count.

- All **balances** must be **counted** at the **same time.**

- All **negotiable securities** must be **available** and **counted** at the time the cash balances are counted.

- At **no time** should the **auditors** be left **alone** with the cash and negotiable securities.

- **All cash** and securities **counted** must be **recorded** on working papers subsequently filed on the current audit file. Reconciliations should be prepared where applicable (for example imprest petty cash float).

3.8 The following procedures should be carried out.

> - **Count cash balances** held and agree to petty cash book or other record:
>   - Count all balances simultaneously
>   - All counting to be done in the presence of the individuals responsible
>   - Enquire into any IOUs or cashed cheques outstanding for unreasonable periods of time
> - **Obtain certificates** of cash in hand from responsible officials
> - **Confirm** that bank and cash **balances** as reconciled above are **correctly stated** in the accounts

3.9 Follow up procedures should ensure that:

> - **Certificates of cash-in-hand** are **obtained** as appropriate.
> - **Unbanked cheques/cash receipts** have subsequently been **paid in** and agree to the bank reconciliation.
> - **IOUs** and cheques cashed for employees have been **reimbursed.**
> - **IOUs or cashed cheques outstanding** for **unreasonable periods** of time have been provided for.
> - The **balances** as **counted** are **reflected** in the **accounts** (subject to any agreed amendments because of shortages and so on).

Question 1

(a) Explain the importance of the bank letter and describe the procedures used to obtain confirmations from the bank.

(b) Describe how you would check a client's bank reconciliation.

Answer

(a) The bank letter is important because it is independent confirmation of a number of important matters in the client's financial statements. It confirms cash and bank balances which may well be a significant asset. It also provides confirmation of customer's assets held as security, customers' other assets held (as custodian) and contingent liabilities. Auditors also ask the bank to give details of other banks and branches that the respondent bank is aware have a relationship with the client.

Audit procedures

(i) Obtain written authority from the client to the bank to disclose the necessary information.

(ii) Send a bank letter in standard form to the bank in sufficient time for it to arrive at least two weeks before the year-end. The letter should state both the year-end date and the previous year-end date, and should refer to the client's granting of authority.

(iii) If additional information over and above what is in the standard letter is requested, send a separate letter requesting that information.

(iv) When confirmation is received from the bank, check that the bank have answered all the questions in the letter.

(v) Follow up all points disclosed in the bank letter.

(b) The following procedures should be carried out.

(i) Obtain standard bank confirmations from each bank with which the client conducted business during the period.

(ii) Check arithmetic of bank reconciliation.

(iii) Trace cheques shown as outstanding from the bank reconciliation to the cash book prior to the year-end and to the after date bank statements and obtain explanations for any large or unusual items not cleared at the time of the audit.

(iv) Verify by checking pay-in slips that uncleared bankings are paid in prior to the year end, and check uncleared bankings are cleared quickly after the year-end.

(v) Verify balances per cash book according to the reconciliation with cash book and general ledger.

(vi) Verify the bank balances with reply to standard bank letter and with the bank statements.

(vii) Scrutinise the cash book and bank statements before and after the balance sheet date for exceptional entries or transfers which have a material effect on the balance shown to be in hand.

(viii) Identify whether any accounts are secured on the assets of the company.

(ix) Consider whether there is a legal right of set-off of overdrafts against positive bank balances.

(x) Determine whether the bank accounts are subject to any restrictions.

Chapter roundup

- **Bank balances** are usually **confirmed directly with the bank** in question. The bank letter can be used to ask a variety of questions, including queries about outstanding interests, contingent liabilities and guarantees.

- **Cash balances** should be **checked** if irregularities are suspected.

Quick quiz

1   Summarise the procedure for obtaining confirmation from a client's bank.

   1   ....

   2   ....

   3   ....

   4   ....

   5   ....

   6   ....

2   Complete these two of the audit tests performed to verify the bank reconciliation.

   (a)   Trace cheques shown as outstanding on the .... to the .... prior to the year end and ....

   (b)   Obtain satisfactory explanations for all items in the .... for which there is no corresponding entry in the .... and ....

3   Give two examples of business where cash floats could be considerable.

   1   ....

   2   ....

4   What planning matters relating to a cash count should be recorded in the current audit file?

   1   ....

   2   ....

   3   ....

Answers to quick quiz

1   See para 1.6

2   bank reconciliation, cash book, after date bank statements

3   hotels
     retail operations

4   Time of count
     Names of client staff attending
     Names of audit staff attending

Now try the questions below from the Exam Question Bank

Number	Level	Marks	Time
16	Exam	20	36 mins

BPP PUBLISHING

Chapter 17

LIABILITIES AND CAPITAL

Topic list	Syllabus reference
1 Trade creditors and purchases	6
2 Accruals	6
3 Long-term liabilities	6
4 Provisions and contingencies	6
5 Capital and other issues	6

Introduction

Some of the liability components of the balance sheet are technically quite difficult in that they are regulated by company law. This mainly applies to share capital and reserves which we examine in part 5. We will try to avoid the more complex legalistic aspects of these items and concentrate on the fundamental auditing procedures involved.

In the case of other liabilities, circularisation for verification purposes is quite rare and other procedures are normally used. This can be one of the most sensitive areas of the audit as it affects the company's liquidity and gearing ratios and these may be closely related to bank borrowing covenants or debenture agreements. Testing for **understatement** and **completeness** is particularly important.

Auditing provisions can be complex due to the complexity of the accounting for them.

Study guide

Section 19

- Describe and tabulate for inclusion in a work program the substantive procedures used in obtaining evidence in relation to current liabilities and accruals, and the related income statement entries

- Explain the purpose of substantive procedures in relation to financial statement assertions concerning current liabilities and accruals

Section 21

- Describe and tabulate for inclusion in a work program the substantive procedures used in obtaining evidence in relation to long-term liabilities and the related income statement entries

- Explain the purpose of substantive procedures in relation to financial statement assertions concerning long-term liabilities.

Exam guide

As long term liabilities are often used to finance fixed assets, these could be examined jointly. Trade creditors could be examined in conjunction with purchase controls.

1 TRADE CREDITORS AND PURCHASES

1.1 As with debtors, creditors are likely to be a material figure in the balance sheet of most enterprises. The purchases cycle tests of controls will have provided the auditors with some assurance as to the completeness of liabilities.

1.2 Auditors should however be particularly aware, when conducting their balance sheet work, of the possibility of **understatement** of **liabilities** to improve liquidity and profits (by understating the corresponding purchases). The primary objective of their balance sheet work will be to ascertain whether **liabilities** existing at the year-end have been **completely** and **accurately recorded**.

1.3 As regards **trade creditors**, this primary objective can be subdivided into two detailed objectives.

- Is there a **satisfactory cut-off** between goods received and invoices received, so that purchases and trade creditors are recognised in the correct year?

- Do trade creditors represent the **bona fide** amounts due by the company?

1.4 Before we ascertain how the auditors design and conduct their tests with these objectives in mind, we need to establish the importance, as with trade debtors, of the list of balances.

Trade creditors listing and accruals listing

1.5 The list of balances will be one of the principal sources from which the auditors will select their samples for testing. The listing should be extracted from the purchase ledger by the client. The auditors will carry out the following substantive tests to verify that the extraction has been properly performed.

- **Check** from the **purchase ledger accounts** to the **list of balances** and *vice versa*
- **Reconcile** the **total** of the list with the **purchase ledger control account**
- **Cast** the **list** of balances and the purchase ledger control account

---

The client should also prepare a detailed schedule of trade and sundry accrued expenses.

Completeness, rights and obligations and existence of trade creditors

1.6 The most important test when considering **trade creditors** is comparison of suppliers' statements with purchase ledger balances.

1.7 When selecting a sample of creditors to test, auditors must be careful not just to select creditors with large year-end balances. Remember, it is errors of **understatement** that auditors are primarily interested in when reviewing creditors, and errors of understatement could occur equally in creditors with low or nil balances as with high.

1.8 When comparing **supplier statements** with **year-end purchase ledger balances**, auditors should include within their sample creditors with nil or negative purchase ledger balances. Auditors should be particularly wary of low balances with major suppliers. Remember the client has no incentive to record liabilities before being invoiced.

1.9 You may be wondering why if as we normally carry out a debtors' circularisation whether we would also circularise creditors. The answer is generally no.

1.10 The principal reason for this lies in the nature of the purchases cycle: third party evidence in the form of suppliers' invoices and even more significantly, **suppliers' statements**, are part of the standard documentation of the cycle. The auditors will hence concentrate on these documents when designing and conducting their tests.

1.11 In the following circumstances the auditors may, however, determine that a circularisation is necessary. In these cases confirmation requests should be sent out and processed in a similar way to debtors' confirmation requests. 'Positive' replies will be required where:

- **Suppliers'** statements are, for whatever reason, **unavailable** or **incomplete**.
- **Weaknesses in internal** control or the nature of the client's business make possible a material misstatement of liabilities that would not otherwise be picked up.
- It is thought that the **client** is **deliberately** trying to **understate creditors**.
- The **accounts** appear to be **irregular** or if the nature or size of balances or transactions is abnormal.

Exam focus point

Testing suppliers' statements is frequently examined in auditing exams.

Purchases and expenses

1.12 When testing purchases and expenses, auditors are testing whether they are for **valid** reasons, that goods and services purchased have provided benefits to the company. They are also checking for **accuracy of recording** so again **cut-off** procedures will be important.

Occurrence and completeness of purchases

1.13 As with sales, **analytical procedures** will be important. Auditors should consider:

- The **level of purchases and expenses** over the year, compared on a month-by-month basis with the previous year
- The effect on value of purchases of **changes in quantities purchased**
- The effect on purchases value of changes in **products** purchased (for example a change in ingredients), or **prices of products**
- How the **ratio of trade creditors to purchases** compares with previous figures
- How the **ratio of trade creditors to stock** compares with previous years' figures

1.14 In addition auditors items may carry out the following additional substantive tests on individual purchases.

- Check **purchases and other expenses recorded** in the **purchase or general ledger or cash book** to supporting documentation (books of prime entry, invoices, delivery notes) considering whether:
  - **Purchases and expenses are valid** (invoices addressed to the client, for goods and services ordered by the client, for the purposes of the business)
  - **Purchases** and expenses have been **allocated** to the correct **purchase or general ledger** account

- Consider **reasonableness of deductions** from purchases or expenses by reference to subsequent events

- Check whether **valid debts** are **recorded** in **purchase ledger** by checking **credit notes**

1.15 One important expense is obviously wages and salaries which we consider below.

Purchases cut-off (completeness)

1.16 The procedures applied by the auditors will be designed to ascertain whether:

- **Goods received** for which **no invoice** has been **received** are **accrued**

- **Goods received** which have been **invoiced** but **not yet posted** are **accrued.**

- **Goods returned** to suppliers **prior** to the **year-end** are **excluded** from **stock** and **trade creditors**

1.17 At the year-end stocktaking the auditors will have made a note of the last serial numbers of goods received notes. Suggested substantive procedures are as follows.

- **Check from goods received notes** with serial numbers before the year-end to ensure that invoices are either:
  - Posted to purchase ledger prior to the year-end, or
  - Included on the schedule of accruals

- **Review the schedule of accruals** to ensure that goods received after the year-end are not accrued

- **Check from goods returned notes prior to year-end** to ensure that **credit notes** have been **posted** to the purchase ledger prior to the year-end or accrued

- **Review large invoices** and **credit notes** included after the year-end to ensure that they refer to the following year

- **Review outstanding purchase orders** for indications of any purchases completed but not invoiced

- **Reconcile daily batch invoice totals** around the year-end to purchase ledger control ensuring batches are posted in the correct year

- **Review** the **control account** around the year-end for **any unusual items**

Purchase of goods subject to reservation of title clauses

1.18 Under certain transactions, the seller may retain legal ownership of goods passed to a 'purchaser'. The requirements are known as 'reservation of title'.

1.19 The cases of *Borden (UK) Limited v Scottish Timber Products*, *Re Bond Worth* and the *Romalpa* case, suggest that a reservation of title clause will only be upheld if it states that the seller has a charge over the goods and the goods, any products made from them and any sale proceeds are kept separately and are readily identifiable.

1.20 Generally, the auditors' approach should be as follows.

> • **Ascertain** how the **client identifies suppliers selling** on terms which **reserve title** by enquiry of those responsible for purchasing and the board
>
> • **Review** and test the **procedures** for **quantifying** or **estimating** the **liabilities**
>
> • **Consider** whether **disclosure** is **sufficient** by itself if the directors have decided quantification is impractical
>
> • **Consider** the adequacy of the **disclosures** in the accounts
>
> • **Review the terms of sale** of **major suppliers** to confirm that liabilities not provided for do not exist or are immaterial

2 ACCRUALS

2.1 Checking the completeness and valuation of sundry accruals is an area that lends itself to **analytical procedures** and reconciliation techniques.

2.2 A variety of sources can indicate possible accruals. These include **last year's accruals**, **expense items** where an accrual would be expected, and **invoices received** and **cash paid** after the year-end.

2.3 Auditors should also use their **knowledge of the business** to consider whether there are accruals which they would expect to be there, but which may not be invoiced or paid until long after the year-end.

2.4 The following substantive procedures are suggested.

> • Check that **accruals** are **fairly calculated** and **verify** by reference to **subsequent payments** and **supporting documentation**
>
> • **Review the profit and loss account** and **prior years' figures** and consider liabilities inherent in the trade to **ensure** that all **likely accruals have been provided**
>
> • **Scrutinise payments** made **after year-end** to ascertain whether any payments made should be accrued
>
> • **Consider basis** for **round sum accruals** and ensure it is consistent with prior years
>
> • **Ascertain** why any **payments on account** are being **made** and **ensure** that the **full liability is provided**

2.5 For PAYE and VAT the following approach should be adopted.

> • **PAYE.** Normally this should represent one month's deductions. Check amount paid to Revenue by inspecting receipted annual declaration of tax paid over, or returned cheque
>
> • **VAT.** Check reasonableness to next VAT return. **Verify last amount paid in year** per cash book to VAT return

Wages and salaries

2.6 Although auditors may test other expenses solely by analytical review, they may carry out more detailed testing on wages and salaries, partly because of the consequences of failure to deduct PAYE and NIC correctly.

2.7 Analytical procedures will nonetheless be used to give some assurance on wages and salaries. Auditors should consider:

- **Wages and salaries levels** month-by-month with **previous years**
- **Effect on wages and salaries of rate changes** during the year
- **Average wage** per month **over the year**
- **Sales/profits** per **employee**
- **Payroll proof in total** (Pay rise × staff changes × staff mix)

2.8 In addition auditors may carry out the following substantive tests.

Occurrence

- **Check individual remuneration** per payroll to **personnel records, records of hours** worked, **salary agreements** etc

- **Confirm existence** of **employees** on payroll by meeting them, attending wages payout, inspecting personnel and tax records, and confirmation from managers

- **Check benefits** (pensions) on payroll to **supporting documentation**

Measurement

- **Check accuracy of calculation of remuneration**

- **Check** whether **calculation of statutory deductions** (PAYE, NIC) is **correct**

- Check **validity** of **other deductions** (pension contributions, share save etc) by agreement to supporting documentation (personnel files, conditions of pension scheme) and **check accuracy** of **calculation** of other deductions

Completeness

- **Check casts** of **payroll records**
- **Confirm** payment of net pay per payroll records to **cheque** or **bank transfer** summary
- **Agree net pay** per cash book to **payroll**
- **Scrutinise payroll** and **investigate unusual items**

Question 1

You have been asked to carry out the audit of the wages system by the senior in charge of the audit of Moonstar Manufacturing Ltd.

Most of the employees are paid their wages weekly in cash. However, directors, senior managers and some office staff have their salaries paid monthly by a direct payment into their bank account. Employees are paid a fixed rate per hour with supplements for overtime. The time employees work is recorded on clock cards, and overtime must be authorised by the works manager. Wage rates are authorised by the managing director, and the grade of an employee is decided by the works manager for all works employees, and the managing director for all other employees.

The personnel department keep a record of when employees start with the company and when they leave. The payroll is prepared by the wages department using a computer, which calculates the employee's gross pay from the hours worked (including overtime), determines the deductions for income tax, national insurance and other non-statutory deductions (pension contributions, savings, union deductions and so on), calculate the net pay and prints the payslip. The wage packets are prepared by the wages department. Employees sign for their pay when they receive their wage packet.

Required

(a) Briefly describe the principal aims in auditing a wages system.

(b) In relation to a starters and leavers test:

(i) Briefly describe the purpose of this test
(ii) Describe how you would carry out the test

(c) List and briefly describe:

(i) The principal audit objectives in carrying out a check of the pay-out of wages
(ii) The checks you would perform in carrying out a wages pay-out test
(iii) The tests you would perform in checking the unclaimed wages system

Answer

(a) Audit of a wages system should seek to ensure that there is an effective system of internal control in operation in order to minimise the likelihood of error, fraud or other irregularity occurring. Division of duties should be present where practicable. One source of weakness in this case is the fact that staff in the wages department are responsible for both preparation of the wage packets and preparation of the payroll.

There are a number of other specific objectives in the audit of the wages system; these are to ensure that:

(i) No errors or irregularities have taken place which are material to the financial statements.

(ii) Wages paid are at the authorised rates for the times actually worked.

(iii) Wages payments are made only to valid employees.

(iv) Deductions from employees' pay are calculated accurately and have been paid over to the appropriate third parties (for example the Inland Revenue, pension scheme or trade union) on time and in the correct amount.

(v) Holiday pay is calculated correctly and paid in accordance with the terms and conditions of individuals' employment contracts.

(b) (i) The main purpose of a test of employees joining and leaving is to ensure that pay in respect of these employees does not extend to periods before they started employment (for joiners) or after they leave employment (for leavers).

(ii) Firstly, I would compile a list of starters and leavers between two dates (perhaps six months apart) from personnel records of staff starting and leaving dates, checking that these records have been authorised by a responsible official.

The payroll at each of these two dates can then be examined and it will be possible to check that for employees leaving between the two dates, there is no pay shown at the later date and that for employees joining there is no pay at the earlier date. If the examination of the payroll at the two dates revealed other apparent starters or leavers, these instances would be investigated.

The payroll would be scrutinised around the date of starting or leaving for a sample of starters and leavers in order to ensure that pay starts or ceases at the appropriate date. This test would need to take into account any special procedures which apply. For example, leavers may be paid final holiday pay early, on the date they cease work but prior to their date of officially ceasing employment. Similarly, special arrangements might apply to the pay of employees joining.

(c) (i) The principal objectives of the auditors in attending a wages payout are to ensure that:

(1) All wage packets are either collected by an apparently bona fide employee or are recorded as unclaimed wages.

(2) No person collects more than one wage packet.

(3) Only wages claimed are signed for as collected.

(4) All unclaimed wages are accounted for by a responsible official.

(5) The wages payout is in general carried out in an orderly way.

(ii) Procedures to be carried out in performing a check on the wages payout include the following.

(1) Ensure that cash counted for wage packets is checked by a second employee and that the total cash is reconciled to the total net cash wages shown on the payroll.

(2) Ensure that names of employees are checked against the payroll before wage packages are removed from the wages department.

(3) Ensure that security measures are in evidence in taking wage packets to the location of the payout (at least two people should do this).

(4) Ensure that appropriate procedures take place when wages are handed out. One person should hand out the wage packets; another should obtain the employee's signature. Each employee should take only the packet bearing his or her name, and should sign as acknowledgement of receipt of the wages. A responsible official should be on hand to identify each employee receiving a wage packet.

(5) Ensure that unclaimed wages are returned to the wages department and that the names of the employees concerned are recorded in the unclaimed wages book. This procedure should be carried out by a responsible official other than the person who prepares the payroll or makes up the wage packets. Employees who are absent at the time of the wages payout should collect their wages from the wages department: other employees should not be permitted to claim the wages of missing employees on their behalf.

(6) Be put upon enquiry for any unusual or untoward occurrences or procedures.

(iii) The tests I would carry out on unclaimed wages would be as follows.

(1) Check that the unclaimed wages book has been regularly and properly written up.

(2) Check that signatures of employees claiming wages which were not collected at the payout are entered in the book.

(3) Test check a sample of employees' signatures to personnel files.

(4) Ensure that wages unclaimed for a certain period (say, two weeks) are banked. The cashier should sign and date the unclaimed wages book for each banking. Agree banking to cash book and general ledger account.

(5) Check that wage packets are present for all employees who have not claimed their wages as recorded in the unclaimed wages book. Consider test counting the contents of a sample of wage packets.

3 LONG-TERM LIABILITIES

3.1 We are concerned here with long-term liabilities comprising debentures, loan stock and other loans **repayable** at a date **more than one year after the year-end.**

3.2 Auditors will primarily try and determine:

- **Completeness:** whether all long-term liabilities have been disclosed

- **Measurement:** whether interest payable has been calculated correctly and included in the correct accounting period

- **Disclosure:** whether long-term loans and interest have been correctly disclosed in the financial statements

3.3 The major complication for the auditors is that debenture and loan agreements frequently contain conditions with which the company must comply, including restrictions on the company's total borrowings and adherence to specific borrowing ratios.

Substantive procedures applicable to all audits

3.4 The following suggested substantive procedures are relevant.

- **Obtain/prepare schedule of loans** outstanding at the balance sheet date showing, for each loan: name of lender, date of loan, maturity date, interest date, interest rate, balance at the end of the period and security

- **Compare opening balances** to previous year's papers

- **Test the clerical accuracy** of the analysis

BPP PUBLISHING

- **Compare balances** to the **general ledger**
- **Check name** of **lender** etc, to **register** of **debenture holders** or equivalent (if kept)
- **Trace additions** and **repayments** to **entries** in the **cash book**
- **Confirm repayments** are in accordance with **loan agreement**
- **Examine cancelled cheques** and **memoranda of satisfaction** for **loans repaid**
- **Verify** that **borrowing limits** imposed either by Articles or by other agreements are **not exceeded**
- **Examine signed Board minutes** relating to **new borrowings/repayments**
- **Obtain direct confirmation** from **lenders** of the amounts outstanding, accrued interest and what security they hold
- **Verify interest charged** for the period and the adequacy of accrued interest
- **Confirm assets charged** have been **entered** in the **register of charges** and **notified** to the **Registrar**
- **Review restrictive covenants** and provisions relating to default:
  - **Review** any **correspondence** relating to the loan
  - **Review confirmation** replies for non-compliance
  - If a **default appears** to exist, **determine** its **effect**, and schedule findings
- **Review minutes, cash book** to **check** if all **loans have been recorded**

4 PROVISIONS AND CONTINGENCIES

4.1 When considering the audit of these two issues, it is important to revise the accounting requirements here first.

FRS 12 *Provisions, contingent liabilities and contingent assets*

KEY TERMS

A **provision** is a liability that is of uncertain timing or amount, to be settled by the transfer of economic benefits.

A **contingent liability** is either

(a) a possible obligation arising from past events whose existence will be confirmed only by the occurrence of one or more uncertain future events not wholly within the entity's control, or

(b) a present obligation that arises from past events but is not recognised because it is not probable that a transfer of economic benefits will be required to settle the obligation or because the amount of the obligation cannot be measured with sufficient reliability.

A **contingent asset** is a possible asset arising from past events whose existence will be confirmed only by the occurrence of one or more uncertain future events not wholly within the entity's control.

4.2 The key distinction in FRS 12 therefore is between provisions which are accrued in the accounts, and contingent assets and liabilities, which are not accrued but which may be disclosed.

Recognition

4.3 A provision should be recognised when an entity has a **present obligation** as a result of a past event, it is **probable** that a **transfer** of **economic benefits** will be **required** to settle the obligation, and a **reasonable estimate** can be made of the amount of the obligation. Unless these conditions are met, no provision should be recognised.

Measurement

4.4 The amount recognised as a provision should be the **best estimate** of the expenditure required to settle the present obligation at the balance sheet date.

Reimbursements

4.5 Where some or all of the expenditure required to settle a provision is expected to be reimbursed by another party, the reimbursement should be recognised only when it is **virtually certain** that the reimbursement will be received if the entity settles the obligation. The reimbursement should be treated as a separate asset.

Changes in provisions

4.6 Provisions should be reviewed at each balance sheet date and adjusted to reflect the current best estimate.

Contingent assets and liabilities

CONTINGENT LIABILITIES		
Where, as a result of past events, there may be a transfer of future economic benefits in settlement of (a) a present obligation or (b) a possible obligation whose existence will be confirmed by the occurrence of one or more uncertain future events not wholly within the entity's control, and		
there is a present obligation that probably requires a transfer of economic benefits in settlement,	there is a possible obligation or a present obligation that may, but probably will not, require a transfer of economic benefits in settlement,	there is a possible obligation or a present obligation where the likelihood of a transfer of economic benefits in settlement is remote,
a provision is recognised and disclosures are required for the provision.	no provision is recognised but disclosures are required for the contingent liability.	no provision is recognised and no disclosure is required.

4.7 A contingent liability also arises in the extremely rare case **where there is a liability** that cannot be recognised because it cannot be **measured reliably**. Disclosures are required for the contingent liability.

CONTINGENT ASSETS		
Where, as a result of past events, there is a possible asset whose existence will be confirmed by the occurrence of one or more uncertain future events not wholly within the entity's control, and		
the inflow of economic benefits is virtually certain,	the inflow of economic benefits is probable but not virtually certain,	the inflow is not probable,
the asset is not contingent.	no asset is recognised but disclosures are required.	no asset is recognised and no disclosure is required.

4.8 The audit tests that should be carried out on provisions and contingent assets and liabilities are as follows.

- **Obtain details** of all **provisions** which have been included in the **accounts** and all **contingencies** that have been disclosed

- **Obtain** a **detailed analysis** of all **provisions** showing opening balances, movements and closing balances

- **Determine** for each material provision **whether** the **company** has a **present obligation** as a result of past events by:
    - Review of **correspondence** relating to the item
    - **Discussion** with the **directors**. Have they created a valid expectation in other parties that they will discharge the obligation?

- **Determine** for each material provision **whether** it is **probable** that a **transfer of economic benefits** will be required to settle the obligation by the following tests.
    - **Check** whether any **payments** have been **made** in the post balance sheet period in respect of the item
    - **Review correspondence** with solicitors, banks, customers, insurance company and suppliers both pre and post year end
    - **Send** a **letter** to the **solicitor** to obtain their views (where relevant)
    - **Discuss** the **position** of similar **past provisions** with the directors. Were these provisions eventually settled?
    - **Consider** the **likelihood** of **reimbursement**

- **Recalculate** all **provisions** made

- **Compare** the **amount provided** with any post year end payments and with any amount paid in the past for similar items

- In the event that it is not possible to estimate the amount of the **provision**, check that this **contingent liability** is **disclosed** in the accounts

- **Consider** the **nature** of the **client's business**. Would you expect to see any other provisions for example, warranties?

Exam focus point

You should appreciate that the problems of accounting for contingencies makes their audit difficult.

5 CAPITAL AND OTHER ISSUES

Share capital

5.1 The issued share capital as stated in the accounts must be **agreed** in total with the **share register**. An examination of transfers on a test basis should be made in those cases where a company handles its own registration work. Where the registration work is dealt with by independent registrars, auditors will normally examine the reports submitted by them to the company, and obtain from them at the year-end a certificate of the share capital in issue.

5.2 Company law prescribe that the directors must:

(a) Have the general powers of management to be able to allot shares.

(b) Not exercise that power without **authority** from the **members**. That authority may either be given by the company's **articles** or by **resolution** passed in **general meeting** (s 80 of the Companies Act).

(c) Respect the **pre-emption rights** of **existing members**. Under s 89 of the Companies Act directors must first offer shares to holders of similar shares in proportion to their holdings. A private company can permanently exclude these rules in its memorandum and articles. Any company can decide by special resolution that the rules should not apply on a specific occasion.

5.3 Auditors should take particular care if there are any movements in reserves that cannot be distributed, and should **confirm** that these movements are **valid**.

5.4 The following suggested substantive procedures are relevant in this area.

Share capital

> - **Agree** the **authorised share capital** with the **memorandum** and **articles of association**
> - **Agree changes** to **authorised share capital** with **properly authorised resolutions**

Issue of shares

> - **Verify any issue** of share capital or other changes during the year with general and board **minutes**
> - **Ensure issue or change** is within the **terms** of the **memorandum** and **articles** of association, and directors possess appropriate authority to issue shares
> - **Confirm** that **cash** or **other consideration** has been **received** or **debtor(s) is included** as called up share capital not paid
> - **Confirm** that any **premium** on issue of shares has been **credited** to the **share premium** account
> - Where a public company has issued shares for **non-cash consideration**, check fair **value** has been **received for** the shares, and that valuation reports have been obtained
> - For **redeemable shares** issued, check their **terms provide** for payment on **redemption**

Transfer of shares

- **Verify transfers of shares** by reference to:
  - Correspondence
  - Completed and stamped transfer forms
  - Cancelled share certificates
  - Minutes of directors' meeting
- **Check the balances** on **shareholders' accounts** in the register of members and the total list with the amount of issued share capital in the general ledger

Dividends

- **Agree dividends** paid and proposed to **authority** in minute books and **check calculation** with **total share capital** issued to ascertain whether there are any outstanding or unclaimed dividends
- **Check dividend payments** with **documentary evidence** (say, the returned dividend warrants)
- **Check** that **dividends do not contravene** the distribution provisions of the **Companies Act 1985**

Reserves

- **Check movements on reserves** to **supporting authority**
- **Ensure that movements on reserves do not contravene** the **Companies Act 1985** and the memorandum and articles of association
- **Confirm** that the **company** can **distinguish** those reserves at the balance sheet date that are **distributable** from those that are **non-distributable**
- **Ensure appropriate disclosures** of movements on reserves are made in the company's accounts

Statutory books

5.5 Suggested substantive procedures are as follows.

Register of directors and secretaries

- **Update permanent file** giving details of directors and secretary
- **Verify** any **changes** with the **minutes** and ensure that the necessary details have been filed at Companies House
- **Verify** that the **number of directors complies** with the **Articles**

Register of directors' interests in shares and debentures

- **Ensure** that **directors' interests** are **noted** on the permanent file for cross-referencing to directors' reports
- **Ensure** that **directors' shareholdings comply** with the **Articles**

Minute books of directors and general meetings

- **Obtain photocopies** or **prepare extracts** from the **minute books** of meetings concerning financial matters, cross-referencing them to appropriate working papers

- **Ensure** that **extracts** of **agreements** referred to in the minutes are **prepared** for the permanent file

- **Check agreements** with the company's seal book where one is kept

- **Note the date** of the last **minute reviewed**

- **Check** that **meetings** have been **properly convened** and that quorums attended them

Register of interests in shares (if applicable)

- **Scrutinise register** and verify that *prima facie* it appears to be in order
- **Ensure** that **significant interests** are **noted on** the permanent file

Register of charges

- **Update permanent file schedule** from the register

- **Ensure** that **any assets** which are **charged** as security for loans from third parties are **disclosed** in the **accounts**

- **Obtain confirmation** that there are **no charges** to be recorded if no entries are recorded in the register

- **Consider carrying out company search** at Companies House to verify the accuracy of the register

Accounting records

- Consider whether the accounting records are adequate to:
    - **Show** and **explain** the **company's transactions**
    - **Disclose** with **reasonable accuracy**, at any time, the **financial position** of the **company**
    - **Comply** with the **Act** by recording money received and expended, assets and liabilities, year-end stock and stock-taking, sales and purchases
    - **Enable** the **directors** to **ensure** that the **accounts give** a **true and fair view**

General ledger and journals

- **Check opening balances** in general ledger to **previous year's audited accounts**

- **Check additions** of general ledger accounts

- **Review general ledger accounts** and ensure significant transfers and unusual items are *bona fide*

- **Review the journal** and ensure that **significant entries** are **authorised** and **properly recorded**

- **Check extraction** and **addition** of **trial balance** (if prepared by the client)

Returns

- **Check** that the **following returns** have been filed properly:
    - Annual return and previous year's accounts
    - Notices of change in directors or secretary
    - Memoranda of charges or mortgages created during the period
    - VAT returns
    - Other tax returns

Directors' service contracts

- **Inspect copies** of directors' service contracts or memoranda.

- **Ensure** that they are **kept** at

    - The **registered office,** or
    - The **principal place of business,** or
    - The place where the register of members is kept, if not the registered office

- Verify that long-term service contracts (lasting more than five years) have been approved in general meeting.

Directors' emoluments

5.6 The auditors have a duty to include in their report the required disclosure particulars of directors' emoluments and transactions with directors, if these requirements have not been complied with in the accounts (s 237).

Audit approach

5.7 The auditors will have carried out an evaluation of salaries payroll procedures, including the system in operation for directors' salaries, earlier in the audit. At the year end, they can probably concentrate on limited substantive work designed to ensure that the final **figures** in the **accounting records** are **complete** and the disclosure requirements in respect of directors have been complied with.

5.8 The auditors should carry out the following general procedures.

- **Ascertain** whether **monies payable or benefits** in kind provided have been **properly approved** in accordance with the company's memorandum and articles of association and that they are not prohibited by the Act

- **Confirm** that all **monies payable** and **benefits receivable** in relation to the current accounting period have been **properly accounted for,** unless the right to any of these has been waived by inspecting:

    - Salary records
    - Service contracts
    - Board minutes
    - Other relevant records

- **Consider** whether the **most common types of benefit** (company cars or cheap loans) may have been **omitted**

- **Review directors' service contracts**

- **Review** the **company's procedures** to ensure that **all directors advise** the board of all disclosable **emoluments**

- **Review** the **procedures** for ensuring that any **payments made to former directors** of the company are **identified** and **properly disclosed**

- **Consider** the **need** for any **amounts** included in directors' remuneration to be **further disclosed** in accordance with the Companies Act 1985 (for example property rented by directors from a company at below market rental)

Valuation of benefits in kind

5.9 In accordance with the Companies Act 1985 the amount to be disclosed for a benefit in kind is its **estimated money value.**

Golden hellos

5.10 Under the Companies Act 1985 rules emoluments in respect of a person's accepting office as director shall be treated as emoluments in respect of his services as director.

Chapter roundup

- The largest figure in current liabilities will normally be trade creditors generally checked by comparison of suppliers' statements with purchase ledger accounts.

- A creditors' circularisation might be appropriate, although they are relatively rare in practice.

- Accruals can be significant in total. Expense accruals will tend to repeat from one year to the next. Auditors should review after-date invoices and payments, and consider whether anything else that would have been expected has not been accrued.

- Long-term liabilities are usually authorised by the board and should be well documented.

- The accounting provisions for provisions and contingencies are complex and that can make them difficult to audit.

- The main concern with share capital and reserves (including distributions) will be that all transactions comply with the Companies Act.

- When auditing statutory books auditors should consider whether:
  - The company has complied with the Companies Act.
  - The records contain information that affects other areas of the audit.

- Auditors should ensure that directors' emoluments have been completely recorded in the accounts.

Quick quiz

1   What are the two primary objectives of balance sheet work on liabilities?

   1   ....

   2   ....

2   Nil balances should not be included in a supplier statement test.

   True   ☐

   False   ☐

3   Give two instances where creditors' circularisation is required.

1   ....

2   ....

4   Give four things auditors should consider when carrying out analytical review on wages and salaries.

1   ....

2   ....

3   ....

4   ....

5   Complete the definition

Long term liabilities comprise ...., ...-............................ and other loans .... at a date .... a year .... the year end.

Answers to quick quiz

1   To ensure (1) completely and (2) accurately recorded

2   False

3   1   Supplier statements are unavailable
    2   Weak internal controls

4   1   Salary rate changes
    2   Average wage by month over the year
    3   Sale/employee
    4   Payroll proof in total

5   debentures, loan-stock, repayable, more than, after.

Now try the questions below from the Exam Question Bank

Number	Level	Marks	Time
17	Exam	20	36 mins

Chapter 18

AUDIT REVIEWS AND FINALISATION

Topic list	Syllabus reference
1 Going concern	6
2 Subsequent events	6
3 Management representations	6
4 Unaudited published information	6
5 Overall review of financial statements	6
6 Problems of accounting treatment	6
7 Analytical procedures	6
8 Completion of the audit	6

Introduction

In this chapter will consider the reviews that take place to complete the audit and the procedures carried out before the audit conclusion is drawn and the opinion reached.

Firstly we consider two key reviews

- Going concern
- Subsequent events

These are both important disclosure issues in the financial statements. If the disclosures are not correct, this will impact on the auditors' report, which is discussed in Chapter 19.

In Chapter 12, in the context of accounting estimates, we discussed how there are some items in financial statements where facts or knowledge is confined to management. In the final stages of the audit, the auditor must consider this evidence, and obtain written representations from directors where necessary.

The remaining reviews are linked by their common aim of giving assurance as to the company's **stability** and the **validity** of the financial statements. The results of analytical procedures will be applied when considering the going concern situation and so on.

Accountancy knowledge is particularly important in this chapter. Auditors need to be able to interpret accounts understand the requirements of specific accounting standards.

These procedures are extremely important; failure to carry them out can lead to the gravest consequences for the auditors. Given this fact, they tend to be fairly standard in most audit approaches. A useful summary of these procedures is given in the checklist at the end of the chapter and you should refer to the checklist throughout this chapter.

Study guide

Section 23

- Explain the importance of going concern reviews
- Describe the procedures to be applied in performing going concern reviews

- Describe the disclosure requirements relating to going concern
- Describe the reporting implications of the finding of going concern reviews

Section 24

Describe the:

- Circumstances in which obtaining management representations is necessary and the matters on which representations are commonly obtained
- Purpose of the subsequent events review
- Procedures to be undertaken in performing a subsequent events review

Section 25

- Describe the importance of the overall review of evidence obtained
- Analyse the problems associated with the application of accounting treatments
- Explain the significance of unadjusted differences

Exam guide

All the reviews are very important to the audit, but particularly going concern. This is highly examinable.

1 GOING CONCERN

1.1 SAS 130 *Going concern basis in financial statements* was developed separately from the bulk of the other auditing standards because of its importance. This arises from the exposure of the auditors should they miss the going concern problems of a client and the difficulties surrounding the determination of going concern status in any given situation.

Going concern as an accounting concept

> **KEY TERM**
>
> The **going concern** concept: the enterprise will continue in operational existence for the foreseeable future. This means in particular that the profit and loss account and balance sheet assume no intention or necessity to liquidate or curtail significantly the scale of operation.

1.2 There are also legal requirements concerning going concern. Under these requirements, the financial statements of an entity are assumed to be prepared on a going concern basis.

1.3 Where the going concern basis is **not** appropriate:

- The entity may not be able to recover the amounts recorded in respect of assets.
- There may be changes in the amounts and dates of maturities of liabilities.

Therefore, if material, the amounts and classification of assets and liabilities would need to be adjusted.

1.4 Consequently, the **directors** must satisfy themselves that the going concern basis is appropriate. Even where it is, further disclosure may be required to give a true and fair view.

The applicability and scope of this SAS

SAS 130.1

When forming an opinion as to whether financial statements give a true a fair view, the auditors should consider the entity's ability to continue as a going concern, and any relevant disclosures in the financial statements.

1.5 The SAS gives guidance to auditors in the context of the going concern basis in financial statements which are required to be properly prepared under CA 1985 and to show a true and fair view. The SAS does **not** give guidance relating to the going concern in any other context, for example, *Cadbury Report* matters.

Foreseeable future

1.6 FRS 18 uses the term 'foreseeable future' but does not define it. The SAS recognises that any consideration of foreseeable future involves 'making a judgement, at a particular point in time, about future events which are inherently uncertain'.

1.7 The SAS suggests that the degree of **uncertainty increases significantly** the **further into the future** the consideration is taken and the 'foreseeable future' depends on the specific circumstances at a point in time.

1.8 As a consequence there can never be any certainty in relation to going concern. The auditors' judgement is only valid at that time and can be 'overturned by subsequent events'.

Consideration of going concern by the directors

1.9 The directors must assess going concern by looking at a period into the future and considering all available and relevant information. The SAS states that a minimum length for this period cannot be specified; it would be 'artificial and arbitrary' as there is no 'cut off point' after which the directors would change their approach.

1.10 FRS 18 requires the directors to make disclosures about the period they have determined to be the 'foreseeable future' if that period is less than one year.

Procedures

1.11 The audit procedures will be based on the directors' deliberations and the information they used. The auditors must assess whether the audit evidence is sufficient and appropriate and whether they agree with the directors' judgement. They should consider:

- The nature of the entity (its size and the complexity of its circumstances, for instance)

- Whether the information relates to future events, and if so how far into the future those events lie

A lengthy appendix to the SAS gives examples of how auditors might apply the SAS in different circumstances.

Audit evidence

> ## SAS 130.2
>
> The auditors should assess the adequacy of the means by which the directors have satisfied themselves that:
>
> (a) it is appropriate for them to adopt the going concern basis in preparing the financial statements; and
>
> (b) the financial statements include such disclosures, if any, relating to going concern as are necessary for them to give a true and fair view.
>
> For this purpose:
>
> (i) the auditors should make enquiries of the directors and examine appropriate available financial information; and
>
> (ii) having regard to the future period to which the directors have paid particular attention in assessing going concern, the auditors should plan and perform procedures specifically designed to identify any material matters which could indicate concern about the entity's ability to continue as a going concern.

Preliminary assessment

1.12 The auditors' approach includes a preliminary assessment, when the overall audit plan is being developed, of the risk that the entity may be unable to continue as a going concern. The auditors should consider.

(a) **Whether the period** to which the directors have paid particular attention in assessing going concern is **reasonable** in the client's circumstances

(b) The **systems**, or other means (formal or informal), **for timely identification of warnings of future risks** and uncertainties the entity might face

(c) **Budget and/or forecast information** (cash flow information in particular) produced by the entity, and the quality of the systems (or other means, formal or informal) in place for producing this information and keeping it up to date

(d) Whether the **key assumptions** underlying the budgets and/or forecasts appear appropriate in the circumstances, including consideration of:

- Projected profit
- Forecast levels of working capital
- The completeness of forecast expenditure
- Whether the client will have sufficient cash at periods of maximum need
- The financing of capital expenditure and long-term plans

(e) The **sensitivity of budgets and/or forecasts** to variable factors both within the control of the directors and outside their control

(f) Any **obligations, undertakings or guarantees** arranged with other entities (in particular, lenders, suppliers and group companies)

(g) The **existence, adequacy and terms of borrowing facilities**, and supplier credit

(h) The **directors' plans** for resolving any matters giving rise to the concern (if any) about the appropriateness of the going concern basis. In particular, the auditors may need to consider whether:

- The plans are realistic
- There is a reasonable expectation that the plans are likely to resolve any problems foreseen

- The directors are likely to put the plans into practice effectively

1.13 The auditors' and directors' procedures can be very simple in some cases, particularly in the case of smaller companies, where budgets and forecasts are not normally prepared and no specific systems are in place to monitor going concern matters.

The auditors' examination of borrowing facilities

1.14 The auditors will usually:

- Obtain confirmations of the existence and terms of bank facilities
- Make their own assessment of the intentions of the bankers relating thereto

1.15 These procedures will become more important if (for example) there is a **low margin** of **financial resources** available to the entity, correspondence between the bankers and the entity reveals that the **last renewal** of facilities was **agreed with difficulty** and a **significant deterioration in cash flow** is projected.

1.16 If the auditors cannot satisfy themselves then, in accordance with the audit reporting standard (SAS 600), they should consider whether the relevant matters need to be:

- **Disclosed in the financial statements** in order that they give a true and fair view
- **Referred to in the auditors' report** (by explanatory paragraph or qualified opinion)

Determining and documenting the auditors' concerns

> ### SAS 130.3
>
> The auditors should determine and document the extent of their concern (if any) about the entity's ability to continue as a going concern. In determining the extent of their concern, the auditors should take account of all relevant information of which they have become aware during their audit.

1.17 The following are given as examples of indicators of an entity's inability to continue as a going concern.

Going concern	
Financial	An excess of liabilities over assets
	Net current liabilities
	Necessary borrowing facilities have not been agreed
	Default on terms of loan agreements, and potential breaches of covenant
	Significant liquidity or cash flow problems
	Major losses or cash flow problems which have arisen since the balance sheet date and which threaten the entity's continued existence
	Substantial sales of fixed assets not intended to be replaced
	Major restructuring of debts
	Denial of (or reduction in) normal terms of trade credit by suppliers
	Major debt repayment falling due where refinancing is necessary to the entity's continued existence
	Inability to pay debts as they fall due

Going concern	
Operational	Fundamental changes to the market or technology to which the entity is unable to adapt adequately
	Externally forced reductions in operations (for example, as a result of legislation or regulatory action)
	Loss of key management or staff, labour difficulties or excessive dependence on a few product lines where the market is depressed
	Loss of key suppliers or customers or technical developments which render a key product obsolete
Other	Major litigation in which an adverse judgement would imperil the entity's continued existence
	Issues which involve a range of possible outcomes so wide that an unfavourable result could affect the appropriateness of the going concern basis

Exam focus point

Any question on going concern is likely to ask you to identify signs that a particular client may not be a going concern.

1.18 Auditors may still obtain sufficient appropriate audit evidence in such situations to conclude that the going concern basis is still appropriate. Further procedures such as discussions with the directors and further work on forecasts may be required.

1.19 Where auditors consider that there is a significant level of concern about the going concern basis, they might write to the directors suggesting the need to take suitable advice.

Written confirmations of representations from the directors

SAS 130.4

The auditors should consider the need to obtain written confirmations of representations from the directors regarding:

(a) the directors' assessment that the company is a going concern; and
(b) any relevant disclosures in the financial statements.

1.20 Representations may be critical in terms of audit evidence. If they do **not** receive such representations the auditors should consider whether:

- There is a limitation of scope in their work and a qualified opinion is required in 'except for' or 'disclaimer' terms.

- The failure of the directors to provide written confirmation could indicate concern.

Assessing disclosures in the financial statements

SAS 130.5

The auditors should consider whether the financial statements are required to include disclosures relating to going concern in order to give a true and fair view.

1.21 The main concern here is **sufficiency** of disclosure where:

- There are going concern worries.

- The future period the directors have considered is less than one year.

1.22 The auditors must assess whether the statements show a true and fair view and hence whether their opinion should be qualified, as well as whether all matters have been satisfactorily disclosed.

Reporting on the financial statements

1.23 The SAS summarises, in flowchart form, how auditors formulate their opinion as to whether the financial statements give a true and fair view and this is shown on a following page.

> ### SAS 130.6
>
> Where the auditors consider that there is a significant level of concern about the entity's ability to continue as a going concern, but do not disagree with the preparation of the financial statements on the going concern basis, they should include an explanatory paragraph when setting out the basis of their opinion. They should not quality their opinion on these grounds alone, provided the disclosures in the financial statements of the matters giving rise to the concern are adequate for the financial statements to give a true and fair view.

1.24 The following matters must be included in the financial statements for disclosure to be regarded as adequate.

- A statement that the financial statements have been prepared on the **going concern basis**

- A statement of the **pertinent factors**

- The **nature** of the concern

- A statement of the **assumptions** adopted by the directors, which should be clearly distinguishable from the pertinent facts

- (Where appropriate and practicable) a statement regarding the directors' **plans for resolving the matters** giving rise to the concern

- Details of any **relevant actions** by the directors

> ### SAS 130 7
>
> If the period to which the directors have paid particular attention in assessing going concern is less than one year from the date of approval of the financial statements, and the directors have not disclosed that fact, the auditors should do so within the section of their report setting out the basis of their opinion, unless the fact is clear from any other references in their report. They should not qualify their opinion on the financial statements on these grounds alone.

1.25 The auditors will also qualify their opinion if they consider that the directors have not taken adequate steps to satisfy themselves that it is appropriate for them to adopt the going concern basis. This will be a limitation in the scope of the auditors' work.

1.26 The audit report will contain the following paragraph if disclosure is considered to be inadequate.

> **Basis of opinion: excerpt**
>
> *Going concern*
>
> In forming our opinion, we have considered the adequacy of the disclosures made in note 1 of the financial statements concerning the uncertainty as to the continuation and renewal of the company's bank overdraft facility. In view of the significance of this uncertainty we consider that it should be drawn to your attention but our opinion is not qualified in this respect.

> **SAS 130.8**
>
> Where the auditors disagree with the preparation of the financial statements on the going concern basis, they should issue an adverse audit opinion.

Going concern presumption is inappropriate

1.27 Where the going concern presumption is **inappropriate**:

- Even disclosure in the financial statements of the matters giving rise to this conclusion is **not** sufficient for them to give a true and fair view.

- The effect on financial statements prepared on that basis is so material or pervasive that the financial statements are seriously misleading.

Accordingly, an **adverse opinion** is appropriate in such cases.

Financial statements not prepared on the going concern basis

> **SAS 130.9**
>
> In rare circumstances, in order to give a true and fair view, the directors may have prepared financial statements on a basis other than that of a going concern. If the auditors consider this other basis to be appropriate in the specific circumstances, and if the financial statements contain the necessary disclosures, the auditors should not qualify their opinion in this respect.

1.28 Under such circumstances, the accounts may be prepared on a basis that reflects the fact that assets may need to be realised other than in the ordinary course of operations. The auditors may wish to refer to the basis on which the financial statements are prepared.

1.29 **Section summary**

- Director and auditor assessment of the going concern basis should take place over the **foreseeable future.**

- Auditors should make a **preliminary assessment** of going concern and be alert during the audit for **signs** of **going concern problems.**

- Specific audit procedures include **assessment** of **client forecasts,** examination of **borrowing facilities** and obtaining **representations** from the directors.

- Auditors may **qualify** the audit report because they disagree with the use of the **going concern basis** or **extent of disclosure.**

- Alternatively auditors may consider it appropriate to give an unqualified opinion with a **fundamental uncertainty** paragraph.

*Going concern and reporting
on the financial statements*

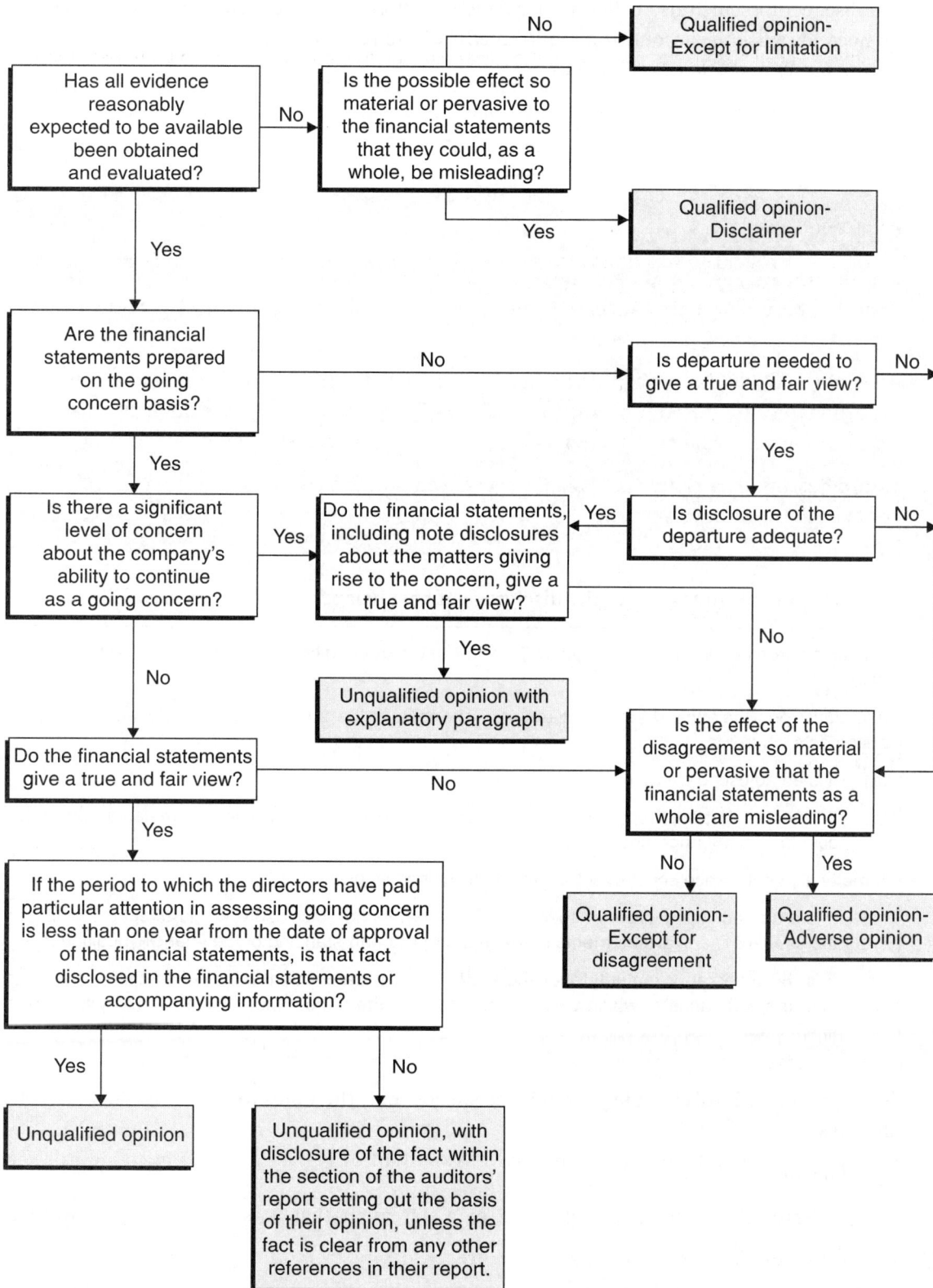

Has all evidence reasonably expected to be available been obtained and evaluated?

→ **No** → Is the possible effect so material or pervasive to the financial statements that they could, as a whole, be misleading?

→ **No** → Qualified opinion- Except for limitation

→ **Yes** → Qualified opinion- Disclaimer

↓ **Yes**

Are the financial statements prepared on the going concern basis?

→ **No** → Is departure needed to give a true and fair view? → **No** →

↓ **Yes**

Is there a significant level of concern about the company's ability to continue as a going concern?

→ **Yes** → Do the financial statements, including note disclosures about the matters giving rise to the concern, give a true and fair view?

← **Yes** ← Is disclosure of the departure adequate? → **No** →

Is departure needed... ↓ **Yes**

Do the financial statements... ↓ **Yes** → Unqualified opinion with explanatory paragraph

Do the financial statements... → **No** ↓

↓ **No**

Do the financial statements give a true and fair view?

→ **No** → Is the effect of the disagreement so material or pervasive that the financial statements as a whole are misleading?

← Is disclosure of the departure adequate ... **No** →

↓ **Yes**

If the period to which the directors have paid particular attention in assessing going concern is less than one year from the date of approval of the financial statements, is that fact disclosed in the financial statements or accompanying information?

Is the effect of the disagreement... → **No** ↓ → Qualified opinion- Except for disagreement

Is the effect of the disagreement... → **Yes** ↓ → Qualified opinion- Adverse opinion

↓ **Yes** → Unqualified opinion

↓ **No** → Unqualified opinion, with disclosure of the fact within the section of the auditors' report setting out the basis of their opinion, unless the fact is clear from any other references in their report.

2 SUBSEQUENT EVENTS

2.1 Before describing the steps taken by the auditors to obtain reasonable assurance in respect of subsequent events (also called post balance sheet events - the terms are interchangeable) we need to revise the accounting requirements of the relevant accounting standard SSAP 17 *Accounting for post balance sheet events.*

SSAP 17

> **KEY TERMS**
>
> **Post balance sheet events** are those events, both favourable and unfavourable, which occur between the balance sheet date and the date on which the financial statements are approved by the board of directors.
>
> **Adjusting events** are post balance sheet events which provide additional evidence of conditions existing at the balance sheet date. They include events which because of statutory conventional requirements are reflected in financial statements.
>
> **Non-adjusting events** are post balance sheet events which concern conditions which did not exist at the balance sheet date.

2.2 Standard practice in respect of the disclosure of post balance sheet events is as follows.

> 'Financial statements should be prepared on the basis of conditions existing at the balance sheet date.
>
> A material post balance sheet event requires changes in the amounts to be included in financial statements where:
>
> (a) It is an adjusting event; or
>
> (b) It indicates that application of the going concern concept to the whole or a material part of the company is not appropriate.
>
> A material post balance sheet event should be disclosed where:
>
> (a) It is a non-adjusting event of such materiality that its non-disclosure would affect the ability of the users of financial statements to reach a proper understanding of the financial position; or
>
> (b) It is the reversal or maturity after the year end of a transaction entered into before the year end, the substance of which was primarily to alter the appearance of the company's balance sheet.'

2.3 In respect of each disclosable post balance sheet event, the notes to the financial statements should state:

- The **nature** of the event

- An **estimate** of the financial effect, or a statement that it is not practicable to make such an estimate

> **Exam focus point**
>
> Knowledge of the relevant accounting requirements is particularly important when dealing with post balance sheet events.

SAS 150 *Subsequent events*

KEY TERMS

Subsequent events are those relevant events (favourable or unfavourable) which occur and those facts which are discovered between the period end and the laying of the financial statements before the members or equivalent.

Relevant events are those which:

- Provide additional evidence relating to conditions existing at the balance sheet date, or

- Concern conditions which did not exist at the balance sheet date, but which may be of such materiality that their disclosure is required to ensure the financial statements are not misleading.

SAS 150.1

Auditors should consider the effect of subsequent events on the financial statements and on their report.

SAS 150.2

Auditors should perform procedures designed to obtain sufficient appropriate audit evidence that all material subsequent events up to the date of their report which require adjustment of, or disclosure in, the financial statements have been identified and properly reflected therein.

Procedures

PROCEDURES TESTING SUBSEQUENT EVENTS	
Enquiries of management	Status of items involving **subjective judgement/** accounted for using preliminary data
	New **commitments**, borrowings or guarantees
	Sales or destruction of **assets**
	Issues of **shares/debentures** or changes in business structure
	Developments involving **risk areas, provisions** and **contingencies**
	Unusual accounting adjustments
	Major events (eg going concern problems) affecting appropriateness of accounting policies for estimates
Other procedures	**Consider procedures** of management for identifying subsequent events
	Read minutes of general board/committee meetings
	Review latest accounting records and finaisial information

2.4 These procedures should be performed as near as possible to the date of the auditors' report. Reviews and updates of these procedures may be required, depending on the length of the time between the procedures and the signing of the auditors' report and the susceptibility of the items to change over time.

Subsequent events discovered after the date of the auditors' report but before the financial statements are issued

2.5 The financial statements are the directors' responsibility. The directors should therefore inform the auditors of any material subsequent events between the date of the auditors' report and the date the financial statements are issued. The auditors do **not** have any obligation to perform procedures, or make enquires regarding the financial statements **after** the date of their report.

> **SAS 150.3**
>
> When, after the date of their report but before the financial statements are issued, auditors become aware of subsequent events which may materially affect the financial statements, they should establish whether the financial statements need amendment, should discuss the matter with the directors and should consider the implications for their report, taking additional action as appropriate.

2.6 When the financial statements are amended, the auditors should extend the subsequent events procedures discussed above to the date of their new report, carry out any other appropriate procedures and issue a new audit report dated the day it is signed.

2.7 The situation where the statements are not amended but the auditors feel that they should be is discussed below.

Subsequent events discovered after the financial statements have been issued but before their laying before the members, or equivalent

2.8 Auditors have no obligations to perform procedures or make enquiries regarding the financial statements **after** they have been issued.

> **SAS 150.4**
>
> When, after the financial statements have been issued, but before they have been laid before the members or equivalent, auditors become aware of subsequent events which, had they occurred and been known of at the date of their report, might have caused them to issue a different report, they should consider whether the financial statements need amendment, should discuss the matter with the directors, and should consider the implications for their report, taking additional action as appropriate.

2.9 The SAS gives the appropriate procedures which the auditors should undertake when the directors revise the financial statements.

- **Carry out the audit procedures** necessary in the circumstances
- **Consider,** where appropriate, whether Stock Exchange or financial services regulations require the **revision to be publicised** or a regulator informed

- **Review the steps taken by the directors** to ensure that anyone in receipt of the previously issued financial statements together with the auditors' report thereon is informed of the situation

- **Issue a new report** on the revised financial statements

2.10 When the auditors issue a **new report** they:

- **Refer in their report to the note to the financial statements** which more extensively discusses the reason for the revision of the accounts

- **Refer to the earlier report** issued by them on the financial statements

- **Date** their new report **not earlier** than the date the revised financial statements are approved

- **Have regard** to the **guidance** relating to reports on revised annual financial statements and directors' reports as set out in APB's Practice Note 8 *Reports by auditors under company legislation in the United Kingdom*

2.11 Where the directors do **not** revise the financial statements but the auditors feel they should be revised, and where the statements have been issued but not yet laid before the members; or if the directors do not intend to make an appropriate statement at the AGM, then the auditors should consider steps to take, on a timely basis, to prevent reliance on their report for example, a statement at the AGM. The auditors have **no** right to communicate to the members directly in writing.

3 MANAGEMENT REPRESENTATIONS

3.1 The auditors receive many representations during the audit and some may be critical to obtaining sufficient appropriate audit evidence. Representations may also be required for general matters, for example, full availability of accounting records.

3.2 Written confirmation of oral representations avoids confusion and disagreement. The written confirmation may take the form of:

- A **representation letter** from **management** (see example below)

- A **letter from the auditors** outlining their understanding of management's representations, duly acknowledged and confirmed in writing by management

- **Minutes of meetings of the board** or directors, or similar body, at which such representations are approved

SAS 440 *Management representations* covers this area.

SAS 440.1

Auditors should obtain written confirmation of appropriate representations from management before their report is issued.

BPP PUBLISHING

Acknowledgement by directors of their responsibility for the financial statements

> ### SAS 440.2
>
> The auditors should obtain evidence that the directors acknowledge their collective responsibility for the preparation of the financial statements and have approved the financial statements.

3.3 Auditors normally do this when they receive a signed copy of the financial statements which incorporate a relevant statement of the directors' responsibilities.

Representations by management as audit evidence

3.4 In addition to representations relating to responsibility for the financial statements, the auditors may wish to rely on management representations as audit evidence.

> ### SAS 440.3
>
> Auditors should obtain written confirmation of representations from management on matters material to the financial statements when those representations are critical to obtaining sufficient appropriate audit evidence.

3.5 Such matters should be discussed with those responsible for giving the written confirmation, to ensure that they understand what they are confirming. Written confirmations are normally required of appropriately senior management.

3.6 Only matters which are material to the financial statements should be included in a letter of representation.

3.7 When the auditors receive such representations they should:

    (a) Seek **corroborative audit evidence**

    (b) Evaluate whether the representations made by management appear **reasonable and are consistent** with other audit evidence obtained, including other representations

    (c) Consider whether the individuals making the representations can be expected to be **well-informed** on the particular matters

3.8 The SAS then makes a very important point.

> 'Representations by management cannot be a substitute for other audit evidence that auditors expect to be available. If auditors are unable to obtain sufficient appropriate audit evidence regarding a matter which has, or may have, a material effect on the financial statements and such audit evidence is expected to be available, this constitutes a limitation in the scope of the audit, even if a representation from management has been received on the matter. In these circumstances it may be necessary for them to consider the implications for their report.'

3.9 There are two instances given in the SAS where management representations **may** be the only audit evidence available.

    • **Knowledge of the facts is confined to management,** for example, the facts are a matter of management intention.

    • **The matter is principally one of judgement or opinion,** for example, the trading position of a particular customer.

3.10 There may be occasions when the representations received do not agree with other audit evidence obtained.

> **SAS 440.4**
>
> If a representation appears to be contradicted by other audit evidence, the auditors should investigate the circumstances to resolve the matter and consider whether it casts doubt on the reliability of other representations.

Basic elements of a management representation letter

3.11 A management representation letter should:

- Be **addressed** to the **auditors**
- **Contain specified information**
- Be **appropriately dated**
- Be **approved by those with specific knowledge** of the relevant matters

3.12 The auditors will normally request that the letter is:

- Discussed and agreed by the board of directors (or equivalent)

- Signed on its behalf by the chairman and secretary before the auditors approve the financial statements.

3.13 The letter will usually be **dated on** the day the financial statements are **approved**, but if there is any significant delay between the representation letter and the date of the auditors' report, then the auditors should consider the need to obtain further representations.

Action if management refuses to provide written confirmation of representations

> **SAS 440.5**
>
> If management refuses to provide written confirmation of a representation that the auditors consider necessary, the auditors should consider the implications of this scope limitation for their report.

3.14 In these circumstances, the auditors should consider whether it is appropriate to rely on other representations made by management during the audit.

Example of a management representation letter

3.15 An **example** of a management representation letter is provided in an appendix to the SAS. It is **not** a standard letter, and representations do not have to be confirmed in letter form.

> (Company letterhead)
>
> (To the auditors)   (Date)
>
> We confirm to the best of our knowledge and belief, and having made appropriate enquiries of other directors and officials of the company, the following representations given to you in connection with your audit of the financial statements for the period ended 31 December 20...
>
> (1)   We acknowledge as directors our responsibilities under the Companies Act 1985 for preparing financial statements which give a true and fair view and for making accurate representations to you. All the accounting records have been made available to you for the purpose of your audit and all the transactions undertaken by the company have been properly reflected and recorded in the accounting records. All other records and related information, including minutes of all management and shareholders' meetings, have been made available to you.
>
> (2)   The legal claim by ABC Limited has been settled out of court by a payment of £258,000. No further amounts are expected to be paid, and no similar claims have been received.
>
> (3)   In connection with deferred tax not provided, the following assumptions reflect the intentions and expectations of the company:
>
>   (a)   capital investment of £450,000 is planned over the next three years;
>
>   (b)   there are no plans to sell revalued properties; and
>
>   (c)   we are not aware of any indications that the situation is likely to change so as to necessitate the inclusion of a provision for tax payable in the financial statements.
>
> (4)   The company has not had, or entered into, at any time during the period any arrangement, transaction or agreement to provide credit facilities (including loans, quasi-loans or credit transactions) for directors or to guarantee or provide security for such matters.
>
> (5)   There have been no events since the balance sheet date which necessitate revision of the figures included in the financial statements or inclusion of a note thereto.
>
> As minuted by the board of directors at its meeting on .... (date)
>
> ....
>
> Chairman   Secretary

3.16   The following notes are provided by the SAS on the example.

- Other signatories may include those with specific knowledge of the relevant matters, for example the chief financial officer.

- Examples of other issues which may be the subject of representations from management include:

- The extent of the purchase of goods on terms which include reservation of title by suppliers

- The absence of knowledge of circumstances which could result in losses on long-term contracts

- The reasons for concluding that an overdue debt from a related party is fully recoverable

- Confirmation of the extent of guarantees, warranties or other financial commitments relating to subsidiary undertakings or related parties

Exam focus point

The most important points to remember about a letter of representation are:

- The circumstances in which it can be used
- The auditors' response if the client fails to agree to it

You should also be able to draft appropriate representations if asked.

Question 1

Management representations are an important source of audit evidence. These representations may be oral or written, and may be obtained either on an informal or formal basis. The auditors will include information obtained in this manner in their audit working papers where it forms part of their total audit evidence.

Required

(a) Explain the nature and role of the letter of representation.

(b) Explain why it is important for the auditors to discuss the contents of the letter of representation at an early stage of the audit.

(c) Explain why standard letters of representation are becoming less frequently used by the auditing profession.

Answer

(a) The letter of representation is a letter normally signed by appropriate directors normally on behalf of the whole board. Such a letter contains representations relating to matters which are material to the financial statements but concerning which knowledge of the facts is confined to management, or where the directors have used judgement or opinion in the preparation of the financial statements.

The precise scope and content of the letter of representation should be appropriate to the particular audit. An example of a typical situation in which representations may be required would be a case in which an employee's legal claim is settled out of court and the directors are asked to set out in writing their view that no further similar claims are expected to be paid. An absence of independent corroborative evidence and the fact that judgement on the part of directors is involved indicates the need for written evidence of the judgement in the letter of representation.

Representations are not a substitute for other necessary audit work, and they do not relieve the auditors of any of their responsibilities. Even where written representations are obtained, the auditors need to decide whether in the circumstances these representations, together with other audit evidence obtained, are sufficient to justify an unqualified opinion on the financial statements.

However, written representations by the directors do form part of the total audit evidence, and form part of the auditors' working papers. Their status as evidence is given weight by the fact that s 389 of the Companies Act 1985 makes it a criminal offence for directors knowingly or recklessly to make false statements to the auditors in the course of their duty.

One function which the letter of representation may also serve, although it is subsidiary to its central purposes, is that such a letter may act as a reminder to the directors of their responsibilities. For example, the letter will remind them of their responsibilities with regard to the truth and fairness of the accounts, and of their responsibility for statements made orally to the auditors but only recorded in writing in the letter of representation.

(b) The letter of representation should not be seen as an afterthought in the audit process, even though the letter should be finally approved and signed on a date as close as possible to the date of the audit report and after all other audit work has been completed.

Discussion of the contents of the letter early in the audit is an important part of the audit planning process. It makes the auditors aware at an early stage of the areas in which representations may be required. It also acts as prior warning to management of errors. This may usefully give management a chance to think carefully about the nature of any representations which are likely to be required in writing, and may encourage directors to become more fully aware of their responsibilities in relation to such written confirmations.

If discussion of the contents of the representation letter are left until the last stages of the audit, senior management may justifiably object that, the matters covered by the letter ought to have been raised earlier by the auditors. Management might object that if this had been done there would have been an opportunity to assemble appropriate corroborative evidence and thus avoid the need for written representations by the directors. Such objections may be made especially where audit deadlines are tight, which is often the case for companies which are part of a group.

BPP PUBLISHING

Lengthy discussions of judgemental matters on which representations are being sought may, if left until the end of the audit process, detract from a good working relationship between the auditors and client management, and in extreme cases management may become reluctant to comply with the auditors' requests.

(c) Some audit firms make use of a standard form of letter of representation. The principal merit of using a standard letter is that, by using a standard for all audit work in the firm, the firm has more assurance that staff on each audit will have considered all of the typical kinds of matter on which written representations are normally sought from clients. Audit staff may benefit from using such a standard letter as a checklist of possible matters to include in a draft letter to discuss with management. However, in all cases there will be a need to 'tailor' the standard letter to suit the needs of the particular audit engagement. This may involve adapting paragraphs of a standard letter, or adding new paragraphs to cover matters special to the assignment.

Instead of using a full standardised letter, some firms make use of 'specimen paragraphs' to be included in draft letters of representation. Such specimen paragraphs offer the advantage of suggesting appropriate wording dealing with common matters on which representations are required. Given the judgmental nature of many such matters, careful wording is important.

As with all standardised audit documentation, there remains the danger that standardisation may encourage a 'mechanical' approach to audit work and this probably explains why many firms are becoming reluctant to use standard forms of letter. Where audit staff fail to use their initiative and imagination, the standard letter may be followed too closely, and important matters may be missed. However, it could be argued that the problem in such cases lies more with a lack of adequate training of audit staff than with the fact that standardised documentation is available.

In presenting a letter of representation to the directors, it is important that the letter is not treated as merely a standard formality. Even if the letter for a particular assignment contains only similar material to that included generally in such letters, and is little different from last year's letter for the same client, each point should be discussed with management in order to encourage the signatories to consider its contents fully.

4 UNAUDITED PUBLISHED INFORMATION

4.1 The APB's SAS 160 *Other information in documents containing audited financial statements* provides guidance for auditors in this area.

4.2 The SAS uses the term 'other information' by which it means financial and non-financial information **other than** the audited financial statements and the auditors' report, which an entity may include in its annual report, either by custom or statute. Examples are:

- A directors' report (required by statute)
- A chairman's statement
- An operating and financial review
- Financial summaries

4.3 Auditors have no responsibility to report that other information is properly stated because an audit is only an expression of opinion on the truth and fairness of the financial statements.

4.4 However, they may be engaged separately, or required by statute, to report on elements of other information, for example, review the directors' statement of compliance with the Cadbury Code. This would be an example of a non-statutory review.

4.5 The SAS then moves on to the auditors' general responsibilities towards 'other information'.

SAS 160.1

Auditors should read the other information. If as a result they become aware of any apparent misstatements therein, or identify any material inconsistencies with the audited financial statements, they should seek to resolve them.

Auditors' consideration of other information

SAS 160.2

If auditors identify an inconsistency between the financial statements and the other information, or a misstatement within the other information, they should consider whether an amendment is required to the financial statements or to the other information and should seek to resolve the matter through discussion with the directors.

4.6 A **misstatement** within other information exists when it is stated incorrectly or presented in a misleading manner.

4.7 An **inconsistency** exists when the other information contradicts, or appears to contradict information contained in the financial statements. This could lead to doubts about audit evidence or even the auditors' opinion.

Unresolved misstatements and inconsistencies

SAS 160.3

If, after discussion with the directors, the auditors conclude

(a) that the financial statements require amendment and no such amendment is made, they should consider the implications for their report;

(b) that the other information requires amendment and no such amendment is made, they should consider appropriate actions including the implications for their report.

4.8 The auditors have a statutory duty to consider a company's directors' report. S 235 Companies Act 1985 states that:

'the auditors shall consider whether the information given in the directors' report for the financial year for which the accounts are prepared is consistent with those accounts; and if they are of opinion that it is not they shall state that fact in their report.'

4.9 Matters which may require resolution or reference in an explanatory paragraph within the auditors' report include:

(a) An **inconsistency between amounts or narrative** appearing in the financial statements and the directors' report

(b) An **inconsistency between the bases of preparation** of related items appearing in the financial statements and the directors' report, where the figures themselves are not directly comparable and the different bases are not disclosed

(c) An **inconsistency between figures** contained in the financial statements **and a narrative interpretation** of the effect of those figures in the directors' report

4.10 Other information may contain misstatements or inconsistencies with the financial statements and the auditors may be unable to resolve them by discussion with the directors. They may need to use an **explanatory paragraph** within the auditors' report to describe the apparent misstatement or material misconsistency.

BPP
PUBLISHING

Timing considerations

4.11 SAS 600 *Auditors' reports on financial statements* (see Chapter 19) requires all other information to be approved by the entity, and the auditors to consider all necessary evidence, before the audit opinion is expressed.

Question 2

You are auditing the financial statements of Hope Engineering Ltd for the year ending 31 March 20X8. The partner in charge of the audit instructs you to carry out a review of the company's activities since the financial year end. Mr Smith, the managing director of Hope Engineering Ltd, overhears the conversation with the partner and is surprised that you are examining accounting information which relates to the next accounting period.

Mr Smith had been appointed on 1 March 20X8 as a result of which the contract of the previous managing director, Mr Jones, was terminated. Compensation of £500,000 had been paid to Mr Jones on 2 March 20X8.

As a result of your investigations you find that the company is going to bring an action against Mr Jones for the recovery of the compensation paid to him, as it had come to light that two months prior to his dismissal, he had contractually agreed to join the board of directors of a rival company. The company's solicitor had informed Hope Engineering Ltd that Mr Jones' actions constituted a breach of his contract with them, and that an action could be brought against the former managing director for the recovery of the moneys paid to him.

Required

(a) Explain the nature and purpose of a review of the period after the balance sheet date.

(b) List the audit procedures which would be carried out in order to identify any material subsequent events.

(c) Discuss the audit implications of the company's decision to sue Mr Jones for the recovery of the compensation paid to him.

Answer

(a) The auditors' active responsibility extends to the date on which they sign their audit report. As this date is inevitably after the year end, it follows that in order to discharge their responsibilities, the auditors must extend their audit work to cover the post balance sheet period.

The objective of the audit of the post balance sheet period is to ascertain whether the directors have dealt correctly with any events, both favourable and unfavourable, which occurred after the year end and which need to be reflected in the financial statements, if those statements are to show a true and fair view and comply with the Companies Act.

The general rule is that, in the preparation of year end financial statements, no account should be taken of subsequent events unless to do so is required by statute or to give effect to retrospective legislation, or to take account of an adjusting event. In accordance with SSAP 17, a material subsequent event may be an *adjusting event* where it provides information about a condition existing at the balance sheet date, for example realisable values of stock, or indicates that the going concern concept is no longer applicable. Additionally, *non-adjusting events* may have such a material effect on the company's financial condition, for example a merger, that disclosure is essential to give a true and fair view.

(b) The audit procedures which should be carried out in order to identify any material subsequent events consist of discussions with management, and may also include consideration of the following.

(i) Procedures should be implemented by management to ensure that all events after the balance sheet date have been identified, considered and properly evaluated as to their effect on the financial statements.

(ii) Relevant accounting records should be reviewed, specifically to identify subsequent cash received from debtors, to check items uncleared at the year end on the bank reconciliation, to check NRV of stocks from sales invoices, and so on. However, window dressing also may be identified.

(iii) Budgets, profit forecasts, cash flow projections and management accounts for the new period should be reviewed to assess the company's trading position.

(iv) Known 'risk' areas and contingencies, whether inherent in the nature of the business or revealed by previous audit experience, or by solicitors' letters, should be considered.

(v)   Minutes of shareholders', directors' and management meetings and correspondence and memoranda relating to items included in the minutes should be reviewed.

(vi) Relevant information which has come to the auditors' attention from sources outside the enterprise, including public knowledge of competitors, suppliers and customers, should be taken into account.

The subsequent events review should be carried out to a date as near as practicable to that of the audit report by making enquiries of management and considering the need to carry out further tests. It should be fully documented and, where appropriate, a letter of representation should be obtained from management.

(c)   The compensation paid to Mr Smith would be disclosed as part of directors' emoluments for the year ended 31 March 20X8. However, the question then arises as to whether or not the financial statements need to take any account of the possible recovery of the compensation payment.

The auditors should first ascertain from the board minutes that the directors intend to proceed with the lawsuit and should then attempt to assess the outcome by consulting the directors, the company's legal advisors and perhaps by taking Counsel's opinion. Only if it seems probable that the compensation will be recovered should a contingent asset be disclosed in the notes to the accounts, along with a summary of the facts of the case. A prudent estimate of legal costs should be deducted.

It could be argued that Mr Smith's breach of contract existed at the balance sheet date and that the compensation should therefore be treated as a current asset, net of recovery costs. However, this would not be prudent, given the uncertainties over the court case.

5   OVERALL REVIEW OF FINANCIAL STATEMENTS

5.1   Once the bulk of the substantive procedures have been carried out, the auditors will have a draft set of financial statements which should be supported by appropriate and sufficient audit evidence.

5.2   SAS 470 *Overall review of financial statements* covers the beginning of the end of the audit process.

SAS 470.1

Auditors should carry out such a review of the financial statements as is sufficient, in conjunction with the conclusions drawn from the other audit evidence obtained, to give them a reasonable basis for their opinion on the financial statements.

5.3   This review requires appropriate skill and experience on the part of the auditors.

Compliance with accounting regulations

SAS 470.2

Auditors should consider whether the information presented in the financial statements is in accordance with statutory requirements and that the accounting policies employed are in accordance with accounting standards, properly disclosed, consistently applied and appropriate to the entity.

5.4   The SAS goes on to list the factors which the auditors should consider when examining the **accounting policies.**

- Policies **commonly adopted** in **particular industries**

BPP PUBLISHING

- Policies for which there is substantial **authoritative support**

- Whether any **departures from applicable accounting standards are necessary** for the financial statements to give a true and fair view

- Whether the **financial statements reflect** the **substance** of the underlying transactions and not merely their form

5.5 The SAS suggests that, when compliance with statutory requirements and accounting standards is considered, the auditors may find it useful to use a **checklist**.

Review for consistency and reasonableness

> **SAS 470.3**
>
> Auditors should consider whether the financial statements as a whole and the assertions contained therein are consistent with their knowledge of the entity's business and with the results of other audit procedures, and the manner of disclosure is fair.

5.6 The SAS lists the principal considerations:

(a) Whether the financial statements adequately reflect the **information** and **explanations** previously obtained and conclusions previously reached during the course of the audit

(b) Whether it reveals any **new factors** which may affect the presentation of, or disclosure in, the financial statements

(c) Whether **analytical procedures** applied when completing the audit, such as comparing the information in the financial statements with other pertinent data, **produce results** which assist in arriving at the overall conclusion as to whether the financial statements as a whole are consistent with their knowledge of the entity's business (see Section 3)

(d) Whether the **presentation** adopted in the financial statements may have been **unduly influenced by the directors' desire** to present matters in a favourable or unfavourable light

(e) The potential impact on the financial statements of the **aggregate of uncorrected misstatements** (including those arising from bias in making accounting estimates) identified during the course of the audit and the preceding period's audit, if any

6 PROBLEMS OF ACCOUNTING TREATMENT

6.1 As noted in the previous section, SAS 470 requires that auditors review the financial statements. One of the things that they are required to assess is whether the **accounting policies are consistently applied.**

FRS 18

6.2 You should be aware of the details of FRS 18 from your 2.5 paper, but we shall revise the pertinent details here.

> **FRS 18 revision**
>
> FRS 18 prescribes the regular consideration of the entity's accounting policies. The **best** accounting policies should be adopted at all times.
>
> This is a move away from the position of SSAP 2 which was that **consistency** was a fundamental accounting concept.
>
> FRS 18 also required that the entity considers how a change in accounting policy will affect the **comparability** of the financial statements and strike a **balance** between selecting the most appropriate policies and presenting coherent an useful policies.

6.3 In light of FRS 18, therefore, the auditor will have to consider the reasonableness of all accounting polices, and when accounting policies have been changed whether

- The new policy is the best policy for the purposes of providing a true and fair view, and

- The financial statements provide a true and fair view as a whole, given the change in policy.

Alternative treatments

6.4 From your accounting studies, you should also be aware that there are some accounting standards which allow a choice of treatments.

6.5 As always, when reviewing the accounting treatment used, the auditors should consider whether they provide a true and fair view. Given that the options in treatment could be:

- Capitalise, or
- Write off

The difference between the two choices of treatment is likely to be **material** to the financial statements.

7 ANALYTICAL PROCEDURES

7.1 In Chapter 12 we discussed how analytical review procedures are used as part of the overall review procedures at the end of an audit.

7.2 Remember the areas that the analytical review at the final stage must cover:

- Important accounting ratios
- Related items
- Changes in products; customers
- Price and mix changes
- Wages changes
- Variances
- Trends in production and sales
- Changes in material and labour content of production
- Other profit and loss account expenditure
- Variations caused by industry or economy factors

7.3 As at other stages, significant fluctuations and unexpected relationships must be investigated and documented.

8 COMPLETION OF THE AUDIT

Summarising errors

> **SAS 220.3**
>
> In evaluating whether the financial statements give a true and fair view, auditors should assess the materiality of the aggregate of uncorrected misstatements.

8.1 The aggregate of uncorrected misstatements comprises:

(a) **Specific misstatements** identified by the auditors, including uncorrected misstatements identified during the audit of the previous period if they affect the current period's financial statements

(b) Their **best estimate** of **other misstatements** which cannot be quantified specifically

8.2 If the auditors consider that the aggregate of misstatements may be material, they must consider reducing audit risk by extending audit procedures or requesting the directors to adjust the financial statements (which the directors may wish to do anyway).

8.3 The auditors should consider the implications for their audit report if:

- The directors refuse to adjust.

- The extended audit procedures do not enable the auditors to conclude that the aggregate of uncorrected misstatements is not material.

8.4 The summary of errors will not only list errors from the current year, but also those in the previous year(s). This will allow errors to be highlighted which are reversals of errors in the previous year, such as in the valuation of closing/opening stock. Cumulative errors may also be shown, which have increased from year to year.

SCHEDULE OF UNADJUSTED ERRORS

		20X2				20X1			
		P & L account		Balance sheet		P & L account		Balance sheet	
		Dr	Cr	Dr	Cr	Dr	Cr	Dr	Cr
		£	£	£	£	£	£	£	£
(a)	ABC Ltd debt unprovided	10,470			10,470	4,523			4,523
(b)	Opening/ closing stock under-valued*	21,540			21,540		21,540	21,540	
(c)	Closing stock undervalued		34,105	34,105					
(d)	Opening unaccrued expense:								
	Telephone*		453	453		453			453
	Electricity*		905	905		905			905
(e)	Closing unaccrued expenses								
	Telephone	427			427				
	Electricity	1,128			1,128				
(f)	Obsolete stock write off	2,528			2,528	3,211			3,211
Total		36,093	35,463	35,463	36,093	9,092	21,540	21,540	9,092
	*Cancelling items	21,540			21,540				
			453	453					
			905	905					
		14,553	34,105	34,105	14,553				

8.5 The schedule will be used by the audit manager and partner to decide whether the client should be requested to make adjustments to the financial statements to correct the errors.

Completion checklists

8.6 Audit firms frequently use checklists which must be signed off to ensure that all final procedures have been carried out, all material amounts are supported by sufficient appropriate evidence, etc. An example is shown below.

	Yes	No	N/A	Reference to points for partner schedule
15 Have all the working papers been cross-referenced?				
16 Do the working papers show comparative figures where appropriate?				
17 Have audit conclusions been drawn for each balance sheet audit area as appropriate?				
18 Has the balance sheet audit programme been completed, initialled and cross-referenced to the working papers?				
19 Have the necessary profit and loss account schedules been prepared and do they agree with the detailed accounts?				
20 Current assets:				
(a) Were debtors circularised and were the results satisfactory?				
(b) Was the client's stocktaking attended and were the results satisfactory?				
(c) Is the basis of stock and work in progress valuation satisfactory and correctly disclosed in the accounts?				
21 Liabilities:				
(a) Were creditors circularised and were the results satisfactory?				
(b) Have all liabilities, contingent liabilities, and capital commitments been fully accounted for or noted in the accounts?				
Audit completion				
22 Have formal representations been obtained or has a draft letter been set up (including representations in respect of each director regarding transactions involving himself and his connected persons required to be disclosed by the Companies Act 1985)?				
23 Have all audit queries been satisfactorily answered?				
24 Post balance sheet event review:				
(a) Has a comprehensive review been performed and evidenced?				
(b) Has the review been carried out at the most recent date possible with regard to the anticipated date of the audit report?				
25 Have all audit queries been satisfactorily answered?				
26 Have all closing adjustments been agreed with the client?				
27 Are you satisfied that all material instances where we have not received the information and explanations we require have been referred to in the points for partner schedule?				

Audit completion checklist

Client:
Period ended:
Instructions:
1 All questions must be answered by ticking one of the columns as appropriate.
2 Any 'No' answer must be referenced to the 'points for partner' schedule.

Section I - To be completed by the manager

	Yes	No	N/A	Reference to points for partner schedule
Permanent audit file				
1 Have the following been updated in the course of the audit:				
(a) Flowcharts and related documentation for:				
(i) computer systems?				
(ii) non-computer systems?				
(b) Internal /key control evaluation questionnaire conclusions?				
(c) Details of the client organisation?				
(d) Financial history?				
2 Is a current letter of engagement in force?				
Transaction (interim) audit file				
3 Were walk-through tests performed to confirm our record of the accounting systems?				
4 Was the audit programme tailored?				
5 Was adequate audit attention given to internal control weaknesses?				
6 Were levels of audit testing (compliance and substantive) appropriate?				
7 Have audit programmes been signed off as complete?				
8 Are there adequate explanations of work done and are conclusions drawn?				
9 Is there evidence of the review of work?				
10 Have weaknesses arising on the interim audit been reported to management in a formal letter?				
11 Has the client replied to the weaknesses already notified in respect of matters arising from the previous year's audit?				
12 Have major internal control weaknesses previously notified been rectified?				
Final (balance sheet) audit file				
13 Have lead schedules been prepared for each audit area and cross-referenced and agreed with the financial statements?				
14 Have all the working papers been initialled and dated by the members of staff who prepared them?				

	Yes	No	N/A	Reference to points for partner schedule
28 **Review of working papers?**				
(a) Have you reviewed all the working papers? (If not, briefly describe review procedure adopted)				
(b) Have arrangements been made for the financial statements to be reviews by:				
(i) a second partner (a brief review or special review)? and/or				
(ii) the audit review panel?				
(c) Has the planning memorandum and, where applicable, client risk evaluation questionnaire been completed?				
Subsidiary and associated companies				
29 Where secondary auditors have been involved in the audit of subsidiary and associated companies, have we:				
(a) Sent our group accounts audit questionnaire?				
(b) Received satisfactory answers? or				
(c) Reviewed and approved the working papers of secondary auditors?				
30 Have all accounts of subsidiary and associated companies been approved by the directors and audited?				
31 If any of the audit reports have been qualified has the fact and nature of the qualification been referred to in the points for partner schedule?				
Financial statements and directors' report				
32 Is the financial statements layout in accordance with the firm's standard accounts pack?				
33 Has the analytical review memorandum been properly completed and are the review conclusions consistent with the conclusions drawn in respect of our other audit work?				
34 Is the reliance placed on analytical review reasonable in the circumstances?				
35 Is any proposed dividend covered by the distributable profits as disclosed in the financial statements?				
36 Has the firm's accounting disclosure checklist been completed to ensure that the financial statements and directors' report comply with:				
(a) the Companies Act 1985?				
(b) Statements of Standard Accounting Practice and Financial Reporting Standards?				
(c) Stock Exchange requirements?				
(d) Other reporting requirements?				

	Yes	No	N/A	Reference to points for partner schedule
37 Has the directors' report been reviewed for consistency with the financial statements?				
38 Has other financial information to be issued with the audited financial statements (eg contained in the Chairman's Statement or Employee Accounts) been reviewed for consistency with the financial statements?				

....
Audit Manager   Date

Section II - To be completed by the reporting partner

	Yes	No	N/A	Comments
1 Has Section I of the checklist been satisfactorily completed?				
2 Have all the points on the 'points for partner' schedule been satisfactorily resolved or are there any material matters outstanding which should be referred to the audit panel?				
3 Has your review of the current and permanent file indicated that the working paper evidence is sufficient to enable you to form an opinion on the financial statements, having regard to the firm's audit manual procedures?				
4 Are the conclusions you have drawn from your overall review of the financial statements based on your knowledge of the client, consideration of the analytical review memorandum, review of post balance sheet events and where appropriate, client risk evaluation questionnaire, consistent with those contained in the detailed working papers?				
5 Have all improvements which you consider could be made in the conduct of future audits been noted on 'points forward' (for consideration at the audit debriefing)?				
6 (a) Are there any specialist areas in which the client could benefit from our expertise, for example tax planning?				
(b) Has the provision of such services been drawn to his attention?				

I confirm that the report of the auditors will be unqualified*/unqualified with an explanatory paragraph*/ qualified* as set out in the attached draft financial statements.

....
Reporting Partner   Date

*Delete as appropriate

Chapter roundup

- Evaluation of going concern is most important. Auditors should consider the **future plans** of directors and any signs of **going concern problems** which may be noted throughout the audit. **Bank facilities** may have to be confirmed.

- When reporting on the accounts, auditors should consider whether the going concern basis is **appropriate,** and whether **disclosure** of going concern problems is **sufficient.**

- Auditors should consider the effect of **subsequent events** (after the balance sheet date) on the accounts.

- Auditors have a responsibility to **review subsequent events** before they sign their audit report, and may have to take action if they become aware of subsequent events between the date they sign their audit report and the date the financial statements are laid before members.

- **Representations from management** should generally be restricted to matters that cannot be verified by other audit procedures.

- Any representations should be **compared** with other evidence and their **sufficiency** assessed.

- **Unaudited published information** includes the **directors' report,** and other statements such as the **chairman's statement** and an **operating and financial review.** Auditors have a statutory responsibility to report inconsistencies between the directors' report and accounts.

- The auditors must perform and document an **overall review** of the financial statements before they can reach an opinion, covering:

  ° Compliance with statute and accounting standards
  ° Consistency with audit evidence
  ° Overall reasonableness

- **Analytical procedures** should be used at the final stage of audit. The review should cover:

  ° Key business ratios
  ° Related items in accounts
  ° The effect of known changes on the accounts

- As part of their completion procedures, auditors should consider whether the **aggregate of uncorrected misstatements** is material.

Quick quiz

1 Complete the definition, using the words given below.

The .... concept: the enterprise will .... in operational .... for the ....

| future, existence, going, continue, foreseeable, concern |

2 Name two instances where the going concern basis is not appropriate.

1 ....

2 ....

3   Complete the table putting the indicators of an entity's inability to continue as a going concern under the correct headings.

Financial	Operational	Other

(a) Litigation
(b) Inability to pay due debts

(c) Fundamental changes to market
(d) Loss of key customers

(e) Denial of trade credit by suppliers
(f) Loss of key management

4   The directors must satisfy themselves that the going concern basis in the financial statements is appropriate.

True   ☐

False   ☐

5   Complete the definition, using the words given in the box below.

.... are those which provide .... evidence relating to the conditions .... and the balance sheet date, or concern .... which .... at the balance sheet, but which may be of such .... that their .... is required to ensure the financial statements are not misleading.

events, existing, relevant, not, conditions, exist, additional, did, disclosure, materiality

6   Name three enquires that should be made of management to test subsequent events.

1   ....

2   ....

3   ....

7   When should auditors issues a new report?

8   Name two instances given in SAS 440 of when management representation may be the only audit evidence available.

1   ....

2   ....

9   Give five examples of what areas analytical review at the final stage should cover.

1   ....

2   ....

3   ....

4   ....

5   ....

10   In which three instances might unaudited published information be referred to in the audit report?

1   ....

2   ....

3   ....

BPP PUBLISHING

Answers to quick quiz

1 going concern, continue, existence, foreseeable future

2 See para 1.3

3

Financial	Operational	Other
(b) (e)	(c) (d) (f)	(a)

4 True

5 relevant events, additions, existing, conditions, did not exist, materiality, disclosure

6 See table before para 4.1

7 When the directors revise the financial statements before they have been issued, but after the date of the auditors' report.

8 See para 5.9

9 See para 7.2

10 See para 4.9

Now try the question below from the Exam Question Bank

Number	Level	Marks	Time
18	Exam	20	36 mins

Part E
Reporting

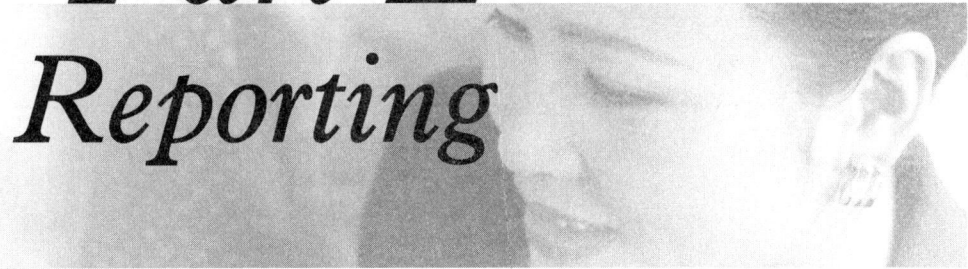

Chapter 19

THE EXTERNAL AUDIT REPORT

Topic list	Syllabus reference
1 SAS 600 *Auditors' report on financial statements*	7
2 Qualifications in audit reports	7
3 Reporting inherent uncertainty	7
4 The audit report as a means of communication	7

Introduction

The **audit report** is the means by which the auditors express their opinion on the **truth and fairness** of a company's financial statements for the benefit principally of the shareholders, but also for other users. Statute has consistently recognised its importance by requiring that certain mandatory statements appear in the report. We considered these mandatory elements in Chapter 2.

SAS 600 was the first step taken by the APB towards closing the 'expectations gap' which was defined in an earlier consultative paper as: 'the difference between the apparent public perceptions of the responsibilities of auditors on the one hand (hence the assurance that their involvement provides) and the legal and professional reality on the other'.

You must remember what the auditor reports on **explicitly** and what the auditor reports on **by exception**.

Study guide

Section 26

* Describe, illustrate and analyse the format and content of unmodified and modified statutory audit reports.

Exam guide

You will not be required to reproduce a full audit report in the exam; however you may be required to describe:

* How the audit report in a specific situation differs from an unqualified audit report, or

* Give extracts from an audit report dealing with uncertainties or disagreements

In December 2001, the requirement was to compare and contract the audit report and the review report.

---

1   SAS 600 AUDITORS' REPORT ON FINANCIAL STATEMENTS   Dec 01

Requirements of the 1985 Act

1.1   Remember that the Companies Act requires the auditors to state **explicitly** (s 235) whether in their opinion the annual accounts have been properly prepared in accordance with the Act and in particular whether a **true and fair view** is given. In addition certain requirements are reported on by exception.

1.2 Auditing standards impose further requirements on the way that the auditor presents his report.

SAS 600.1

Auditors' reports on financial statements should contain a clear expression of opinion, based on review and assessment of the conclusions drawn from evidence obtained in the course of the audit.

1.3 The auditors' report should be placed before the financial statements. The directors' responsibilities statement (explained later) should be placed before the auditors' report.

Basic elements of the auditors' report

SAS 600.2

Auditors' reports on financial statements should include the following matters:

(a) a title identifying the person or persons to whom the report is addressed;

(b) an introductory paragraph identifying the financial statements audited;

(c) separate sections, appropriately headed, dealing with:

(i) respective responsibilities of directors (or equivalent persons) and auditors;
(ii) the basis of the auditors' opinion;
(iii) the auditors' opinion on the financial statements;

(d) the manuscript or printed signature of the auditors; and

(e) the date of the auditors' report.

1.4 The example of an unqualified audit report from an appendix to the SAS, as amended by Bulletin 2001/02 is given here.

Independent auditors' report to the shareholders of XYZ Limited

We have audited the financial statements of (name of entity) for the year ended ... which comprise (state the primary financial statements such as the profit and loss account, the balance sheet, the cash flow statement, the statements of total recognised gains and losses) and the related notes. These financial statements have been prepared under the historical cost convention (as modified by the revaluation of certain fixed assets) and the accounting policies set out therein.

Respective responsibilities of directors and auditors

The director's responsibilities for preparing the annual report and the financial statements in accordance with applicable law and United Kingdom Accounting Standards are set out in the statement of director's responsibilities.

Our responsibility is to audit the financial statements in accordance with relevant legal and regulatory requirements and United Kingdom Auditing Standards.

We report to you our opinion as to whether the financial statements give a true and fair view and are properly prepared in accordance with the (Companies Act 1985). We also report to you if, in our opinion, the director's report is not consistent with the financial statements, if the company has not kept proper accounting records, if we have not received all the information and explanations we required for our audit, or if information specified by law regarding directors remuneration and transactions with the company is not disclosed.

We read other information contained in the annual report and consider whether it is consistent with the audited financial statements. This other information comprises only (the Director's Report, the Chairman's Statement, the Operating and Financial Review). We consider the implications for our report if we become aware of any apparent misstatements or material inconsistencies with the financial statements. Our responsibilities do not extend to any other information.

Basis of audit opinion

We conducted our audit in accordance with United Kingdom Auditing Standards issued by the Auditing Practices Board. An audit includes examination, on a test basis, of evidence relevant to the amounts and disclosures in the financial statements. It also includes an assessment of the significant estimates and judgements made by the directors in the preparation of the financial statements, and of whether the accounting polices are appropriate to the company's circumstances, consistently applied and adequately disclosed.

We planned and performed our audit so as to obtain all the information and explanations which we considered necessary in order to provide us with sufficient evidence to give reasonable assurance that the financial statements are free from material misstatement, whether caused by fraud or other irregularity or error. In forming our opinion we also evaluated the overall adequacy of the presentation of information in the financial statements.

Opinion

In our opinion the financial statements give a true and fair view of the state of the company's affairs as at ... and of its profit (loss) for the year then ended and have been properly prepared in accordance with the (Companies Act 1985).

Registered auditors Address

Date

1.5   The report recommended for a **listed company** is also reproduced here. The significant differences from the standard report are highlighted in grey.

Independent auditors' report to the shareholders of YXZ plc

We have audited the financial statements of (name of entity) for the year ended ... which comprise (state the primary financial statements such as the profit and loss account, the balance sheet, the cash flow statement, the statements of total recognised gains and losses) and the related notes. These financial statements have been prepared under the historical cost convention (as modified by the revaluation of certain fixed assets) and the accounting policies set out therein.

Respective responsibilities of directors and auditors

The director's responsibilities for preparing the annual report and the financial statements in accordance with applicable law and United Kingdom accounting standards are set out in the statement of director's responsibilities.

Our responsibility is to audit the financial statements in accordance with relevant legal and regulatory requirements, United Kingdom Auditing Standards and the Listing Rules of the Financial Services Authority.

We report to you our opinion as to whether the financial statements give a true and fair view and are properly prepared in accordance with the (Companies Act 1985) (Companies (Northern Ireland) Order 1986). We also report to you if, in our opinion, the director's report is not consistent with the financial statements, if the company has not kept proper accounting records, if we have not received all the information and explanations we required for our audit, or if information specified by law or the Listing Rules regarding directors remuneration and transactions with the company (and other members of the group) is not disclosed.

We review whether the Corporate Governance Statement reflects the company's compliance with the seven provisions of the Combined Code specified for our review by the Listing Rules, and we report if it does not. We are not required to consider whether the board's statement on internal control cover all risks and controls, or form an opinion on the effectiveness of the (company's) (group's) corporate governance procedures or its risk and control procedures.

> We read other information contained in the annual report and consider whether it is consistent with the audited financial statements. This other information comprises only (the Director's Report, the Chairman's Statement, the Operating and Financial Review and the Corporate Governance Statement). We consider the implications for our report if we become aware of any apparent misstatements or material inconsistencies with the financial statements. Our responsibilities do not extend to any other information.
>
> **Basis of audit opinion**
>
> We conducted our audit in accordance with United Kingdom Auditing Standards issued by the Auditing Practices Board. An audit includes examination, on a test basis, of evidence relevant to the amounts and disclosures in the financial statements. It also includes an assessment of the significant estimates and judgements made by the directors in the preparation of the financial statements, and of whether the accounting polices are appropriate to the company's circumstances, consistently applied and adequately disclosed.
>
> We planned and performed our audit so as to obtain all the information and explanations which we considered necessary in order to provide us with sufficient evidence to give reasonable assurance that the financial statements are free from material misstatement, whether caused by fraud or other irregularity or error. In forming our opinion we also evaluated the overall adequacy of the presentation of information in the financial statements.
>
> **Opinion**
>
> In our opinion the financial statements give a true and fair view of the state of the (group's and the) company's affairs as at ... and of (the group's) (its) profit (loss) for the year then ended and have been properly prepared in accordance with the (Companies Act 1985) .
>
> *Registered auditors Address*
>
> *Date*

1.6   The SAS recommends the use of standard format as an aid to the reader, including headings for each section, for example 'Qualified opinion'. The title and addressee and the introductory paragraph are fairly self explanatory.

Statements of responsibility and basic opinion

SAS 600.3

(a) Auditors should distinguish between their responsibilities and those of the directors by including in their report:

    (i) a statement that the financial statements are the responsibility of the reporting entity's directors;

    (ii) a reference to a description of those responsibilities when set out elsewhere in the financial statements or accompanying information; and

    (iii) a statement that the auditors' responsibility is to express an opinion on the financial statements.

(b) Where the financial statements or accompanying information (for example the directors' report) do not include an adequate description of directors' relevant responsibilities the auditors' report should include a description of those responsibilities.

Example wording of a description of the directors' responsibilities for inclusion in a company's financial statements

1.7   A description of the directors' responsibilities is given in an example in an appendix. It can be produced by the directors or included by the auditors in their report.

Company law requires the directors to prepare financial statements for each financial year which give a true and fair view of the state of affairs of the company and of the profit or loss of the company for that period. In preparing those financial statements, the directors are required to:

(a)   select suitable accounting policies and then apply them consistently;

(b)   make judgements and estimates that are reasonable and prudent;

(c)   state whether applicable accounting standards have been followed, subject to any material departures disclosed and explained in the financial statements (large companies only);

(d)   prepare the financial statements on the going concern basis unless it is inappropriate to presume that the company will continue in business (if no separate statement on going concern is made by the directors).

The directors are responsible for keeping proper accounting records which disclose with reasonable accuracy at any time the financial position of the company and to enable them to ensure that the financial statements comply with the Companies Act 1985. They are also responsible for safeguarding the assets of the company and hence for taking reasonable steps for the prevention and detection of fraud and other irregularities.

This wording can be adapted to suit the specific situation.

Explanation of auditors' opinion

SAS 600.4

Auditors should explain the basis of their opinion by including in their report:

(a)   a statement as to their compliance or otherwise with Auditing Standards, together with the reasons for any departure therefrom;

(b)   a statement that the audit process includes:

(i)   examining, on a test basis, evidence relevant to the amounts and disclosures in the financial statements;

(ii)   assessing the significant estimates and judgements made by the reporting entity's directors in preparing the financial statements;

(iii) considering whether the accounting policies are appropriate to the reporting entity's circumstances, consistently applied and adequately disclosed;

(c)   a statement that they planned and performed the audit so as to obtain reasonable assurance that the financial statements are free from material misstatement, whether caused by fraud or other irregularity or error, and that they have evaluated the overall presentation of the financial statements. (SAS 600.4)

1.8   Other than in exceptional circumstances, a departure from an auditing standard is a limitation on the scope of work undertaken by the auditors (see later).

Expression of opinion

SAS 600.5

An auditors' report should contain a clear expression of opinion on the financial statements and on any further matters required by statute or other requirements applicable to the particular engagement.

1.9 An unqualified opinion on financial statements is expressed when in the auditors' judgement they give a true and fair view (where relevant) and have been prepared in accordance with relevant accounting or other requirements. This judgement entails concluding whether:

(a) The financial statements have been prepared using **appropriate consistently applied accounting policies**.

(b) The financial statements have been **prepared** in accordance with **relevant legislation, regulations** or **applicable accounting standards** (and that any departures are justified and adequately explained in the financial statements).

(c) There is **adequate disclosure** of all information relevant to the proper understanding of the financial statements.

Date and signature of the auditors' report

SAS 600.9

(a) Auditors should not express an opinion on financial statement until those statements and all other financial information contained in a report of which the audited financial statements form a part have been approved by the directors, and the auditors have considered all necessary available evidence.

(b) The date of an auditors' report on a reporting entity's financial statements is the date on which the auditors sign their report expressing an opinion on those statements.

1.10 If the date on which the auditors sign the report is later than that on which the directors approve the financial statements, then the auditors must check that the post balance sheet event review has been carried out up to the date they sign their report and that the directors would also have approved the financial statements on that date.

Forming an opinion on financial statements

1.11 Appendix 1 of the SAS considers the process of forming an audit opinion using the flowchart shown on the next page. The flowchart is drawn up on the basis that the directors make no further amendments to the financial statements following the audit.

1.12 The principal matters which auditors consider in forming an opinion may be expressed in three questions.

- Have they **completed all procedures necessary** to meet auditing standards and to obtain all the information and explanations necessary for their audit?

- Have the financial statements been **prepared in accordance** with the **applicable accounting requirements**?

- Do the financial statements, as prepared by the directors, give **a true and fair view**?

FORMING AN OPINION ON FINANCIAL STATEMENTS

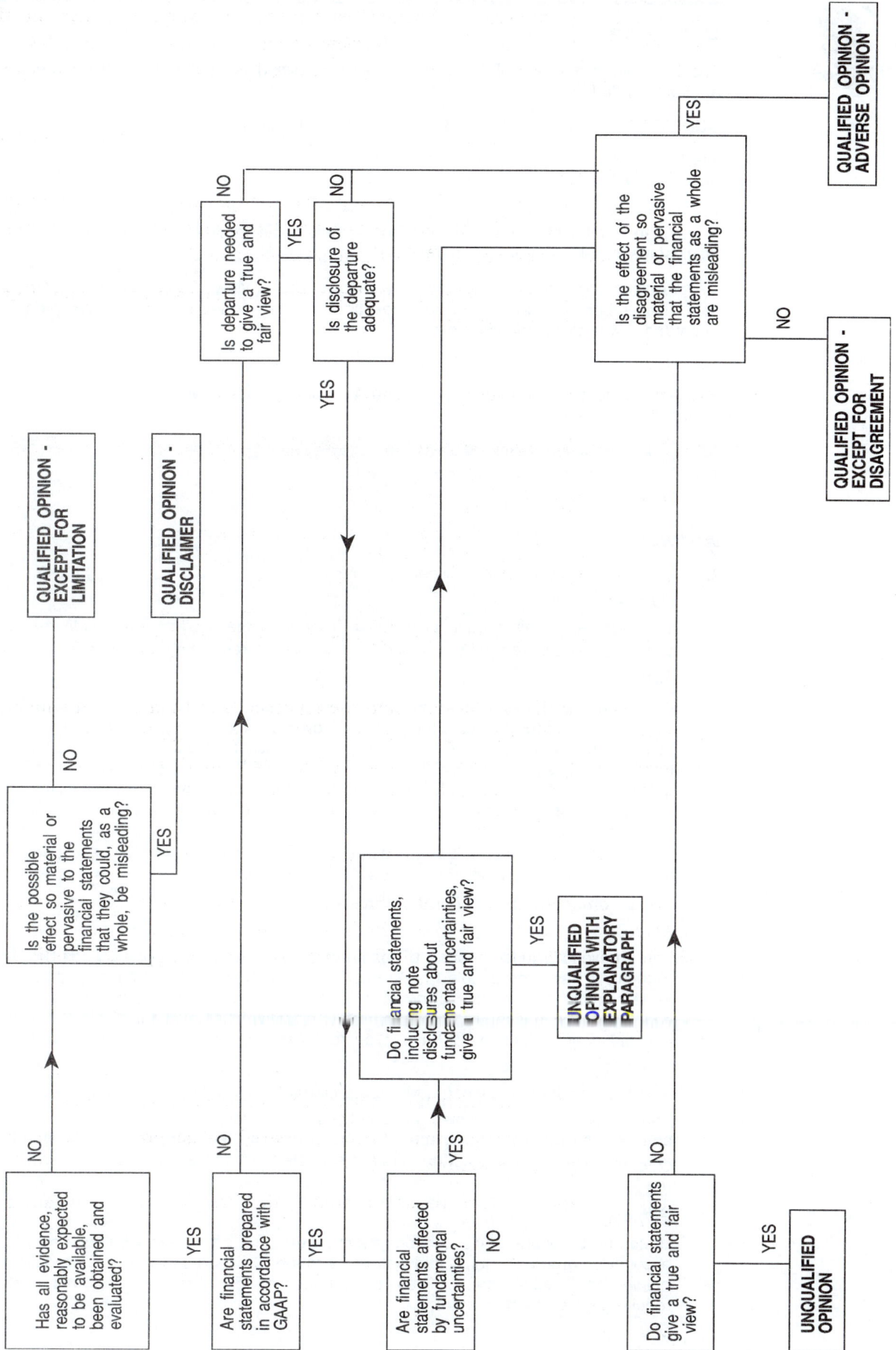

BPP
PUBLISHING

Question 1

The following is a series of extracts from an unqualified audit report which has been signed by the auditors of Kiln Ltd.

AUDITORS' REPORT TO THE SHAREHOLDERS OF KILN LIMITED

We have audited *the financial statements on pages .... to ....* which have been prepared under the historical cost convention.

We have conducted our audit *in accordance with Auditing Standards* issued by the Auditing Practices Board. An audit includes examination on a test basis of evidence relevant to the amounts and disclosures in the financial statements.

In our opinion the financial statements give a true and fair view of the state of the company's affairs as at 31 December 20X3 and of its profit for the year then ended and have been properly prepared in accordance with the Companies Act 1985.

Required

Explain the purpose and meaning of the following phrases taken from the above extracts of an unqualified audit report.

(a)   '... the financial statements on pages .... to ....'
(b)   '... in accordance with Auditing Standards.'
(c)   'In our opinion ...'

Answer

(a)   '*...the financial statements on pages 8 to 20...*'

Purpose

The purpose of this phrase is to make it clear to the reader of an audit report the part of a company's annual report upon which the auditors are reporting their opinion.

Meaning

An annual report may include documents such as a chairman's report, employee report, five year summary and other voluntary information. However, under the Companies Act, only the profit and loss account, balance sheet and associated notes are required to be audited in true and fair terms. FRS 1 requires a cash flow statement and FRS 3 requires a statement of total recognised gains and losses which, under auditing standards, are audited in true and fair terms. Thus the page references (for instance, 8 to 20) cover only the profit and loss account, balance sheet, notes to the accounts, cash flow statement and statement of total recognised gains and losses. The directors' report, although examined and reported on by exception if it contains inconsistencies, is not included in these page references.

(b)   '*...in accordance with Auditing Standards...*'

Purpose

This phrase is included in order to confirm to the reader that best practice, as laid down in Auditing Standards, has been adopted by the auditors in both carrying out their audit and in drafting their audit opinion. This means that the reader can be assured that the audit has been properly conducted, and that should he or she wish to discover what such standards are, or what certain key phrases mean, he or she can have recourse to Auditing Standards to explain such matters.

Meaning

Auditing Standards are those auditing standards prepared by the Auditing Practices Board.

These prescribe the principles and practices to be followed by auditors in the planning, designing and carrying out various aspects of their audit work, the content of audit reports, both qualified and unqualified and so on. Members are expected to follow all of these standards.

(c)   '*In our opinion ...*'

Purpose

Under the Companies Act, auditors are required to report on every balance sheet, profit and loss account or group accounts laid before members. In reporting, they are required to state their *opinion* on those accounts. Thus, the purpose of this phrase is to comply with the statutory requirement to report an opinion.

Meaning

An audit report is an expression of opinion by suitably qualified auditors as to whether the financial statements give a true and fair view, and have been properly prepared in accordance with the Companies Act. *It is not a certificate*; rather it is a statement of whether or not, in the professional judgement of the auditors, the financial statements give a true and fair view.

2   QUALIFICATIONS IN AUDIT REPORTS

2.1   Qualified audit reports arise when auditors do not believe that they can state without reservation that the accounts give a true and fair view.

The qualification 'matrix'

2.2   SAS 600 gives the circumstances in which each sort of qualification would be appropriate. Where the auditors are unable to report affirmatively on the matters contained in the paragraphs about which they have reservations, they should give:

- A full explanation of the reasons for the qualification

- Whenever possible, a quantification of its effect on the financial statements

- Where appropriate, reference should be made to non-compliance with relevant legislation and other requirements

2.3   The standard stresses the fact that **a qualified audit report should leave the reader in no doubt as to its meaning and its implications for an understanding of the financial statements**.

2.4   The APB takes the view that the nature of the circumstances giving rise to a qualification of the auditor's opinion will generally fall into one of two categories:

- Where there is a **limitation in the scope of work** which prevents the auditors from forming an opinion on a matter (uncertainty - see SAS 600.7), or

- Where the auditors are able to form an opinion on a matter but this **conflicts** with the view given by the financial statements (disagreement - see SAS 600.8)

2.5   Either case, uncertainty or disagreement, may give rise to alternative forms of qualification. This is because the uncertainty or disagreement can be:

- Material but not fundamental
- Of fundamental importance to the overall true and fair view

The standard requires that the following forms of qualification should be used in the different circumstances outlined below.

QUALIFICATION MATRIX

Nature of circumstances	Material but not fundamental	Fundamental
Limitation in scope	Except for .. might	Disclaimer of opinion
Disagreement	Except for ...	Adverse opinion

Except for ... might	Auditors disclaim an opinion on a particular aspect of the accounts which is not considered fundamental.
Disclaimer of opinion	Auditors state they are unable to form an opinion on truth and fairness.
Except for	Auditors express an adverse opinion on a particular aspect of the accounts which is not considered fundamental.
Adverse opinion	Auditors state the accounts do not give a true and fair view.

Limitations on the scope of an audit

2.6   One source of uncertainties is **limitations in the scope of the audit**. Scope limitations will arise where the auditor is unable for any reason to obtain all the information and explanations which he considers necessary for the purpose of his audit, arising from:

    (a)   Absence of proper accounting records

    (b)   An inability to carry out audit procedures considered necessary as, for example, where the auditor is unable to obtain satisfactory evidence of the existence or ownership of material assets

---

SAS 600.7

When there has been a limitation on the scope of the auditors' work that prevents them from obtaining sufficient evidence to express an unqualified opinion:

(a)   the auditors' report should include a description of the factors leading to the limitation in the opinion section of their report;

(b)   the auditors should issue a disclaimer of opinion when the possible effect of a limitation on scope is so material or pervasive that they are unable to express an opinion on the financial statements;

(c)   a qualified opinion should be issued when the effect of the limitation is not as material or pervasive as to require a disclaimer, and the wording of the opinion should indicate that it is qualified as to the possible adjustments to the financial statements that might have been determined to be necessary had the limitation not existed.

2.7   When giving this type of qualified opinion, auditors should assess:

- The **quantity and type of evidence** which may reasonably be expected to be available to support the figure or disclosure in the financial statements

- The **possible effect** on the financial statements of the matter for which insufficient evidence is available

2.8   SAS 600 gives the following examples.

Example 8. Qualified opinion: limitation on the auditors' work

(Basis of opinion: excerpt)

.... or error. However, the evidence available to us was limited because £... of the company's recorded turnover comprises cash sales, over which there was no system of control on which we could rely for the purposes of our audit. There were no other satisfactory audit procedures that we could adopt to confirm that cash sales were properly recorded.

In forming our opinion we also evaluated the overall adequacy of the presentation of information in the financial statements.

Qualified opinion arising from limitation in audit scope

Except for any adjustments that might have been found to be necessary had we been able to obtain sufficient evidence concerning cash sales, in our opinion the financial statements give a true and fair view of the state of the company's affairs as at 31 December 20.. and of its profit (loss) for the year then ended and have been properly prepared in accordance with the Companies Act 1985.

In respect alone of the limitation on our work relating to cash sales:

(a)   we have not obtained all the information and explanations that we considered necessary for the purpose of our audit; and

(b)   we were unable to determine whether proper accounting records had been maintained.

Example 9. Disclaimer of opinion

(Basis of opinion: excerpt)

.... or error. However, the evidence available to us was limited because we were appointed auditors on (date) and in consequence we were unable to carry out auditing procedures necessary to obtain adequate assurance regarding the quantities and condition of stock and work in progress, appearing in the balance sheet at £... . Any adjustment to this figure would have a consequential significant effect on the profit for the year.

In forming our opinion we also evaluated the overall adequacy of the presentation of information in the financial statements.

Opinion: disclaimer on view given by financial statements

Because of the possible effect of the limitation in evidence available to us, we are unable to form an opinion as to whether the financial statements give a true and fair view of the state of the company's affairs as at 31 December 20.. or of its profit (loss) for the year then ended. In all other respects, in our opinion the financial statements have been properly prepared in accordance with the Companies Act 1985.

In respect of the limitation on our work relating to stock and work-in-progress:

(a)   we have not obtained all the information and explanations that we considered necessary for the purpose of our audit; and

(b)   we were unable to determine whether proper accounting records had been maintained.

Note. Because of the length of the audit report, we have only shown those parts of each qualified report which differ from the unqualified report shown in Section 2.

2.9   In March 1999 the APB published SAS 601 *Imposed limitation of audit scope* which provides guidance for auditors when the directors or those who appoint the auditors place limitations upon the scope of the audit

> **SAS 601.1**
>
> If the auditors are aware, before accepting an audit engagement, that the directors of the entity, or those who appoint its auditors, will impose a limitation on the scope of the audit work which they consider likely to result in the need to issue a disclaimer of opinion on the financial statements, they should not accept that engagement, unless required to do so by statute.

2.10   The SAS points out that agreeing to such a limitation would **threaten** the **independence** of auditors and make it impossible for them to meet the requirements of auditing standards.

2.11   The APB also believes that in accepting such a limited engagement, the auditors are complicit in the client evading the spirit of the legal requirement to be audited. The SAS points out that even if there is a requirement for an entity to appoint auditors, this does not automatically mean that there is a requirement on the auditors to accept appointment.

> **SAS 601.2**
>
> If the auditors become aware, after accepting an audit engagement, that the directors of the entity, or those who appointed them as auditors, have imposed a limitation on the scope of their work which they consider likely to result in the need to issue a disclaimer on the financial statements, they should request the removal of the limitation. If the limitation is not removed, they should consider resigning from the audit engagement.

BPP PUBLISHING

2.12 If the auditors do not consider it necessary to resign but do issue a disclaimer, the audit report should give full details of why the disclaimer was given.

Circumstances giving rise to disagreements

2.13 The explanatory notes suggest that circumstances giving rise to disagreement include the following.

- **Inappropriate accounting policies**

- **Disagreement** as to the **facts or amounts** included in the financial statements

- **Disagreement** as to the **manner or extent of disclosure** of facts or amounts in the financial statements

- **Failure to comply** with **relevant legislation** or other **requirements**

2.14 SAS 110 suggests also that the auditors conclude that a suspected or actual fraud has a material effect on financial statements and the auditors disagree with the disclosure (or lack of) in relation to it, they may qualify.

SAS 600.8

Where the auditors disagree with the accounting treatment or disclosure of a matter in the financial statements, and in the auditors' opinion the effect of that disagreement is material to the financial statements:

(a) the auditors should include in the opinion section of their report:

    (i) a description of all substantive factors giving rise to the disagreement;
    (ii) their implications for the financial statements;
    (iii) whenever practicable, a quantification of the effect on the financial statements;

(b) when the auditors conclude that the effect of the matter giving rise to disagreement is so material or pervasive that the financial statements are seriously misleading, they should issue an adverse opinion;

(c) in the case of other material disagreements, the auditors should issue a qualified opinion indicating that it is expressed except for the effects of the matter giving rise to the disagreement.

Example 7. Qualified opinion: disagreement

Qualified opinion arising from disagreement about accounting treatment

Included in the debtors shown on the balance sheet is an amount of £Y due from a company which has ceased trading. XYZ plc has no security for this debt. In our opinion the company is unlikely to receive any payment and full provision of £Y should have been made, reducing profit before tax and net assets by that amount.

Except for the absence of this provision, in our opinion the financial statements give a true and fair view of the state of the company's affairs as at 31 December 20.. and of its profit (loss) for the year then ended and have been properly prepared in accordance with the Companies Act 1985.

Example 10. Adverse opinion

Adverse opinion

As more fully explained in note ... no provision has been made for losses expected to arise on certain long-term contracts currently in progress, as the directors consider that such losses should be off-set against amounts recoverable on other long-term contracts. In our opinion, provision should be made for foreseeable losses on individual contracts as required by Statement of Standard Accounting Practice 9. If losses had been so recognised the effect would have been to reduce the profit before and after tax

---

for the year and the contract work in progress at 31 December 20.. by £.. .

In view of the effect of the failure to provide for the losses referred to above, in our opinion the financial statements do not give a true and fair view of the state of the company's affairs as at 31 December 20.. and of its profit (loss) for the year then ended. In all other respects, in our opinion the financial statements have been properly prepared in accordance with the Companies Act 1985.

3   REPORTING INHERENT UNCERTAINTY

Inherent and fundamental uncertainty

KEY TERMS

An **inherent uncertainty** is an uncertainty whose resolution is dependent upon uncertain future events outside the control of the reporting entity's directors at the date the financial statements are approved.

A **fundamental uncertainty** is an inherent uncertainty where the magnitude of its potential impact is so great that, without clear disclosure of the nature and implications of the uncertainty, the view given by the financial statements would be seriously misleading.

SAS 600.6

(a)   In forming their opinion on financial statements, auditors should consider whether the view given by the financial statements could be affected by inherent uncertainties which, in their opinion, are fundamental.

(b)   When an inherent uncertainty exists which:

(i)   in the auditors' opinion is fundamental; and
(ii)   is adequately accounted for and disclosed in the financial statements;

the auditors should include an explanatory paragraph referring to the fundamental uncertainty in the section of their report setting out the basis of their opinion.

(c)   When adding an explanatory paragraph, auditors should use words which clearly indicate that their opinion on the financial statements is not qualified in respect of its concepts.

3.1   The following points are relevant.

(a)   Inherent uncertainties about the outcome of future events frequently affect, to some degree, a wide range of components of the financial statements at the date they are approved.

(b)   In forming an opinion, auditors take into account:

*   The **appropriateness of the accounting policies**

*   The **adequacy of the accounting treatment**

*   **Estimates and disclosures of inherent uncertainties** in the light of evidence available at the date they express their opinion

3.2   Inherent uncertainties are regarded as **fundamental** when they involve a **significant level of doubt** about the validity of the **going concern basis** or other matters whose potential effect on the fundamental statements is unusually great. A common example of a fundamental uncertainty is the outcome of major litigation. There may also be a fundamental uncertainty over a suspected or actual fraud.

3.3 The auditor will need to consider:

- The possibility that the **estimate** included in the accounts may be **subject to change**

- The **possible range of values** it may take

- The **consequences** of that range of potential values on the view shown in the financial statements

---

Example 4. Unqualified opinion with explanatory paragraph describing a fundamental uncertainty.

Fundamental uncertainty (insert just before opinion paragraph)

In forming our opinion, we have considered the adequacy of the disclosures made in the financial statements concerning the possible outcome to litigation against B Limited, a subsidiary undertaking of the company, for an alleged breach of environmental regulations. The future settlement of this litigation could result in additional liabilities and the closure of B Limited's business, whose net assets included in the consolidated balance sheet total £... and whose profit before tax for the year is £.... Details of the circumstances relating to this fundamental uncertainty are described in note .... . Our opinion is not qualified in this respect.

Question 2

During the course of your audit of the fixed assets of Eastern Engineering plc at 31 March 20X4 two problems have arisen.

(a) The calculations of the cost of direct labour incurred on assets in course of construction by the company's employees have been accidentally destroyed for the early part of the year. The direct labour cost involved is £10,000.

(b) The company has received a government grant of £25,000 towards the cost of plant and equipment acquired during the year and expected to last for ten years. The grant has been credited in full to the profit and loss account as exceptional income.

(c) Other relevant financial information is as follows.

	£
Profit before tax	100,000
Fixed asset additions	133,000
Assets constructed by company	34,000
Fixed asset at net book value	666,667

Required

(a) List the general forms of qualification available to auditors in drafting their report and state the circumstances in which each is appropriate.

(b) State whether you feel that a qualified audit report would be necessary for each of the two circumstances outlined above, giving reasons in each case.

(c) On the assumption that you decide that a qualified audit report is necessary with respect to the treatment of the government grant, draft the section of the report describing the matter (the whole report is not required).

(d) Outline the auditors' general responsibility with regard to the statement in the directors' report concerning the valuation of land and buildings.

Answer

(a) SAS 600 *Auditors' report on financial statements* suggests that the auditors may need to qualify their audit opinion under one of two main circumstances:

    (i) limitation in scope of the auditors' examination; and

    (ii) disagreement with the treatment or disclosure of a matter in the financial statements (including inherent uncertainties).

For both circumstances there can be two 'levels' of qualified opinion:

(i) *material but not fundamental,* where the circumstances prompting the uncertainty or disagreement is material but confined to one particular aspect of the financial statements, so that it does not affect their overall value to any potential user;

(ii) the more serious qualification where the extent of the uncertainty or disagreement is such that it will be *fundamental* to the overall view shown by the financial statements, ie the financial statements are or could be misleading.

The general form of qualification appropriate to each potential situation may be seen by the following table.

Circumstance	Material but not fundamental	Fundamental
Limitation of scope	Except for ... might	Disclaimer of opinion
Disagreement	Except for ...	Adverse opinion

(b) Whether a qualification of the audit opinion would be required in relation to either of the two circumstances described in the question would depend on whether or not the auditors considered either of them to be material. An item is likely to be considered as material in the context of a company's financial statements if its omission, misstatement or non-disclosure would prevent a proper understanding of those statements on the part of a potential user. Whilst for some audit purposes materiality will be considered in absolute terms, more often than not it will be considered as a relative term.

(i) *Loss of records relating to direct labour costs for assets in the course of construction*

The loss of records supporting one of the asset figures in the balance sheet would cause a limitation in scope of the auditors' work. The £10,000, which is the value covered by the lost records, represents 29.4% of the expenditure incurred during the year on assets in course of construction but only 6% of total additions to fixed assets during the year and 1.5% of the year end net book value for fixed assets. The total amount of £10,000 represents 10% of pre-tax profit but, as in relation to asset values, the real consideration by the auditors should be the materiality of any over- or under-statement of assets resulting from error in arriving at the £10,000 rather than the total figure itself.

Provided there are no suspicious circumstances surrounding the loss of these records and the total figure for additions to assets in the course of construction seems reasonable in the light of other audit evidence obtained, then it is unlikely that this matter would be seen as sufficiently material to merit any qualification of the audit opinion. If other records have been lost as well, however, it may be necessary for the auditors to comment on the directors' failure to maintain proper books and records.

(ii) *Government grant credited in total to profit and loss account*

The situation here is one of disagreement, since best accounting practice, as laid down by SSAP 4, requires that capital-based grants should be credited to the profit and loss account over the useful life of the asset to which they relate.

This departure from SSAP 4 does not seem to be justifiable and would be material to the reported pre-tax profits for the year, representing as it does 22.5% of that figure.

Whilst this overstatement of profit (and corresponding understatement of undistributable reserves) would be material to the financial statements, it is not likely to be seen as fundamental and therefore an 'except for' qualified opinion would be appropriate.

(c) *Qualified audit report extract*

'As explained in note ... government grants in respect of new plant and equipment have been credited in full to profits instead of being spread over the lives of the relevant assets as required by Statement of Standard Accounting Practice 4; the effect of so doing has been to increase profits before and after tax for the year by £22,500.

Except for ...'

(d) The auditors' general responsibility with regard to the statement in the directors' report concerning the valuation of land and buildings is to satisfy themselves that this is consistent with the treatment and disclosure of this item in the audited financial statements. If the auditors are not satisfied on the question of consistency then an appropriate opinion will be required following their audit report.

4 THE AUDIT REPORT AS A MEANS OF COMMUNICATION

4.1 Unqualified audit reports may not appear to give a great deal of information. The report says a lot, however, by implication.

4.2 The real problem here is that, unfortunately, most users do not know that this is what an unqualified audit report tells them.

4.3 This difference between the actual and the public perception is part of what is called the 'expectation gap'. The question remains: how can we make the **meaning** of an unqualified audit report clear to the user? The Auditing Practices Board (APB) came up with a new audit report SAS, as we saw in the earlier sections of this chapter.

4.4 The APB made it clear that the new audit report was to be seen as a step towards closing the 'expectation gap' which was defined in an earlier consultative paper as 'the difference between the apparent public perceptions of the responsibilities of auditors on the one hand (and hence the assurance that their involvement provides) and the legal and professional reality on the other'.

4.5 The APB stressed that the above definition is not definitive and that the expectations gap is not a 'static phenomenon'. However, the Board has addressed specific issues.

(a) **Misunderstandings of the nature of audited financial statements,** for example that:

- The balance sheet provides a fair valuation of the reporting entity.

- The amounts in the financial statement are stated precisely.

- The audited financial statement will guarantee that the entity concerned will continue to exist.

(b) **Misunderstanding as to the type and extent of work undertaken by auditors.**

(c) **Misunderstanding about the level of assurance provided by auditors,** for example that:

- An unqualified auditors' report means that no frauds have occurred in the period.

- The auditors provide absolute assurance that the figures in the financial statements are correct (ignoring the concept of materiality and the problems of estimation).

4.6 Note that the Cadbury Report *The Financial Aspects of Corporate Governance* also recommends many of the suggestions made in SAS, particularly the statement of both directors' and auditors' responsibilities.

Exam focus point

Questions about audit reports could be about possible qualifications in specific situations.

Chapter roundup

- The Companies Act requires **specific reference** in the audit report to:

  ° The truth and fairness of the state of the company's affairs at the period-end
  ° The truth and fairness of the profit or loss
  ° Whether the accounts have been properly prepared in accordance with the Companies Act

- The Companies Act requires certain matters to be reported on by **exception.**

- The main elements of an **unqualified audit report** under SAS 600 are:

  ° A **title** identifying the addressee

  ° An **introductory paragraph** identifying the **financial statements audited**

  ° Sections dealing with:

    - **Responsibilities** of directors and **auditors**
    - **Basis** of the auditors' opinion
    - A **clear statement of opinion**

- Auditors may qualify their audit opinion on the grounds of **disagreement or limitation of scope**; these may be **material** or **fundamental.**

- Auditors are principally concerned with the correct **treatment** and **disclosure** of **inherent** and **fundamental uncertainties**, which relate to uncertain future events.

- Auditors should include an **explanatory paragraph** in their audit report if **fundamental uncertainties** exist.

Quick quiz

1 What are the three explicit opinions and the five implied opinions of the audit report?

1	....	1	....
2	....	2	....
3	....	3	....
		4	....
		5	....

2 Complete the standard opinion paragraph.

In our opinion the .... give a ....
.... of the state of the company's affairs as at 31.XX.XX and of its ....
(............) for .... and have been ....
.... in accordance with the Companies Act 1985.

3 The statement of directors' responsibilities is always included in the auditors' report.

True ☐

False ☐

4 Complete the diagram by filling in the type of report that would be issued in each situation.

FORMING AN OPINION ON FINANCIAL STATEMENTS

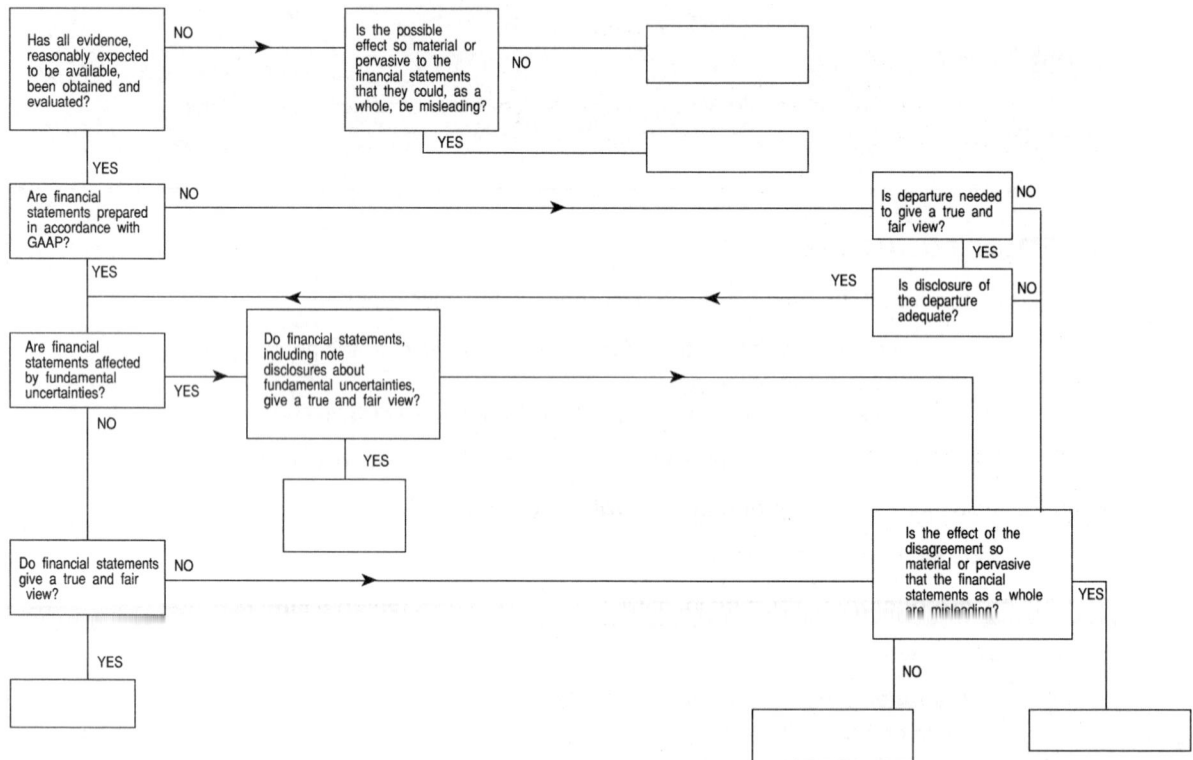

Has all evidence, reasonably expected to be available, been obtained and evaluated? — NO → Is the possible effect so material or pervasive to the financial statements that they could, as a whole, be misleading? — NO → [ ]

YES (from possible effect box) → [ ]

Are financial statements prepared in accordance with GAAP? — NO → Is departure needed to give a true and fair view? — NO

YES → Is disclosure of the departure adequate? — NO

Is departure needed to give a true and fair view? — YES

Are financial statements affected by fundamental uncertainties? — YES → Do financial statements, including note disclosures about fundamental uncertainties, give a true and fair view? — YES → [ ]

Do financial statements give a true and fair view? — NO → Is the effect of the disagreement so material or pervasive that the financial statements as a whole are misleading? — YES → [ ]

NO → [ ]

YES → [ ]

5 Draw the qualification matrix

6 Complete the definition

An .... uncertainty is an uncertainty whose resolution is dependent upon ....
.... outside the control of the reporting entity's directors at ....
.... the financial statements are ....

7   Give three examples of misunderstandings which contribute to the expectations gap.

1   …………………………………………..

2   …………………………………………..

3   …………………………………………..

Answers to quick quiz

1 **Expressly**	**By implication**
State of the company's affairs	Proper accounting records
Company's profit and loss	Accounts in agreement with records
Consolidation (if applicable)	Information and explanations received
	Directors' emoluments disclosed right
	Directors' report consistent with accounts

2   financial statements, true and fair view, profit (loss) the year then ended, properly prepared

3   False

4

FORMING AN OPINION ON FINANCIAL STATEMENTS

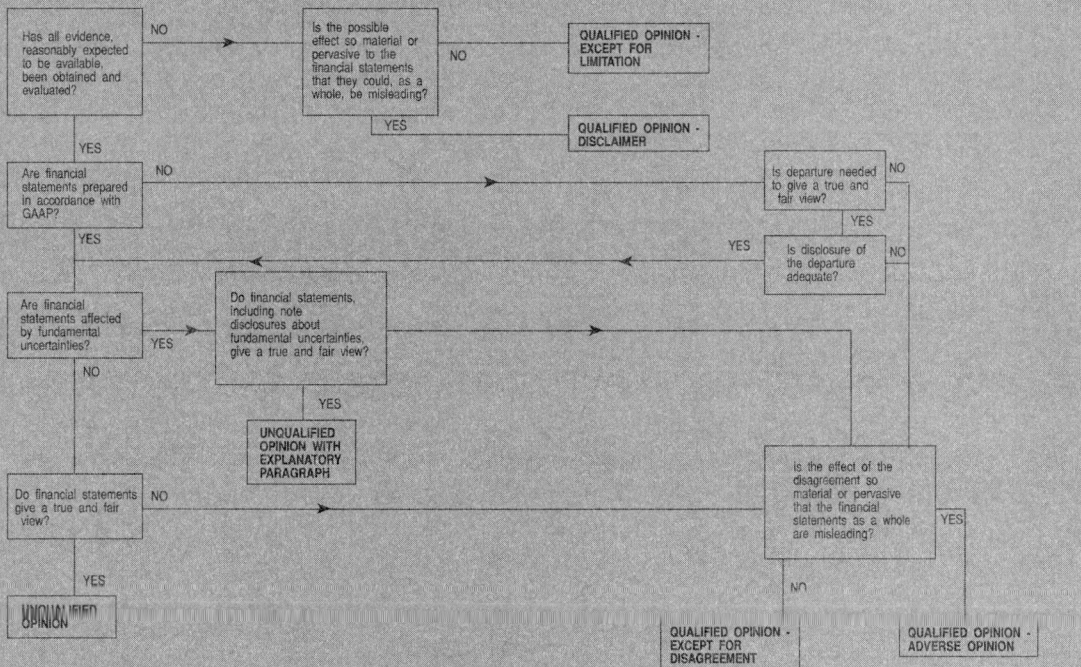

5   QUALIFICATION MATRIX

Nature of circumstances	Material but not fundamental	Fundamental
Disagreement	Except for .. might	Disclaimer of opinion
Limitation in scope	Except for ...	Adverse opinion

BPP PUBLISHING

Except for . . . might	Auditors disclaim an opinion on a particular aspect of the accounts which is not considered fundamental.
Disclaimer of opinion	Auditors state they are unable to form an opinion on truth and fairness.
Except for	Auditors express an adverse opinion on a particular aspect of the accounts which is not considered fundamental.
Adverse opinion	Auditors state the accounts do not give a true and fair view.

6   inherent, uncertain future events, the date, approved

7   See para 5.7

Now try the question below from the Exam Question Bank

Number	Level	Marks	Time
19	Exam	20	36 mins

Chapter 20

NON STATUTORY REPORTS

Topic list	Syllabus reference
1 External review reports	7
2 Specific reports to management	7
3 Communication of audit matters to those charged with governance	7
4 Reporting control weaknesses	7

Introduction

In Chapter 19 we looked at the formal statutory audit report to members. In this chapter we will look at the other reports arising from audits and reviews.

As there is no formal requirements in the UK for reporting on the results of **external reviews**, we shall look briefly at the **international guidance**, found in ISA 910, *Engagement to Review Financial Statements*.

Auditors, both internal and external, also **report to management** about issues arising from audit work undertaken. Theses reports might be in response to a **specific issue**, which they have been asked to report on, or they might be a more **general comment on potential business and system improvements**.

The external auditors' '**report to those charged with governance**' is an example of such a 'general' report. While it not a statutory, it is **mandatory** for external auditors to provide such a report under **auditing standards**.

Guidance is given on such reporting in SAS 610, which was recently revised. The old standard provided some helpful guidance on **reporting weaknesses in control** to the management of an enterprise. Although this guidance is not longer in the auditing standards, we shall consider it in section 4 because it continues to be good guidance to auditors providing such reports.

Study guide

Section 10

- Describe and analyse the format and content of an external review report.

Section 27

Describe, illustrate and analyse the format and content of

- Unmodified and modified internal audit and internal review reports
- Reports dealing with recommendations for the enhancement of business performance

Sections 11-15

- Explain and illustrate how structural and operational weaknesses in

    ○ Sales and purchases systems
    ○ Payroll systems
    ○ Stock systems
    ○ Revenue and capital expenditure systems
    ○ Bank and cash systems

    should be reported to management

BPP PUBLISHING

Exam guide

You are unlikely to be asked to draft a report, but might have to outline what points should be included in a report given a particular scenario, or discuss the level of assurance given in such a report. In December 2001, the external review report was contrasted with the audit report, and in the controls question, the candidate was asked to set out control weaknesses in report format.

---

1 EXTERNAL REVIEW REPORTS   Dec 01

1.1 The concept of an **external review** was introduced in Chapter 1. It is an exercise, similar to an audit, which is designed to give a reduced degree of assurance concerning the proper preparation of a set of financial statements.

1.2 There is no current UK guidance on review engagements, so here we shall consider the international guidance, ISA 910, *Engagements to Review Financial Statements*. Remember that, as discussed in Chapter 1, negative assurance is given on review assignments.

> **ISA 910.25/26**
>
> The review report should contain a clear written expression of **negative assurance**. The auditor should review and assess the conclusion drawn from the evidence obtained as the basis for the expression of negative assurance.
>
> Based on the work performed, the auditor should assess whether any information obtained during the review indicates that the financial statements do not give a true and fair view (or 'are not presented fairly, in all material respects,') in accordance with the identified financial reporting framework.

No matters have come to the attention of the auditor

1.3 In this case, the auditor should give a clear expression of negative assurance in his report. An example of an unqualified review report is given in the appendix to the ISA, and it is reproduced here.

> **Form of Unqualified Review Report**
>
> REVIEW REPORT TO...
>
> We have reviewed the accompanying balance sheet of ABC Company at December 31, 20XX, and the related statements of income and cash flows for the year then ended. These financial statements are the responsibility of the Company's management. Our responsibility is to issue a report on these financial statements based on our review.
>
> We conducted our review in accordance with the International Standard on Auditing (or refer to relevant national standards or practices) applicable to review engagements. This Standard requires that we plan and perform the review to obtain moderate assurance as to whether the financial statements are free of material misstatement. A review is limited primarily to inquiries of company personnel and analytical procedures applied to financial data and thus provides less assurance than an audit. We have not performed an audit and, accordingly, we do not express an audit opinion.
>
> Based on our review, nothing has come to our attention that causes us to believe that the accompanying financial statements do not give a true and fair view (or 'are not presented fairly, in all material respects,') in accordance with International Accounting Standards.
>
> *Date*   *AUDITOR*
>
> *Address*

Matters have come to the attention of the auditor

1.4 If matters have come to the attention of the auditor, he should **describe those matters**. The matters may have the following effects.

Impact	Effect on report
Material	Express a **qualified** opinion of negative assurance
Pervasive	Express an **adverse** opinion that the financial statements do not give a true and fair view

1.5 The auditor may feel there has been a limitation in the scope of the work he intended to carry out for the review. If so, he should **describe the limitation**. The limitation may have the following effects.

Impact	Effect on report
Material to one area	Express a **qualified** opinion of negative assurance due to amendments which might required if the limitation did not exist
Pervasive	Do not provide any assurance

2 SPECIFIC REPORTS TO MANAGEMENT

2.1 As discussed in Chapter 1, auditors may be engaged to undertake assignments other than the statutory audit. Auditors are skilled professionals and a business may want to use that skill to comment on a specific area of their business.

2.2 Such an assignment might commonly be given to the internal audit department to undertake, but if the assignment is confidential, or the business does not have an internal department, the directors might ask their external auditors to undertake such special work.

2.3 As outlined in Chapter 3, auditors could therefore be asked to perform an internal review in any area of the entity's operations. Some further examples are given in the box below.

> - Accounting systems
> - Debtors and cash collection
> - Computer systems
> - Stock holding and purchasing
> - Quality control
> - Internal audit function

2.4 Such assignments are carried out on an entirely different basis to an external audit. in an external audit, auditors report to the shareholders on the truth and fairness of the financial statements. Their report is a comment on the stewardship of the directors.

2.5 In an assignment such as those given below, the auditor or internal auditor is serving a function for management. They are reviewing the function of an aspect of the business, usually in response to a specific objective or question.

Reporting on internal review assignment

2.6 There are **no formal requirements** for such reports in the UK as there are for the statutory audit. The statutory audit report is a highly stylised document which is substantially the same for any audit. A report from the auditors in relation to a review assignment can take any form. However, some points should be borne in mind.

2.7　There is a generally accepted format for reports in business, which is laid out below. This format makes reports useful to readers as it highlights the conclusions drawn and gives easy reference to the user.

Standard report format

TERMS OF REFERENCE

EXECUTIVE SUMMARY – summarising conclusions drawn from assignment

INTRODUCTION

BODY OF THE REPORT

APPENDICES FOR ANY ADDITIONAL INFORMATION

2.8　If the report is in response to specific premise or question, the report will either confirm that opinion or deny it. It is possible to think of this as a modified or unmodified opinion.

KEY TERMS

A **modified opinion** is one which denies the original premise which forms the basis of the report.

An **unmodified opinion** is one which confirms that the premise which forms the basis of the report is reasonable.

2.9　EXAMPLE

Silver Saucepans Ltd has asked their auditors to undertake a special assignment on their credit control systems. They want to know if the system is operated efficiently and if cash in respect of debtors is received as promptly as possible.

The auditors have undertaken a review of the credit control system and discovered that:

- Controls over ordering are weak, with few new customers being credit checked and given credit limits.

- Customers whose balance sheet has negative equity have been given substantial credit.

- The credit controller regularly bypasses the set system for contacting debtors and arranging payment terms and instead depends to a large extent on debtors contacting her.

2.10　In the above example, the auditors who have undertaken the review would give a modified opinion. They would have to conclude that the system is not operated efficiently and cash is received less promptly than is possible in certain circumstances.

2.11　If the terms of the assignment require it, the report could then go on and make recommendations. In this case, there are two clear recommendations that could be made.

- Undertake a system of credit checks an assigning credit limits
- Ensure that the credit controller carries out her job in accordance with company policy

3 COMMUNICATION OF AUDIT MATTERS TO THOSE CHARGED WITH GOVERNANCE

KEY TERMS

Those charged with governance are those persons entrusted with the supervision, control and direction of an entity. Those charged with governance include the directors of a company or other body, the partners, proprietors, committee of management or trustees or other forms of entity, or equivalent persons responsible for directing the entity's affairs and preparing its financial statements.

Management is those persons who have executive responsibility for the conduct of the entity's operations and the preparation of its financial statements.

3.1 **External auditors** are required by auditing standards to communicated matters arising from the audit with those charged with governance. Guidance is given in SAS 610 *Communication of audit matters to those charged with governance*.

SAS 610.1

Auditors should communicate relevant matters relating to the audit of the financial statements to those charged with governance of the entity. Such communications should be on a sufficiently prompt basis to enable those charged with governance to take appropriate action.

3.2 In Chapter 5 we discussed the importance of ensuring mutual understanding between client and auditor concerning the terms of the engagement. This SAS points to the need for **mutual understanding** of the **scope of the audit** and the **respective responsibilities** of the auditors and those charged with governance in the entity.

3.3 It is also important to the audit process that the two parties **share available information,** and that the auditors can make **constructive observations** to the entity.

The communication process

3.4 Many of the factors in the communication process, such as, 'to whom?' 'when?' 'how often?', will depend on the size of the entity and the environment in which it operates.

3.5 The SAS gives the following guidance.

SAS 610.2

Auditors should plan with those charged with governance the form and timing of communications to them and determine whether there are particular persons to whim they should communicate certain matters.

3.6 The **addressees** of such a communication might be the **board of directors,** or the **audit committee.** The SAS states that, **ordinarily,** before discussing matters with those charged with governance, the auditors are likely to **discuss them with management.**

3.7 Similarly, the **form** of the communication will depend upon circumstances. It may be **written** or **oral**. Matters to consider are:

- The size, structure, and communication process of the entity
- The nature, sensitivity and significance of the matters arising
- Statutory or regulatory requirements
- Arrangements made by the parties, as outlined above

Relevant matters

Matters of independence and objectivity

SAS 610.3

At least annually, for all audit engagements where the audited company is a listed company, auditors should:

(a) disclose in writing to the audit committee, and discuss as appropriate:

- all relationships between the audit firm and its related entities and the client entity and its related entities that may reasonable be thought to bear on the firm's independence and the objectivity of the audit engagement partner and the audit staff; and

- the related safeguards that are in place; and

(b) where this is the case, confirm in writing to the audit committee that, in their professional judgement, the firm is independent within the meaning of the regulatory and professional requirements and the objectivity of the audit engagement partner and audit staff is not impaired.

Planning matters

SAS 610.4

Auditors should communicate to those charged with governance an outline of the nature and scope, including, where relevant, any limitations thereon, of the work they propose to undertake and the form of the reports they expect to make.

3.8 Such matters might include materiality, material misstatements, approach to internal controls, extent to which external auditors intend to rely on internal auditors and any work to be undertaken by other auditors.

Audit findings

SAS 610.5

Auditors should communicate to those charged with governance:

(a)   expected modifications to the auditors' report;

(b)   unadjusted misstatements;

(c)   material weaknesses in the accounting and internal control systems identified during the audit;

(d)   their views about the qualitative aspects of the entity's accounting practices and financial reporting;

(e)   matters specifically required by other Auditing Standards to be communicated to those charged with governance; and

(f)   any other relevant matters relating to the audit.

3.9   The auditors should discuss significant misstatements with those charged with governance. It might be that the auditors want the financial statements amended, while the directors do not want to make amendments.

3.10   If this is the case, the SAS advises that the auditors seek confirmation of their reasons.

SAS 610.6

Auditors should seek to obtain a written representation from those charged with governance that explains their reasons for not adjusting material misstatements brought to their attention by the auditors.

Third parties

3.11   There may be occasion when third parties are interested in the report to those charged with governance. The auditor should ensure that the recipients of the letter understand that it is not intended for third parties.

3.12   It might be appropriate to include a **disclaimer** in the letter, stating that it is for the sole use of the addressee and must not be quoted or referred to without the written consent of the auditor.

4   REPORTING CONTROL WEAKNESS   Dec 01

4.1   One of the matters which the external auditor is required to report on by SAS 610 is the area of weaknesses in control systems. This was the area that the old SAS 610 concentrated on.

4.2   Although this guidance has now been withdrawn as mandatory audit practice, the advice it contained is relevant to external and internal auditors alike reporting on control weakness, so we shall consider it here.

Report to management   **Pilot paper**

4.3   External auditors should report any weaknesses discovered in the system of internal control to the management of the company as part of their audit communications. This report usually takes the form of a **letter**, but other types of report are acceptable.

4.4   Such a report to management is **not** a substitute for a qualified audit report (see Chapter 19), when such a qualification is required. Inconsistencies between reports to management and the auditors' report should be avoided.

Material weaknesses in the accounting and internal control systems

4.5   When material weaknesses in the accounting and internal control systems are identified during the audit, auditors should **report them in writing** to management on a **timely basis**.

4.6   A **material weakness** is one which may result in a **material misstatement** in the financial statements. If it is corrected by management, it need not be reported, but the discovery and correction should be documented

4.7   To be effective, the report should be made **as soon as possible** after **completion** of the audit procedures. A written report is usual, but some matters may be raised orally with a file note to record the auditors' observation and the directors' response.

4.8   Where no report is felt to be necessary, the auditors should inform the directors that no material weaknesses have been found.

4.9   Where the audit work is performed on more than one visit, the auditors will **normally report** to management **after the interim audit work** has been completed as well as after the final visit.

Other matters

4.10   If the auditors choose not to send a formal letter or report but consider it preferable to discuss any weaknesses with management, the discussion should be **minuted** or otherwise recorded in writing. Management should be provided with a copy of the note.

4.11   The auditors should explain in their report that it **only** includes those matters which **came to their attention** as a result of the audit procedures, and that it **should not be regarded as a comprehensive statement of all weaknesses** that exist or all improvements that might be made.

4.12   The auditors should request a **reply** to all the points raised, indicating what action management intends to take as a result of the comments made in the report.

4.13   If **previous points** have **not been dealt with effectively** and they are still considered significant, the auditors should enquire why action has not been taken.

4.14   The report may contain matters of varying levels of significance and thus make it difficult for senior management to identify points of significance. The auditors can deal with this by giving the report a **'tiered' structure** so that major points are dealt with by the directors or the audit committee and minor points are considered by less senior personnel.

4.15   Other points to note about such a report are as follows.

- The recommendations should take the form of **suggestions** backed up by **reason and logic**.

- The letter should be in **formal terms** unless the client requests otherwise.

- **Weaknesses** that **management** are aware of but **choose not to do anything about** should be **mentioned** to protect the auditors.

- If management or staff have **agreed to changes,** this should be mentioned in a letter.

Specimen letter

4.16 A specimen letter is provided below which demonstrates how the principles described in the previous paragraphs are put into practice. This could form part of a more extensive communication to those charged with governance as discussed in section 3.

Exam focus point

You may be asked to draft paragraphs for such a report in the exam. You should follow the format we have used. The pilot paper contained 6 marks on items to be included in a report to management.

SPECIMEN MANAGEMENT LETTER

AB & Co
Certified Accountants
29 High Street
London, N10 4KB

The Board of Directors,
Manufacturing Co Limited,
15 South Street
London, S20 1CX

1 April 20X8

Members of the board,

Financial statements for the year ended 31 May 20X8

In accordance with our normal practice we set out in this letter certain matters which arose as a result of our review of the accounting systems and procedures operated by your company during our recent interim audit.

We would point out that the matters dealt with in this letter came to our notice during the conduct of our normal audit procedures which are designed primarily for the purpose of expressing our opinion on the financial statements of your company. In consequence our work did not encompass a detailed review of all aspects of the system and cannot be relied on necessarily to disclose defalcations or other irregularities or to include all possible improvements in internal control.

1 *Purchases: ordering procedures*

Present system
During the course of our work we discovered that it was the practice of the stores to order certain goods from X Ltd orally without preparing either a purchase requisition or purchase order.

Implications
There is therefore the possibility of liabilities being set up for unauthorised items and at a non-competitive price.

Recommendations
We recommend that the buying department should be responsible for such orders and, if they are placed orally, an official order should be raised as confirmation.

---

2   *Purchase ledger reconciliation*

Present system

Although your procedures require that the purchase ledger is reconciled against the control account on the nominal ledger at the end of every month, this was not done in December or January.

Implications

The balance on the purchase ledger was short by some £2,120 of the nominal ledger control account at 31 January 20X8 for which no explanation could be offered. This implies a serious breakdown in the purchase invoice and/or cash payment batching and posting procedures.

Recommendations

It is important in future that this reconciliation is performed regularly by a responsible official independent of the day to day purchase ledger, cashier and nominal ledger functions.

3   *Sales ledger: credit control*

Present system

As at 28 February 20X8 debtors account for approximately 12 weeks' sales, although your standard credit terms are cash within 30 days of statement, equivalent to an average of about 40 days (6 weeks) of sales.

Implications

This has resulted in increased overdraft usage and difficulty in settling some key suppliers accounts on time.

Recommendations

We recommend that a more structured system of debt collection be considered using standard letters and that statements should be sent out a week earlier if possible.

4   *Preparation of payroll and maintenance of personnel records*

Present system

Under your present system, just two members of staff are entirely and equally responsible for the maintenance of personnel records and preparation of the payroll. Furthermore, the only independent check of any nature on the payroll is that the chief accountant confirms that the amount of the wages cheque presented to him for signature agrees with the total of the net wages column in the payroll. This latter check does not involve any consideration of the reasonableness of the amount of the total net wages cheque or the monies being shown as due to individual employees.

Implications

It is a serious weakness of your present system, that so much responsibility is vested in the hands of just two people. This situation is made worse by the fact that there is no clearly defined division of duties as between the two of them. In our opinion, it would be far too easy for fraud to take place in this area (eg by inserting the names of 'dummy workmen' into the personnel records and hence on to the payroll) and/or for clerical errors to go undetected.

Recommendations

(i)   Some person other than the two wages clerks be made responsible for maintaining the personnel records and for periodically (but on a surprise basis) checking them against the details on the payroll;

(ii)   The two wages clerks be allocated specific duties in relation to the preparation of the payroll, with each clerk independently reviewing the work of the other;

(iii) When the payroll is presented in support of the cheque for signature to the chief accountant, that he should be responsible for assessing the reasonableness of the overall charge for wages that week.

Our comments have been discussed with your finance director and the chief accountant and these matters will be considered by us again during future audits. We look forward to receiving your comments on the points made. Should you require any further information or explanations do not hesitate to contact us.

This letter has been produced for the sole use of your company. It must not be disclosed to a third party, or quoted or referred to, without our written consent. No responsibility is assumed by us to any other person.

We should like to take this opportunity of thanking your staff for their co-operation and assistance during the course of our audit.

Yours faithfully

ABC & Co

Question 1

During the post-audit meeting at Auckland Limited, one of the directors has asked why auditors produce a management letter, as he thought that the auditors only produced an audit report.

Write a letter to the director, Mr Venkataraghavan, indicating why auditors produce a management letter, and describe briefly its advantages and disadvantages.

Answer

Mr A Venkataraghavan
Auckland Limited
51 Central Street
Westnorth, Southshire
WN2 1SW

21 July 20X0

Dear Mr Venkataraghavan

I am writing to answer your queries about the purposes of a management letter.

Purposes

Auditors are required by auditing guidance to communicate audit matters with those charged with governance. The main purposes of a management letter are for us as auditors to communicate information and suggestions:

(a) On the design and operation of internal control systems and to make suggestions for their improvement

(b) For improvements in the economy and efficiency of the use of the company's resources

(c) On adjusted or unadjusted errors in the accounts or on specific accounting policies

(d) Of problems during the audit which may have prolonged the audit and resulted in increased costs

(e) Of significant differences between the financial accounts and management accounts which may limit the usefulness of the management accounts

(f) Of any results of our analytical procedures which we believe will be of use to management

These matters would not necessarily lead to the audit report being qualified, but we believe our suggestions in these areas will benefit management.

Advantages and disadvantages

The main advantages of a management letter are:

(a) The letter shows that we have been doing during the audit and what we have found. It is thus a very important means of communication between ourselves and yourselves.

(b) The letter contains suggestions we make having used our experience and knowledge of the business environment.

(c) As indicated above, the suggestions we make cover matters other than those which are mentioned in our audit report.

Yours faithfully

ABC & Co

Chapter roundup

- In the UK, there is no guidance on reporting on external review assignments. There is international guidance, however.

- Assurance is given in the form of negative assurance. Apart from this, the internationally accepted format is very similar to the statutory audit opinions.

- Reports made as a result of internal audits or reviews may take two forms:
  - Specific reports in response to a particular issue
  - General reports concerning business performance

- There are not formal reporting requirements for internal review reports in the UK.

- A specific example of a general report could be the external auditors' communication of audit matters to those charged with goverance, which is a by-produce of the controls testing stage of the external audit.

- Guidance on the format of such communications is given in SAS 610 *Communication of audit matters to those charged with governance.*

- The old guidance about reporting to management, while no longer mandatory for external auditors can be useful for internal and external auditors alike when reporting on control weakness.

Quick quiz

1   Complete the definition.

.... is moderate assurance given by auditors when no matters have come to their attention to indicate .... do not give a .... and .... view.

2   Give three examples of an entity's operations which could be subject to an internal review.

1   ....

2   ....

3   ....

3   There are formal reporting requirements in the UK for internal review reports.

True   ☐

False   ☐

4   What are the six matters which a report under SAS 610 should contain?

1   ....

2   ....

3   ....

4   ....

5   ....

6   ....

5   Auditors can never be liable to third parties on the basis of information contained within the report communicating audit matters to those charged with governance.

True   ☐

False   ☐

Answers to quick quiz

1   Negative assurance, financial statements, true, fair

2   See para 1.3

3   False

4   Unexpected modifications to the audit report
    Unadjusted misstatements
    Material weaknesses in accounting and internal control systems
    Qualitative aspects of accounting policies and financial reporting
    Other matters required to be communicated by other auditing standards
    Other relevant matters

5   False - so they are advised to insert disclaimers and limitations on their liability in the report

Now try the question below from the Exam Question Bank

Number	Level	Marks	Time
20	Introductory	n/a	20 mins

Part F
Not for profit organisations

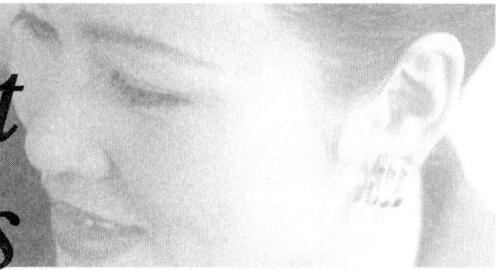

Chapter 21

NOT FOR PROFIT ORGANISATIONS

Topic list	Syllabus reference
1 Charities	6
2 Public sector	6

Introduction

This chapter looks at the audit of two not for profit organisations. Remember, that such entities may be required to have a **statutory audit** under legislation. Alternatively, they may choose to have a **non statutory audit** under the terms of a charitable deed, or as part of good practice.

Once thing an auditor should do when conducting a non statutory audit is confirm that a statutory opinion is not required.

The points made in this chapter about the issues inherent in these entities are **relevant for any kind of assurance work in not for profit organisations**, that is, internal auditors and external auditors undertaking audits or reviews. These entities will have inherent features, the most obvious being the difference in objective of the entity, which will **affect the way the work is carried out**.

Study guide

Section 28

- Apply audit and review techniques to small not-for-profit organisations

- Explain how the audit and review of small not-for profit organisations differed from the audit and review of for-profit organisations.

Exam guide

The study guide refers to questions being about small not-for-profit organisations, so it seems reasonable to expect one.

1   CHARITIES

1.1   Charities are a common form of not-for-profit organisations, so we will consider them first.

1.2   Section 96(1) of the Charities Act 1993 states that, unless the context otherwise requires, 'charity' means:

> '... Any institution, corporate or not, which is established for charitable purposes and is subject to the control of the High Court in the exercise of the court's jurisdiction with respect to charities'.

1.3   A layman's guide to the meaning of 'charitable purposes' was given by Lord MacNaghten in *Pemsel's Case* in 1891 where he suggested four main divisions.

- The relief of poverty
- The advancement of education

- The advancement of religion
- Other purposes beneficial to the community not above

Legal status and constitution

1.4 The objects of a charity will be set out in its constitution. Clearly, the activities performed by the charity should accord with its objects, but they must also be within the categories of charitable purposes defined above.

Regulatory bodies

1.5 If the Charity Commissioners are satisfied that an institution applying for registration is established for exclusively charitable purposes they will register it.

Fiscal provisions affecting charities

1.6 The auditors should ensure that they are aware of any **changes in legislation** which may alter the various forms of relief and tax advantages which may be enjoyed by charities.

Contents of accounts

1.7 The Charity Statement of Recommended Practice (SORP) states that the accounts should comprise:

(a) A **statement of financial activities** (SOFA) that shows all resources made available to the charity and all expenditure incurred and reconciles all changes in its funds

(b) Where the charity is required to prepare accounts in accordance with the 1985 Companies Act, or similar legislation, or where the governing instrument so requires, a **summary income and expenditure account** (in addition to the SOFA) in certain circumstances

(c) A **balance sheet** that shows the assets, liabilities and funds of the charity. The balance sheet (or its notes, see (e) below) should also explain, in general terms, how the funds may or, because of restrictions imposed by donors, must be utilised

(d) A **cash flow statement**, where required by FRS 1

(e) **Notes**

Duties of the statutory auditors

1.8 The auditors are required to give an opinion as to the **truth and fairness** of the accounts, and state whether they comply with the relevant regulations. Many of the usual 'exception reporting' rules apply.

Practice Note

1.9 The Auditing Practices Board published a Practice Note *'The Audit of Charities'* in October 1996. This covered the main problems faced by charity auditors and also how SASs apply to the audit of charities. Although the Practice Note is not examinable, it provides **practical illustrations** of how SASs can be applied in practice, and hence is discussed here.

1.10 Where an audit is required, its scope should be defined in a suitably worded **letter of engagement**. Where an opinion is not to be expressed on the truth and fairness of the financial statements but as to whether they comply with regulations governing the charity's operations, the precise wording of these regulations will govern the scope of the engagement.

The auditors' operational approach

1.11 Where the charity is a company, a friendly or an industrial and provident society or in many cases where it is incorporated by special Act of Parliament, the minimum audit requirements are laid down by statute.

1.12 In other cases, the constitutional documents should be examined to determine audit requirements and discussions held with the trustees of the charity.

Problem areas

Donations

1.13 Donations can cause several problems for charities.

(a) Unlike the income of commercial entities, donations will not be supported by invoice or equivalent documentation.

(b) The level of donations cannot be predicted accurately; people's pattern of giving may change, and it is difficult to establish a relationship between donations and other figures in the accounts.

(c) Valuing assets given in kind can be difficult.

Trustees therefore need to institute appropriate controls.

Legacies

1.14 These may give rise to problems of income recognition. Charities should include legacies in their accounts when they become entitled to them and the amounts can be measured.

Grants

1.15 Grants are usually made for specific purposes and are subject to conditions, which, if the charity breaks them, can have serious consequences.

Restricted funds

1.16 Tests will need to be designed to confirm that these funds have been correctly accounted for, and applied in accordance with, the conditions or restrictions attached to them. Different materiality levels may be applied to specific funds from those used on the figures on the main fund.

Grants to beneficiaries

1.17 The auditors should confirm that the *bona fides* of the recipient has been established. For example, the auditors will look for evidence of the *bona fides* of a sample of grants made by the charity, and scrutinise all grants of an unusual size or nature.

Branches

1.18 Charities' use of branches vary. The accounting and audit treatment of branches vary according to their legal form, but the charities' SORP does require branches to be included within the charities' main accounts. Auditors will be particularly concerned with the degree of control exercised by charities over branches.

Planning

1.19 However, some specific issues are work raising here. When planning the audit of a charity the auditors should particularly consider the following.

- The **scope** of the audit
- Recent **recommendations** of the **Charity Commissioners** or the other regulatory bodies
- The **acceptability of accounting policies** adopted
- **Changes in circumstances** in the sector in which the charity operates
- **Past experience** of the effectiveness of the charity's accounting system
- **Key audit areas**
- The **amount of detail included** in the financial statements on which the auditors are required to report

Inherent risk

Key factors include:

- The complexity and extent of regulation
- The significance of donations and cash receipts
- Difficulties of the charity in establishing ownership and timing of voluntary income where funds are raised by non-controlled bodies
- Lack of predictable income or precisely identifiable relationship between expenditure and income
- Uncertainty of future income
- Restrictions imposed by the objectives and powers given by charities' governing documents
- The importance of restricted funds
- The extent and nature of trading activities must be compatible with the entity's charitable status
- The complexity of tax rules (whether Income, Capital, Value Added or local rates) relating to charities
- The sensitivity of certain key statistics, such as the proportion of resources used in administration
- The need to maintain adequate resources for future expenditure while avoiding the build up of reserves which could appear excessive

Control risk

Key factors include:

- The amount of time committed by trustees to the charity's affairs
- The skills and qualifications of individual trustees
- The frequency and regularity of trustee meetings
- The form and content of trustee meetings
- The independence of trustees from each other
- The division of duties between trustees
- The degree of involvement in, or supervision of, the charity's transactions on the part of individual trustees

Control environment

Key elements are:

- A recognised plan of the charity's structure showing clearly the areas of responsibility and lines of authority and reporting

- Segregation of duties

- Supervision by trustees of activities of staff where segregation of duties is not practical

- Competence, training and qualification of paid staff and any volunteers appropriate to the tasks they have to perform

- Involvement of the trustees in the recruitment, appointment and supervision of senior executives

- Access of trustees to independent professional advice where necessary

- Budgetary controls in the form of estimates of income and expenditure for each financial year and comparison of actual results with the estimates on a regular basis

- Communication of results of such reviews to the trustees on a regular basis

Internal controls

1.20   Small charities will generally suffer from internal control weaknesses common to small enterprises, such as **lack of segregation of duties** and use of **unqualified staff**. Shortcomings may arise from the staff's lack of training and also, if they are volunteers, from their attitude, in that they may resent formal procedures.

1.21   The auditors will have to consider particularly carefully whether they will be able to obtain adequate assurance that the accounting records do reflect all the transactions of the enterprise.

1.22   In considering internal controls the auditors should bear in mind any related reporting requirements. For example, the Friendly Societies Act 1974 requires the auditors to state in their report if a satisfactory system of control over transactions has not been maintained.

1.23   The sorts of internal control which might be typical of a number of charities are given in the Practice Note.

Cash donations	
Source	*Examples of controls*
Collecting boxes and tins	Numerical control over boxes and tins
	Satisfactory sealing of boxes and tins so that any opening prior to recording cash is apparent
	Regular collection and recording of proceeds from collecting boxes
	Dual control over counting and recording of proceeds
Postal receipts	Unopened mail kept securely
	Dual control over the opening of mail
	Immediate recording of donations on opening of mail or receipt
	Agreement of bank paying-in slips to record of receipts by an independent person

Other donations

Source	Examples of controls
Deeds of covenant	Regular checks and follow-up procedures to ensure due amounts are received
	Regular checks to ensure all tax repayments have been obtained
Legacies	Comprehensive correspondence files maintained in respect of each legacy,
	Regular reports and follow-up procedures undertaken in respect of outstanding legacies
Donations in kind	In case of charity shops, separation of recording, storage and sale of stock

Other income

Source	Examples of controls
Fund-raising activities	Records maintained for each fund-raising event
	Other appropriate controls maintained over receipts
	Controls maintained over expenses as for administrative expenses
Central and local government grants and loans	Regular checks that all sources of income or funds are fully utilised and appropriate claims made
	Ensuring income or funds are correctly applied

Use of resources

Resource	Examples of controls
Restricted funds	Separate records maintained of relevant revenue, expenditure and assets
	Terms controlling application of fund
	Oversight of application of fund money's by independent personnel or trustees
Grants to beneficiaries	Records maintained, as appropriate, of requests for material grants received and their treatment
	Appropriate checks made on applications and applicants for grants, and that amounts paid are intra vires
	Records maintained of all grant decisions, checking that proper authority exists, that adequate documentation is presented to decision-making meetings, and that any conflicts of interest are recorded
	Control to ensure grants made are properly spent by the recipient for the specified purpose, for example requirements for returns with supporting documentation or auditors' reports concerning expenditure, or monitoring visits

Audit evidence

1.24 When designing substantive procedures for charities the auditors should give special attention to the possibility of:

- **Understatement or incompleteness** of the **recording of all income** including gifts in kind, cash donations, and legacies

- **Overstatement of cash grants or expenses**

- **Misanalysis** or misuse in the application of funds

- **Misstatement** or omission of **assets** including donated properties and investments

- The existence of **restricted or uncontrollable funds** in foreign or independent branches

1.25 Completeness of income can be a particularly problematic area. The Practice Note highlights the main areas auditors may check:

- Loss of income through fraud
- Recognition of income from professional fund raisers
- Recognition of income from branches, associates or subsidiaries
- Income from informal fundraising groups
- Income from grants

Overall review of financial statements

1.26 The auditors must consider carefully whether the **accounting policies** adopted are **appropriate** to the activities, constitution and objectives of the charity, and are consistently applied, and whether the financial statements adequately disclose these policies and fairly present the state of affairs and the results for the accounting period.

1.27 In particular the auditors should consider the basis of disclosing income from fund-raising activities (for example net or gross), accounting for income and expenses (accruals or cash), the capitalising of expenditure on fixed assets, apportioning administrative expenditure, and recognising income from donations and legacies.

1.28 Charities without significant endowments or accumulated funds will often be dependent upon future income from voluntary sources. In these circumstances auditors may question whether a going concern basis of accounting is appropriate.

Reporting

Unqualified audit report expressed in 'true and fair' terms

REPORT OF THE AUDITORS TO THE TRUSTEES OF XYZ CHARITY

We have audited the financial statements on pages … to … which have been prepared under the historical cost convention [as modified by the revaluation of certain fixed assets] and the accounting policies set out on page …

Respective responsibilities of trustees and auditors

As described on page … you are responsible as trustees for the preparation of the financial statements. It is our responsibility to form an independent opinion, based on our audit, on those statements and to report our opinion to you. We have been appointed as auditors under section 43 of the Charities Act 1993 and report in accordance with regulations made under section 44 of that Act.

Basis of opinion

We conducted our audit in accordance with Auditing Standards issued by the Auditing Practices Board. An audit includes examination, on a test basis, of evidence relevant to the amounts and disclosures in the financial statements. It also includes an assessment of the significant estimates and judgements made in the preparation of the financial statements, and of whether the accounting policies are appropriate to the charity's circumstances, consistently applied and adequately disclosed.

We planned and performed our audit so as to obtain all the information and explanations which we considered necessary in order to provide us with sufficient evidence to give reasonable assurance that the financial statements are free from material misstatement, whether caused by fraud or other irregularity or error. In forming an opinion we also evaluated the overall adequacy of the presentation of information in the financial statements.

Opinion

In our opinion the financial statements give a true and fair view of the charity's state of affairs as at 31 December 20.. and of its incoming resources and application of resources in the year then ended and have been properly prepared in accordance with the Charities Act 1993.

Registered auditors   *Address*

Date

1.29   The Charities Practice Note should be read in conjunction with SAS 600.

1.30   The form of auditors' report and the persons to whom it will be addressed will depend on the constitution of the particular charity concerned.

1.31   For example, the auditors' report on the financial statements of a charity registered under the Companies Act is determined in accordance with the provisions of that Act and addressed to the members or appropriate governing body.

1.32   In other cases, where charities are not governed by statute, the auditors' report will be determined in accordance with the terms of the auditors' appointment. For example, it may be appropriate for the auditors' to report only that the financial statements have been prepared in compliance with regulations governing the charity's operations.

Question 1

You have recently been appointed audit of Links Famine Relief, a small registered charity which receives donations from individuals to provide food in famine areas in the world.

The charity is run by a voluntary management committee, which has monthly meetings, and it employs the following full-time staff:

(a)   A director, Mr Roberts, who suggests fund raising activities and payments for relief of famine, and implements the policies adopted by the management committee

(b)   A secretary (and bookkeeper), Mrs Beech, who deals with correspondence and keeps the accounting records

You are planning the audit of income of the charity for the year ended 5 April 20X7 and are considering the controls which should be exercised over income.

The previous year's accounts, to 5 April 20X6 (which have been audited by another firm) show the following income.

	£	£
Deeds of covenant by bankers order		14,745
Tax reclaimed on covenants (1/3 of net income)		4,915
		19,660
Donations through the post		63,452
Autumn Fair		2,671
Other income		
Legacies	7,538	
Bank deposit account interest	2,774	
		10,312
		96,095

Notes

(a)   Income from deeds of covenant is stated net. Each person who pays by deed of covenant has filled in a deed of covenant form, which is kept by the secretary, Mrs Beech.

(b)   All deeds of covenant are paid by banker's order - they are credited directly to the charity's bank account from the donor's bank. Donors make their payments by deed of covenant either monthly or annually.

(c)   The tax reclaimed on deeds of covenant is 1/3 of the net value of the covenants, and relates to covenant income received during the year - as the tax is received after the year-end, an appropriate debtor is included in the balance sheet. The covenant treasurer, who is a voluntary (unpaid) member of the management committee, completes the form for reclaiming the income tax, using the deed of covenant forms (in (a) above) and he checks to the full-time secretary's records that each donor has made the full payment in the year required by the deed of covenant.

(d)   Donations received through the post are dealt with by Mrs Beech, the full-time secretary. These donations are either cheques or cash (bank notes and coins). Mrs Beech prepares a daily list of donations received, which lists the cheques received and total cash (divided between the different denominations of bank note and coin). The total on this form is recorded in the cash book. She then prepares a paying-in slip and banks these donations daily. When there is a special fund-raising campaign, Mrs Beech receives help in dealing with these donations from voluntary members of the management committee.

(e)   The Autumn Fair takes place every year on a Saturday in October - members of the management committee and other supporters of the charity give items to sell (for example food, garden plants, clothing) - a charge is made for entrance to the fair and coffee and biscuits are available at a small charge. At the end of the fair, Mrs Beech collects the takings from each of the stalls, and she banks them the following Monday.

(f)   Legacies are received irregularly, and are usually sent direct to the director of the charity, who gives them to Mrs Beech for banking - they are stated separately on the daily bankings form (in (d) above).

(g)   Bank deposit account interest is paid gross by the bank, as the Links Famine Relief is a charity.

Required

List and briefly describe the work you would carry out on the audit of income of the charity, the controls you would expect to see in operation and the problems you may experience for the following sources of income, as detailed in the income statement above.

(a)   Deeds of covenant by bankers order
(b)   Tax reclaimed on covenants
(c)   Donations received through the post
(d)   Autumn Fair
(e)   Other income

Answer

The audit consideration in relation to the various sources of income of the Links Famine Relief charity would be as follows.

(a)   *Deeds of covenant*

This type of income should not present any particular audit problem as the donations are made by banker's order direct to the charity's bank account and so it would be difficult for such income to be 'intercepted' and misappropriated.

Specific tests required would be as follows.

(i) Check a sample of receipts from the bank statements to the cash book to ensure that the income has been properly recorded.

(ii) Check a sample of the receipts to the deed of covenant forms to ensure that the full amount due has been received.

Any discrepancies revealed by either of the above tests should be followed up with Mrs Beech.

(b) *Tax reclaimed on covenants*

Once again this income should not pose any particular audit problems. The auditors should check the claim form submitted to the Inland Revenue and ensure that the amount of the claim represents $1/3$ of the net value of the covenants recorded as having been received.

(c) *Donations received through the post*

There is a serious problem here as the nature of this income is not predictable and also because of the lack of internal check with Mrs Beech being almost entirely responsible for the receipt of these monies, the recording of the income and the banking of the cash and cheques received. The auditors may ultimately have to express a qualified opinion relating to the uncertainty surrounding the completeness of income of this type.

Notwithstanding the above reservations, specific audit tests required would be as follows.

(i) Check the details on the daily listings of donations received to the cash book, bank statements and paying-in slips, ensuring that the details agree in all respects and that there is no evidence of any delay in the banking of this income.

(ii) Check the donations received by reference to any correspondence which may have been received with the cheques or cash.

(iii) Consider whether the level of income appears reasonable in comparison with previous years and in the light of any special appeals that the charity is known to have made during the course of the year.

(iv) Carry out, with permission of the management committee, surprise checks to vouch the completeness and accuracy of the procedures relating to this source of income.

(d) *Autumn fair*

Once again there is a potential problem here because of the level of responsibility vested in one person, namely Mrs Beech.

Specific work required would be as follows.

(i) Attend the event to observe the proper application of laid down procedures and count the cash at the end of the day.

(ii) Check any records maintained by individual stallholders to the summary prepared by Mrs Beech.

(iii) Check the vouchers supporting any expenditure deducted from the proceeds in order to arrive at the net bankings.

(iv) Agree the summary prepared by Mrs Beech to the entry in the cash book and on the bank statement.

(e) *Other income*

The unpredictable nature of legacies means that as with donations, it will be difficult to check the completeness of this source of income. There should be no particular problem relating to bank deposit interest.

Specific work required would be as follows.

(i) Check legacies received to entries in the cash book, paying-in slips, bank statements and any other supporting evidence, such as correspondence with the executors of the donor's estate.

(ii) Check bank deposit interest to the bank statement and obtain direct confirmation of the amount involved from the charity's bankers.

2   PUBLIC SECTOR

2.1   Another type of organisation which might operate as not-for-profit organisations are public sector organisations. We will consider these briefly here also.

2.2   The public sector in the UK comprises a great variety of organisations. They all **must have their accounts audited by an independent external auditor,** in order to provide external accountability to the community at large.

2.3   In the public sector there is a **tendency for an external audit to cover a much wider scope than in the private sector.** The scope of public sector audit includes not only auditing of **financial records** and auditing to check **compliance with regulations** but also auditing the **achievement of economy, efficiency and effectiveness.**

2.4   The audit is an important part of public accountability and it provides an independent check on how **public funds** have been raised and spent. More specifically audit is needed to ensure that:

- **Public funds** have been **spent** on **proper, authorised purposes** and **legally within statutory powers.**

- Organisations **install and operate controls** to limit the possibility of corrupt practice, fraud and poor administration.

- Arrangements are in place to secure **economy, efficiency and effectiveness** in the use of resources.

External auditors in the public sector

2.5   The table below summarises the position on who acts as auditor in the various parts of the public sector.

	National Audit Office	Audit Commission	Monopolies and Mergers Commission	Private sector firms
Central departments	All	-	-	-
Non-departmental public bodies	Most	-	-	A few
Nationalised industries	-	-	VFM	All
Local authorities	-	Most	-	Some
Health authorities	Rights of access and inspection	Most	-	Some
Universities	Rights of access and inspection	-	-	All

The regulatory framework

2.6   The public sector is subject to a **high degree of regulation** including statutory regulations and detailed administrative requirements. For most public sector audits, the scope and objectives of the audit are affected by the **interests and requirements of certain third party organisations** such as audit **supervisory bodies** and **government sponsoring departments** which have specific regulatory responsibilities.

Exam focus point

Not-for-profit organisations can be very large organisations or they can be small. If you are given a question on a small not-for-profit organisations, remember to bear in mind the points madeabout smaller entities throughout this Text.

Chapter roundup

- Guidance is given on the audit of charities in a Practice Note, 'The audit of charities'.

- The problem area when auditing charities is often income.

  ○   Little documentation
  ○   Unpredictability
  ○   Valuation

- There are specific risks attaching to charities stemming from issues such as:

  ○   Regulation
  ○   Uncertainty of income
  ○   Size

- Internal controls can be a problem in charities particularly small ones, with segregation of duties being a particular problem.

Quick quiz

1   Give three reasons why income can be a problem when auditing charities.

1   ....

2   ....

3   ....

2   Complete the table, giving two examples of controls in each area.

Cash donations	Other donations	Other income

3   All limited companies must have a statutory audit.

True   ☐

False   ☐

Answers to quick quiz

1   See para 1.13

2   See para 1.23

3   False

Now try the question below from the Exam Question Bank

Number	Level	Marks	Time
21	Exam	20	36 mins

The scenario and requirement of this question have been analysed in some detail in the Exam Question Bank because as well as being a question on a not for profit organisation, it is an example of a question where you are asked to identify **audit risks**, which is a key skill for the exam.

Exam question bank

Examination standard questions are indicated by mark and time allocations.

1 PRINCETOWN AND YALE   *15 mins*

Princetown and Yale are in partnership. Previously accounts have been prepared by their bookkeeper but as their business is growing they are considering asking your firm to act as auditors to the partnership.

Required

(a)   State how a non-statutory audit could assist the partnership.

(b)   Identify the major difficulty you could potentially face in a non-statutory audit, and state how you would try to overcome it.

2 STANDARDS   *30 mins*

You are required to discuss the advantages and disadvantages of accounting and auditing standards to auditors and the consequences of such standards being enforceable by statute.

3 ROLE OF INTERNAL AUDIT (20 marks)   *36 mins*

(a)   You are a member of the internal audit team at Golden Holdings plc, a listed company. The board of directors wants to raise the profile of the internal audit department in the company. They have asked the internal audit department to give a series of seminars on the corporate governance and the role of internal audit in achieving corporate objectives to other members of staff.

The head of internal audit has asked you to prepare some notes on this subject.

Required

Prepare the notes which the head of internal audit wants.   (12 marks)

You should cover the following matters:

(i)   The Board of Directors
(ii)   Accountability
(iii)   The meaning of risk management

(b)   After the seminars, the various departments of Golden Holdings have been asked to carry out risk management brainstorming sessions to identify risks in each of their departments and to design internal control systems to reduce those risks. The sales director, Wayne, has asked you if you will attend the brainstorming session in the sales department and whether you will assist them in the risk identification and management process.

Required

Draft a memorandum to the Sales Director, answering his questions.   (8 marks)

You should cover the following matters

(i)   Whether you will attend the meeting, and in what capacity.

(ii)   Whether you attend the meeting or not, what involvement you, as a member of the internal audit team, will have in the risk management exercise.

4 OBJECTIVITY (20 marks)   *36 mins*

(a)   Explain the concept of objectivity, with reference to

(i)   External auditors
(ii)   Internal auditors, who are members of ACCA,

outlining any general threats to objectivity that exist.   (8 marks)

(b)   *Scenario 1*

Bakers Ltd is an audit client of Hinkley Innes, a firm of Chartered Certified Accountants. The firm has had the audit of Bakers for 17 years and the fee represents 7% of firm income. Bakers is considering a major new project and has asked the firm if it would be happy to undertake some one off consultancy work for the firm. It is possible that the fee income for this contract would represent 10% of that year's income for Hinkley Innes. The new business services partner, who

BPP
PUBLISHING

heads up a new division of the firm, is keen to take on the work, as this would represent his best contract yet.

Scenario 2

Peter works in the purchasing department of Murphy Manufacturing plc. He has been instrumental in setting up control systems in the purchasing department as part of a recent risk management exercise. He has a poor relationship with his immediate supervisor, the Purchasing Director. Murphy Manufacturing has just advertised the post of trainee internal auditor. Peter is interested in the work that internal audit do, having liased substantially with the department during the recent controls exercise. No formal accountancy qualifications are required for the post, because the successful candidate will be put through accountancy training. Peter has had a chat with the head of internal audit concerning the post and is seriously considering making an application.

Required

Discuss the threats and the safeguards to objectivity that could be implemented in the two situations given above. (12 marks)

5 NEW ENGAGEMENT
30 mins

Effective audit planning is essential to ensure both quality of service to the client and the minimising of risk to the practitioner.

Required

(a) What general points should auditors consider before accepting a new audit client?
(b) What is the purpose of the letter of engagement; what major matters should it refer to?

6 GLO (20 marks)
36 mins

Glo-Warm Ltd is a company which manufactures various heating products which it sells to both High Street and catalogue retailers.

The balance sheets for the years ended 2001 and 2002 are set out below. Last year, materiality was set at £10,000.

	2002 £'000	2002 £'000	2001 £'000	2001 £'000
Fixed Assets				
Tangible Fixed Assets		20		21
Investments		2		2
Current Assets				
Stock	52		179	
Debtors	78		136	
Cash at bank	12		34	
Cash in hand	1		1	
	143		350	
Creditors: amounts falling due within one year				
Trade creditor	121		133	
Bank loan	5		5	
	126		138	
Net current assets		17		212
Creditors: amounts falling due after more than one year				
Bank loan		(20)		(25)
Provision*		(20)		-
Total (liabilities)/assets		(1)		210
Capital and reserves				
Share capital		2		2
Profit and loss account		(3)		208
		(1)		210

*The provision of £20,000 consists entirely of a warranty provision.

Required

(a) Without carrying out any calculations, discuss whether the materiality level used in 2001 will be appropriate for this year's audit, giving reasons for your answer. (3 marks)

(b) Explain audit risk. (3 marks)

(c) Review the balance sheet given above and set out the areas on which audit work should be concentrated, giving reasons in each case. (14 marks)

7 USING THE WORK OF AN EXPERT (20 marks) *36 mins*

An auditing standard has been issued, SAS 520 *Using the work of an expert.*

You are carrying out the audit of Ravenshead Construction plc. The company's business includes large civil engineering contracts (the construction of buildings and roads). It also owns investment properties which are let to third parties and these comprise offices and industrial buildings.

During the year ended 31 October 20X6 the company received a substantial claim for damages from Netherfield Manufacturing plc for faults in a building it had constructed. This claim includes the cost of repairs and damages, as the customer alleges that the building cannot be used because of the faults, so alternative accommodation has had to be found. The company has obtained advice on the likely outcome of this claim from a local solicitor.

In the year end accounts the investment properties had been revalued by an independent valuer and the long-term contract work in progress has been valued by an employee of the company who is a qualified valuer.

Required

Describe the matters you would consider and the other evidence you would obtain to enable you to assess the reliability of the work of experts in the following cases:

(a) Legal advice obtained from the local solicitor on the outcome of the claim by Netherfield Manufacturing (7 marks)

(b) Valuation of the investment properties by the independent valuer (7 marks)

(c) Valuation of the long-term contract work in progress by the internal valuer (6 marks)

8 AUDIT EVIDENCE (20 marks) *36 mins*

(a) For each of the following substantive tests you are required to state, together with any limitations, whether they provide strong or weak evidence of the completeness, existence, accuracy and valuation and (where applicable) ownership of the asset or liability at the financial year end.

 (i) Inspecting inventories and testing perpetual records by making test counts and noting damaged, obsolete and slow moving items (6 marks)

 (ii) Vouching fixed assets additions to supporting documentation (3 marks)

 (iii) Verification of bank balances by bank confirmation request (4 marks)

(b) Explain why it is important that audit evidence is fully documented and list the details relating to the audit tests which should be recorded in the working papers. (7 marks)

9 INTERNAL CONTROLS (20 marks) *36 mins*

(a) State four objectives of an internal control system. (4 marks)

(b) Internal and external auditors may review internal control systems. Explain the reason for their reviews, distinguishing between them. (6 marks)

(c) Suggest the work an internal auditor could carry out to check procedures in a purchase system to minimise the risk of fraud and error. (5 marks)

(d) If the risk of fraud and error is assessed as higher than normal, how would that affect the work of an external auditor and an internal auditor? (5 marks)

10 FENTON DISTRIBUTORS (20 marks)   *36 mins*

Fenton Distributors Ltd is a small company which maintains its sales, purchase and nominal ledgers on a small PC, using a standard computerised accounting package. The company buys products from large manufacturers and sells them to shops which either sell or hire them to the general public. The products include drain clearing machines, portable generators, garden cultivators and wallpaper strippers.

You have been asked to carry out an audit of the nominal ledger system to verify that items are accurately recorded in the year. At the end of the year, the nominal ledger produces a trial balance, which is used to prepare the annual accounts.

The company employs a bookkeeper, who is responsible for posting the sales and purchase ledgers, and maintaining the nominal ledger. Data is posted to the nominal ledger as follows.

(a) At the start of the financial year, all the balances on the nominal ledger accounts are set to zero (using the standard year-end procedure of the computer package).

(b) The following procedures relate to purchase transactions.

(i) When invoices are posted to the purchase ledger, the purchase analysis code (for the nominal ledger), the purchases value and the VAT value are entered. The total invoice value is posted to the purchase ledger.

(ii) At the end of the month, the computer posts the following items to the nominal ledger.

(1) The total of each category of invoice expense and VAT for purchase invoices and credit notes posted in the month (at the same time the computer prints details of the individual invoices making up the total of each invoice expense and VAT for the month).

(2) The total of purchase ledger cash payments, discount received and adjustments posted to the purchase ledger in the month (the computer prints details of the individual items comprising the total cash discount and adjustments for the month).

(3) Where there is no account in the nominal ledger relating to the items being posted, the computer posts the items to a creditors suspense account. Also, all adjustments are posted to the suspense account.

(c) Sales ledger data is posted to the nominal ledger in a similar way to purchase ledger data.

(d) Journals are posted manually to the nominal ledger for:

(i) The opening balances at the start of the year
(ii) Other cash book items (other than sales and purchase ledger cash)
(iii) Petty cash payments
(iv) Wages analysis (details are obtained from the computerised payroll system)
(v) Adjustments, which include:

(1) Correction of errors

(2) Dealing with items in the sale and purchase ledger suspense accounts (adjustments posted to the ledger, and items where there is no account in the nominal ledger)

All these journals are written manually in an accounts journal book, and they must be authorised by the managing director before posting. The opening balances are posted to the nominal ledger when the previous year's accounts have been approved by the auditors. Although the employee wages are calculated using another computer package, the total wages expense is posted to the nominal ledger manually. The wages expense is calculated from the payroll's monthly summary, using a spreadsheet package, and the wages expense is analysed into directors, sales, warehouse and office wages (or salaries).

Your are required to list and describe the audit work you would perform on the computerised nominal ledger system, and in particular:

(a) The checks you would perform to verify the accuracy of purchases transactions which are posted to the nominal ledger.   (5 marks)

(b) The checks you would perform to verify the validity and accuracy of journals posted to the nominal ledger. Also, you should briefly describe any other checks you would perform to verify the accuracy of the year end balances on the nominal ledger.   (15 marks)

Note. You should assume that sales transactions are accurately recorded and correctly posted to the nominal ledger.

11 CHEQUE PAYMENTS AND PETTY CASH (20 marks)   *36 mins*

Mr A Black has recently acquired the controlling interest in Quicksand Ltd, who are importers of sportswear. In his review of the organisational structure of the company Mr Black became aware of weaknesses in the procedures for the signing of cheques and the operation of the petty cash system. Mr Black engages you as the company's auditor and requests that you review the controls over cheque payments and petty cash. He does not wish to be a cheque signatory himself because he feels that such a procedure is an inefficient use of his time. In addition to Mr Black, who is the managing director, the company employs 20 personnel including four other directors, and approximately three hundred cheques are drawn each month. The petty cash account normally has a working balance of about £300, and £600 is expended from the fund each month. Mr Black has again indicated that he is unwilling to participate in any internal control procedures which would ensure the efficient operation of the petty cash fund.

Required

(a) Prepare a letter to Mr Black containing your recommendations for good internal control procedures for:

    (i)   Cheque payments   (9 marks)
    (ii)   Petty cash   (7 marks)

    (Marks will be awarded for the style and layout of the answer.)

(b) Discuss the audit implications, if any, of the unwillingness of Mr Black to participate in the cheque signing procedures and petty cash function.   (4 marks)

12 ANALYTICAL REVIEW   *20 mins*

Explain the purpose of analytical review and at what stages of the audit it should be carried out.

13 BOSTON MANUFACTURING (20 marks)   *36 mins*

You are the audit assistant assigned to the audit of Boston Manufacturing. The audit senior has asked you to plan the audit of fixed assets. He has provisionally assessed materiality at £72,000.

Boston Manufacturing maintain a register of fixed assets. The management accountant reconciles a sample of entries to physical assets and vice versa on a three-monthly basis. Authorisation is required for all capital purchases. Items valued less than £10,000 can be authorised by the production manager, item costing more than £10,000 must be authorised by the Managing Director. The purchasing department will not place an order for capital goods unless it has been duly signed.

The company has invested in a large amount of new plant this year in connection with an 8 year project for a government department.

The management accountant has provided you with the following schedule of fixed assets:

	Land and buildings £	Plant and equipment £	Computers £	Motor vehicles £	Total £
Cost	*				
At 31 March 2001	500,000	75,034	30,207	54,723	659,964
		250,729	1,154		251,883
Additions					
At 31 March 2002	500,000	325,763	31,361	54,723	911,847
Accumulated depreciation					
At 31 March 2001	128,000	45,354	21,893	25,937	221,184
Charge for the year	8,000	28,340	2,367	13,081	51,788
At 31 March 2002	136,000	73,694	24,260	39,018	272,972
Net realisable value					
At 31 March 2002	364,000	252,069	7,101	15,705	638,875
At 31 March 2001	372,000	29,680	8,314	28,786	438,780

*Of which, £100,000 relates to land.

Required

(a) Without undertaking any calculations, assess the risk of the tangible fixed assets audit, drawing reasoned conclusions. (6 marks)

(b) Outline the audit procedures you would undertake on fixed assets in respect of the following assertions:

    (i)   Existence (3 marks)
    (ii)   Valuation (excluding depreciation) (4 marks)
    (iii)   Completeness (3 marks)

(c) Describe how you would assess the appropriateness of the depreciation rates. (4 marks)

14 SITTING PRETTY (20 marks) 36 mins

Sitting Pretty Ltd is a small, family run company that makes plastic chairs in a variety of shapes and colours for children and 'fun at heart' adults. It buys in sheets of plastic which can be cut and bent into the correct shape and a plastic leg that is custom made by another company to Sitting Pretty's requirements. All off-cut plastic is sent back to the supplier who melts it down and re-uses it, for which Sitting Pretty receive a 10% discount off their purchase price.

For the stocktake, the factory manager ensures that no work in progress is outstanding and closes down production for the day. The factory workers come in early on the day of the stocktake to count the stock, and they are entitled to go home as soon as stock is counted. Good controls have always been maintained over the stocktake in previous years. There are no perpetual stock records. Raw materials are all kept in the stores and are only taken out when they are required for production. Finished goods are kept in the end of the factory, near the delivery exit.

You are the audit assistant assigned to attend the stocktake. You have just rung the factory manager and he has mentioned that on the day of the stocktake a large consignment of plastic is going to be delivered. It is the only day that his supplier can make the delivery, and he needs the material to continue with production on the day after the stocktake.

The audit engagement partner has told you that he is aware that Sitting Pretty changed the specification of their customised leg recently, after a series of complaints over the stability of their chairs. Last year's stock was valued at £200,000 in the balance sheet, of which £30,000 related to raw material stocks.

Finished goods are all carried at the same valuation as each other as there is very little difference between the stock ranges. Planning materiality for this year has been set at £5,000 on the grounds, at this stage, that the figures are expected to be similar to last years.

Required

(a) Explain the importance of the stocktake in this situation. (3 marks)

(b) Prepare notes for your audit supervisor detailing the procedures you propose to undertake in relation to your stocktake attendance. (7 marks)

(c) Outline the procedures which should be taken in relation to cut off at the final audit. (5 marks)

(d) List the audit procedures you would carry out on the valuation of stock at the final audit. (5 marks)

15 BRIGHT SPARKS (20 marks) 36 mins

Bright Sparks Ltd distributes domestic electrical equipment from one warehouse. Customers are mainly installers of such equipment, but there is a 'cash and carry' counter in the warehouse for retail customers. The warehousemen are responsible for raising invoices and credit notes relating to credit sales as well as handling cash sales.

You have carried out your interim audit in respect of the year ending 31 December 20X0 which included a circularisation of 80 debtors as at 30 September 20X0 selected from a total credit customer list of 1,000. Replies were received from all debtors circularised. The interim audit work disclosed the following.

(a) Of the 80 customers accounts circularised, 8 disagreed but could be reconciled by bringing into account payments stated by the customers concerned to have been made before 30 September 20X0 but which in each case were recorded in Bright Sparks Ltd's books between 14 and 18 days after the dates stated by the customers as the date of payment.

(b) Your tests suggested that some 25% of credit customers were allowed settlement discounts of 2½% although payments were consistently received after the latest date eligible for discount.

(c) A large number of credit notes were raised representing approximately 12% of the total number of invoices raised. A review of the copy credit notes indicated that they usually arose from arithmetical and pricing errors on invoices raised.

You are required to set out the conclusions you would draw as a result of the interim audit and the work you would plan to carry out at the final audit on debtors at 31 December 20X0 based upon those conclusions.

16 NEWPIECE (20 marks)   *36 mins*

Your firm is the auditor of Newpiece Textiles Limited and you are auditing the financial statements for the year ended 31 October 19X7. The company has a turnover of £2.5 million and a profit before tax of £150,000.

(a) The company has supplied you with the following bank reconciliation at the year end. You have entered the 'date cleared' on the bank reconciliation, which is the date the cheques and deposits appeared on the November's bank statement.

				£	£
Balance per bank statement at 31 October 19X7					(9,865)
Add: deposits not credited					
CB date		*Type*	*Date cleared*		
31 Oct		SL	3 Nov	11,364	
24 Oct		CS	3 Nov	653	
27 Oct		CS	4 Nov	235	
28 Oct		CS	5 Nov	315	
29 Oct		CS	6 Nov	426	
30 Oct		CS	7 Nov	714	
31 Oct		CS	10 Nov	362	
					14,069
Less: uncleared cheques					
CB date	*Cheque no*	*Type*	*Date cleared*		
30 Oct	2163	CP	3 Nov	1,216	
31 Oct	2164	PL	18 Nov	10,312	
31 Oct	2165	PL	19 Nov	11,264	
31 Oct	2166	PL	18 Nov	9,732	
31 Oct	2167	PL	20 Nov	15,311	
31 Oct	2168	PL	21 Nov	8,671	
31 Oct	2169	PL	19 Nov	12,869	
31 Oct	2170	PL	21 Nov	9,342	
31 Oct	2171	CP	3 Nov	964	
					(79,681)
Balance per cash book at 31 October 19X7					(75,477)

Notes

1   'CB date' is the date the transaction was entered in the cash book

2   Type of transaction

SL   sales ledger receipt
CS   receipt from cash sales
PL   purchase ledger payment
CP   cheque payment (for other expenses)

3   All cheques for purchase ledger payments are written out at the end of the month.

Required

(i) Describe the matters which cause you concern from your scrutiny of the bank reconciliation.

(ii) Describe the investigations you will carry out on the items in the bank reconciliation which cause you concern.

(iii) Describe the adjustments you will probably require to be made to the financial statements if your investigations confirm the problems you have highlighted in (i) above. (10 marks)

(b) The manager in charge of the audit has asked you to consider the petty cash system and recommend what audit work may be necessary. You have found that petty cash is recorded in a hand written analysed petty cash book and it is not kept on an imprest system. From the petty cash book you have recorded the petty cash expenditure for each month.

		£
1996		
	November	855
	December	6,243
1997		
	January	972
	February	796
	March	893
	April	751
	May	986
	June	695
	July	749
	August	8,634
	September	948
	October	849
	Total	23,371

Required

(i) Advise the audit manager as to the desirability of performing further substantive procedures on petty cash. You should consider materiality and audit risk in relation to the petty cash system. (4 marks)

(ii) Assuming the audit manager decides that further audit work is necessary, describe the detailed substantive tests of transactions and balances you should carry out on the petty cash system. (6 marks)

17 **TRURO ELECTRONICS (20 marks)** *36 mins*

You are the audit senior in charge of the audit of Truro Electronics plc.

Required

State the audit procedures you would carry out to verify the following items appearing in the balance sheet at 31 March 20X8.

(a) Trade creditors £3,200,000
(b) Bank overdraft £2,100,000
(c) Corporation tax creditor £5,200,000
(d) Accruals £2,300,000
(e) Value Added Tax creditor £1,700,000

18 **GOING CONCERN (20 marks)** *36 mins*

Carrington Joinery Ltd is a private company, owned by its directors, which manufactures wooden window frames, doors and staircases for domestic houses. It has prepared draft accounts for the year ended 30 September 20X6 and you are concerned that they indicate serious going concern problems. The profit and loss accounts and balance sheets for the last five years (each ended 30 September) are given below.

PROFIT AND LOSS ACCOUNTS

	20X2	20X3	20X4	20X5	20X6
	£'000	£'000	£'000	£'000	£'000
Sales	625	787	1,121	1,661	1,881
Cost of sales	(478)	(701)	(962)	(1,326)	(1,510)
Gross profit	147	86	159	335	371
Other expenses	(88)	(86)	(161)	(240)	(288)
Interest	(6)	(9)	(58)	(90)	(117)
Net profit/(loss)	53	(9)	(60)	5	(34)

BALANCE SHEETS

	20X2	20X3	20X4	20X5	20X6
	£'000	£'000	£'000	£'000	£'000
Fixed assets	89	161	544	600	587
Current assets					
Stock	67	133	181	307	449
Debtors	91	240	303	313	364
	158	373	484	620	813
Current liabilities					
Creditors	90	317	355	490	641
Bank overdraft	10	65	211	269	365
Hire purchase creditor	14	28	98	92	59
	114	410	664	851	1,065
Net assets	133	124	364	369	335
Capital and reserves					
Share capital	17	17	17	17	17
Reserves	116	107	47	52	18
	133	124	64	69	35
Long term loan	-	-	300	300	300
	133	124	364	369	335

The company has been in business for about fifteen years. In January 20X3 it decided to build a new factory on a site leased from the local authority which would allow a major increase in sales. This new factory with new machinery was completed a year later. The factory was financed by a long-term loan of £300,000 from a merchant bank and an increase in the bank overdraft.

The loan from the merchant bank is secured by a fixed charge on the leasehold factory and the bank overdraft is secured by a second charge on the leasehold factory, a fixed charge on the other fixed assets and a floating charge on the current assets.

The company purchases its main raw material, wood, from timber wholesalers. It sells about 75% of its production to about twelve local and national builders of new domestic houses. The remaining sales are mainly to smaller builders with a very few sales to local builders merchants.

Required

(a) In relation to the accounts above, list and briefly describe the factors which indicate that the company may not be a going concern. You should also highlight certain figures and calculate relevant ratios in the accounts. (13 marks)

Note. You will only be given credit for going concern problems which can be determined from the accounts above.

(b) Describe the investigations and checks you would carry out, in addition to those described in part (a) above, to determine whether the company is a going concern. (7 marks)

19 **WISEGUYS NATIONAL BAKERIES (20 marks)**   *36 mins*

You firm acts as auditors of Wiseguys National Bakeries Ltd. The finance director has prepared the financial statements of the company for the year ended 31 December 20X3 which show a pre-tax profit of £450,000. You have been advised that the board of directors has approved the financial statements and decided that no amendments should be made thereto.

As partner responsible for the audit, you have noted the following matters during your review of the financial statements and the audit working papers.

(a) The freehold property which was included in cost in previous years' balance sheets has now been restated at a professional valuation of £1,250,000 carried out during the year. You are satisfied with the valuation, the relevant figures have been adjusted and the necessary information disclosed in the notes to the accounts.

(b) An amount of £45,000 due from a customer in respect of sales during the year is included in debtors but, from information made available to you, you conclude that no part of this debt will be recovered. No provision has been made against this amount.

(c) The financial statements do not disclose the fact that a director was indebted to the company for an amount of £22,000 during the period of six weeks commencing 1 February 20X3.

(d) A substantial claim was lodged against the company arising from a major breach of contract and alleged damage to a customer's business. No provision has been made for legal costs or compensation payable as it is not possible to determine with reasonable accuracy the amounts, if any, which may become payable. A satisfactory explanation of the circumstances is given in the notes to the accounts.

Required

Write a letter to the directors explaining how you propose to deal with the above matters in your audit report.

20 **EXTERNAL REVIEW REPORTS** *20 mins*

(a) Define negative assurance.

(b) Explain why an auditor gives negative assurance as a result of a review engagement.

(c) Explain what formats the external review report might take if:

    (i) Matters have come to the attention of the auditor which indicate a true and fair view is not given.

    (ii) There has been a limitation in the scope of the auditor's work.

You are an audit assistant in the firm Rogers and Smith. You have been asked to plan the audit of 'Tap!' for the year ended 30 June 2002. It is the first time your audit firm has audited the charity, which has not been audited previously. The trustees have expressed interest in receiving a 'value added' audit and are particularly interested in business advice, especially in the area of systems controls.

'Tap!' is a registered charity that raises money for projects building wells in Africa through musical entertainment in the UK. The group consists of volunteers who travel around the country, putting on variety shows of music and dance, the proceeds of which are put towards building the wells. The main show is an tap dance production, acting out the difficulties many people face when they are not near a clean water supply.

The administrative offices of 'Tap!' are located in Leicester. It owns a house, donated by legacy in the past, where the administration is carried out and where the volunteers stay during off periods.

A large proportion of 'Tap!"s income comes from box office receipts which are taken by the theatre at which they are performing. The theatres usually waive their standard terms for use of the premises and merely take a 10% commission on ticket receipts to cover light and heat and other such expenses. Income usually comes in after every booking in the form of a lump sum cheque from the theatre, together with a break down of takings and commission.

Tap also receives donations towards the work. These come from a variety of sources:

- Cash donations from buckets passed around at the interval of each performance
- Cash donations on the (rare) occasion that the team do street performances
- Cash donations made over the phone or by post by interested donors

The troupe consists largely of volunteers so they are only paid expenses for their work. The cost of housing the group while they are on the road is borne by the charity. The charity employs an administrator who organises bookings, handles publicity and co-ordinates all the finances.

Required

(a) Discuss the risks arising for the audit of the year ending 30 June 2002. (8 marks)

(b) Outline the audit procedures you would undertake in respect of cash income in the financial statements. (6 marks)

(c) Outline some controls over cash which the charity should implement. (6 marks)

Approaching the answer

You should read through the requirement before working through and annotating the question as we have so that you are aware what things you are looking for.

> First time audit for firm so little CAKE knowledge and experience.

> Impact on opening balances and comparatives.

You are an audit assistant in the firm Rogers and Smith. You have been asked to plan the audit of 'Tap!' for the year ended 30 June 2002. It is the first time your audit firm has audited the charity, which has not been audited previously. The trustees have expressed interest in receiving a 'value added' audit and are particularly interested in business advice, especially in the area of systems controls.

> Not just a simple audit. This may make the engagement too risky – given the potential bad publicity that could result if there were problems with the audit.

> High degree of regulation. Do we have any experience in this field?

> Where is the audit evidence? Also, is expenditure in line with the Trust Deed.

'Tap!' is a registered charity that raises money for projects building wells in Africa through musical entertainment in the UK. The group consists of volunteers who travel around the country, putting on variety shows of music and dance, the proceeds of which are put towards building the wells. The main show is an tap dance production, acting out the difficulties many people face when they are not near a clean water supply.

> Is this common? Are there restrictions on expenditure? Also ensure accounts are correct for disclosures.

The administrative offices of 'Tap!' are located in Leicester. It owns a house, donated by legacy in the past, where the administration is carried out and where the volunteers stay during off periods.

> How accounted?

> Trust?

A large proportion of 'Tap!'s income comes from box office receipts which are taken by the theatre at which they are performing. The theatres usually waive their standard terms for use of the premises and merely take a 10% commission on ticket receipts to cover light and heat and other such expenses. Income usually comes in after every booking in the form of a lump sum cheque from the theatre, together with a break down of takings and commission.

> Again cash. Also, poor in future years for analytical evidence. Lack of good evidence available.

> Cash income - risky

> Trust for completeness

Tap also receive donations towards the work. These come from a variety of sources:

> Again cash. Also, what are the controls here? Completeness has to be a problem.

- Cash donations from buckets passed around at the interval of each performance
- Cash donations on the (rare) occasion that the team do street performances
- Cash donations made over the phone or by post by interested donors

> No salaries

> Expenditure issues again.

The troupe consists largely of volunteers so they are only paid expenses for their work. The cost of housing the group while they are on the road is borne by the charity. The charity employs an administrator who organises bookings, handles publicity and co-ordinates all the finances.

> Not a specialist? But drafting complex accounts.

> You should have been noticing and annotating risks as you have worked through the scenario. Try and categorise them in your mind (Inherent Control, Detection)

Required

> Note you are looking specifically for **audit** risks.

(a) Discuss the risks arising for the audit of the year ending 30 June 2002. (8 marks)

(b) Outline the audit procedures you would undertake in respect of cash income in the financial statements. (6 marks)

> Only cash income!!

(c) Outline some controls over cash which the charity should implement. (6 marks)

> A standard requirement, but you must **tailor** your answer to the scenario.

> Think of control objectives and then design reasonable controls that meet the objective. There are more control problems in the scenario than you need to identify/solve for the marks.

Answer plan

Then organise the things you have noticed and your points arising into a coherent answer plan. Not all the points you have noticed will have to go into your answer – you should spend a few minutes thinking them through and prioritising them.

(a) Audit risks

Overall risk of being auditor to a charity in terms of potential bad publicity in the event of problems arising on the audit.

Inherent risk	Control risk	Detection risk
Cash – susceptible to loss or theft.	Appears to be very little control over cash.	First year audit – lack of detailed knowledge of the business on the part of the auditor.
Charity – high degree of regulation		First ever audit of the charity – need to take extra care over audit of opening balances, implications for comparatives, audit report.
Lack of an accounting specialist drafting the accounts		Whereabouts of audit evidence – some may be posted to Leicester – is it all retained there?
Completeness of income appears to be a problem		
Disclosure of income – net or gross of commission		
Expenditure – substantiating, in accordance with Trust Deed?		

(b) **Audit procedures**

Income from box office takings

Verified to bank records/statement from the theatre. Possible to circularise the theatres to get them to verify numbers of seats sold so as to gain a little more assurance about the completeness of income?

Income from buckets

Are there any original records of cash counts? Verify from them to the banking documentation if so.

Income from other donations

Original documents such as letters/forms or original records of cash received should be traced to banking documentation and bank records.

(c) **Controls over cash**

Box office

The theatre should try and get more assurance re completeness of income. Is it possible to get a schedule of seats sold from the theatres – this should be available on their system.

Buckets

Two people should collect and count to avoid loss, misappropriation and/or error.

The money should be made more secure both during collection and between banking: use collecting tins, have a transportable safe and bank frequently.

An initial record of the cash count should be kept, signed by both the counters.

Other income

Other income should be recorded on pre-numbered forms to help ensure completeness.

The Trustees should carry out a periodic review of the work of the administrator to protect both the charity and the administrator.

Exam answer bank

1   **PRINCETOWN AND YALE**

> *Tutorial note.* This is not an exam standard question but it includes the simple benefits of an audit which you must understand and be able to outline. However remember that in a small company, these same benefits could also be provided by an alternative assurance service, perhaps a review. You need to be able to evaluate the difference between the levels of assurance given.

(a)   A non-statutory audit could assist the partnership of Princetown and Yale in the following ways.

(i)   It would highlight any weaknesses in the partnership's systems, and should provide constructive suggestions for improvements.

(ii)   It would help to substantiate the partnership accounts in case of any disagreement between the partners or any query arising as to the results shown in the accounts.

(iii)   Audited accounts carry more weight with interested third parties such as the Inland Revenue, Customs and Excise and bankers or other potential sources of loan finance or credit.

(b)   There is a risk that, in the absence of statutory guidance, auditors and clients have different expectations of the non-statutory audit. For instance, as discussed in (b) above, the client may expect the audit to be aimed at detecting fraud. A letter of engagement should be sent by the client to the auditors, having been discussed and agreed by both parties, setting out the areas to be covered by the audit. This should help to ensure that the client understands what degree of comfort the audit will give, and that the auditors are aware of the client's requirements.

2   **STANDARDS**

> *Tutorial note.* Although not exam style, this is a useful discussion about important issues which could be examined. The examiner has stated that an understanding of the overall regulatory environment is essential. Auditing standards were specifically examined in December 2001.

The major *advantages* of accounting standards and auditing standards can be summarised as follows.

(a)   *Accounting standards*

(i)   They reduce the areas of uncertainty and subjectivity in accounts.

(ii)   They narrow the areas where different accounting policies can be adopted.

(iii)   They increase the comparability of financial statements.

(iv)   They codify what is considered in most circumstances to be best accounting practice.

(v)   They give an indication of the interpretation of the concept 'true and fair' in many circumstances.

(b)   *Auditing standards*

(i)   They give a framework for all audits around which a particular audit can be developed.

(ii)   They help to standardise the approach of all auditors to the common objective of producing an opinion.

(iii)   They assist the court in interpretation of the concept of 'due professional care' and may assist auditors when defending their work.

(iv)   They increase public awareness of what an audit comprises and the work behind the production of an audit report.

(v)   They provide support for auditors in a dispute with clients regarding the audit work necessary.

The possible *disadvantages* include the following.

(a)   *Accounting standards*

(i)   They are considered to be too rigid in some areas and too general in others, making their application difficult in some circumstances.

(ii)   They can be onerous for small companies to adopt.

  (iii) Their proliferation could be said to increase proportionately the number of qualified audit reports thereby reducing the impact of such qualifications.

  (iv) They can create divisions within the profession of those who agree and those who disagree with a particular standard.

  (v) They would be difficult to change once they become statutory as alterations to company law can take years rather than months to enact.

(b) *Auditing standards*

  (i) It may appear that they impinge on, rather than assist, professional judgement.

  (ii) They are considered by some to stifle initiative and developments of new auditing methods.

  (iii) They may create additional and unnecessary work and thus raise fees, particularly on the audit of small companies.

If either type of standard were to be enforceable by statue it would mean that there would be government intervention in areas currently controlled solely by the profession itself. This might ultimately lead to a diminished role in self-regulation. To be enforceable by statute the standards would have to be applicable to all circumstances and thus need to be very general and broad in their instructions. This might reduce their usefulness to the auditors. Auditors might spend unnecessary time ensuring that they have complied with the law rather than considering the quality of their service to their clients.

Finally, it should be considered whether full statutory backing for standards would force auditors into narrow views and approaches which might gradually impair the quality of accounting and auditing practices.

Note. A legal opinion on truth and fairness, accounting standards and the law in the *Foreword to Accounting Standards* strengthens the legal backing for accounting standards and UITF pronouncements.

3 ROLE OF INTERNAL AUDIT

> *Tutorial note.* The examiner has recently written an article on the role of internal audit in risk management, and has stated that it is an important area both in practice and in this syllabus. It is important that you get to grips with the all the issues relating to internal audit and risk management.
>
> Part (a) of this question requires you to state what you know about the background corporate governance issues and any requirements which companies must meet. Note that Golden Holdings is a listed company, so things such as the Combined Code are mandatory.
>
> Part (b) requires you to apply the role of internal audit in a practical situation. It demands that you draw some conclusions about what your role will be. You should provide reasoning for the conclusions you draw, so that the marker can credit you both for your conclusions and your thought-processes. As internal auditor you have been asked to educate the senior management about the role of internal audit, so in practice it would be appropriate for you to appraise the director of your reasoning.

(a) **Notes on the role of internal audit**

  (i) *Requirements in relation to the Board of Directors*

   As a listed company, Golden Holdings is bound by the requirements of the Combined Code. This contains the following requirements:

    • Board must meet regularly
    • There should be a clearly accepted division of responsibilities
    • Positions of Chief Executive and Chairman should be distinct
    • A formal schedule of matters for referral to the Board should exist
    • Non-executive directors should form 1/3 of the Board

   Companies should also set up remuneration committees comprised of non-executive directors to determine executive remuneration. Committee should report annually to the shareholders setting out the company's policy to remuneration and making disclosures about director's remuneration packages.

These recommendations specifically relate to listed companies, and if listed companies do not comply with the recommendations, they must explain themselves. However, they also represent good practice for other companies.

(ii) *Requirements in relation to accountability*

The Combined Code contains the following matters in relation to accountability:

- Directors must explain their responsibility for preparing accounts
- Directors must report on the going concern status of the company
- The Board should establish an audit committee

In addition, the financial statements must be audited by an independent auditor who qualifies for the position under legislation. The company is required as part of the annual report to include a narrative statement of how it has applied the principles of the combined code.

(iii) *Risk management*

The Combined Code requires that the directors review the effectiveness of internal control systems at least annually.

Internal control systems are maintained to enable the business to operate efficiently, to ensure that assets are safeguarded and that reliable records are maintained. An internal control system reduces risk to a company.

As such, an internal control system is part of a company's risk management. Directors are required to review the system as part of their risk management exercise, to ensure that the system is still reducing risks, and that all risks have been considered.

The directors are also required to appraise the need for an internal audit department annually. Internal audit have a role in monitoring the risk management of an entity.

(b) **Sales department brainstorming session**

MEMORANDUM

To: Sales director

(i) I should be able to come along to your brainstorming session in July. However, it is probably best that I attend in an **advisory and interested capacity** only.

As we shall be involved in monitoring the systems which the sales department put into place to mitigate risks in the business, it is **inappropriate** for me to get **too involved** in the initial systems **design stage**, as this will **impair my future objectivity** when **monitoring** how the system is operating and achieving its objectives.

(ii) In terms of **assessing risks**, I am not best qualified to undertake this role. You guys work in the department everyday, **you are the specialists** and should be able to identify the major risks arising in the department.

Just to give you a better idea of what my role can be, I can say that internal audit are able to provide three things:

- **Objective assurance** on the operation of systems once you have them up and running
- Assistance in **setting up a process to help you identify risks**
- Assistance in **strengthening the control process** once you have identified risks.

In other words, if you are struggling to identify risks at the meeting, I can give you some pointers on how to go about it, but after that my job will be looking at the systems you come up with, and helping you improve them continually.

See you at the meeting, if not before,

Internal auditor

4   OBJECTIVITY

(a)   **Objectivity**

Objectivity is defined by the ACCA as being 'a state of mind which has regard to all considerations relevant to the task in hand but no other. It pre-supposes intellectual honesty.'

(i)   **External auditors**. Objectivity is usually hallmarked by '**independence**' in the case of external auditors. The auditor must 'be, and be seen to be, independent'. ACCA provides a number of guidelines as to how an auditor should maintain his independence.

(ii)   **Internal auditors**. Internal auditors are usually employees of the people they report to, so independence is a more difficult issue to understand here. However, it is vital that they maintain objectivity towards their tasks within a company, so they must **avoid conflicts of interest** and maintain **integrity in their relationships** with other staff members.

In particular, as an ACCA member, an internal auditor is bound by the ACCA's Fundamental Principles and Rules of Professional Conduct. Objectivity is a fundamental principle.

Threats to objectivity

The following are all threats to objectivity:

- **Personal interest** (for example, fear of losing fees or a good relationship with a client/fellow staff member)

- **Review of own work** (for example, if an auditor audits financial statements he has compiled, or an internal auditor monitors systems he has designed)

- **Disputes** (for example, with a client, or where an audit firm advocates for its client, or where an internal auditor has a personal issue with a staff member)

- **Long association or undue sympathy** (for example, through close personal relationships)

- **Intimidation** (this is linked to self-interest. For example, fear of losing a client or an internal auditor losing his job)

(b) **Two situations**

Scenario 1

(i) **Threats**

The situation raises three potential threats to objectivity.

The first is the issue that the firm has had a **long association** with the audit client. It is unclear whether the same engagement staff have been associated with the entity in that time.

The second is that the firm has been offered the opportunity to carry out work other than audit for the firm. ACCA guidance states that **provision of other services** can affect objectivity.

Connected to the previous point is the fact that a **self-interest threat** arises through the **substantial fee income** that this client may generate in the current year. ACCA's guideline in respect to recurring income is that 15% of office income from one client is likely to adversely affect objectivity (for a Ltd company). The income in this year is likely to be 17%, but much of that is not recurring. However, the firm should consider that the result of the consultancy might be that the business expands and the audit fee might rise in the future. They should lay down contingency plans.

(ii) **Safeguards**

In relation to the other services, the key inherent safeguard is that it is a **one off project**, as stated above. It appears that it will also be carried out by a **department other than the audit department**, which will help to maintain objectivity.

In terms of the audit, as the client has been associated with the audit firm for a number of years, the firm should consider laying out procedures for **rotation of the engagement partner** in relation to the client, so that the relationship cannot become too close over time.

If this is considered inappropriate, it might consider instituting a **second partner review** as another measure to maintain objectivity.

Scenario 2

(i) **Threats**

If Peter was to get the job in the internal audit department, there would be considerable threat of **self-review** as he would have to monitor the systems which he has set up in the purchasing department.

As Peter is a current employee of the company, there is also a risk that his objectivity towards an internal audit role would be affected by his **relationships with fellow employees**.

This is particularly the case with regard to his relationship with his current boss, the **Purchasing Director**, as he has a **poor relationship** with him. As a member of the internal audit department, Peter would in all likelihood have to report directly on matters relating to this director.

(ii) **Safeguards**

If Peter gets the job, an important safeguard would be that he **did not work on matters relating to the purchasing department for a period of time**, or perhaps until the systems have been reviewed again and/or the Purchasing Director moves on.

It would also be important to address the issue of objectivity as part of the recruitment process. The issue of **relationships with staff** would have to be **discussed** and **understood**.

Lastly, it would is important to have **objectivity in the recruitment process**. As Peter has had an informal discussion with the head of Internal Audit, the head of Internal Audit should ensure that other staff members are included in the recruitment process.

5 NEW ENGAGEMENT

Tutorial note. This question is not exam standard but the considerations it covers could form part of a larger, scenario question on accepting audit and ethical considerations, for example.

(a) Prospective auditors should consider the following before accepting a new audit appointment.

(i) Do I have the technical competence to carry out the assignment?

(ii) Will I have the time and resources (including staff) to carry out the work?

(iii) Could there be a conflict of interest involved?

(iv) Do there appear to be any professional reasons why I should not take up the appointment?

(b) The auditing standard SAS 140 *Engagement letters* states that: 'The auditors and the client should agree on the terms of the engagement, which should be recorded in writing'. This will help to avoid misunderstandings between the client and the auditors.

The engagement letter also provides written confirmation of the auditors' acceptance of their appointment, of the scope of the audit and of the form of the audit report.

The following important items should be included in the letter of engagement.

(i) A statement of management's responsibilities to keep proper accounting records and to prepare the financial statements

(ii) A statement of management's responsibility for the detection of fraud

(iii) A description of the auditors' responsibilities in forming their opinion on the financial statements

(iv) An explanation of the scope of the audit, stating that it will be carried out in accordance with auditing standards

(v) An explanation that weaknesses in internal controls will be reported to management in a letter

(vi) An explanation of the need to obtain written management representations in certain circumstances

(vii) Details of the basis for charging and paying for fees

(viii) Applicable law governing the letter (usually CA 1985) and a statement that neither party has the right to object to any action in the courts

(ix) A request that the directors agree the terms of the letter

6 GLO

Tutorial note. In part (a) you must discuss the issues raised by the question. It is not appropriate to answer a 3 mark question by saying 'no, it will not be appropriate.' The question asks you to discuss, so you must explain your reasoning and come to a conclusion.

Part (b) should represent easy marks. However, remember to explain what you know swiftly to bank those marks and then move on to section (c) where a large number of marks are available for identifying risk areas in practice.

In part (c) you need to identify what looks odd in the balance sheet because this will indicate that it is potentially a risk area requiring a higher level of audit work. However, you should not just read through the balance sheet and compile an answer which lists the balance sheet areas in balance sheet order, explaining they are risky because 'stock has fallen' etc.

You should explain **why things may be risky** for the audit, in other words, **explain what the balance sheet movement may indicate**. Stock may have fallen because a large amount of stock held at a third parties wasn't included in the stocktake, or because of a tremendous recent marketing push. The first explanation shows the risk that the financial statements are materially misstated in terms of stock completeness.

You should **structure your answer** in terms of what you feel is the **greatest risk**. This may involve **making links between the various lines of the balance sheet** and pulling together an **overview of the situation**. In our answer below, we highlight the issue of going concern. There is no point in auditing the balance sheet in its current form if the going concern basis is inappropriate, therefore going concern is a key risk in this audit. There are various indicators that the going concern assumption may be inappropriate: fall in value in the whole balance sheet, retained loss, fall in cash position, suggestion of fall in activity.

(a) **Materiality**

It is **never appropriate** to apply the prior year's materiality figure to the current year figures. Materiality should be assessed in each year.

If the financial position has not changed much, and the results are very comparable with the prior year, it is possible that the materiality assessed year on year is very similar, but this does not mean that the auditors should not assess it for each audit. When assessing materiality, the auditor must consider **all known factors at the current date**. In this case, the position has changed considerably, increasing the risk of the audit, which may lower materiality in itself.

As the **balance sheet position** has **changed considerably**, so when materiality is assessed, it is unlikely that it will be similar to the prior year. Using the information available, **materiality is likely to be assessed extremely low** in monetary terms, due to the overall decrease in assets and the loss that appears to have been made in the year. It is also possible that given the current balance sheet position, the balance sheet figures will not be used to assess materiality in this year.

(b) **Audit risk**

Audit risk is the risk that the auditor will give an inappropriate opinion on financial statements. It is made up of three different elements of risk:

- **Inherent risk**: the risks arising naturally in the business and specific accounts/transactions
- **Control risk**: the risk that the accounting system will fail to detect and prevent errors
- **Detection risk**: the risk that the auditors will not detect material misstatements

Detection risk is comprised of **sampling risk** (the risk that the auditors' conclusion drawn from a sample is different to what it would have been, had the whole population been tested) and **non-sampling risk** (the risk that auditors may use the inappropriate procedures or misinterpret evidence).

Inherent and control risk are assessed by the auditors. Detection risk is then set at a level which makes overall audit risk acceptable to them.

(c) **Specific audit areas of risk**

A review of this balance sheet suggests that audit work should be directed in the following areas:

Going concern

The **balance sheet has reduced considerably in value** since the previous year. Net current assets has fallen from £212,000 to £17,000, and the total position in 2002 is **net liabilities**, albeit this is only marginal. Although the profit and loss account has not been reviewed, the balance sheet shows a **retained loss** for the year of £211,000.

Net assets shows a **reduction in both stock and debtors**, which **suggest a decrease in activity**, although trade creditors does not seem to have fallen so considerably. However, this could be accounted for by Glo-Warm not paying its suppliers in a similar fashion to the previous year. It will be **necessary to review** the **profit and loss account** to substantiate whether activity has reduced.

The **cash position has also worsened**, with cash falling by £22,000. The cash flow statement should reveal more detail about this fall. However, the company has paid of £5,000 of its bank loan, reducing over all net debt.

In summary, audit work should be directed at going concern as **several indicators of going concern problems** exist in the balance sheet. This will be further amplified when the profit and loss account is available.

Stock

Stock has been mentioned above in the context of going concern. Audit work should be directed at stock specifically as this **balance has fallen significantly** from the previous year, which seems **odd in a manufacturing company**. There is no suggestion on the balance sheet for why this should be so (for example, debtors are not correspondingly high, suggesting high pre-year end sales, and creditors are not correspondingly low, suggested low pre-year end purchases). It may be that the stocktake did not include every item of stock. Alternatively it could simply point to a fall in activity (discussed above).

Warranty provision

A provision of £20,000 has been included in 2002 for warranties. The reasons for this must be investigated and the auditors must check that it has been accounted for correctly in accordance with FRS 12.

It seems **odd that a warranty provision should suddenly appear in a balance sheet**. It suggests a change in the terms of contracts given to customers, or a change in the customers themselves (with different terms then applying). Alternatively it suggests that **FRS 12** has been **wrongly applied in the current year, or should have been applied in the previous year**, and was not.

Other material items

As stated above, given the indications of loss and the reduction in total asset value, it is likely that materiality will be assessed low in monetary terms. In this case, most balances on the balance sheet are likely to be material (excluding investments and cash in hand which appear to be very low risk).

However, as the bank loan is likely to have good audit evidence available, the most risky of the other balances are **trade debtors** and **trade creditors**, for reasons discussed above in going concern. More detail is required to make a judgement about the risk of tangible fixed assets.

7   **USING THE WORK OF AN EXPERT**

> *Tutorial note.* Note that as well as considering the independence and qualifications of experts, auditors should consider the scope of the expert's work and carry out *some* confirmation work on the expert's opinion. You do not need (and would not expected to have) a detailed knowledge of valuation of long-term contracts to be able to answer Part (c)

(a)   In assessing the reliability of the legal advice obtained from a local solicitor on the outcome of the claim by Netherfield Manufacturing plc, the auditors should consider the following.

  (i)   The materiality of the claim is important as the significance to the company of the amount involved would clearly affect the extent of the audit work required.

  (ii)   The qualification, experience, reputation and standing of the local solicitor would be relevant. Presumably the solicitor would be qualified, but it would also be necessary to consider his suitability to advise on this type of claim. The experience of the solicitor and his firm and their reputation in this field of litigation would be an important factor in determining the extent of reliance to be placed on the solicitor's advice. In particular, consideration should be given as to whether the solicitor had advised the company in respect of similar litigation in the past and how reliable his advice had proved to be on those earlier occasions.

  (iii)   The independence of the solicitor must be checked as any suggestion that the solicitor or his firm had any direct connection with the company or its management would tend to reduce somewhat the reliability of the evidence provided.

  (iv)   The nature and extent of the evidence provided by the company to the solicitor, and on which he has based his opinion, should be carefully reviewed to ensure that the solicitor's decision appears to have been based upon all relevant facts available to the company.

(v)   The solicitor's opinion should be examined and its reasonableness assessed, in the light of the auditor's knowledge and experience of similar cases against both Ravenshead and other clients engaged in similar activities.

(vi)   If the auditors consider the amount of the claim to be material, and there is uncertainty in relation to the outcome of the claim and/or the solicitor's evidence, the auditors should consider recommending to the client that a second opinion from an independent specialist in the field be obtained. If the client was not agreeable to this action or if the auditors still considered there to be material uncertainty, then a qualification of the audit report would probably be required.

(b)   The factors to be considered by the auditors in assessing the reliability of the valuation of investment properties by an independent valuer would be as follows.

(i)   The independence of the valuer should be considered in a similar way to that of the local solicitor, and for the same reasons.

(ii)   The qualification, reputation and experience of the valuer should be considered. The valuer should be a qualified member of a professional valuation body with experience of valuing similar properties within the same geographical area as the properties owned by Ravenshead. If the valuer does not have experience of the type of properties held by the company or of the areas in which they are located, then the value of his evidence is likely to be considerably reduced. The reputation of the valuer or his firm would also affect the reliability of his evidence so far as the auditors are concerned, with the likelihood that more reliance could be placed on a valuation made by a large firm with a good reputation, than one obtained from a little-known small firm.

(iii) The actual valuation of the properties by the valuer should be carefully examined. The auditors would need to satisfy themselves that a reasonable basis for the valuation had been adopted. Typically, an open market value based upon existing usage would be expected. The valuation of leasehold properties should be assessed in the light of the remaining length of the leases and the value of freehold properties would be affected by whether or not they are leased and, if they are, the remaining period of the leases, the amount of the rental income and the frequency of rent reviews.

(iv)   Any change in the valuation of the properties since the time of the previous valuation should be assessed. The validity of any significant changes in the valuation of the properties should be considered in the light of any statistical or other evidence available for similar properties.

(v)   The reasonableness of the valuations should be considered against any profits or losses made on any properties disposed of in recent times, as this could be a good indication of any tendency to over or under value the properties to a material extent, either over or under valuation being likely to distort the truth and fairness of the financial statements.

(vi)   The reasonableness of the valuations could also be considered by the auditors comparing the valuations with those used by other clients holding similar properties in the same locations.

(c)   The matters to be considered when assessing the valuation of the long-term contract work in progress by an internal valuer would be as follows.

(i)   How material is this asset in the financial statements: as it is likely to be highly material, it needs to be valued accurately.

(ii)   The basis of the valuation should be carefully checked to consider the extent to which it appears to comply with the requirements of SSAP 9.

(iii) Recognition of the fact that, as the valuer is an employee of Ravenshead, this will reduce the reliability of the evidence provided. However this may be countered to a certain extent by the fact that the valuer should have a more detailed knowledge of the work in progress than it would perhaps ever be possible for an independent valuer to obtain.

(iv)   Confirmation should be sought that the valuer had actually visited all of the contract sites, or otherwise obtained satisfactory evidence as to the stage of completion of the contracts in order to provide himself with a reliable basis for their valuation.

(v)   The valuer's basis of determining costs to date should be ascertained and the auditor would need to be satisfied as to the reliability of the company's records in this respect and, in particular, that a consistently applied satisfactory basis of overhead recognition had been employed.

      (vi)   The valuer's estimates of the further costs to completion of the contracts should be carefully reviewed and confirmation obtained that reasonable allowance had been made for increases in the costs of material and labour having regard to the current and projected rates of inflation.

8   AUDIT EVIDENCE

> *Tutorial note.* Each of the numbered sections in this question could form part of a question on auditing a specific balance sheet area. In such a question, you could be asked to set out the audit procedures you would undertake (what evidence would you seek) and ask for an assessment of the quality and quantity of that evidence, (that is, how much evidence do you need and why).

(a)   (i)   Inspecting inventories and testing perpetual records by making test counts provides:

        (1)   Strong evidence of completeness with the limitation that items not physically in stock or on the perpetual records will not be identified. This may apply to goods in the receiving area at the time of the stocktake

        (2)   Strong evidence of existence

        (3)   Strong evidence of accuracy

        (4)   Weak evidence of valuation, and

        (5)   Weak evidence of ownership as stock items may be on consignment or help under Romalpa conditions.

    (ii)   Vouching fixed asset additions to supporting documentation provides:

        (1)   Weak evidence of completeness as such a test will not highlight omissions only overstatement

        (2)   Weak evidence of existence as, although the additions were purchased by the company, there is no evidence that they are physically held by the company at the year end

        (3)   Strong evidence of accuracy

        (4)   Strong evidence of valuation in respect of cost but not for any subsequent fall in value, and

        (5)   Strong evidence of ownership as the purchases will be invoiced in the company name. However, this assumes no subsequent sales or transfers.

    (iii)   Verification of bank balances by bank confirmation request provides strong evidence for existence, accuracy, valuation and ownership for balances at the particular bank circularised. However, only weak evidence is given of completeness, because undetectable balances may be held at other banks. The same applies to liens.

(b)   Audit evidence should be fully documented so that the auditor has a written record of the work and conclusions thereon on which he has based his audit opinion.

    Documentation also acts as a means of quality control on the work done providing evidence for the reviewer. (Per SAS 240 work delegated should be reviewed in a manner which provides reasonable assurance that the work is performed competently). It is particularly important in litigation situations.

    The details relating to the audit tests which should be regarded are as follows.

    (i)   Detailed audit tests carried out, the reasons for the timing and level of the tests and the objectives of the tests

    (ii)   Notes of errors or exceptions found and action taken

    (iii)   Conclusions drawn by staff who performed the tests

9   INTERNAL CONTROLS

> *Tutorial note.* Parts (a) and (b) to this question should be reasonably straight-forward. Part (c) requires you to set out the work that the internal audit department would routinely do to reduce the risk of fraud and error. Remember that one of the risks facing the purchases department is that fraud may be perpetrated: internal controls have been put in place to ensure that this risk is reduced. Therefore, on a routine basis, this would fall within the role of the internal audit department checking that controls are operating effectively. In your answer to part (c) then, you should identify what controls would exist to mitigate against fraud and set out the procedures that internal audit would carry out to test their effectiveness.
>
> In part (d), you are asked how a risk assessment would affect the work of both internal and external auditors. You are not asked specifically for procedures that would be carried out. You should therefore note that as a higher than normal risk has been identified, more work would be carried out than usual. For the external auditor this would mean a higher number of the same procedures, for the internal auditor, it might mean a special investigation. However, you could also note that internal audit might disguise their special operations as normal operations so as not to alert the suspected party that they are investigating him. If fraud was expected to have a material impact on the financial statements, the external auditors would carry out some procedures that they might not have otherwise carried out (for example, a creditors' circularisation). You should note these in your answer.

(a)   **Four objectives of an internal control system**

SAS 300 outlines the following objectives of internal control systems:

- To enable management to carry on the business of the company in an orderly and efficient manner

- To satisfy management that their policies are being adhered to

- To ensure that the assets of the company are safeguarded

- To ensure, as far as possible, that the enterprise maintains complete and accurate records

(b)   **Review of internal control systems**

External auditor

As part of his audit, the external auditor is required to **ascertain the system and controls**. Once the system has been ascertained, the external auditor will walkthrough the systems to ensure that they operate as he has been led to believe that they do.

The auditor will then determine his **audit approach**. If he is planning to rely on the controls in the system, he has to evaluate the controls in the accounting system to assess whether they are **reliable enough to produce financial records which are free of material misstatement**. In other words, he is assessing whether the systems achieve the fourth objective given above.

He will conduct tests of controls to ensure that the controls have operated properly in the year. If these tests produce good results, the auditor can rely on the systems and undertake reduced substantive testing on the financial statements.

The auditor will decide not to undertake tests of controls if the controls do not appear effective, or it is more cost effective to undertake high substantive procedures.

Internal auditor

Internal audit is an appraisal or monitoring activity established by the directors. It functions, amongst other things, by **examining and evaluating the adequacy and effectiveness of components of the accounting and internal control systems**.

Internal audit therefore review and test internal control systems to assess whether the systems are **achieving the four objectives** stated above.

Conclusion

The external auditor is interested in the internal control systems which help to produce the financial statements which he is auditing. Internal auditors are interested more generally in internal controls to ensure that they meet their objectives of helping the business to operate effectively and reduce risks.

(c) **Internal auditor work**

The sort of frauds which could be carried out in a purchases system are: processing non-businesses expenses as business expenses or paying fictional suppliers inflated prices.

The work an internal auditor could carry out to check procedures in the purchase system and to lessen the risk of fraud and error is as follows:

(i) Check individual purchases to the invoice, agreeing the details to the purchase order and delivery note. If these items are not available this should be noted.

(ii) Review individual purchases to ensure that they are related to **business expenses**. If an item appears questionable, it should be investigated further.

(iii) Review the **prices paid** for purchases and ensure that alternative supply options have been considered (either on an individual basis, or on a yearly basis)

(iv) Test **cheque payments** to ensure that they **related to approved invoices**

(v) Perform **reconciliations to supplier statements** to ensure that payments have been made to the **correct suppliers for genuine invoices**

(vi) Check reconciliations made between the purchase ledger and the purchase control account to ensure that **all differences have been investigated and reconciled**.

(vii) Review the purchase ledger on a regular basis to ensure that there are **no unusual or unexplained balances or debits**.

(d) **Risk of fraud and error**

The auditors should consider the reasons that the risk of fraud and error has been assessed as high, as this will affect the work that they do. The factors that cause each set of auditors to assess risk as high may be different.

External auditors' work

SAS 110 *Fraud and error* states that 'auditors should plan and perform their audit procedures and evaluate and report the results thereof, recognising that fraud or error may materially affect the financial statements...when planning the audit the auditors should assess the risk that fraud or error may cause the financial statements to contain material misstatements'.

In this case, the risk has been assessed and it appears to be higher than normal. This means that the external auditor will have to perform **additional procedures** to **reduce the risk that the financial statements are materially misstated** as a result of fraud. The additional risk would mean that materiality was assessed lower. This would result in a greater proportion of transactions and balances being subject to evidence gathering.

If a purchase ledger fraud was suspected, the external auditors would **circularise creditors**, to obtain third party evidence as to the value of creditors at the year end. If a sales ledger fraud was suspected, they would conduct a debtors' circularisation, or extend the sample from previous years.

They would scrutinise the ledgers for indications of suppliers or customers who may be connected to management.

The external auditors might also carry out detailed transactions tests such as have been outlined above in part (c) to be carried out by internal audit.

Internal auditors' work

Internal auditors might assess the risk of fraud or error as high if they had **specific suspicions** about a particular member of staff. This would direct their additional work.

Investigating fraud would be a special project for the internal audit department, outside of the scope of their normal work. However, it is possible that they would want the operation to be covert, so as to ensure that the person suspected would not be alerted to their suspicions. The special project would involve scrutinising past records, looking for **evidence of controls having been bypassed**, particularly evidence of authorisation not being sought. This would be done by scrutinising documents for evidence of controls being kept, for example, authorising initials, or 'paid' stamps. They would interview staff to assess whether if controls are maintained as they should be. They would also observe the system operating at the current time.

They might also run company searches on all the suppliers on their central suppliers' register to ensure that they did not appear to be connected to members of staff.

If the suspicions of fraud were strong, the company might hire specialist forensic practitioners to assist the internal audit department's investigations.

10 FENTON DISTRIBUTORS

> *Tutorial note.* In (b) significant emphasis is placed on testing unusual or suspicious items (particularly the adjustment journals). Note also the importance of accounting controls at the year-end. Correct categorisation of expenses is important from the viewpoint of the statutory accounts (directors' emoluments), and in ensuring the quality of management information, which the auditors may use for analytical procedures.

(a) To verify the accuracy of the purchases transactions posted to the nominal ledger I would perform the following checks.

   (i)   I would check that the bookkeeper was up to date with the monthly posting of all purchases transactions to the nominal ledger.

   (ii) Specific checks on purchase transactions will include the following.

   (1) Purchase transactions will be traced from the invoice to the nominal ledger and the analysis and analysis code will be checked.

   (2) The total invoice value will be traced to the nominal ledger.

   (3) The category of invoice expense and the expense amount will be checked to confirm that it appears correctly on the detailed computer list for the month concerned.

   (4) The total of the items on the detailed list will be checked to the nominal ledger.

   (5) Transactions will also be traced backwards from the entries in the nominal ledger making up the monthly total posted to the purchase ledger back to both the detailed analysis and the individual invoice.

   (6) The amount of the invoice expense will be agreed with the amount posted to the nominal ledger.

   The tests above check accounting entries forwards and backwards within the system and any errors would be fully investigated as to their type, cause, materiality and pattern.

   (iii) The test checks on the detailed list and total postings of cash payments, discounts received and adjustments will follow the same procedure as for invoices and credit notes. The monthly cash book total will be checked to the total posted from the purchase ledger to the nominal ledger.

   (iv) A check on the analysis and coding of purchase invoices will be carried out to establish the level of accuracy achieved. Particular care will be taken to see that the expense category 'purchases' is correctly identified and coded from invoices and is not confused with other categories, for example stationery, rates, gas and telephone. Incorrect analysis and/or coding may be indicated where the expense category is high or low in comparison with its budget to date.

   Large variations between actual and budget on expense categories should be test checked to verify that they are not due to errors in analysis, coding or posting.

(b) To verify the validity and accuracy of the journals posted to the nominal ledger I would carry out the following checks.

   (i)   Firstly, I would check the opening balances at the start of the financial year. To do this I would check the value of each trial balance item on the opening trial balance back to the closing entries on the previous year's accounts. After this, each item would be checked to the nominal ledger ensuring that both the value and analysis are correct. These opening postings should be the first entries in the new year as all nominal ledger balances should have been set to zero, and this should be confirmed.

   (ii) Other cash book items would be test checked to the nominal ledger to confirm that postings are correct as to value and expense category. Large items would require a larger sample size and large, unusual or suspicious items should all be checked and evidenced by supporting documentation or Board approval.

(iii) The year-end balances of cash and bank on the nominal ledger should be agreed with the year-end balances in the cash book. This would require the last month to be checked as the closing balances at all previous month-ends will have been checked already.

(iv) The checks on petty cash payments transactions would include the following.

(1) Check that transactions are supported by vouchers and correctly posted to the right nominal ledger account. This would include checking that transactions are valid and coded to the correct expense category.

(2) Check that petty cash transactions are within any limits, regarding the type of expenditure or maximum value, established by management.

(3) Check that the petty cash balance in the nominal ledger at the end of each month and at the financial year-end agrees with the balance in the petty cash book.

(v) The wages expense is posted manually to the nominal ledger from the monthly payroll summaries by means of a journal. To verify that the journals are correctly posted I would select several journals and check the following matters.

(1) The totals of the analysis columns on the monthly summary shown on the spreadsheet should be posted to the journal, and forward to the nominal ledger.

(2) The breakdown of wages expense into directors and the several departmental categories will be checked. The correct identification of directors' pay is important as this requires statutory disclosure. I would obtain the current list of directors. I would add up the totals in the analysis columns to confirm the summary total, and consider its reasonableness.

(3) Amounts owing at the year-end for PAYE, NI, accrued pay, superannuation and other deductions will be verified and any reconciliation drawn up by the bookkeeper agreed.

(4) Any additions to, or amendments of, weekly wages records posted to the nominal ledger through the adjustments journal will be fully investigated and their validity established.

(5) The analysis of wages expense for the year will be compared with the budget and an explanation will be sought for any significant variances.

(vi) Adjustment journals are potentially a high-risk area and any checks would include the following.

(1) Check that all the manually written adjustment journals were authorised by the managing director and supported by documentation and proper narratives.

(2) Check journals are posted in numerical order and there should be no missing numbers gaps in the postings.

(3) Examine all large adjustments and the reasons given for the errors. These will be traced to the nominal ledger to ensure that postings do correct the errors.

(4) Investigate closely recurring errors to establish their cause and whether these can be avoided in future by management action.

(5) Examine the purchase ledger suspense account (creditors suspense) and trace all postings in and out.

(6) Where there was no account in the nominal ledger, check back to the purchase invoice, establish the account number and verify that the item has been posted from the suspense account to the correct account.

(7) Where the adjustment is due to the wrong account number being used, check that the journal correctly transfers the item to the right account.

(8) Where the bookkeeper has created contra entries between the purchase ledger and the sales ledger, check that the creditor/debtor company concerned is posted with a purchase ledger and sales ledger contra of the same value.

(9) All other adjustments will be checked for validity and supporting documentation.

Reasons will be established for postings that increase or reduce purchase ledger balances.

(vii)   Year-end balances on the nominal ledger would be further checked as follows.

(1)   Any balances remaining on the purchase ledger and sales ledger suspense accounts should be itemised on a supporting schedule and the existence of each item justified.

(2)   Nominal ledger balances for the cash book, petty cash book, sales ledger and purchase ledger should agree to, or be reconciled to, the cash book, petty cash book, total sales ledger and total purchase ledger balances at the year end. I will check that any difference is reconciled and explained. It may be that further adjustments are required to reduce or eliminate a difference.

(3)   All fixed asset movements should be checked, including purchases, sales, revaluations and depreciation.

(4)   All outstanding liabilities should be verified and their size reviewed for reasonableness.

(5)   The bank reconciliation should establish the correctness of balances on all types of bank account, ie loan, current, deposit, special transactions and so on.

(6)   A review of the financial statements would be carried out to ensure that material changes in assets, expenses, revenues, liabilities and share capital are justified and explained. Justification would be sought in both relative and absolute terms.

11   CHEQUE PAYMENTS AND PETTY CASH

> *Tutorial note.* This question asks you to asses the controls over a particular area of a business. As such, it could have been posed to either an internal or an external auditor – remember that either would be possible in the exam. Notice that the answer refers to the objectives of the suggested controls as well as the controls themselves. Thinking through the control objectives in any given area will help you to suggest relevant controls. In another situation, it might help you to explain why current controls are weak.

(a)   A Black Esq   MNO & Co
Managing Director   3 Green Street
Quicksand Limited   Anytown
12 Kelvin Street
Anytown   Date

Dear Mr Black

You recently requested that we should advise you on good internal controls over cheque payments and petty cash. We should like to make the following recommendations.

The main objectives of control over payments are to ensure that payments are made only in respect of valid transactions and that they are suitably authorised.

The following control procedures will contribute toward attaining these objectives.

Cheque payments

(i)   Cheques should be raised only on the basis of authorisation, for example a purchase invoice which has been suitably authorised.

(ii)   Cheques should be signed by people other than those who approve invoices.

(iii)   There should be two independent signatories for each cheque, for instance, two directors might act as signatories. Signatories should inspect the documents supporting the cheque to ensure that the details agree. They should also mark the document so that it cannot be reused.

(iv)   Cheques should be restrictively crossed.

(v)   Unused cheques should be kept in a secure place. Cheques should never be signed in blank.

(vi)   Cheques should be under sequential control and all numbers should be accounted for. Spoilt cheques should therefore be retained.

(vii)   When cheques have been signed, they should be despatched immediately.

Petty cash

(i)   Petty cash payments should be made only on the basis of suitably authorised vouchers, which should be under sequential control. Vouchers should be retained for subsequent references. Where independent evidence is also available, for example invoices and receipts, this should be retained.

(ii)   An imprest system should be used to control petty cash. This means that the petty cash float is maintained at a specific amount and is reimbursed at regular intervals on the basis of vouchers showing the payments which have been made. It is suggested that the float should be kept at a level of £300 and be reimbursed on a weekly basis.

(iii)   The petty cash float should be subject to a periodic surprise counts by a responsible person not involved with the petty cash system. The balance on hand should be reconciled to the imprest account by reference to the vouchers not yet reimbursed.

(iv)   The size of individual payments out of petty cash should be subject to a maximum to be agreed by the directors.

(v)   Staff should not be allowed to cash personal cheques or borrow from petty cash.

I hope that the above information is useful to you in designing your systems of internal control. If you require any more information, please let me know.

Yours sincerely,

A Smith

(b)   Mr Black presumably feels that involvement in cash and cheque controls will be time-consuming, and that he is too busy to be involved in it. He may feel that he does not want to play a direct part in the petty cash function. Because of the small amounts involved, he may wish to delegate this function to another director. He should appreciate, however, that involvement at least in the authorisation of cheque payments would help to ensure that he is aware of major transactions in his business. He might consider the possibility of authorising cheques in excess of a given amount; this would minimise the demands on his time, while exercising control and keeping him informed of significant outgoings from the business.

Auditors may wish to consider whether Mr Black's lack of involvement may be symptomatic of insufficient attention being given to financial matters by the board.

12   ANALYTICAL REVIEW

> *Tutorial note.* This is not an exam standard question, but it is a useful look at what analytical procedures are and when they should be used. It is easy to fall into a trap of thinking that analytical procedures are only relevant at the start and end of the audit. This is not the case. They are valid procedures to use in the audit of every balance sheet area, and so might fall into an answer setting out procedures for the audit of any area.

Analytical review involves studying **significant ratios**, **trends** and other **statistics** and investigating any unusual or expected variations. The precise nature of these procedures and the manner in which they are documented will depend on the circumstances of each audit.

What determines comparisons made

The comparisons which can be made will depend on the **nature**, **accessibility** and **relevance** of the data available. Once the auditors have decided on the comparisons which they intend to make in performing analytical procedures, they should determine what **variations** they expect to be disclosed by them.

Investigation and evaluation of results

Unusual or **unexpected variations**, and expected variations which fail to occur, should be **investigated**. **Explanations** obtained should be **verified** and **evaluated** by the auditor to determine whether they are consistent with his understanding of the business and his general knowledge. Explanations may indicate a change in the business of which the auditors were previously unaware in which case they should reconsider the adequacy of their audit approach. Alternatively, they may indicate the possibility of misstatements in the financial statements; in these circumstances the auditors will need to **extend** their **testing** to determine whether the financial statements do contain **material misstatements**.

Analytical review at different stages of the audit

Auditors use analytical review in **audit planning** to help them **understand** the **client's business** and to identify **areas** of particular **audit risk**. Analytical procedures help auditors decide on the **nature, timing** and **extent** of **audit procedures**. Auditors can use various sources of information at the planning stage, including **budgets, management accounts** and **bank** and **cash records**.

Auditors may use analytical procedures as substantive tests. Various factors determine how much they will do so. These include the **level** of **detail** available, the **predictability** of the **data** being studied, and the **objectives** of the **audit tests**.

At the final stage of the audit auditors will use analytical procedures (such as ratio analysis and comparisons with previous years) to help them draw a **conclusion** about the accounts. Auditors will carefully review the results of the procedures undertaken to see whether they are **consistent** with the **results** of **other audit procedures** and the auditors' **knowledge** of the **business**.

13 BOSTON MANUFACTURING

> *Tutorial note.* In part (a), where you are required to assess the risk of the tangible fixed assets section of the audit, you should assess each of the components of audit risk in relation to the information given to you and then draw a conclusion about overall audit risk. However, this does not mean you should give detailed definitions of each component of audit risk. That will not gain you any marks in this question. The requirement clearly asks you to assess audit risk in this situation. You need to understand what each component is in order to be able to assess the risk here, but this question requires application of your understanding, not explanation.
>
> Part (b) is a very typical auditing question at this level. You should expect a question requiring you to set out appropriate procedures relating to any of the balance sheet areas you have studied. You should have a good knowledge of the sort of tests you are likely to carry out in respect of each balance sheet assertions, however, remember also to use information given to you in the question to direct you in the specific case.
>
> For example, in this situation, there has been a heavy investment in plant in the year. A high proportion of the total fixed assets figure relates to this new plant. Information given to you about these assets should affect your answer to part (c) when you consider how the depreciation rate should be set and assessed. However, it is also clearly relevant to part (b). Knowing that depreciation on the new plant should in the region of £25K should point you towards the fact that there may be plant which is fully written down in the financial statements. This may in fact be plant which has been replaced by the new plant. If the plant is not in use, it should not be included in the balance sheet.

(a) **Risk in the tangible fixed asset audit**

Control risk

The controls over fixed assets at Boston Manufacturing appear to be strong. The company maintains and reconciles a fixed asset register and there are authorisation procedures in operation. These controls should be tested, and if they prove effective, control risk could be assessed low.

Inherent risk

The tangible fixed assets are material on the basis of the proposed materiality level. There has been a substantial movement on the plant and equipment account this year, but this appears to be supported by the information given by the management accountant. There appear to be no disposals in the year, which may indicate that they have been omitted, or that obsolete items are included in the register. It is also unclear whether land is being depreciated. It would be inappropriate if it was being depreciated. Overall, the inherent risk seems to be medium.

Detection risk

Given that inherent risk has been assessed as moderate and control risk has been assessed as low, detection risk will be assessed as higher. However, there is usually good evidence in relation to existence and valuation of fixed assets and these are the key assertions which the auditors are interested in. There will also be scope to carry out good analytical procedures, such as proof in total of depreciation.

Conclusion

The audit of fixed assets appears to be medium to low risk.

(b) **Audit procedures**

(i) **Existence**

In many cases it is self-evident that land and buildings exist. However, it is important for the auditors to verify all components of land and buildings contained within the balance sheet, if they are on a site different to the one which the auditors are primarily attending, for example. Land and buildings should also be verified to **title deeds** to ensure that they **not only exist**, but that **they are owned** by the client.

The other classes of asset should be **inspected**. A sample of assets from the **register should be agreed to the physical asset**. There may be scope to rely on the work that the management accountant has undertaken here. The auditor should check a reconciliation which the accountant has undertaken. The auditors should make use of any identification marks on assets recorded in the register, for example, security tages or bar codes which are kept on assets to distinguish them. The auditor should inspect the **condition** of the assets and ensure that they are **in use**.

The motor vehicles should be **reconciled in terms of number of vehicles existing at the opening and closing positions**. Again, to ensure that they not only exist, but are owned by the company, the auditors should check the **registration documents** to ensure that the company is the registered owner.

For all the above assets, the external auditor should also review the insurance provision for the assets. This gives **third party evidence** of the existence of assets as the insurer would not insure a non-existing asset.

(ii) **Valuation (excluding depreciation)**

Land and buildings appear to be stated at historic **cost** as the schedule does not contain the words 'or valuation'. The auditors should **confirm** that this is the case with the management accountant. The cost can then be **agreed to brought forward figures** as there have been no additions in the year. These figures will have been audited in the previous year. If the assets are held at valuation, the auditors must ensure that the requirements of FRS 15 in relation to revaluations are being complied with.

Similarly, as there have been no movements in the year, **motor vehicles** can be agreed to the **opening position**.

To audit the valuation of **plant and computers**, the auditors should **agree the opening position**. They should then **obtain a schedule of additions** to fixed assets, which can be **agreed to purchase invoices** to verify valuation.

Lastly, the auditors should investigate whether the cost figures include any **fully-written down assets**. This is implied by the fact that the depreciation charge on plant excluding additions is low. If so, the auditor should find out whether these assets **are still in use**, and if not, consider whether they **should be excluded** from the cost and accumulated depreciation figures contained within the notes to the accounts. Excluding them would have a net effect on the reported figure of £0.

(iii) **Completeness**

The schedule of fixed assets prepared should be reconciled to:

*   The **opening position** (that is, the previous balance sheet)
*   The **closing position** (what is disclosed in the financial statements)
*   The **underlying records** (the nominal ledger)

If the fixed asset register contains details of the cost and accumulated depreciation of each asset, the **register should also be reconciled to the schedule**. Explanations should be sought for any differences.

The additions of the schedule should also be checked to ensure that the opening and closing positions reconcile within the schedule.

The auditors should also carry out a test on some of the **individual additions**, tracing the transaction through the system, from purchase orders to delivery notes and invoices and through the ledgers to the financial statements to ensure that additions have been included completely.

(c) **Depreciation**

(i) **Appropriateness**

The appropriateness of the rates should be considered and discussed with management. **Relevant factors** to consider are matters such as;

- The **replacement policy** for the asset
- The pattern of **usage** in the business
- The **purpose of the asset** being owned

In this instance, the auditors should establish the rationale behind the depreciation rates applied, particularly in the case of plant. In the case of the plant purchased this year, the depreciation rate applied is 10%. However, the assets have been purchased in relation to an 8 year project, so 12.5% might be a more appropriate rate.

(ii) **Audit procedures**

Depreciation on **buildings** can be verified by agreeing the purchase date of the buildings to last year's file or historic invoices/purchase documents and the valuation applied to the building portion.

For the other classes of asset, depreciation should be agreed for individual assets, as it is not possible to agree them in total. The auditors should obtain a **breakdown of the charges** for the year. They should be able to **recalculate the depreciation** from details in the fixed asset register and compare the results.

14 SITTING PRETTY

Tutorial note. This question covers all the important aspects of stock; existence, valuation and cut off. Part (b), which is for the most marks, requires you to plan the stocktake attendance. As you are planning, you should look for risk areas given to you in the question, just as you would in a more standard planning question.

In part (a) don't just give a standard answer about the importance of a stocktake (although this should form part of your answer). The question asks you to be specific about this situation.

The Study Text gives three useful steps in planning a stocktake attendance (on page 268) so you should bear these in mind, although not all the matters it mentions there are important in this case. You must practice being able to use standard lists of matters to consider but to *apply* them to a given scenario.

Similarly in parts (c) and (d), do not just write down everything you know about auditing cut off and valuation of stock. You must tailor your answer to the facts given in the question. In part (d), therefore, you will have to make a comment about the 10% discount, for example.

(a) **Importance of the stocktake**

The stocktake provides important **audit evidence** as to the **existence** and **completeness** of stock included in the financial statements.

In this case, the stocktake is particularly important because the **company does not maintain perpetual stock records**. As no perpetual records are maintained, the only basis for the stock entries in the financial statements is the results of this stocktake.

Stocks are **generally material** to the balance sheet of a manufacturing company and they are also one of the **higher risk areas** on the balance sheet. The stocktake provides important audit evidence reducing the risk of a material misstatement in relation to stock.

(b) **Planning for attendance**

Gain knowledge: I must review the notes of last year's stocktake and I must contact the factory manager to obtain details of this year's. I must review this year's details to ensure that the stocktake appears to be planned efficiently and effectively.

> *Tutorial note*. It is possible you assumed that this part of planning was already completed as the question tells you that you have just rung the factory manager. If so, you should have stated that assumption, or to cover yourself as we have, noted that this is a requirement. However, you should not have spent long on this aspect of the question.

Assess key factors: There are various key factors given in the scenario:

(i) **Nature and volume of the stocks**. There should be no WIP, so I will count raw materials (approximately 10% of the stock) and finished goods. However, raw material plastic should be low because a delivery is required to continue with production.

(ii) **Possible obsolescence**. I must make a note of the number of old chair legs maintained in raw materials as these are no obsolete, a new specification having been agreed.

(iii) **Cut off issues**. I need to ensure that the delivery on the day is isolated and that I obtain details of the delivery made during the stocktake. I need to determine whether this should be included as deliveries for the year, but most of all ensure that it does not get counted twice (as it arrives, and if it is put into stores). I should also obtain copies of the relevant documents, for example, the last invoices in the year and the last goods received and despatched notes.

(iv) **Off-cuts**. I need to consider whether any off cuts are maintained on site and whether these are being included in the stocktake. As the company receives a discount relating to them, they are unlikely to legally be considered Sitting Pretty's and so should not be included.

(v) **Staff issues**. It appears that the stocktake is undertaken by the people who work in the factory and handle the stock on a daily basis. This is not best practice, although in practical terms it is difficult to avoid. However, I should discuss this with the factory manager to assess whether staff can be allocated to counting stock they have not produced. Also, as the staff are allowed to go home as soon as the stocktake is completed, there is a risk that the stocktake will be rushed and mistakes will be made. The manager should ensure that it is made clear that the stocktake should be thorough and that no one will leave before checks on the thoroughness of the counts have been made.

Plan procedures: I need to determine my sample sizes and whether there is a need for expert assistance at this stocktake.

(i) **Procedures**. I will carry out test counts, checking from a sample of items to the count sheets and a sample of items from the count sheets to the physical items.

(ii) **Samples**. There are no higher value items that I should concentrate particularly on. Materiality for the year has been set at £5,000 currently. Dividing last year's figures for stock by this materiality level would give a sample size of 6 items for raw materials and 34 items for finished goods. I need to determine the batches in which stock is valued to ensure that I count the correct items. I need to assess the levels of stock when I arrive to ascertain whether this remains appropriate.

(c) **Cut off at final audit**

General procedures

The audit team should take a **sample of delivery notes** for sales and purchases on either side of the year end and **trace** these to **invoices** and **ledgers** and **stock** records to ensure that **sales and purchases have been included in the correct period** and that **stock is accounted for where appropriate**. (That is, sales have not be counted twice and purchases have been included in stock.) As the factory has been shut down, there is a lower risk that sale cut off is inappropriate than purchase cut off.

Stocktake delivery

Once it is determined whether this delivery should count as this year's stock (which it should if the stocktake was the year end date), the delivery information should be traced to purchase invoices and ledgers to ensure that the purchase is recorded in the year and that the creditor is accounted for in the year. The stock should then be included also.

Other matters

If **stock returns** are material, the stock returns after the year end should be reviewed to ensure that items are not included as sales in the year and that the stock is added to the stock figure unless it is now obsolete, whereupon it should be written off.

(d)   **Valuation of stock**

The auditors should obtain the client's working papers relating to the valuation of stock. Items which the auditor sampled at the stocktale should already have been verified to the stocktake records as part of the verification of existence.

Cost

The auditors should then **trace a sample of items to purchase invoices** to ensure that **cost has been correctly applied**. Cost of purchase (per SSAP 9) excludes trade discounts and rebates, so the auditors should ensure that the valuation **cost excludes the 10% discount** received for returning the off-cuts of plastic.

The auditors should then ensure that for a sample of finished goods items, **costs of conversion** (comprising costs of labour and overheads) have been included. This should be on a comparable basis to the previous year and therefore can be audited by analytical review.

Net realisable value

The auditors should ensure that **cost is lower than net realisable value** by tracing their sample to **after date sales**. If no invoices are yet available, the auditors can make confirmations by reviewing sales orders and price lists.

Obsolete

Lastly, the auditors should ensure by review and by discussion with management that stock which has been identified as **obsolete** at the stocktake has **not been attributed value** and has been **scrapped**.

Analytical procedures

The auditors will undertake general analytical procedures to ensure that the stock figure stacks up. This could include calculating ratios such as stock turnover and ensuring that they stack up with the facts that have been presented them in the course of the stock audit.

15   BRIGHT SPARKS

> *Tutorial note*. This question looks at the issue of control problems arising from an interim audit and then it asks you to draw conclusions for the final audit. The second part of this question is in effect a planning exercise. It requires you to look at specific procedures as a result of what has been done at the interim stage, however, you also need to include some more general procedures in your answer. This question is slightly unusual in that an interim audit has already been done. In an exam you are more likely to have to set out procedures from scratch. However, this question is also good practice in evaluating the results of procedures performed. This could also be examined, perhaps in the context of drawing conclusions for the audit report.

(a)   *Conclusions to be drawn as a result of the interim audit*

The following weaknesses exist in the company's systems.

(i)   In any system of internal control, one person should not be able to process a whole transaction:

(1)   Authorisation
(2)   Execution
(3)   Recording

The most serious deficiency in the company's system is that warehousemen can:

(1)   Sell goods
(2)   Receive cash from cash sales
(3)   Raise sales invoices for credit sales
(4)   Raise credit notes

Moreover, there appears to be no procedure for checking any of their work. Since the accounting records are written up on the evidence of these invoices and credit notes, any errors made by the warehousemen will be carried into the records. It may also be the case that the issue of credit notes is not authorised by a senior member of staff.

Possible consequences

(1)   Errors on invoices may not be detected except by customers

(2) Risk of unauthorised or fraudulent invoices or credit notes being raised without detection

(3) Risk of goods leaving the premises without being invoiced, whether through error or fraud (this is particularly dangerous in a business such as this, with a variety of high-value items)

(4) Time wasted by needless disagreements with customers about amounts owing

(ii) There appears to be a weakness in the recording of cash received by the company. The dates recorded in the books are presumably the dates when the entries were written up. If so, there is clearly an excessive delay in recording cash received, and possibly also in banking it. There may also be no record of cash received made when incoming mail is opened.

Possible consequences

(1) Errors and defalcations can arise where a cash received system is weak.

(2) The longer the gap between receipt and recording, the more likely it is that discrepancies can occur.

(3) Specific possibilities:

- Falsification of records leading to misappropriation of cash (teeming and lading)

- Mislaying of cheques if not banked promptly

- Errors in the records, especially concerning dates

(iii) Stricter control is needed over the granting of cash discounts (assuming that it is the actual receipt of cash which is later than the due date, not merely the late recording of same).

Possible consequence

Discounts given to a standard list of customers who may be friends of staff or regular customers, not necessarily prompt payers.

(b) *Audit work on debtors at the final audit*

(i) *Second circularisation*

(1) Consider circularising all debtors, or at least a larger sample than before of debtors not circularised at 30 September.

(2) Circularise, and investigate disagreeing replies. Discover if reasons are similar to those given at 30 September circularisation.

(ii) To gain further evidence about the rights and obligations and existence of debtors

(1) Check the sales invoices which make up the balances with backing documentation, for example purchase orders and despatch notes (if the latter exist).

(2) Ascertain extent of cash received from debtors after the year-end; reconcile the individual invoices to ensure that no discrepancies exist.

(3) Obtain explanations for invoices remaining unpaid after subsequent invoices have been paid.

To gain evidence about the valuation of debtors, I would review the cash received after date and would also carry out the following tests.

(1) Check calculation of outstanding invoices.

(2) Carry out further tests on settlement discounts and ascertain whether the position has improved or deteriorated since the time of the interim audit.

(3) Confirm necessity/adequacy of provision against write-off of specific debts by review of correspondence, solicitors' debt collection, agencies' letters, liquidation statements.

(4) Consider whether amounts owed may be not recovered where there have been round sum payments on account or invoices unpaid after subsequent invoices paid.

(5) Review customer files/correspondence from solicitors and debtors' circularisation results for evidence of potential bad debts.

(6) Confirm any general provisions for bad debts, considering how well previous year's provision considering predicted actual bad debts and whether the formula used is reasonable and consistent with previous years.

I would check the completeness of debtors by carrying out cut-off tests at 31 December to ensure that all goods leaving the premises by that date (and only those) have been included in sales. I would also check that all returns of goods after the year-end relating to 20X0 sales have been correctly recorded.

Other general tests include:

(1) Agree the opening balance on the sales ledger control account with the previous year's working papers to ensure all the necessary adjustments were put through last year.

(2) Scrutinise sales ledger control for unusual entries.

(3) Check list of debtor balances to and from sales ledger, and reconcile with sales ledger control account.

(4) Carry out analytical procedures, particularly reviewing changes in the debtor turnover period, and changes in the age profile of debtors.

(5) Check that trade debtors have been separately disclosed in the notes to the accounts.

16   NEWPIECE

Tutorial note. The bank reconciliation is extremely important when auditing bank. It links the good, third party evidence of a bank letter to the client's actual position after timing differences. If a question on auditing bank comes up, it is likely to involve procedures relating to auditing a bank reconciliation, so this is good practice. Part (b) looks at some audit considerations in relation to petty cash.

Always remember to consider (and write down that you have) materiality with regard to petty cash. It is often immaterial, and this should affect the audit approach you take.

(a) (i) The matters that are of concern in the bank reconciliation are as follows

(1) **Delay in banking cash sales.** Cash received does not appear to have been banked until a week after the cash was received. A **teeming** and **lading fraud** could have occurred, where an embezzlement of receipts is covered up by an apparent delay in banking subsequent receipts.

(2) **Delay in presentation of cheques by suppliers.** Most suppliers would bank cheques within seven to ten days. However payments to the majority of suppliers entered on October 31 have not been cleared for over two weeks. Cheques, although entered prior to the year-end, may not therefore have been sent to suppliers until some time after the year-end. The reason for doing this would be to **improve** the appearance of the company's **liquidity** in its accounts, by decreasing cash and creditors, and hence improving the company's current and acid test ratios.

(ii) **Cash sales**

The following tests should be carried out.

(1) **Compare** the **date** on the **bank statement** with the **date** stamped on the **paying-in slip**. If the dates are the same or a day apart, then that is strong evidence of when the cheques were actually banked.

(2) **Compare amounts banked** with **cash records** for the day (invoices or the till roll).

(3) **Compare sales ledger cash received** per **cash book** with **daily listing** of cash received.

(4) Carry out **further investigations** if there does appear to be a **significant delay** between **collecting** and **banking cash**. Investigations should cover other periods of the year and the situation at the date of the audit.

(5) If there is **unbanked cash** at the date of the **audit**, **inspect** this **cash**. Failure to produce this cash would be strong evidence of fraud.

Uncleared payments

The following tests should be carried out.

(1) **Ask cashiers** and others involved in sending cheques out **when** the **cheques** were **actually sent.**

(2) **Obtain suppliers' statements** after the year-end, and **check** the **date** the **cash** is **shown as received.** If this date is similar to the date shown on the bank statement, the cheques would probably have been sent out after the year-end.

(iii) (1) If the **cash receipts** represent monies that have been **embezzled,** these **receipts** should be **excluded** from the **cash balances** at the year-end (£2,705). If the **money** is **irrecoverable,** it should be charged as an **expense** in the profit and loss account; if it appears to be **recoverable,** it should be charged as an **amount owing.**

(2) **Cash** and **creditors** should be **increased** as it appears that the true date of the cheques, the date that the cheques were sent to suppliers, was after the year-end. Thus the bank balance and creditors due within one year should be increased by £77,501, the total of cheques 2164 to 2170.

Thus the true cash book balance will be £681 overdrawn.

(b) (i) **Materiality**

Two commonly used measures of materiality are **1% of turnover** and **5% of profit** before tax. For Newpiece these two measures would suggest materiality levels of £25,000 and £7,500 respectively. Total petty cash expenditure is well over the profit measure and slightly under the turnover measure, and this indicates that on balance it should be audited. However about £15,000 of total expenditure occurred in two months. This suggests that testing should be concentrated on these months, with a briefer review taking place of other months, since material fraud and error is unlikely to occur during those months.

Audit risk

Petty cash is a high risk audit area for the following reasons.

(1) Cash is the **most liquid asset**, and hence there is a high risk of defalcation.

(2) **Supporting documentation** for payments may be **limited.**

(3) The failure to keep petty cash on an imprest system means that it may **not** be **subject** to **regular management review.**

(4) Risk would be increased by a **large petty cash balance** (say over £1,000), as this would offer greater opportunity for fraud.

(ii) The audit tests that will be carried out are as follows.

Initial procedures

(1) **Agree opening balances** to working papers for last year.

(2) **Check additions** in **petty cash book.**

(3) **Check that petty cash book totals** have been **posted** to the **general ledger.**

(4) **Check** that **payments** in the **main cash book** shown as payments to **petty cash** have been shown as receipts in the **petty cash book.**

Review of unusual items and analytical review

(1) **Review cash payments** in the **general ledger** and **investigate unusual transactions.**

(2) **Carry out analytical procedures** on **balances** by **comparing amounts** with **cash flow forecasts.**

Transactions (to test existence, completeness and rights and obligations)

(1) **Verify individual payments** in petty cash book (concentrating on the larger items) to **supporting documentation** and check that employee has acknowledged receipt of cash.

(2) **Check cash cut-off** procedures have been performed by **reviewing reconciliation** at the year-end, and checking that all reconciling items can be satisfactorily **explained** and have **subsequently been cleared**.

Cash counts (to verify existence, completeness, rights and obligations and valuation)

(1) **Count all balances simultaneously** and **agree** to **petty cash book** or other record.

(2) **All counting** should be **done** in the **presence** of the **individuals responsible**. They should sign at the end of the count to acknowledge funds returned are complete.

(3) **Enquire** into any **IOUs** or **cashed cheques** outstanding for unreasonable periods of time.

(4) **Obtain certificates** of **cash in hand** from responsible officials.

(5) **Confirm** that bank and cash **balances** as reconciled above are **correctly stated** in the **accounts**.

Follow-up procedures should include the following tests.

(1) **Obtain certificates** of **cash-in-hand** as appropriate.

(2) **Check unbanked cheques/cash receipts** have subsequently been **paid in** and **agree** to the **bank reconciliation**.

(3) **Check IOUs** and **cheques cashed** for **employees** have been **reimbursed.**

(4) **Check IOUs** or **cashed cheques outstanding** for **unreasonable periods** of time have been **provided for**.

(5) **Check** the **balances** as **counted** are **reflected** in the **accounts** (subject to any agreed amendments because of shortages and so on).

Presentation and disclosure

Check presentation of cash balances in the accounts is **correct.**

17   TRURO ELECTRONICS

> *Tutorial note.* Again we have focused our answer round the financial statement assertions. This answer is longer than you would be expected to produce in an exam. The question is not really exam style – in the exam you might be asked a similar requirement, but probably in the context of a fuller audit scenario.

The substantive procedures that might be performed to verify the specified balance sheet items are as follows.

(a)   *Trade creditors: £3,200,000*

We should carry out the following general tests on trade creditors

(i)   Agree the opening balance on the purchase ledger control account with the previous year's working papers to ensure all the necessary adjustments were put through last year.

(ii)   Obtain a list of purchase ledger balances in respect of the year-end and:

(1)   Test check to and from purchase ledger accounts to list of balances.

(2)   Check total of list with control account balance at year-end (obtain explanations if any reconciliation necessary).

(3)   Cast list of balances and control account.

(iii)   Carry out analytical review of statistics such as ratio of trade creditors to purchases and gross profit ratio; compare to previous periods and obtain explanations for major variances.

(iv)   Scrutinise ledger balances for unusual entries especially items that are large and occur around the year-end.

Reconciliation of suppliers' statements with purchase ledger balances will be a key test of rights and obligations, valuation and existence. A creditors' circularisation should be carried out if suppliers' statements for significant creditors are not available.

The following tests should be carried out to check creditors are completely recorded.

(i)   Check purchases cut-off.

    (1)   Check from goods received notes with serial numbers before the year-end to ensure that invoices are either:

        °   Posted to purchase ledger prior to the year-end; or
        °   Included on the schedule of accruals.

    (2)   Review the schedule of accruals to ensure that goods received after the year-end are not accrued.

    (3)   Check from goods returned notes prior to year-end to ensure that credit notes have been posted to the purchase ledger prior to the year-end or accrued.

    (4)   Review large invoices and credit notes included after the year-end to ensure that they refer to the following year.

    (5)   Reconcile daily batch invoice totals around the year-end to purchase ledger control account ensuring batches are posted in the correct year.

    (6)   Review purchase ledger control account around the year-end for any unusual items.

(ii)   Compare current listing of creditors with that of the previous year and note any significant changes, for example changes in major suppliers, proportion of debit balances.

We should also check that trade creditors are disclosed separately in the notes to the accounts, and other necessary disclosures (for example amounts payable by instalments) made.

(b)   *Bank overdraft: £2,100,000*

The bank letter will provide vital evidence concerning the financial statement assertions that relate to the bank overdraft We should carry out the following tests that relate to the bank letter and the year-end bank reconciliation.

(i)   Check arithmetic of bank reconciliation.

(ii)   Trace cheques shown as outstanding from the bank reconciliation to the cash book prior to the year-end and to the after date bank statements and obtain explanations for any large or unusual items not cleared at the time of the audit.

(iii)   Verify by checking pay-in slips that uncleared bankings are paid in prior to the year end, and check uncleared bankings are cleared quickly after the year-end.

(iv)   Verify balances per cash book according to the reconciliation with cash book and general ledger.

(v)   Verify the bank balances with reply to standard bank letter and with the bank statements.

(vi)   Scrutinise the cash book and bank statements before and after the balance sheet date for exceptional entries or transfers which have a material effect on the balance shown to be in hand.

(vii)   Obtain explanations for all items in the cash book for which there are no corresponding entries in the bank statement and vice versa.

The following tests relate specifically to rights and obligations.

(i)   Ensure that bank overdraft is within company's agreed limit with the bank.

(ii)   Consider balance in terms of:

    (1)   Right of set-off with other balances

    (2)   Any security granted for the borrowing (if there is a charge over the assets it should be registered)

    (3)   The company's borrowing limits per its articles and authorisation in the directors' minutes

We should consider the classification of the overdraft in the accounts as current or longer term, and check that it has been disclosed separately in the notes to the accounts.

(c)   *Corporation tax creditor: £5,200,000*

The main emphasis will be checking the calculation and reasonableness of the provision. The auditors will carry out the following tests:

(i) Obtain and recompute corporation tax computation for the current year, check that current year's provision has been computed at the correct rate, and reconcile the tax charge in the profit and loss account with tax at current rate applied to the profit before tax.

(ii) Check position regarding computations for previous years; note agreed computations and verify that provisions for computations not yet agreed appear reasonable. (*Note*. The provision of £5,200,000 may be in respect of more than one accounting period.).

(iii) Confirm tax paid to receipts from Inland Revenue.

The following tests should be carried out to check the completeness of the provision and also rights and obligations:

(i) Ensure that all disallowable items have been identified and added back by reviewing the financial and management accounts in conjunction with our own detailed working papers.

(ii) Review correspondence with the Inland Revenue for unusual items.

We should also check that the taxation provision is separately disclosed in the accounts, ensuring that the balance is properly identified as tax currently payable (within one year).

(d) *Accruals: £2,300,000*

We should obtain the list of accruals and check the list to the accounting records to confirm its accuracy.

We should check the valuation of accruals by carrying out the following tests:

(i) Verify the amounts of accruals by reference to subsequent payments and supporting documentation (this also provides evidence of rights and obligations).

(ii) Consider basis for any round sum accruals and ensure it is consistent with prior years.

(iii) Carry out analytical review of accruals.

The main emphasis on testing accruals will be on testing that accruals have been completely provided. We shall carry out the following tests.

(i) Scrutinise payments made and invoices received after year-end to ascertain whether any further accruals are necessary.

(ii) Compare with prior year's list of accruals. Investigate any items brought forward and items normally paid in arrears not included on current year's list.

(iii) Ascertain why any payments on account are being made and ensure full liability has been provided.

(iv) Consider whether there are any items which might not be invoiced until a long time after the year-end.

We should also check that accruals are disclosed separately in the notes to the accounts.

(e) *VAT creditor: £1,700,000*

The following tests should be carried out on the valuation of the creditor:

(i) Check that VAT accrual is correct amount outstanding by checking to returns/accounting records.

(ii) Ensure that no non-deductible tax is reclaimed.

(iii) Vouch payments or refunds of VAT to cash book from VAT returns.

We should perform the following tests to confirm the completeness of the creditor, also to confirm rights and obligations:

(i) Obtain VAT returns for the period, and check returns have been properly prepared and filed promptly (attention should be paid to the default surcharge provisions for late submission of returns or late payment of VAT due).

(ii) Test VAT totals from prime records to monthly/quarterly summaries and test cast summaries and scrutinise for unusual items.

(iii) Review correspondence with HM Customs & Excise and results of any recent control visits.

18   GOING CONCERN

> *Tutorial note.* Part (a) demonstrates what can be deduced from the calculations for example short-term funds used to purchase fixed assets and delayed payments to creditors. It is vital when you approach questions like this that you do not spend so long calculating ratios that you fail to make comments and draw conclusions from your work. Equally, having been asked in the question to undertake some calculations, it would be wrong not to do so. You must apply judgement in the balance between calculations and analysis in your answer, remembering that you will score better marks for analysis. Of course, to get those marks, you must have something to analyse …

Workings

The following significant accounting ratios are based on the accounts provided in the question.

	20X2	20X3	20X4	20X5	20X6
Gross profit (%)	23.50	10.90	14.20	20.20	19.70
Other expenses: sales (%)	14.10	10.90	14.40	14.40	15.30
Interest: sales (%)	0.90	1.10	5.20	5.50	6.20
Net profit (%)	8.50	(1.10)	(5.40)	0.30	(1.80)
Current ratio	1.39	0.91	0.73	0.73	0.76
Liquidity ratio	0.80	0.59	0.46	0.37	0.34
Gearing	0.18	0.75	9.52	9.58	20.69
Stock (months)	1.68	2.28	2.26	2.77	3.57
Debtors (months)	1.75	3.66	3.24	2.26	2.32
Creditors (months)	1.73	4.83	3.80	3.54	4.09

Notes

$$\text{Stock age} = \frac{\text{Year end stock}}{\text{Cost of sales}} \times 12$$

$$\text{Debtors age} = \frac{\text{Year end debtor}}{\text{Sales}} \times 12$$

$$\text{Creditors age} = \frac{\text{Year end creditor}}{\text{Sales}} \times 12$$

$$\text{Gearing} = \frac{\text{Long-term loans} + \text{Bank overdraft} + \text{Hire purchase}}{\text{Shareholders' funds}}$$

(a)   The various factors in the accounts which may be indicative of going concern problems are as follows.

(i)   Only losses or low profits are being made; the company is not generating sufficient funds to finance the expansion required.

(ii)   There has been a dramatic increase in the level of overdraft over the last year, there seems little prospect of the borrowing being reduced and the security is threatened.

(iii)   There are signs of overtrading as the expansion has been financed by borrowings and the increase in current assets is being financed by creditors.

(iv)   The gearing is high and increasing, with very little security being available for the loans.

(v)   There is a low current ratio; short term funds are being used to finance long term assets.

(vi)   The liquidity ratio is low and decreasing and the company's ability to meet its liabilities on demand must be very questionable.

(vii)   Stock levels are increasing, suggesting that one or more of the following problems may exist: deteriorating sales, poor stock control, obsolete or slow moving stocks.

(viii) The value and age of creditors is increasing: some creditors must be having to wait a considerable time before being paid and it can only be a matter of time before pressure is put on the company by one or more of its creditors.

(ix)   High and increasing interest charges make the company very vulnerable, especially in a period of recession and high interest rates.

    (x)   The fluctuating gross profit would suggest that the company's profit margins are under pressure. The present level of gross profit does not seem sufficient given the company's high level of expenses.

(b)   The other important steps to be taken by the auditors in determining whether or not the company may be properly regarded as a going concern at the year end would include:

    (i)   Review carefully the cash and profit forecasts for the next year to see if they suggested any improvement in the company's position; consider the basis of preparation of these forecasts and whether they appear comprehensive.

    (ii)   Seek some evidence that the company's bank is prepared to continue supporting the company.

    (iii)   Review the level of post balance sheet trading to see if this supports the forecasts and show any signs of improvement in the company's position.

    (iv)   Examine correspondence files for any evidence that creditors might be putting pressure on the company for repayment of monies owing.

    (v)   Consider how the company's position compares with similar companies in the same business.

    (vi)   Discuss generally the situation with management and review any recovery plans which they may have in mind.

19   WISEGUYS NATIONAL BAKERIES

> *Tutorial note.* The question does *not* ask you to draft the necessary qualifications in the audit report (a question in the exam might).
>
> The question does require an explanation of the reasons for qualifying and not qualifying the audit report; it is particularly important here that the explanations are clear, since they are being addressed to a client who might be sensitive about having a qualified audit report.

S J Lee & Co
Castle House, 67-70 Knights Road
London EC1

Mr N Morris
Finance Director
Wiseguys National Bakeries Ltd
Wiseguys House
Woodley Industrial Estate
Woodley, Beds

28 February 20X4

Dear Mr Morris,

Financial statements: year ended 31 December 20X3

Thank you for your letter dated 21 January 20X4 and copy of the minutes of your board meeting at which the above financial statements were approved. We note also that it was resolved that no amendments should be made to the statements as approved.

We must, nevertheless, point out that there are certain matters which we have noted during our review of the financial statements and, subject to further discussion, these may well require suitable reference in our audit report when this is finalised in due course. These matters are accordingly listed below.

1   *Freehold property*

In past years this property has been shown in the statement at its original cost, whereas it is now restated at £1,250,000 as professionally valued during the year. We are satisfied as to the basis of the revaluation, adjustment to and disclosure within the financial statements. As a result no further reference to the property revaluation will be required in our audit report.

2   *Doubtful debt provision*

It is our belief that no part of the debt of £45,000 due from XYZ Ltd will be recovered by the company. Since the financial statements which the directors have approved include no provisions against this debt, it will be necessary for us to state that:

(a)   No provision has been made against an amount of £45,000 owing by the customer.

(b)   We believe such amount to be irrecoverable.

(c)   Except for the failure to make such provision, in our opinion a true and fair view of the state of the company's affairs and its results is given by the financial statements.

3   *Loan to a director*

Since the director's indebtedness of £22,000, which subsisted during a six week period, has not been disclosed in the financial statements in accordance with the provisions of the Companies Act 1985, we are obliged under the Act to include in our report a statement giving the required particulars.

The particulars include:

(a)   The name of the director
(b)   The fact of his indebtedness
(c)   The amount due (including any interest) ie £22,000

4   *Alleged breach of contract*

Because of the potential materiality of the uncertainty concerning the amount of compensation (possibly including costs) which it appears will be payable following the major breach of your contract with LMBN Ltd, we feel it will be necessary for our report to refer to the explanatory note in the financial statements in which this contingent liability is disclosed under a fundamental uncertainty paragraph.

This paragraph simply draws closer attention to this matter. It is not a qualification of our opinion.

Should you and your co-directors wish to discuss these matters further, please do not hesitate to contact us. If it is believed that, in the light of the above comments, amendments to the accounts should be made, it will, of course, be necessary for the board to re-approve the amended financial statements.

However, should the board still consider that no amendments are to be made, it will be necessary for us to draft our audit report incorporating the various matters referred to in this letter. A copy of the proposed report will be forwarded for your information.

Yours sincerely

For S J Lee & Co.

20   **EXTERNAL REVIEW REPORTS**

> *Tutorial note.* This question is not exam standard. However, the review report was examined in a 'compare and contrast to the audit report situation' in December 2001 and it is vital you are comfortable with the report. This question is useful consolidation, therefore.

(a)   Negative assurance is when the auditor gives assurance that nothing has come to his attention which indicates that the financial statements have not been prepared according to the applicable framework and that they do not show a true and fair view. It is assurance in the absence of any evidence to the contrary.

(b)   A review engagement is designed to enable an auditor to express an opinion on financial statements on the basis of lower level procedures than would be undertaken for an audit.

It follows, therefore that the level of assurance given after such an assignment will be lower than for an audit assignment. Insufficient evidence has been obtained to give 'reasonable assurance', only a limited amount of assurance can be given.

(c)   (i)   If matters have come to the attention of the auditor, he should **describe those matters**. The matters may have the following effects.

Impact	Effect on report
Material	Express a **qualified** opinion of negative assurance
Pervasive	Express an **adverse** opinion that the financial statements do not give a true and fair view

(ii) The auditor may feel there has been a limitation in the scope of the work he intended to carry out for the review. If so, he should **describe the limitation**. The limitation may have the following effects.

Impact	Effect on report
Material to one area	Express a **qualified** opinion of negative assurance due to amendments which might required if the limitation did not exist
Pervasive	Do not provide any assurance

21   'TAP!'

> *Tutorial note.* In part (a) you are asked to discuss the audit risks in the scenario. Remember that there will be some inherent risk in the audit from the fact that this client is a charity (such as additional regulatory requirements and unusual income) but there these are not exclusively the inherent risks. Don't put an imaginary 'charity hat' on to the exclusion of everything else. Breaking your answer down into the components of audit risk helps to structure your answer. If you are thinking in terms of the components of risk as you read through the scenario, it might help you see the various risks that are contained in the scenario. Don't be afraid to mark your question paper as well – scribble things down as they strike you.
>
> Part (b) should be fairly straightforward. Remember, when suggesting audit procedures, be explicit about what you are going to do. Don't just 'check invoices'. Explain which invoices and why.
>
> In part (c) you should be able to think of many more than 5 marks worth of controls which the charity could implement over cash, as you have not been told of any that they have. Remember to think in terms of control objectives – why is a control needed and what is it trying to achieve? Then you will be suggesting relevant controls. Try and be realistic as well. The Trustees want genuine business advice, not crazy schemes.

(a) **Audit risks**

There is a higher audit risk associated with a charity as in the event of problems arising and litigation taking place, the audit firm could experience a significant amount of bad publicity.

> This 'overall' risk comes before all the others

Inherent risks

(i) **Cash**. The charity operates with a high number of cash and cheque transactions. A substantial part of their **income** comes from cash donations. Put another way, it is likely that very little of their income comes from direct bank transfers. Also, it is likely that many of the **expenses** which 'Tap!' incurs are also cash expenses. Cash is **risky for audit purposes** because it is **susceptible to loss, miscounting or misappropriation**.

(ii) **Charity**. The theatre company is a charity, and is therefore subject to a high degree of **regulation**. This raises the risk for our audit.

(iii) **Accounting specialist**. The charity employs an administrator, but there is no mention of an accountant. It is **unclear who is going to draft the charity accounts** (which must comply with specialist requirements) but it does not appear that a specialist exists to undertake this job. This increases the risk of errors existing in the accounts.

(iv) **Completeness of income**. As the charity appears to have **no control** over the primary collection of income from box office receipts, there is a significant **risk that income is understated** and that the theatres have not accounted properly to the theatre.

(v) **Disclosure of income**. The disclosure of income must be considered. It is unlikely to be appropriate to show the 'net income from theatres' figure. Rather, the gross income less commission should probably be disclosed.

(vi) **Expenditure**. The charity expenses may be well-recorded, or they may be **difficult to substantiate** – this is not clear. It may also be difficult to substantiate payments made to build wells in Africa. We currently have no knowledge about how that aspect of the charity operates. It will be important to check that expenditure is made in accordance with the trust deed. Some necessary administrative expense will not necessarily be conducive to the aims of the charity. We must ensure that it is all analysed correctly.

Control

There currently appear to be **no controls over cash** in the charity.

Detection

This is a **first year audit**, so there is little knowledge of the business at present. It is also the **first ever audit** of the charity, so the comparatives are unaudited. We must make this clear in our report, and we will need to undertake more detailed work on the **opening balances**. As the charity is to a large degree **peripatetic**, we may find audit evidence difficult to obtain, if it has not be properly returned to the administrative offices.

Conclusion

This appears to be a high risk first year audit. It is likely to result in a qualified audit opinion.

(b) **Audit procedures**

Income from box office takings

Income from box office can be **verified to the statement from the theatre** and the **bank statements** to ensure that it is complete. The **commission** can be agreed by **recalculation**.

It might be necessary to **circularise** a number of the theatres and request **confirmation of the seats sold** for each performance to ensure that income is completely stated on the return from the theatre. [However, if theatres have been defrauding the charity, they are unlikely to confirm this to the auditors. This may have to be an area which is aided by stronger controls over income.]

Income from buckets (theatres and streets)

We must discover whether the charity fill out 'counting sheets' when the buckets of money are originally counted. If so, the **money in buckets can be verified from the original sheet to the banking documentation**.

However, in the **absence of strong controls** over the counting, it will be **impossible to conclude that this income is complete**.

Income from other donations

Donations made over the phone should have been noted on documents then retained at the administrative offices. Donations made by post should have **original documents**. A sample of these should be **traced to banking documentation** and bank statements.

Again, in the **absence of originating documentation**, it will be **difficult to conclude that income is fairly stated**.

(c) **Controls over cash**

Tutorial note. Three good suggestions should be sufficient to gain you 6 marks. We have included others as there are a large number of suggestions that can be made.

Income from box office takings

It would be a good control over completeness of income to request a **schedule of seats sold** from the theatres for every night a performance is given. This is likely to be information that theatres can print off their systems with no trouble. This will lead to the theatre company having more assurance as to the completeness of income.

Income from buckets

As this income is highly susceptible to loss or misappropriation, strong controls should be put in place:

(i) **Number of people**. If possible, the charity should assign **two people** to each bucket during the collection phase and two people should count the money in the bucket at the end of the day. These people will act as a **check on each other** to ensure that cash is kept more secure.

Structuring your answer by components of risk makes it logical/easy to read

---

Do not be afraid to conclude that there may be insufficient evidence

---

(ii)   **Security**. The security arrangements for buckets should be strong. The charity could invest in a **transportable safe** in which to store the money between collection and banking. It might also be wise to use **collecting tins** rather than buckets, as this simple measure would ensure that the cash was less open to the public. The cash should also be **banked frequently**. It should not be kept not banked for 24 hours after collection.

(iii) **Recording**. A record should be made of cash counts and it should be signed by both the people that undertook the count. These can provide an initial record of the cash takings.

Other income

The controls over other income will be restricted by the number of staff at the Leicester office. It appears that only the administrator may work there regularly. If this is the case, it is going to be difficult to introduce supervision into the cash operations.

All phone donations should be **recorded on pre-numbered documentation** so as to give evidence of completeness.

As the administrator largely works alone, it would be a good idea for the Board of Trustees to carry out a cyclical review of the work of the administrator. This would provide a useful protection from problems for both the charity and the administrator.

> Make sure your suggestions are relevant and possible

Index

Note: **Key Terms** and their references are given in **bold**

BPP
PUBLISHING

See overleaf for information on other
BPP products and how to order

ACCA Order

To BPP Publishing Ltd, Aldine Place, London W12 8AW

Tel: 020 8740 2211

Fax: 020 8740 1184

email: publishing@bpp.com

online: www.bpp.com

Mr/Mrs/Ms (Full name)

Daytime delivery address

Postcode

Daytime Tel

Date of exam (month/year)

	6/02 Texts	1/02 Kits	9/01 Passcards	MCQ Cards	Tapes	Videos	7/02 i-Learn	7/02 i-Pass	Virtual Campus
PART 1									
1.1 Preparing Financial Statements	£20.95	£10.95	£5.95	£5.95	£12.95	£25.00	£34.95	£24.95	£90.00
1.2 Financial Information for Management	£20.95	£10.95	£5.95	£5.95	£12.95	£25.00	£34.95	£24.95	£90.00
1.3 Managing people	£20.95	£10.95	£5.95		£12.95	£25.00	£34.95	£24.95	£90.00
PART 2									
2.1 Information Systems	£20.95	£10.95	£5.95		£12.95	£25.00	£34.95	£24.95	£90.00
2.2 Corporate and Business Law	£20.95	£10.95	£5.95		£12.95	£25.00	£34.95	£24.95	£90.00
2.3 Business Taxation FA 2001 (for 12/02 exam)	£20.95	£10.95	£5.95		£12.95	£25.00	£34.95	£24.95	£90.00
2.4 Financial Management and Control	£20.95	£10.95	£5.95		£12.95	£25.00	£34.95	£24.95	£90.00
2.5 Financial Reporting	£20.95	£10.95	£5.95		£12.95	£25.00	£34.95	£24.95	£90.00
2.6 Audit and Internal Review	£20.95	£10.95	£5.95		£12.95	£25.00	£34.95	£24.95	£90.00
PART 3									
3.1 Audit and Assurance Services	£20.95	£10.95	£5.95		£12.95	£25.00			
3.2 Advanced Taxation FA 2001 (for 12/02 exam)	£20.95	£10.95	£5.95		£12.95	£25.00			
3.3 Performance Management	£20.95	£10.95	£5.95		£12.95	£25.00			
3.4 Business Information Management	£20.95	£10.95	£5.95		£12.95	£25.00			
3.5 Strategic Business Planning and Development	£20.95	£10.95	£5.95		£12.95	£25.00			
3.6 Advanced Corporate Reporting	£20.95	£10.95	£5.95		£12.95	£25.00			
3.7 Strategic Financial Management	£20.95	£10.95	£5.95		£12.95	£25.00			
INTERNATIONAL STREAM									
1.1 Preparing Financial Statements	£20.95	£10.95	£5.95	£5.95					
2.5 Financial Reporting	£20.95	£10.95	£5.95						
2.6 Audit and Internal Review	£20.95	£10.95	£5.95						
3.1 Audit and Assurance Services	£20.95	£10.95	£5.95						
3.6 Advance Corporate Reporting	£20.95	£10.95	£5.95						
Success in your Research and Analysis Project – Tutorial Text (8/02)	£20.95								
Learning to Learn (7/02)	£9.95								

Subtotal £ ___

POSTAGE & PACKING

Study Texts

	First	Each extra	
UK	£3.00	£2.00	£
Europe*	£5.00	£4.00	£
Rest of world	£20.00	£10.00	£

Kits/Passcards/Success Tapes

	First	Each extra	
UK	£2.00	£1.00	£
Europe*	£2.50	£1.00	£
Rest of world	£15.00	£8.00	£

MCQ cards

	£1.00	£1.00	£

CDs each

UK	£2.00	£
Europe*	£2.00	£
Rest of world	£10.00	£

Breakthrough Videos

	First	Each extra	
UK	£2.00	£2.00	£
Europe*	£2.00	£2.00	£
Rest of world	£20.00	£10.00	£

Grand Total (incl. Postage) £ ___

I enclose a cheque for ___
(Cheques to BPP Publishing)

Or charge to Visa/Mastercard/Switch

Card Number ___

Expiry date ___

Start Date ___

Issue Number (Switch Only) ___

Signature ___

REVIEW FORM & FREE PRIZE DRAW

All original review forms from the entire BPP range, completed with genuine comments, will be entered into a draw on 31 January 2003 and 31 July 2003. The names on the first four forms picked out will be sent a cheque for £50.

Name: _____ Address: _____

_____

How have you used this Text?
(Tick one box only)

☐ Home study (book only)

☐ On a course: college _____

☐ With 'correspondence' package

☐ Other _____

Why did you decide to purchase this Text?
(Tick one box only)

☐ Have used complementary Study Text

☐ Have used BPP Texts in the past

☐ Recommendation by friend/colleague

☐ Recommendation by a lecturer at college

☐ Saw advertising

☐ Other _____

During the past six months do you recall seeing/receiving any of the following?
(Tick as many boxes as are relevant)

☐ Our advertisement in *ACCA Student Accountant*

☐ Our advertisement in *Pass*

☐ Our brochure with a letter through the post

Which (if any) aspects of our advertising do you find useful?
(Tick as many boxes as are relevant)

☐ Prices and publication dates of new editions

☐ Information on Text content

☐ Facility to order books off-the-page

☐ None of the above

Which BPP products have you used?

Text	☑	MCQ cards	☐	i-Learn	☐
Kit	☐	Tape	☐	i-Pass	☐
Passcard	☐	Video	☐	Virtual Campus	☐

Your ratings, comments and suggestions would be appreciated on the following areas.

	Very useful	Useful	Not useful
Introductory section (Key study steps, personal study)	☐	☐	☐
Chapter introductions	☐	☐	☐
Key terms	☐	☐	☐
Quality of explanations	☐	☐	☐
Case examples and other examples	☐	☐	☐
Questions and answers in each chapter	☐	☐	☐
Chapter roundups	☐	☐	☐
Quick quizzes	☐	☐	☐
Exam focus points	☐	☐	☐
Question bank	☐	☐	☐
Answer bank	☐	☐	☐
List of key terms and index	☐	☐	☐
Icons	☐	☐	☐
Mind maps	☐	☐	☐

	Excellent	Good	Adequate	Poor
Overall opinion of this Text	☐	☐	☐	☐

Do you intend to continue using BPP Products?   ☐ Yes   ☐ No

Please note any further comments and suggestions/errors on the reverse of this page. The BPP author of this edition can be e-mailed at: catherinewatton@bpp.com

Please return to: Katy Hibbert, ACCA Range Manager, BPP Publishing Ltd, FREEPOST, London, W12 8BR

REVIEW FORM & FREE PRIZE DRAW (continued)

TELL US WHAT YOU THINK

Because the following specific areas of the text contain new material/cover tricky topics/cover highly examinable topics etc, your comments on their usefulness are particularly welcome.

- Internal audit (Chapters 3, 11, 20)

- Audit planning and risks (Chapter 7)

Please note any further comments and suggestions/errors below.

FREE PRIZE DRAW RULES

1 Closing date for 31 July 2003 draw is 30 June 2003. Closing date for 31 January 2003 draw is 31 December 2002.

2 No purchase necessary. Entry forms are available upon request from BPP Publishing. No more than one entry per title, per person. Draw restricted to persons aged 16 and over.

3 Winners will be notified by post and receive their cheques not later than 6 weeks after the draw date.

4 The decision of the promoter in all matters is final and binding. No correspondence will be entered into.